W9-CAZ-253

Fondue Neuchâtel (page 42)

Opposite: **Beef Stifado** (page 311)

Above: **Chipotle and Orange Pork Ribs** (page 357)

Above: **Ragoût of Peas and Artichokes with Tarragon** (page 146)
Opposite: **Gingered Carrot–Sweet Potato Soup** (page 93)

Opposite: **New Orleans–Style Vanilla Bread Pudding with Whiskey Sauce** (page 382)
Above: **Mexican Coffee with Brandy and Kahlúa** (page 73)

Above: **Osso Buco** (page 332)

Opposite: **Poached Peaches with Brandied Custard Sauce** (page 403)

Opposite: **Country Tomato Sauce with Roasted Vegetables** (page 119)
Above: **Rolled Turkey Breast with Prosciutto** (page 280)

Above: **Red Cabbage with Red Wine, Apricots, and Honey** (page 132)
Opposite: **Buttery Rosemary Pecan Halves** (page 48), **Walnuts and Ginger** (page 50), **Curry Mixed Nuts** (page 52)

Opposite: **Pinto Bean Chili with Mexican Sausage** (page 232)
Above: **Mushroom-Gorgonzola Risotto in Radicchio Wraps with Balsamic Syrup** (page 172)

Chicken with Glazed Walnuts and Grand Marnier (page 264)

Not
Your Mother's®
Slow Cooker Recipes
for Entertaining

Also by Beth Hensperger and Julie Kaufmann

Not Your Mother's Slow Cooker Cookbook

The Ultimate Rice Cooker Cookbook

Also by Beth Hensperger

Not Your Mother's Slow Cooker Recipes for Two

The Gourmet Potluck

The Bread Lover's Bread Machine Cookbook

The Best Quick Breads

Bread for Breakfast

Bread Made Easy

The Pleasure of Whole Grain Breads

The Bread Bible

Breads of the Southwest

Beth's Basic Bread Book

Bread for all Seasons

Baking Bread

Bread

Not
Your Mother's®
Slow Cooker Recipes
for Entertaining

Beth Hensperger
and Julie Kaufmann

The Harvard Common Press
Boston, Massachusetts

The Harvard Common Press
535 Albany Street
Boston, Massachusetts 02118
www.harvardcommonpress.com

Copyright © 2007 by Beth Hensperger and Julie Kaufmann
Photographs copyright © 2007 by Eskite Photography

All rights reserved. No part of this publication may be reproduced or transmitted in any form or by any means, electronic or mechanical, including photocopying, recording, or any information storage or retrieval system, without permission in writing from the publisher.

Printed in the United States of America
Printed on acid-free paper

Library of Congress Cataloging-in-Publication Data
    Hensperger, Beth
        Not your mother's slow cooker recipes for entertaining / Beth Hensperger and Julie Kaufmann.
            p.   cm.
        ISBN 978-1-55832-311-7 (hardcover : alk. paper)—ISBN 978-1-55832-312-4 (pbk. : alk. paper)
        1. Electric cookery, Slow.   2. Entertaining.   I. Kaufmann, Julie.   II. Title.
        TX827.H3915   2007
        641.5'884—dc22   2007002510

Special bulk-order discounts are available on this and other Harvard Common Press books. Companies and organizations may purchase books for premiums or resale, or may arrange a custom edition, by contacting the Marketing Director at the address above.

Cover photographs—front: Cherry-Glazed Pork Pot Roast with Herbs, page 342; spine: Fondue Neuchâtel, page 42; back, from left to right: Rolled Turkey Breast with Prosciutto, page 280; Poached Peaches with Brandied Custard Sauce, page 403; and Country Tomato Sauce with Roasted Vegetables, page 119

Book design by Ralph Fowler / rlf design
Cover and interior photographs by Eskite Photography
Food styling by Andrea Lucich
Prop styling by Carol Hacker

10 9 8 7 6 5 4

Not Your Mother's is a registered trademark of The Harvard Common Press.

*For Agra, who guided me into new channels of growth and was
there from the beginning through to the end of this project, providing me
with not only inspiration, but also great entertainment*

—Beth Hensperger

*For Mom and Aunt Rowie, who introduced me
to the pleasures of cooking*

—Julie Kaufmann

*And to you, our gentle reader, who gets as much entertainment
in the kitchen preparing the recipes as you do in expressing
the essence of graceful entertaining after the guests arrive.
Use this book often and make it your own.*

Acknowledgments

The authors would like to thank everyone who contributed moral support, thoughtful guidance, and delicious recipes to this book. Special thank-yous to recipe testers Bobbe Torgerson, literary agent Martha Casselman, Nancyjo Riekse, Batia Rabec, and Vivien "Bunny" Dimmel.

Thank you to Kathy Benson, director of marketing services at West Bend Housewares; Chuck Williams of Williams-Sonoma; Susan Jones, marketing director at Hamilton Beach/Proctor-Silex, Inc.; and Yvonne Olson of Hamilton Beach/Proctor-Silex, Inc., for providing the big slow cookers used for testing these recipes.

Additional thanks go to all of our friends, neighbors, and cookbook peers who contributed ideas, recipes, and encouragement—we have acknowledged them individually in the recipes.

Thank you to our publisher, Bruce Shaw, who made it possible for you to hold this book in your hands; to Pam Hoenig, our accomplished first editor, who deserves her own byline for her sound advice and long hours of labor initially guiding this many-year, multi-volume project; and to Valerie Cimino, who refined the manuscript into its final shape and voice with her own panache.

Contents

Acknowledgments   vii

Introduction   xi

So You're Giving a Party   •   1

Appetizer Dips, Savory Fondues, and
Party Nuts   •   27

The Electric Punch Bowl   •   55

Company Soups from the Slow Cooker   •   83

Slow Cooker Savory Sauces   •   105

Slow-Cooked Vegetables   •   125

Slow-Cooked Grains and Stuffings ○ 163

Not from the Slow Cooker Accompaniments ○ 187

The New-Fashioned Bean and Chili Pot ○ 209

Poultry, Game Birds, and Rabbit ○ 247

Beef, Veal, and Venison ○ 295

Pork and Lamb ○ 339

Slow Cooker Puddings, Cakes, and Breads ○ 377

Fruit Desserts and Compotes ○ 397

Dessert Fondues, Sweet Sauces, and
Chocolate Truffles ○ 421

Measurement Equivalents   445
Index 447

Introduction

While the virtues of slow-cooking techniques are widely acknowledged and millions use the slow cooker as part of daily food preparation, the slow cooker is often seen as a humble and homey appliance. It is that, but it is so much more. The slow cooker is a kitchen appliance extraordinaire for preparing and serving foods for entertaining. Whether you are an old hand at party-giving or a nervous newcomer, there is always pleasure to be had in mulling over a menu and finding dishes that will fit the occasion, and here we present to you a book full of possibilities.

Once entertaining was synonymous with formality and setting the dining room table with seldom-used silver and china. But with changing lifestyles and a bounty of inexpensive seasonal foods, entertaining can mean anything from a backyard picnic to a kitchen gathering to an elegant sit-down dinner or a festive holiday meal. Entertaining can be one of the great joys of life and a satisfying form of creativity.

One of the keys to any type of entertaining is creating a feeling of relaxed hospitality, and one way to achieve that ambiance is to prepare recipes ahead of time. A slow cooker entrée, such as a chili, stew, ragoût, or braised chicken dish, needs only some store-bought bread, a piece of cheese, a nice salad, and sorbet or berries and biscotti to become a satisfying and welcoming luncheon or dinner. Slow cooker side dishes are perfect complements to outdoor grilled or indoor oven-roasted meats and fish. We also serve pasta to our guests with one of our luscious slow-cooked sauces. Make the sauce ahead of time and then just cook the pasta and toss the salad. Get ready to dish up seconds.

A fondue party? Yes, fondue is firmly back in fashion for intimate parties, and your slow cooker makes an excellent fondue pot. Having lunch afloat? Plug in your slow cooker in the galley for a simple, delicious meal that simmers below while you linger on deck. Out for an early appointment or a youth soccer game? Fill the slow cooker, turn it on, and come home later to a welcome meal that will satisfy the most finicky of young and old guests. Our recipes take easily available, inexpensive ingredients and make them worthy of any occasion. The simplest of meals is frequently just as enjoyable as one with exotic and unfamiliar recipes.

Once you have mastered the skill of cooking in a slow cooker, you can assemble and cook a dish that does not require any tending. In fact, you can leave the house or go to bed without worry. Today's heavy, fully glazed stoneware cooking vessels are so versatile and attractive that you can, in most instances, assemble and refrigerate the ingredients for a dish at night and, in the morning, fill the crockery insert and place it into the metal housing containing the heating elements. Turn on the cooker, let it cook for hours, then serve the meal

directly from it. Think of it as a large oven-to-table casserole or soup tureen.

Since slow cookers are so versatile, your guests can enjoy meals that reflect the fragrant aromas and potent spices of India, Mexico, Italy, the American Southwest, or Morocco. You can highlight the fresh summer harvest with roasted summer vegetables, or stay cozy in January with a special beef stew with roots or baked beans. Bring the slow cooker outside to serve your easy-to-eat ribs and wings at a poolside party. Slow cookers prepare a great version of Elizabeth Taylor's Chili (page 234) on the hottest of days, without changing the temperature of your kitchen an iota or using the oven, to be served in the cool of the early evening with margaritas, warm tortillas, and a big salad. Slow cookers prepare succulent meals for an elegant sit-down dinner or a fancy, substantial cocktail party as easily as they do side dishes for buffets, one of the simplest methods of entertaining, where guests just help themselves.

Entertaining is not just about preparing and serving good food—it is a form of self-expression. Once you give a successful gathering of any type, you will be inspired to create more occasions. You plan an event and a meal that you yourself want to enjoy, and your confidence is evident with the way you deliver and share that meal. It is an effort that is greatly rewarded. The no-fuss assembly inherent in slow cooker dishes helps you to be efficient with your time in the kitchen and imaginative in your choice of ingredients. The slow-cooking process is worry-free after loading the crockery insert, leaving you available to handle other details or relax before your guests arrive. Slow-cooking is not just a technique, a piece of equipment, or a place in the kitchen, but a frame of mind as well.

We think of our entertaining dishes as simple yet impressive. So send out the invitations, make your lists, and prepare for your guests to enjoy one of the slow cooker creations within. Whether you are serving four or 24, happy slow-cooking!

So You're Giving a Party

We designed *Not Your Mother's Slow Cooker Recipes for Entertaining* as a companion to *Not Your Mother's Slow Cooker Cookbook*. From simple daily meals to ones made with ingredients that are a little bit more special for entertaining, from dishes that take a few extra steps to those that have everything placed in the pot at one time, we have created recipes to appeal to every type of cook, every single day of the year, and that are suitable for all occasions. Here we focus on more

convenient slow cooker recipes for meals that will feed a crowd as well as your family.

Take your time to read through this book and see which recipes inspire you. Make notes for future reference, feeling free to pick and choose, and mix and match, when composing menus. We encourage you to mark up your book; it is a tool meant to be used. There is no set way to entertain, so you can be creative here.

Learn to trust yourself. Think about the recipes, make your lists, and then experiment with preparing them. Combine these recipes with ones from other books and your favorites, finding the balance that is right for you.

In writing this book, we wanted to continue to enjoy the pleasures of home cooking and the good, nourishing food it provides. We wanted to create a cookbook where good cooks go for inspiration, to appeal to both the practical and the perfectionist in everyone. We wanted to take advantage of the global culinary melting pot and all its appetizing contrasting flavors, yet respect old-fashioned hospitality and culinary regionalism, the kind of cooking that is the basis for American cuisine today. We want you to adapt your mother's and grandmother's recipes based on our instructions. And we want you to jot a record of your efforts in the margins of recipes you go back to year after year.

We want to be part of your stash of favorite recipes. But yes, if you are an occasional cook with little tolerance for the kitchen, we can help you to serve a great meal, like a lamb stew or oxtail daube, with the aid of your slow cooker. The slow cooker can ease the anxiety of home entertaining. Since there are no rules for how you need to serve your meal, you can skip appetizers and serve a main course and dessert and still be deemed a fabulous cook.

In the writing of this book, we looked to world cuisines for inspiration, seeking foods that have traditionally been cooked in closed ceramic pots or casseroles. These are the basis for our one-pot meals for crowds. We found, and adapted to the slow cooker, many wonderful, soul-satisfying recipes made special for today's entertaining. The low temperature and long cooking time of such dishes allow for the toughest, often most inexpensive "country" cuts of meat (unsuitable for fast high-heat sautés and grilling) to be cooked to a luscious tenderness without loss of the natural juices. They end up very special.

Bean dishes, long-simmered tomato sauces, and other flavorful vegetable dishes are also slow cooker naturals. The slow cooker is one of the best ways to cook beans, lentils, and split peas to perfection. Remember, this style of cooking depends on artful combination and technique rather than expensive or remarkable ingredients. No matter what your budget or space requirements, the slow cooker can help make your gathering a huge success.

Party Styles

There are three main styles of parties that encompass most occasions—buffets; cocktail parties; and sit-down dinners, luncheons, and brunches. Special occasions, such as a shower, Super Bowl party, wedding, or holiday, usually will be planned and executed in one of these styles. We have included recipes for every type of entertaining need, from appetizers, side dishes, and sauces to roasts, stews, and desserts. You can make dishes as simple or elaborate as you like by substituting ingredients or complementing the meal with additional side dishes, salads, breads, and desserts.

There are two types of buffets. One we call the grazing buffet, where people can stand or sit as desired, encouraging mingling and informality. This is good for small groups and small rooms. If people are eating off their laps, be sure to serve food that can be consumed with only a fork, such as ragoûts, stews, pastas, salads, and casseroles. If you serve a complex stew, complement the meal with a simple vegetable or plain salad. A more formal buffet, like at a wedding, is when guests help themselves but are all seated at tables. If you have your slow cooker plugged in on the buffet table, be aware of where the cord is; you want the table close to the wall so no one will trip over the cord or pull the slow cooker off the table. If you are using a dining room table in the center of the room, use the slow cooker unplugged or move it to a sideboard for safety. If there is any problem, you can always set up the food in the kitchen. For a nice, bountiful-looking buffet, cover the entire table with bowls and platters of food, flowers, candles, and other decorations. Save room at one end for plates, napkins, and flatware.

Cocktail parties are the easiest way to entertain with a sense of formality, especially if you are short on time or have a very tight budget. There is customarily a time limit, usually around two hours, where the guests have a drink or two and nibble out of hand or off a small plate. You can serve the appetizers by setting up a buffet or having trays passed in the room. If you have trays passed, you will need some extra help in the form of servers. We like to serve appetizers with cocktails, since we can mix and match complementary finger foods, such as seafood and meat, with some cheeses and raw vegetables. We recommend six different appetizers for a group of up to 12 people; for 12 to 25 people, offer 10 appetizers; and for 25 to 50 people, about a dozen different ones. Plan on three servings of each appetizer per person, although generally we find that each person eats about a dozen appetizers over a two-hour period. If you are serving a few bites before a dinner, keep it very light: one appetizer, such as hummus or some spiced nuts, will do. The small slow cooker is great for dips and a medium-size round or oval one is perfect for fondue set up on a buffet table. The large slow cooker is a must for effortlessly serving a beautiful cauldron of a hot party drink.

Sit-down dinners and luncheons can be formal or informal, while brunches are typically informal. They commence at a set time and seats are typically assigned. The usual number for each table is six to eight people, or a dozen at most. A formal meal is served in courses from the kitchen with china and silverware. A server and cleanup person are often employed so the host/hostess can sit with the guests and also enjoy the party. In these scenarios, the slow cooker can be set on KEEP WARM until serving time. An informal dinner can be any type of food served in any manner, such as a chili and assorted toppings, set on the table all at once. Instead of courses, there can be a main dish and then dessert, skipping appetizers or even a salad.

Remember that cooking for a large number of people will always take longer than cooking for your family or a few people. Because space is limited in most apartments and homes, the slow cooker is perfect for food preparation because it takes up so little space and gives you an extra burner when necessary.

Your New Slow Cooker

You may be buying your very first slow cooker, replacing an old one, or adding to your collection. The new machines are a great improvement over those on the market even five years ago, and with such an inexpensive appliance, it is painless to go ahead and upgrade. When shopping, do check inside the box to make sure all parts are intact and that the shape of the cooker, which may be different from what is pictured on the outside of the box, is what you want.

At home, after removing the slow cooker and manufacturer's booklet from the box, place the slow cooker on your countertop. Remove the lid and stoneware insert and wash them in hot soapy water, taking care not to scratch them. Both the lid and the insert are dishwasher safe. Dry them thoroughly and place them on the countertop.

Inspect the inside of the metal base to familiarize yourself with the design. The low-wattage, wraparound heating coils are sandwiched between the inner and outer metal walls for indirect heat; the heat source never makes direct contact with the stoneware crock. The coils inside the base heat up, and the space between the base wall and crock heats up and transfers that heat to the stoneware. The slow cooker cooks at a temperature between 200° and 300°F.

Now, put the stoneware insert back into the base by sliding it into place. We like to line up the handles on the insert and base.

Put on the lid and leave the cooker on the counter until you are ready to cook something. Next, read the manufacturer's booklet, highlighting warranty information and customer service phone numbers, and fill out the warranty card. Make a note in the back of this book regarding the model and capacity, a note that is especially useful since, as time goes on, you may forget what size your crock is.

We recommend that you stay in the house during your first use of this appliance to assess how it works and observe the cooking process. Slow cookers do not have a thermostat, so if you are concerned about temperature, use an instant-read thermometer inserted into the meat or cooking liquid. There will never be a specific temperature given in our recipes because the slow-cooking process is based on the wattage and time. The contents will take 1 to 2 hours to heat up to a simmer, which is much slower than any other cooking process, so be prepared for it. Many cooks turn the cooker to the HIGH heat setting for 1 to 2 hours to bring the temperature up as quickly as possible to 140°F—the temperature at which bacteria can no longer proliferate in food—then switch to LOW for the remainder of the cook time. The LOW setting uses 80 to 185 watts and cooks in the temperature range of 170° to 200°F. The HIGH heat setting is double the wattage, 160 to 370 watts, and cooks at a temperature of about 280°F, with slight variations related to the size of the cooker, the temperature of the food, and how full the crock is. Any time you lift the lid to check the contents or to stir, you release the accumulated steam that cooks the food, and it will take approximately 20 minutes for the temperature in the cooker to return to the original level.

With your first use, be prepared for the smell, and perhaps light smoke, that will be emitted from the heating elements as they heat for the first time and any manufacturing residues are burned off. This is normal. We have found that new machines can emit a metal-like smell for about one full hour. It is best to use your stove fan or open a window or a door, or employ a combination of the two, to allow the smell to dissipate as rapidly as possible. During cooking, the outside of the metal base housing will become hot to the touch, so keep it away from children and walls or low cabinets.

The stoneware insert will slowly reach the same temperature, although we find we can touch both briefly without oven mitts to check the temperature. If you are transferring the whole dish to a buffet or potluck, just carry the entire portable unit by its handles, then plug it in and set to LOW to reheat the food. (There are optional accessories available, such as a rubber latch that keeps the lid in place while transporting, and an insulated carrying case designed by one manufacturer.)

About the Slow Cooker Crock

On a whim back in the 1970s, Beth bought an oversized 7-quart Vallauris *marmite* clay pot. She had no idea that the primitive-looking, shiny brown earthenware was famous for preparing the great slow-cooked peasant dishes of France. Tall, deep, straight-sided earthenware cooking pots (metal pots just won't give the right flavor) are designed specifically for long-cooking stews and thick soups such as pot-au-feu and potage. The large round slow cooker is nearly identical to that venerable piece of crockery, updated for a modern kitchen. The appeal is the same; crockery casseroles do not heat up quickly, but, once hot, they will retain their even heat for hours.

The modern slow cooker uses two basic shapes of thick, sturdy stoneware cooking vessel inserts, round and oval, based on the designs of the deep European clay cooking pots. Both are superb vessels for slow-cooking. The shapes encourage condensation, but, with their tight-fitting lids, prevent the contents from evaporating. It is important when you are first cooking in the slow cooker to remember to use less liquid than for conventional cooking methods, since there is no evaporation. The key here is to remember the principles of self-basting: The condensation under the lid adds an extra ½ to 1 cup of liquid during the cooking process.

The first, most familiar, slow cooker is the round shape. This is the best shape for soups, beans, stews, and risottos. It reminds us of a classic flowerpot, with a rather small surface area on the bottom; tall, slightly outwardly sloping sides; and a larger open top area with a see-through, tempered-glass lid that forms an airtight container when the contents are heated. The first slow cookers had flimsy Lexan plastic lids, but they are now smoothly domed tempered glass, a fabulous improvement that allows for the heat to reflect down and envelop the contents in moist heat from all sides.

The first stoneware inserts were not removable and, hence, a hassle to clean. All the models we inspected during the writing of this book now have inserts that remove easily for cleaning, and are even dishwasher-safe. The first cookers were only available in 3½- or 4-quart round shapes and did not have lips suitable to be used as handles. All the stoneware inserts now have handles so that you can easily lift and lower the pot. In older models, the insulated metal housing came in scary colors like psychedelic orange, avocado green, and mustard yellow or were overly decorated or cutesy, but today's cookers come in a pale soft white with a simple border, or a stunning stainless steel that looks elegant with its black stoneware insert. An empty medium-size round crock weighs approximately 6 pounds.

In the last few years, the oval roaster shape has appeared. Based on the classic French terrine (whose root is the French word for earth, *terre,* hence, earthenware pot) with lower, wider sides like the traditional round *poêlon* casserole, it is a bit more shallow and compact than the round shape and especially well suited for holding large cuts of meat, such as a pork roast, leg of lamb, or whole poultry. In black or soft beige colors, it is a handsome casserole by any definition. It has more

surface area on the bottom than the round model, so take that into consideration when timing; stews and soups will cook slightly faster in an oval cooker than in a round one.

There are also slow cookers with metal inserts. These models, designed for multitasking, such as popping corn and deep-frying, do not work as well as the stoneware inserts because of food sticking to them and the cooking pot getting way too hot to handle. For those reasons we prefer the stoneware cookers. But remember that stoneware cannot, under any circumstance, be used with direct heat on the stovetop for browning or finishing off, and cannot be placed in the freezer; it will crack. It can, however, be used in the oven with great success as a casserole dish or for baking bread, at temperatures up to 400°F.

With new technologies constantly finding their way into countertop appliances, look for slow cookers that go beyond the traditional manual mode we have all become used to. New models feature integrated probes, which are perfect for cooking large cuts of meat (Hamilton Beach was the first to come out with this feature) and will cause the cooker to automatically switch to KEEP WARM when the desired temperature is reached. Other models have a built-in digital timer: You can set cooking times at half-hour increments for up to 12 hours on either HIGH or LOW heat. If you are out of the house all day, these features may be right for your style of cooking.

Slow Cooker Sizes and Uses for Entertaining

The electric slow cooker is a valuable appliance for entertaining due to its versatility. Whether you need a buffet chafing dish for chicken wings or meatballs, an additional stovetop burner when your oven and regular stove are maxed out, or a convenient electric punch bowl, there is a slow cooker size to fit each need.

Do you need any special size slow cooker for entertaining purposes? Not really. The slow cooker is available in a wide range of volume capacities, from 1-quart to 7-quart, and each has its specific occasion and use. It is up to you to decide which size you need depending on the number of people you want to serve and what types of foods you are making. Hard-core slow cooker users usually have two or three sizes, as well as different shapes, which we recommend if you entertain a lot.

There are three basic slow cooker sizes: small, medium, and large, and we designate the proper cooker to use in each recipe. Most sizes come in a choice of round or oval (even the very smallest ones do, depending on the manufacturer), but be sure to check inside the box when purchasing; we have found that the picture on the outside of the box sometimes is not the shape within.

The smallest cooker is dubbed the "Little Dipper," because it is perfect for hot dips, side dishes, dessert and savory sauces, and small amounts of fondue for entertaining. We prefer the 1- or 1½-quart size (usually round)—marketed in the past by Rival as the Crock-Ette and easy to find on the shelves—since it gives a bit more room for hands to do the dipping. Hamilton Beach has added the Party Crock! Cookset to its line. This is a slow cooker designed specifically for entertaining, with a detachable dish in a luscious shade of pumpkin. The 1½-quart round insert cooks in its housing, then is placed on a cast-iron warming stand fueled by a tea candle (no power cord!). We will be seeing a lot more specialty slow cookers in the future designed with convenient entertaining in mind. Remember that this size is too small for cooking regular soups and stews. When we indicate "small" in a recipe, you can use the 1½- to 3-quart capacity round or oval slow cooker.

Medium is the most popular size of slow cooker, and before you even make your first dish you will know why: It is an easily manageable size, comfortable to lift and manipulate, and it fits nicely on the counter or in the dishwasher. When we indicate "medium" in a recipe, we are referring to the 3- to 4½-quart model. The 3-quart oval became a very popular model for us during our recipe-testing for this book. This size is perfect for four to six servings, holds a 3- to 3½-pound roast or cut-up chicken, and makes a medium-size pot of pasta sauce or pot of ribs. This is also a good size for two people who like leftovers, which can be reheated or frozen. Meatloaf can be made in either a round or an oval shape, but note that the shape of the finished dish will reflect which model cooker you used.

When we indicate a "large" cooker in a recipe, we mean a 5- to 7-quart model. The most popular are the 5- and 6-quart sizes. These are designed for families and for entertaining groups. It is the best punch bowl you can imagine (no more messy stovetop). You can make chili or soup for 20 in a 7-quart slow cooker. The large oval is essential if you are cooking a lot of boneless chicken breasts; you want room to lay the chicken in one layer so it won't get soggy. It is also best for large cuts of meat, such as brisket and corned beef, pot roasts, and whole poultry, and large-quantity stews like *boeuf bourguignon*. The large size is convenient when using another mold or casserole insert, such as for steamed pudding, so that the mold does not touch the sides of the stoneware. If you are adjusting a recipe designated for a medium-size cooker, increase the cooking time by 1½ to 2 hours and increase your ingredients by 50 to 100 percent, depending on whether you are using a 5-, 6-, or 7-quart cooker.

The latest Rival models in 5- and

Slow Cooker Sizes at a Glance

Little Dipper: 1- or 1½-quart capacity

Small: 1½-, 2-, or 2½-quart capacity

Medium: 3, 3½-, 4-, or 4½-quart capacity

Large: 5-, 5½-, 6-, or 7-quart capacity

6-quart cookers include the programmable Smart-Pot. The Smart-Pot, available in 5-quart round and 6-quart oval sizes and white or brushed chrome finishes, cooks on the HIGH setting for 4 or 6 hours or on the LOW setting for 8 or 10 hours. When the cooking time is up, the Smart-Pot will automatically shift to a KEEP WARM setting (which is recommended for no more than 4 hours), so your meal is waiting for you when you are ready to eat. This is a good item for entertaining because as you serve your appetizers, your dinner can wait in the slow cooker. If you want to cook for different times than the automated settings allow (i.e., less time on LOW or a longer time on HIGH), you'll have to be there to turn the pot off or on. You cannot pre-program with a Smart-Pot, because the food will spoil too rapidly.

Look for dramatic designer-style models of large slow cookers if you entertain a lot and like to serve right out of the crock. Hamilton Beach makes an attractive two-toned copper and stainless-steel 6-quart oval model with full-grip handles for easy carrying. One of our favorites is a 5.3-quart cooker made by Breville, a little-known Australian company that specializes in top-of-the-line small appliances (look for it online at www.amazon.com). It has a brushed stainless-steel exterior with a brown housing interior and a dark brown crock; it looks very dignified on a buffet table. Cuisinart has a 6-quart rectangular model with a stainless-steel insert. Although the quality is fantastic and the design is lovely, we tend to prefer stoneware

Is a Slow Cooker Safe?

The slow cooker, a countertop appliance, cooks foods slowly at a relatively low temperature—between 170° and 280°F. The low heat helps less expensive, leaner cuts of meat become tender and experience less shrinkage (high heat shrinks protein in meat and leads to more loss of the natural juices). The direct, multidirectional heat from the pot, lengthy cooking time, and concentrated steam created within the tightly covered container combine to destroy bacteria and make the slow cooker a safe way to cook foods.

crocks, because the stainless becomes very hot around the edges and especially in the pointed corners.

Equipment for Slow Cooker Entertaining

To make all-in-one meals in your slow cooker, you will need a few pieces of equipment, mostly for preparing the ingredients and serving. These are what we consider the basics, and they generally are in the most modestly equipped kitchen. Remember that you want to avoid using metal utensils in your slow cooker when possible, because they may scratch and damage the insert.

For use in the slow cooker:

- Wooden spoons and heat-resistant plastic or silicone oversized spoons and slotted spoons, for stirring

- Heat-resistant spatulas of different sizes, for stirring and scraping down the sides of the cooker

- Long-handled kitchen fork, for removing meat

- Meat baster, for skimming fat off the surface

- Gravy skimmer (which looks like a measuring cup with the spout coming from the bottom instead of the top), for skimming stocks and sauces

- Instant-read thermometer, for checking doneness of meat or the temperature of the contents of the crock

- Set of thick oven mitts, for handling the crock while hot

For serving and storage:

- Large, heat-resistant plastic ladle, for transferring stews and sauces

- Food mill or conical strainer, for sauces

- Long-handled serving spoons, a 12-inch slicing/carving knife, gravy and sauce ladles

- Metal tongs, for removing roasts

- Aluminum foil, for tenting food while thickening sauces

- Platters or large shallow bowls, if serving food outside the cooking vessel

- A variety of sizes of airtight refrigerator and freezer storage containers, for leftovers and stocks

Our Tried and True Rules of the Pot

We first introduced you to the rules of the pot in *Not Your Mother's Slow Cooker Cookbook*. We feel the information is so important that we must include it here as well.

Once you become familiar with the techniques involved with using your slow cooker, you will probably wonder how you ever did without it as an essential kitchen appliance. But at first you are in a brave new world, and learning a new technique takes a bit of time and attention to detail. Once we got past the idea of the slow cooker as a "magic pot" (that is, that you randomly throw in some raw ingredients and they are magically transformed into a fabulous meal), and began using the slow cooker to its best advantage, we gained a new respect for this appliance. Please be sure to read this section before your first cooking forays and to use it as a reference

Is a Slow Cooker Efficient?

The slow cooker is user-friendly and very economical, using about the same amount of energy on the LOW setting as a 75-watt light bulb. It takes much less electricity to use a slow cooker than a conventional gas or electric oven. On the HIGH setting, you will use less than 300 watts. It is an excellent alternative method of cooking on extremely hot days when energy alerts recommend reduced use of electrical appliances, and it won't heat up your kitchen the way an oven does.

guide thereafter, because there are some very important guidelines for safe cooking.

- Many instruction booklets say never to lift the lid during the cooking process. On one hand, that is a good rule; on the other hand, it is next to impossible. As the contents of the slow cooker heat up and create steam, a natural water seal is created around the rim of the lid to form a vacuum. The rim of the lid will stick in place when gently pulled. This is important for the even cooking of the food within. But a recipe might call for adding ingredients halfway or near the end of the cooking time, or you might want to check your food for doneness at some point. It is fine to do this, but always remember that by breaking the lid seal and allowing the steam to escape, the temperature within is reduced. When you replace the lid, it takes 20 to 30 minutes for the internal temperature of the contents to come back to the proper cooking temperature. You can easily check the contents visually through the glass lid. There is no need to stir or turn the food, unless a recipe specifies that you do so.

- Unless you are cooking on the wrong setting, have used too much or too little liquid, have let a dish cook too long, or have overfilled the crockery insert, there will be no burning, sticking, or bubbling over. However, these things can occur if you have the cooker set on HIGH with the cover off to encourage evaporation of liquid, so keep an eye on it under those circumstances.

- Never preheat a crockery insert when empty. Load the crock with the ingredients and then turn on the heat or plug the cooker in to start the heating process.

- The cord on the slow cooker is deliberately short to minimize danger from tangling or tripping. You may use a heavy-duty extension cord *only* if it has a marked electrical rating at least as great as the electrical rating of your cooker.

- When beginning to cook or to hasten the cooking process, switch from the LOW to the HIGH heat setting. The cooking time on HIGH is about half of what it is when the setting is on LOW. One hour on HIGH is equivalent to approximately 2 to 2½ hours on LOW, or twice as fast. Our recipes specify the best heat setting for the best results. Although old slow cooker recipes were often printed with both a HIGH and a LOW temperature setting and two different cooking times for convenience, we have found that the new slow cookers are much more efficient and run at slightly higher temperatures than older cookers. Check the wattage of your unit; there are slight differences among manufacturers. Some recipes turn out better on LOW, with its gentle, rolling simmer, than with the vigorous simmer on HIGH. Many cooks always start their cookers on HIGH for about an hour to get a good start on the cooking, and then switch to LOW for the remainder of the cooking time.

- The glass lid becomes quite hot during the cooking process. Use a potholder to remove it, if necessary, and handle it with care to avoid burns. The lid is dishwasher-safe.

- Most recipes need at least a bit of liquid to cook properly in the slow cooker. Liquid measures vary drastically in our recipes, from a few tablespoons to cover the bottom of the crock to submerging the food completely in liquid. Each recipe will be specific on these points. Fill the cooker with the solid ingredients, place in the base, and then add the liquid to avoid splashing or lifting an overly heavy crock.

- Ideally, slow cooker crockery inserts should be filled half full to no more than 1 full inch from the rim. The best practice is to fill the insert one-half to three-fourths full, because the heating elements are around the sides of the cooker; this will give you the most even cooking.

- Tender vegetables overcook easily, so add them during the last 30 to 60 minutes of cooking. The same goes for seafood. For the most control over seasoning, add fresh herbs during the last hour and dried herbs and spices at the beginning of cooking time. Remember that the flavors will concentrate, so do not add too much; you can always add more at the end of cooking. More fresh herbs, as well as salt and pepper, are often added at the end.

- Unless otherwise noted in the recipe, thaw frozen foods before placing them in the slow cooker so that the food temperature can reach 140°F as soon as possible. This is very important; frozen foods can slow the heating of the cooker and leave your stew or braise at too low a temperature for too long a time to be safe to eat.

- Although the crockery insert can be used in a conventional oven, it cannot be used on a gas or electric stovetop; it will break if it comes into direct contact with a heating element. If you are browning ingredients, such as meat, do so in a sauté pan, skillet, or saucepan as directed in the recipe, then transfer to the crock. The manufacturer's directions will specify whether the crock is ovenproof, microwave-safe, or able to be put under a broiler.

- Once the dish is completely cooked, you can keep the food hot by switching to the LOW or KEEP WARM setting. Food can be held safely for up to 2 to 4 hours, depending on the dish, on the KEEP WARM setting before eating. Many programmable digital cookers switch automatically to the KEEP WARM setting when the cooking time is up. Do not use the KEEP WARM setting, if you have one, for cooking; the temperature is too low to cook foods safely.

- At the end of the cooking time, remove the lid and stir well with a wooden or plastic spoon. If your dish is not cooked to your preference, replace the lid, set the temperature setting to HIGH, and cook in additional increments of 30 to 60 minutes until the food is cooked to your liking.

- If you are not serving food directly out of the cooker, use heavy oven mitts to carefully lift the hot crock with its contents out of the cooker and transfer it to a trivet or folded towel.

- When the food is cooked and ready to be served, turn the cooker to the OFF setting and/or unplug the unit. Many older slow cookers and small units do not have an OFF setting; off is when the unit is unplugged.

- Transfer leftovers to proper refrigerator or freezer storage containers within 2 hours after finishing cooking. Do not store your cooked food in the crockery insert, because the insert can crack with the difference in temperature.

- Never store the stoneware crock in the freezer. The crock can crack if you add a lot of frozen food or submerge it in cold water while it is still hot from the cooking cycle. Be sure to let the crock come to room temperature before washing it; never pour cold water into a hot crock. If your crock becomes cracked or deeply scratched, contact the manufacturer for replacement instructions.

- The crock can be washed by hand with nonabrasive dish soap and a nylon scrubber or brush or placed in the dishwasher.

- If you are not at home during the entire cooking process and you discover that the power has gone out, throw away the food even if it looks done and steer your party to the local pizza parlor, or order in. If you are at home, finish cooking the ingredients immediately by some other means: on a gas stove, on the outdoor grill, or at a neighbor's house where the power is on. If you are at home and the food was completely cooked before the power went out, the food will remain safe for up to 2 hours in the cooker with the power off.

- Cold cooked food should not be reheated in the crockery insert, because it will not reach a safe internal temperature quickly enough to render the food safe to eat. However, cooked food can be brought to steaming on the stove or in a microwave and then put into a preheated slow cooker to keep it hot until serving. To preheat the crockery insert, fill it with warm, not boiling, water, and then let it stand for a few minutes. Pour out the water and dry the insert, then add the food and set the temperature accordingly.

- Never immerse the metal housing of the slow cooker in water or fill it with liquid; you must always have the crockery insert in place to cook. To clean, let the base come to room temperature, then wipe the inside and the outside with a damp, soapy sponge and dry with a towel so as not to damage the finish. Make sure the bottom is clean inside and free of food particles or spillage.

Preparing Raw Ingredients for the Slow Cooker

Always defrost meat or whole poultry before putting it into a slow cooker, or else it will not cook properly and safely in the allotted time. Certain recipes do require the use of fully frozen poultry pieces, which is okay; this prevents the delicate flesh of poultry parts from overcooking. Choose to make foods with a high moisture content, such as chilis, soups, meat and vegetable stews, and thick meat and vegetable sauces. Cut food into evenly sized chunks or small pieces to ensure thorough cooking. Do not use a non-recommended size of slow cooker for large pieces of meat, such as a roast or a whole chicken, because the food will cook so slowly and unevenly that it could remain in the bacterial "danger zone" for too long. When preparing large pieces of meat, follow the recipes and slow cooker recommendations carefully.

When we indicate how to prepare and cut any raw ingredient, we are working within the following guidelines:

minced: $\frac{1}{16}$ inch

chopped: $\frac{1}{8}$ inch to $\frac{1}{4}$ inch

coarsely chopped: $\frac{1}{4}$ inch to $\frac{1}{2}$ inch

thinly sliced: $\frac{1}{8}$ inch thick

sliced: $\frac{1}{8}$ inch to $\frac{1}{4}$ inch thick

thickly sliced: $\frac{1}{2}$ inch thick

diced: $\frac{1}{2} \times \frac{1}{2}$-inch squares

cubed: 1×1-inch squares

Filling the Slow Cooker with the Right Amount of Food

Using the proper amount of ingredients for the size of your cooker is of the utmost importance. Fill the stoneware insert no less than half full and no more than two-thirds full to allow for expansion during cooking. The vessel needs to be at least half full due to the positioning of the heat coils around the walls of the cooker. Vegetables cook more slowly than do meat and poultry in a slow cooker, so if you are using them both, put the vegetables in first, at the bottom and around the sides of the cooking vessel, in layers. Then add the meat and cover the food with liquid, such as broth, water, tomato sauce, or barbecue sauce. Keep the lid in place during the cooking, briefly removing only to stir the food or check for doneness. Keeping the lid in place is essential for proper cooking of the contents.

Temperature Settings

Different machines have different settings, and being able to manipulate these settings to your liking is important. For the best results, if you are not already schooled in this method of cooking, you must experiment with different cooking times, temperature variables, and ingredients to yield results that appeal to your personal preferences. The small slow cookers tend to have one heat setting—LOW.

This is a safety precaution, because of the cooker's small size. Some have an OFF setting, and some must be unplugged to turn them off.

Standard medium-size and large slow cookers have two heat settings—LOW and HIGH. Foods take different times to cook depending on the setting used. Certainly, foods will cook faster on HIGH than on LOW. However, for all-day cooking or for less-tender cuts, we recommend LOW. If possible, turn the cooker to HIGH for the first hour of cooking to increase the temperature as fast as possible, and then adjust to LOW or the setting called for in your recipe. However, it's safe to cook foods on LOW for the entire cooking time.

Because of food safety considerations, the slow cooker does not allow you to pre-program the cooking start time. So you can't fill the pot with food, leave home, and have the pot go on an hour or two later. While food is cooking and once it's done, food will stay safe as long as the cooker is operating. The stoneware insert will retain heat for a full hour after turning off the machine.

The new Smart-Pot machines, available from Rival in medium and large sizes, have a digital face and can be programmed for a designated amount of cooking time. There are HIGH and LOW buttons as well as two buttons for increasing or decreasing the cooking time. When the food has been cooked for the programmed amount of time, the pot will switch automatically to KEEP WARM. These pots are really a convenience for away-from-home-all-day cooking.

Slow Cooker Cook Times

Beth, with a background in baking, was used to variations in baking times of only 5 to 10 minutes, so at first it was hard to adapt to the idea of a 2-hour, or longer, window of doneness. But with more experience using the slow cooker, this anxiety disappeared. We suggest that you check food for doneness at least once toward the middle of the cooking time, then again around the minimum time suggested, especially the first time you make a dish (this can make the difference between a nicely shaped crock-baked apple and applesauce). We encourage you to note the final cooking time in the margin of the recipe for future reference. While testing recipes, we found that five people, all with different models and slightly different sizes of slow cookers, who were buying their ingredients in different regions of the country at different times of year, all had slightly different cooking times within our recommended time window.

For the sake of an effortless party, we suggest that you try a dish out on your family before making it the star attraction at your next get-together. Or make the dish the day before the party, to avoid any last-minute mistakes, and then reheat it for the festivities.

Guide to Internal Temperatures

There is always a bit of leeway when determining whether a particular food is completely cooked, or cooked to your preference. This is a skill usually acquired through years of cooking with your senses. But professional chefs consider the gauging of the internal temperature of meats and poultry the most reliable way to tell when a food has reached a particular stage of doneness. When using a slow cooker, especially when you are a novice with the appliance, it is important to get the cooking temperature to 140°F as soon as possible, and then to be sure that the meat or poultry is totally cooked before eating. Just because it has cooked for hours does not mean it is done. Because of the lack of browning, you rely less on visual cues. You are looking at, smelling, and touching to ascertain the proper level of doneness. An instant-read thermometer or an accurate meat thermometer is the tool that we recommend as basic equipment in every slow cooker kitchen. This is particularly important when cooking larger pieces of meat or whole poultry. A beef roast that is approximately 125°F in its interior will always be rare, whether braised in a slow cooker, grilled outdoors, or roasted in a conventional oven, and regardless of how long it took to reach that temperature. Use the chart (page 16) as a guide for judging when your meat and poultry are done when using a slow cooker.

•• Is It Done Yet? ••

Type of Meat	Rare	Medium	Well Done
Beef	125° to 130°F	140° to 145°F	160°F
Veal	Not recommended	140° to 145°F	160°F
Lamb	130° to 140°F	140° to 145°F	160°F
Pork	Not recommended	145° to 150°F	160°F
Poultry and game birds	Not recommended	170° to 175°F	180°F
Venison	125° to 130°F	140° to 145°F	160°F

Note: Cook chicken and turkey to an internal temperature of 170° to 180°F.

Useful Cooking Techniques for the Slow Cooker

Because of the types of dishes you will be making in your slow cooker, you'll most likely find the following techniques of great use.

How to Get the Fat Out

When you've made a meat stew, a braised dish, or a stock or soup, you will often want to remove as much fat as possible from the liquid. Here are the several methods we recommend.

If you are not serving the dish until the next day, your task is simple: For stocks, refrigerate the liquid, uncovered, in a bowl. For braises, refrigerate the cooled liquid in an uncovered container separate from the meat and other ingredients. For stews with many components, this may not be possible. Just let the dish cool, then refrigerate the entire thing, covered. The next morning, you can spoon off any con-gealed fat, which will have risen to the top and solidified. Many cooks like to leave a small amount of the fat behind for flavor instead of removing all of it.

If you are using a stock right away, pour the liquid from the hot crock into a heatproof glass bowl or measuring cup (such as Pyrex). Wait several minutes for the fat to rise to the top of the liquid. You will be able to see a translucent, yellowish layer floating on top of the liquid.

Now you have two options: Remove the fat from the liquid or remove the liquid from the fat. To remove the fat, use a large, shallow metal spoon and carefully spoon off the clear fat, discarding it as you go. This isn't a perfect solution; you will inevitably spoon off some of the liquid you are trying to save or you will leave some fat floating on top. If there is very little fat, you can float a paper towel in the liquid for a few seconds. It will absorb the topmost layer, and then can be thrown away.

The second approach is to sneak the liquid out from under the layer of fat. One way to do this is with a turkey baster. Place a clean container large enough to hold the degreased liquid next to the container holding the liquid. Squeeze the turkey baster bulb and lower the open end straight down to the bottom of the container with the liquid. Release the bulb, and the baster will fill with the liquid from the bottom of the container. Bring the baster straight up out of the container, still holding it pointed end downward and being careful not to put pressure on the bulb, and aim the baster into the clean container. Squeeze the bulb and squirt in the liquid. Repeat until there is just fat remaining in your original container.

A brilliant little gadget called a degreaser is a worthwhile investment if you find yourself degreasing liquids often. It's like a measuring cup, but with a spout from the bottom instead of the top. To use it, pour in the liquid you are trying to degrease and wait several minutes for the fat to rise to the top. Then pour off the grease-free liquid from the bottom, stopping just before the fat layer can sneak into the spout.

How to Thicken

The slow cooker naturally produces a lot of moisture during cooking, and while we often like eating our soups, stews, and leftover liquid from roasting *au naturel*, we like to have the option of thickening it, too. Here are the most common ways to prepare and use thickening agents and enrichments. You can use them interchangeably for the most part. Your choice may depend on dietary preferences and the type of ingredients needing to be thickened, or your own cooking style.

Flour is the most commonly used thickener. You dredge meat in it before browning or sprinkle it in the pan afterward, then stir in liquid and pour it all into the slow cooker. You can use bleached or unbleached all-purpose, whole wheat, or whole wheat pastry flours interchangeably. Flour can also be added at the end of cooking by making a slurry, with 1 to 2 tablespoons of flour mixed with an equal amount of water per cup of liquid, depending on how thick you want your dish. Turn the cooker to HIGH, stir the slurry into the hot liquid, re-cover, and cook until thick, 10 to 15 minutes, or cook a bit longer on LOW.

Roux is the term for equal parts of flour and butter cooked to form a paste. Melt the butter in a shallow pan over medium heat, then whisk in the flour. Stir for a few minutes to cook the flour slightly. Add some liquid and stir until smooth. Stir roux into your soup, stew, or leftover liquid until thickened and no longer murky. For a soup, use the ratio of 1 tablespoon each of butter and flour to 1 cup of liquid, and for a stew or sauce, 2 tablespoons each of butter and flour to 1 cup of liquid. Turn the cooker to HIGH, stir the roux into the hot liquid, re-cover, and cook until thick, 10 to 15 minutes, or cook a bit longer on LOW.

Beurre manié also utilizes flour and butter and is one of our favorite methods of thickening. It is an uncooked paste of flour and butter and it will transform the thinnest of sauces into a luscious one. To make a *beurre manié*, place an equal amount of soft butter and flour in a bowl or small food processor. Using a fork or pulsing motion, mash them together until the mixture becomes a semifirm mass. *Beurre manié* can be made ahead, divided into portions, then wrapped in plastic and stored in the refrigerator for up to 1 week, or in the freezer for up to 1 month (it can be used frozen). For a soup, use the ratio of 1 tablespoon each of butter and flour to 1 cup of liquid, and for a stew, 2 tablespoons each of butter and flour to 1 cup of liquid. Turn the cooker to HIGH, stir the *beurre manié* into the hot liquid, re-cover, and cook until thick, 10 to 15 minutes, or cook a bit longer on LOW.

Butter used alone will thicken a soup or sauce slightly and, of course, will add lots of flavor. Add at the end of cooking and stir gently a few times.

How to Read Our Recipes

Our recipes are designed to be easy to read. We also want you to be able to easily spot important information while cooking. After the title of the recipe comes the headnote. Do not skip reading this; it contains information on the food or type of dish and any special points or techniques. We often put serving suggestions or complementary food suggestions here.

The next line is the yield, a suggestion for approximately how many servings the recipe makes, using a moderately sized single portion as a guide. Serving sizes are notoriously subjective; they do not take into account the big eater who has multiple helpings, nor children's portions or leftovers, so pay attention here and adjust with regard to your specific needs.

Then comes information on the size of the slow cooker best suited to the recipe based on our testing. If you want to double the recipe, consider using a larger machine, and if you cut the recipe in half, downsize your cooker, depending on the type of recipe. Remember that the small slow cookers often only have a LOW setting, so if the dish must be cooked on HIGH, such as many of the bean recipes, a smaller machine will not be appropriate.

The machine setting and cook time are next, separated from the body of the recipe for easy reference. We suggest writing down the approximate finish time or setting a timer. Check your food near the end of the cooking time for the most control over texture and degree of finish.

Adapting Conventional Recipes to the Slow Cooker

If you are an experienced slow cooker user, you will have already learned that adapting conventional recipes for use in the slow cooker requires keeping a few things in mind.

- Slow cooker recipes require less liquid than recipes that use conventional cooking methods because evaporation is so markedly reduced. In general, we have found that slow cooker recipes require ½ to 1 cup less liquid than conventional recipes do. As moisture condenses from the food, it accumulates under the lid. These moisture droplets then fall onto the food, self-basting it. The liquid will not boil away or evaporate, so, combined with the food juices, you will end up with more liquid than when you began. When converting a recipe for the first time, we usually reduce the liquid by half, then add more as necessary at the end of cooking (for example, to thin a soup or bean dish), making the appropriate adjustment notes on the recipe.

○ Herbs and spices take on a new dimension in the slow cooker. With the long cooking times and concentration during cooking, fresh herbs tend to disintegrate and taste washed out, while dried herbs become overpowering and bitter. Start with half the amount of dried herbs and spices called for in a recipe and taste for seasoning an hour before serving. Season with salt, pepper, additional dried herbs if desired, and fresh herbs at that time.

○ Of course, the biggest difference is in the timing. A stew that calls for an hour on the stove will take approximately 6 to 8 hours on the LOW setting

·· Recipe Time Conversion Chart ··

We use this handy conversion chart as a guide for translating traditional cooking times into slow cooker times. All times are approximate. When making a recipe for the first time, be sure to check for doneness halfway through and near the end of the cooking time, making notes for future reference. Certain recipes will cook just as well on HIGH for half the amount of time as on LOW. Generally, 1 hour of cooking on the HIGH setting is equal to 2½ hours on LOW. While early slow cooker recipes all designated both LOW and HIGH cook times, we have found that most every dish cooks best on one or the other. Our recipes give directions for the temperature that gives the best results.

If a Recipe Reads	Slow Cooker Time on LOW	Slow Cooker Time on HIGH
15 minutes	2 to 2½ hours	1 to 1½ hours
30 minutes	3 to 4 hours	2 to 2½ hours
45 minutes	5 to 6 hours	3 to 3½ hours
60 minutes	6 to 8 hours	4 to 4½ hours
90 minutes	9 to 10 hours	5 to 5½ hours
2 hours	10 to 12 hours	6 to 6½ hours
3 hours	14 to 18 hours	7 to 7½ hours

·· High Altitude Slow-Cooking ··

There are special guidelines for slow-cooking at altitudes more than 3,000 feet above sea level. Just remember that the higher you go, the less compressed the air is and the lower the temperature at which water boils. Figure your food will take approximately 25 percent more time to come up to the proper cooking temperature and to cook.

The rule is to increase the oven temperature 1°F for every 100 feet of altitude, but in the slow cooker the temperature is preset, so you need to cook all foods on HIGH and increase the cooking time slightly. Use the LOW heat setting for warming.

Use the following chart as a guideline. Be sure to take notes on the adjustments you make to recipes for future reference.

Altitude Adjustment	3,000 feet	5,000 feet	7,000 to 8,000 feet
Cooking temperature	HIGH	HIGH	HIGH
Decrease in liquid per cup in recipe	1 to 2 tablespoons	2 to 3 tablespoons	3 to 4 tablespoons

of the slow cooker. This is a big difference, and once you make the adjustment, you will love the flexibility. Please refer to the Recipe Time Conversion Chart (page 19) as a guide.

The Panic-Proof Pantry for Slow Cooker Entertaining

"Well stocked" translates to "well prepared." You do not need to have a connoisseur mentality to cook good food, just a sense of organization and the desire to cook with ingredients that appeal to you. We are great proponents of having a full pantry, by purchasing ingredients before you need them. In the most modest pantry these days it is not unusual to see canned coconut milk next to jarred salsa and hot sauce, harissa next to *herbes de Provence*, extra-virgin olive oil with sesame oil and grape leaves. Oh, and then there are the favorite barbecue sauces, dried fruit, and soy sauce. If you do not make your own stocks, have on hand cans of your favorite vegetable and meat broths.

We have included in this book a wide variety of dishes suitable for entertaining: very easy, quick-to-assemble recipes (boneless chicken breasts in two hours) as well as those that are a bit more sophisticated (cassoulet or lamb shanks) and take a bit more time (but not necessarily more effort). All rely on your pantry. Our panic-proof slow cooker pantry is designed for on-the-spot slow-cooking and contains items that are, above all, versatile and make vivid, delicious combinations. For parties or company dinners, make lists from the recipes you are going to prepare and check against your pantry to see what you need to buy.

The Cupboard

Vinegars: Stock red and white wine vinegar, white and dark balsamic vinegar, champagne vinegar, apple cider vinegar, malt vinegar, and herb vinegars such as tarragon or basil.

Oils: In addition to regular and light extra-virgin olive oils, keep a light vegetable oil such as safflower or canola; regular, toasted, and hot sesame oils; and a few nut oils, such as walnut and hazelnut, that are also good for vinaigrettes, drizzling over finished dishes, and sautéing vegetables. Walnut oil is a great all-purpose cooking oil and is nutritionally healthy like olive oil.

Tomatoes: The slow cooker uses a lot of tomato products because they are a wonderful and versatile flavor medium. Canned tomatoes come in a wide variety of preparations (whole, diced, pureed) and are so convenient; often, canned whole or diced peeled tomatoes are better than out-of-season market ones. Keep dehydrated and olive oil–packed sun-dried tomatoes, too. Tomato paste is useful for keeping sauces from being too thin, and always keep one good commercial tomato sauce on hand for those on-the-spot rib dishes or a ragù.

Beans: Stock canned cannellini beans, red kidney beans, pinto beans, garbanzo beans, and black beans, as well as canned refried beans for dips. Also keep on hand dried beans, such as flageolets verts, black turtle beans, anasazi beans, cranberry beans, navy beans, pintos, lentils, split peas, and Great Northern beans.

Stock and broth: Buy chicken, beef, and vegetable broths and clam juice for soups, stews, vegetable dishes, and risottos.

Mushrooms: Once only a gourmet item, dried mushrooms are excellent everyday slow cooker ingredients. A well-stocked supermarket now has an entire selection, usually in a corner of the produce department, including dried porcini, morels, and cèpes. Look for shiitake in the Asian food section. Dried mushrooms keep indefinitely and reconstitute easily for sauces, risottos, and stews.

Dried pastas: Although we use limited amounts of pasta in slow cooker dishes, because it tends to get gummy if not carefully prepared, noodles are a wonderful side dish or bed for most sauces and stews. Fit the shape to your dish; try linguine, spaghetti, and stubby macaronis such as penne, fusilli, and shells, as well as egg noodles and Japanese udon.

Rice: Converted rice and wild rice hold up beautifully in the long cooking process. Italian Arborio and Vialone nano are used for slow cooker risottos.

Keep white basmati, Japanese-style short-grain white rice (Calrose), short-grain brown rice, and wild rice as the basics for a delicious starchy side dish.

Dried fruits: Keep apricots, prunes, raisins, dried cranberries, and dried tart cherries for desserts and compotes, as well as for use in Moroccan tagines and many quick chicken dishes.

Chocolate: Stock semisweet or bittersweet chocolate chips, unsweetened chocolate, and good old-fashioned Hershey bars for mole and slow cooker chocolate sauces.

Preserves, jams, and jellies: Orange marmalade is great for ribs and glazes. Also stock some uncommon preserves, such as whole sour cherries, currant jelly, quince jelly, and lime or ginger marmalade.

Essential sundries: Canned evaporated milk, your favorite barbecue sauce, jarred roasted red peppers, canned roasted green chiles, jarred salsa, tuna packed in olive oil or spring water, olives (green, black niçoise, Greek oil-cured, canned ripe California), grape leaves, and capers all make good additions to sauces, soups, and stews. Also stock all-purpose flour, cornmeal, and granulated and brown sugar.

The Refrigerator

Standards: These include butter, milk, eggs, heavy cream, sour cream, and crème fraîche or yogurt for sauces. Keep bacon or pancetta, too, for soups and stews, and vacuum-packed sausages.

Sauces and condiments: Stock soy sauce, hot pepper sauce, Worcestershire sauce, and maple syrup.

Vegetables: Keep durable cabbage, apples, potatoes, carrots, celery, garlic, shallots, onions, and turnips on hand for soups, vegetable dishes, and stews.

Cheeses: Chèvre (goat cheese) is flavorful and versatile. Keep Parmesan, Asiago, or Romano for grating. We also use lots of cheddar, Monterey Jack, mozzarella, Muenster, and Gorgonzola.

The Freezer

Meat: Stock individually wrapped bone-in and boneless chicken breasts (the quintessential desperation cooking food), chicken wings, turkey breast or tenderloins, veal or lamb stew meat, beef or pork ribs, pork tenderloin, pork roast, and sausage.

Nuts: These are the original store-it-away-forever food and are used for sauces, desserts, hors d'oeuvres, and garnishing. The basics are pine nuts, walnuts, almonds, and pecans. We keep nuts and seeds in the freezer.

Miscellaneous indispensables: You'll be grateful to have frozen artichoke hearts, peas, and spinach; also frozen ravioli and tortellini, unsalted butter, and frozen berries such as raspberries or blueberries.

Herbs

We love herbs, both fresh and dried, and the special aromatic flavor they impart to a dish. The basic rule in using herbs is to use a bit less than usual if you are using dried and put them into the pot with the initial ingredients. Fresh are more volatile and delicate over the long cooking process, tending to break down, so we often add them at the end, or add a portion during the cooking and the remainder at the end. The ultimate test, of course, is how you like it; please adjust the recipe to your palate, especially if you like more or less flavoring. Since dried herbs are often stronger in flavor than fresh, the approximate substitution proportion is to use one-third the amount of the dried as you would of the fresh. That is, if a recipe calls for 1 tablespoon of minced fresh basil, you would use 1 teaspoon dried.

Where to get your fresh herbs? Some people love having a small kitchen garden with a sunny patch devoted just to their favorite herbs. Chives, mint, oregano, parsley, and sage grow nicely in pots indoors all winter. Other cooks are just as happy to buy their herbs in the produce section at the supermarket. While most supermarkets have a section devoted to dried herbs, home-dried herbs are really special (page 24). We also adore buying dried herbs by mail-order from Penzeys Spices (www.penzeys.com).

The following is a list of our most used fresh herbs.

Fresh basil, oregano, marjoram, savory, sage, thyme, rosemary, and bay leaf: These herbs are often called for in Mediterranean and American cooking.

⋅⋅ Salt: The Most Important Seasoning ⋅⋅

Salt is an important addition to food, accenting and balancing the natural flavors. In slow-cooking, very few recipes call for salt in the beginning of cooking, but the majority call for it at the end, so you can taste and make your adjustments at that time. This is because the flavors in slow-cooking become more concentrated during the long cook times, and salt, as with other seasonings, will intensify. Stirring in salt at the end of cooking gives it time to "melt" into the dish and harmonize the flavors. Always add the salt for beans at the end of cooking, otherwise they will toughen and never cook to the desired soft texture. If your ingredients contain capers, anchovy paste, olives, fish sauce, miso, preserved lemon, ham or bacon, Parmesan cheese, or soy sauce, take care adding salt; you may not need any, because these ingredients are salty by nature.

Many cooks especially love thyme flowers and stems. California bay leaves are double the strength of Turkish bay leaves, so be sure to check what type you have to avoid too strong a flavor.

Fresh tarragon, chervil, chives, and dill: These herbs are prevalent in European cooking, especially tarragon and chervil. Tarragon is best harvested before it flowers, and chive flowers are delicious.

Fresh parsley: Parsley is an all-purpose herb that is best used fresh. We always use flat-leaf parsley, also called Italian parsley, because it is less chewy than the curly variety.

Fresh mint: There are many types of mint, all of which are delicious, and the stems are as good as the leaves.

Fresh cilantro: Also called coriander or Chinese parsley, this is an herb that transcends all boundaries. It is as at home in Chinese and Thai cuisine as it is in Mexican. It looks like a delicate parsley and tastes peppery and refreshing.

How to Dry Fresh Herbs

The end of summer is the time to gather fresh outdoor herbs and dry them for storage and use during the winter. This method works especially well with bay leaf, oregano, savory, marjoram, sage, tarragon, thyme, lemon verbena, and rosemary. Drying breaks down the cell structure, evaporates the water in the leaves, and concentrates the essential oils that compose the herb's flavor (that is why dried herbs are stronger than fresh ones).

Harvest your herbs depending on the part of the plant you want to use: Remove flowers when the buds open but are not fully in bloom, and remove leaves when they are young and tender. Use kitchen shears; never pull them out or tear them. Gently wash the leaves with cool to tepid water, because hot water can dissolve precious aromatic oils; dry and remove undesirable leaves, and let the herbs dry overnight.

Remove the whole leaves from the stem and spread the leaves on a double layer of paper towels placed on a plate or flat basket so that the air can circulate; for larger amounts, lay the leaves on old screens or use a controlled-temperature stacked dehydrator at 95°F for 2 to 4 hours. Let the leaves air-dry at room temperature for three days to one week in a clean area, away from direct sunlight.

For small amounts of dried herbs, you can use your microwave. Place a small amount of herbs on a paper towel, spreading them out. Dry at 1-minute intervals, watching constantly so that the herbs do not overheat, because they can experience spontaneous combustion. The leaves should become crisp and brittle, but be careful not to overdry them, because that will destroy the oils, vitamins, and minerals.

No matter which drying method you use, store the herbs in brown paper bags in a cupboard for up to 6 months; when

• • A Glass for the Pot • •

Wine is the world's most common beverage, along with beer, these days. It is remarkably compatible with food, not only as an accompaniment, but also as a highly versatile ingredient because it blends so nicely with myriad foods.

Note that we use table wines of all sorts, both during the assembly of ingredients and when loading the slow cooker, and at the end of cooking time, when we often take advantage of fortified wines to add another dimension of flavor. When you add wine at the beginning of cooking, some of the alcohol will burn off and leave the delicious flavor elements; if you add it at the end of cooking, the alcohol content will basically remain. We also often deglaze a pan with wine after meat or poultry has been browned. The boiling wine loosens the bits of cooked meat from the pan, and everything dissolves together, becoming the base for a delicious sauce.

There are rules for adding wine to your stews and braises. First, never cook with a wine that you would find unsuitable for drinking. Never use those "cooking wines" that can ruin a stew faster than a bad cook in an ill-equipped kitchen. Slow-cooking concentrates the qualities of the wine, and you will notice all sorts of flavors that can add up to an artificial or a cloying taste. You don't have to use any expensive or rare wines for cooking. There is a gigantic world of moderately priced wines from which to choose, so worry not.

Leftover opened bottles of red wine are great to use in cooking. Even if a red wine has sat for weeks and oxidized a bit, it will make your braised oxtails sing. White wine should be used right after it has been opened or within a day, even if it has been refrigerated. After that, it is a throwaway because it is so perishable. Dry table wines can be used for the most part interchangeably in recipes, but never substitute a sweet dessert wine for a dry wine; you will ruin your dish.

Select a wine that complements your dish. We often make suggestions in our recipes, especially if a dish's flavor depends upon a certain wine. Red wine is stronger than white, so it is not often used in fish sauces, but it can be used interchangeably in poultry dishes just fine. If you use a sparkling wine or Champagne, expect that the effervescence will fade and the wine will act like a still white wine. Many cooks first choose what they want to drink with their dinner, then opt for a cheaper version for the pot. This works well if you are buying an expensive import; then just substitute a domestic version of that wine. If you are planning ahead, it is a nice way to be a bit economical.

you need herbs, just pull a few leaves out of the bag, crushing them before using.

How to Freeze Fresh Herbs

For a close-to-fresh flavor, wash the leaves and strip them from the stem, as for drying. Chop the leaves or leave them whole, as desired. Place them in small plastic freezer bags and freeze for up to one year. Break off portions to use as needed. The herbs can be used frozen or defrosted, but they must be used as soon as possible. Do not refreeze them. This method is especially good for mint, cilantro, basil, sage, marjoram, epazote, and chives.

Appetizer Dips, Savory Fondues, and Party Nuts

Hot Artichoke Dip with Pita Crisps o 29

Layered Artichokes and
Green Chiles o 30

Hot Spinach Dip o 31

Always Smooth Chili con Queso o 31

Smoky Black Bean and
Cheddar Dip o 33

Jacquie's Black Bean–
Jalapeño Dip o 33

Chili Olive Dip o 34

Creamy Refried Bean Dip o 35

Hot Crab Supreme o 36

Bagna Cauda o 37

Hot Sausage Dip o 38

Caramel Brie o 39

Welsh Rabbit o 40

Tomato Fondue o 41

Fondue Neuchâtel o 42

Champagne Fondue o 43

Buttermilk Fondue o 44

Fondue with Sparkling
Apple Cider o 45

Tamari Almonds o 46

Malabar Almonds o 47

Buttery Rosemary Pecan Halves o 48

Maple-Glazed Pecans o 49

Spicy Walnuts o 50

Walnuts and Ginger o 50

Sugared Walnuts o 51

Curry Mixed Nuts o 52

Retro Party Mix o 52

Appetizers and hors d'oeuvres are the prelude to a meal or are part of a little meal made up of many parts served at the same time, such as a grazing buffet. They are immensely popular, yet often there is the dilemma of what to make. We say keep it simple.

If you are offering a taste of this and that before a meal just to ward off hunger while chatting, one appetizer will usually do. If you are having only appetizers for a gathering, then a number of them, balanced among meats, vegetables, cheeses, breads, nuts, and rich and lean foods, are in order. While appetizers tend to be trendy, we have our perennial nibbly favorites, namely, oozy hot dips served with colorful fresh veggies or crisp chips, and salty, tasty nuts.

Dips have always been easy to manage, and they feed a large group effortlessly. The slow cooker has made this even more true. Mix together the ingredients right in the ceramic insert, then let the cooker warm the mixture, and serve it hot right out of the crock. Dips can sit all evening on LOW or KEEP WARM. The recipes we've collected here are tried and true and represent a range of international flavors, with classics such as bagna cauda, refried bean dip, and a host of lovely fondues, which are also suitable to serve as a light meal with a salad. Serve fondues with toasted baguette slices, fresh bread, or any number of veggies or chips for dipping.

We always make sure to put out a small bowl of some sort of flavored spiced nuts for parties, because they go well with so many drinks. The slow cooker toasts nuts beautifully, with little risk of burning them. Wonderful for holiday entertaining, spiced nuts also make great hostess gifts and are delicious when tossed into salads.

Hot Artichoke Dip with Pita Crisps

T his is the most popular dip we make. It is good hot or warm, or even cooled to room temperature. If you want a no-added-fat version of the pita crisps, just brush the smooth side of the pita with a beaten-until-foamy egg white instead of the oil. ○ *Makes about 2¼ cups to serve 8*

COOKER: Small round
SETTING AND COOK TIME: LOW for 1½ to 3 hours

6 pita pocket breads
⅓ cup olive oil
4 green onions (white and green parts)
One 8-ounce package cream cheese, softened
1 cup freshly grated Parmesan cheese
One 13.75-ounce can artichoke hearts packed in water, drained
½ cup regular or low-fat mayonnaise, or regular or low-fat plain yogurt
    drained in a coffee filter–lined strainer until thick
Dash of hot red pepper sauce

1. Preheat the oven to 300°F. Line a baking sheet with parchment paper. Split each pita open, making 2 rounds. Brush the smooth side of each round with olive oil. Place on the baking sheet. Bake until crisp, about 20 minutes. Let cool on racks, then break each round into 5 irregular pieces. If they lose their crispness before serving, reheat in the oven for a few minutes.

2. Place the green onions in a food processor and chop. Add the cream cheese and Parmesan and process until smooth. Add the artichokes and process until coarsely chopped. Add the mayonnaise and hot sauce and pulse until just incorporated.

3. Scrape the dip into the slow cooker. Cover and cook on LOW until the dip is hot throughout, 1½ to 3 hours.

4. Set the slow cooker in the entertaining area. Set on LOW, leave the cover off, and dip with the pita bread crisps.

Layered Artichokes and Green Chiles

ere is another excellent variation on artichoke dip, this time layered. This is good with tortilla chips or pita bread crisps (see preceding recipe). We use a 2½-quart small slow cooker. ○ *Serves 8*

COOKER: Small round
SETTING AND COOK TIME: LOW for 2 to 3 hours

One 13.75-ounce can artichoke hearts packed in water, drained and chopped
1½ cups shredded mild or sharp cheddar or Muenster cheese
2 ounces fresh goat cheese, crumbled
One 16-ounce jar marinated artichoke hearts, drained and chopped
One 4-ounce can diced roasted green chiles, drained
⅓ cup regular or low-fat mayonnaise
Tortilla chips or pita bread crisps for serving

1. Coat the inside of the slow cooker crock with nonstick cooking spray or grease with olive oil. Make a single, even layer of each ingredient in the following order: the water-packed artichoke hearts, a third of the cheddar cheese, half of the goat cheese, the chopped marinated artichoke hearts, then the green chiles. Spread the top with the mayonnaise, completely covering the vegetables. Sprinkle with the remaining cheddar cheese and goat cheese.

2. Cover and cook on LOW until the dip is hot throughout, 2 to 3 hours.

3. Set the slow cooker in the entertaining area. Set on LOW, leave the cover off, and dip with tortilla chips or pita bread crisps.

Hot Spinach Dip

There are many versions of spinach dip, and this is one of the best. Try it with chips or crudités. It is so decadently satisfying that it's worth making at least once a year for guests . . . and yourself! ○ *Makes about 3 cups to serve 12*

COOKER: Small round
SETTING AND COOK TIME: LOW for 1½ to 3 hours

One 12-ounce package frozen chopped spinach, thawed and squeezed dry
One 8-ounce package cream cheese, cubed
¼ cup freshly grated Parmesan or Asiago cheese
1 cup shredded whole-milk mozzarella cheese
Potato chips and assorted raw vegetables for serving

1. In a food processor, combine the spinach, cream cheese, and Parmesan and process until smooth, stopping to scrape down the bowl as necessary.

2. Scrape the dip into the slow cooker and fold in the mozzarella cheese to evenly distribute. Cover and cook on LOW until the dip is hot throughout and the cheese melted, 1½ to 3 hours.

3. Set the slow cooker in the entertaining area. Set on LOW, leave the cover off, and dip with chips and veggies.

Always Smooth Chile con Queso

This is a favorite recipe from food writer Elaine Corn, co-owner of Bamboo Restaurant in Sacramento, California, but a native of El Paso, Texas. She loves only white cheese for her melted queso. The fresh green chiles are worth the extra effort of roasting and peeling; they make the dip fantastic. It is important to sauté the onions and chiles properly before adding them to the cheese, because they will not cook further. This is great party food. ○ *Makes about 2½ cups to serve 10 to 12*

COOKER: Medium round

SETTING AND COOK TIME: LOW for 1 to 1½ hours

1½ pounds Monterey Jack cheese, cubed
¼ cup (½ stick) unsalted butter
2 medium-size white onions, finely chopped
1 tablespoon finely minced garlic
10 green Anaheim or California chiles (see Note), roasted (page 135),
    peeled, seeded, and coarsely chopped
2 jalapeño chiles, seeded and minced
Dash of salt (optional)
Freshly ground black pepper to taste
Tortilla chips for serving

1. Place the cheese in the slow cooker; cover and set on LOW. Stir frequently until melted.

2. Meanwhile, in a large skillet over medium heat, melt the butter, then add the onions and cook, stirring, until quite limp and transparent but not browned, about 5 minutes. Add the garlic and cook a minute or two more. Add the Anaheim and jalapeño chiles and cook, stirring, about 5 minutes more. Add the salt, if desired, and season with pepper.

3. Scrape the mixture into the slow cooker and stir to combine with the melted cheese. Cover and keep on LOW for up to 1 hour.

4. Set the slow cooker in the entertaining area. Set on LOW, leave the cover off, and dip tortilla chips into the queso.

Note: Instead of the fresh chiles, you can substitute three 4-ounce cans roasted whole green chiles, drained and coarsely chopped.

Smoky Black Bean and Cheddar Dip

his easy dip is earthy and filling. The smoky-hot flavor comes from a chipotle chile. Feel free to add more chile if you like. Serve with tortilla chips, raw multicolored bell pepper strips, jicama, and cherry tomatoes for dipping. Everyone will be asking you for the recipe.

○ *Makes about 2½ cups to serve 8 to 10*

COOKER: Small round
SETTING AND COOK TIME: LOW for 1½ to 3 hours

One 19-ounce can black beans, drained, or 2 cups cooked black beans
¼ of an individual canned chipotle chile in adobo, cut into small pieces,
    plus 1 teaspoon of the adobo sauce from the can
3 cups shredded medium-sharp cheddar cheese
Corn chips and assorted raw vegetables for serving

1. In a food processor, process the black beans and chile with its sauce together until smooth, stopping to scrape down the bowl as necessary.

2. Scrape the dip into the slow cooker and fold in the cheese to evenly distribute. Cover and cook on LOW until the dip is hot throughout and the cheese melted, 1½ to 3 hours.

3. Set the slow cooker in the entertaining area. Set on LOW, leave the cover off, and dip the chips and veggies.

Jacquie's Black Bean–Jalapeño Dip

his is what Latin-food specialist Jacquie Higuera McMahan calls "a velvety concoction." It is from her self-published book, *The Healthy Mexican Cook Book* (1994), one of our favorite cookbooks. She spreads it inside tacos, smears it on crusty French bread or *bolillos*, the torpedo-shaped sandwich rolls of Mexico, from a local *panadería*, or just dips into it with chips. Be sure to buy mild ground chili powder if you are seeking a mildly spicy dip. Medium or hot ground chili powder will give the dip more punch.

○ *Makes about 2 cups to serve 8 to 10 as an appetizer or 4 as a sandwich filling*

COOKER: Small round
SETTING AND COOK TIME: LOW for 1½ to 3 hours

One 19-ounce can black beans, drained, or 2 cups cooked black beans
2 cloves garlic, minced
2 jalapeño chiles, seeded and minced
1 tablespoon freshly squeezed lime juice
1 tablespoon cider vinegar
2 teaspoons red chili powder of your choice (see above)
¼ teaspoon ground cumin
One 3-ounce package cream cheese
Corn chips and sliced French bread for serving

1. Coat the inside of the crock with nonstick cooking spray or grease with olive oil.

2. In a food processor, combine the beans, garlic, chiles, lime juice, vinegar, chili powder, cumin, and cream cheese and process until well combined and smooth.

3. Transfer the mixture to the crock. Cover and cook on LOW until the dip is hot throughout and the cheese melted, 1½ to 3 hours.

4. Set the slow cooker in the entertaining area. Set on LOW, leave the cover off, and dip the chips or serve with a spreader for the bread.

Chili Olive Dip

B eth's sister whips up dips like this for every party she gives, whether four or a dozen guests are coming over. The combination of the chili with the cream cheese is really tasty, so don't miss this one. ○ *Makes about 3 cups to serve 12*

COOKER: Small round
SETTING AND COOK TIME: LOW for 2 to 3 hours

Two 7-ounce cans chili with beans
Two 3-ounce packages cream cheese, cubed
½ cup sliced California black olives
¼ cup canned diced green chiles, drained
Sliced green onions for garnish
Corn chips for serving

1. Combine the chili, cream cheese, olives, and chiles in the slow cooker and stir until smooth. Cover and cook on LOW until the dip is hot throughout and the cream cheese melted, 2 to 3 hours.

2. Set the slow cooker in the entertaining area. Set on LOW, leave the cover off, sprinkle with the green onions, and dip the chips.

Creamy Refried Bean Dip

 his is a nice dip to make for a crowd. It's creamy and spicy—a nice contrast to the crisp and salty chips. ⦿ *Makes about 5 cups to serve 20 to 25*

COOKER: Medium round or oval
SETTING AND COOK TIME: LOW for 1½ to 3 hours

One 16-ounce can refried beans
1 cup picante sauce of your choice
½ cup regular or low-fat sour cream
1 tablespoon chili powder
¼ teaspoon ground cumin
One 3-ounce package cream cheese, diced
1 cup shredded Monterey Jack cheese
1 cup shredded cheddar cheese
Tortilla chips for serving

1. Combine the beans, picante sauce, sour cream, chili powder, and cumin in the slow cooker and stir until smooth. Fold in the cream cheese and Jack and cheddar cheeses. Cover and cook on LOW until the dip is hot throughout and the cheeses melted, 1½ to 3 hours.

2. Set the slow cooker in the entertaining area. Set on LOW, leave the cover off, and dip the tortilla chips.

Hot Crab Supreme

his warm crab dip is rich and decadent, the perfect party food. Serve it directly from the slow cooker insert with cubes of French bread and provide little plates and long bamboo picks for easy dipping and dunking. Do not use low-fat or nonfat mayonnaise or sour cream in this recipe.

Makes about 8 cups to serve 16 to 24

COOKER: Medium round or oval
SETTING AND COOK TIME: LOW for 2 to 2 1/2 hours;
    crabmeat added during the last 20 minutes

1 quart mayonnaise
2 cups sour cream
1/4 cup dry sherry
3 tablespoons freshly squeezed lemon juice
1/4 cup chopped fresh Italian parsley
2 pounds fresh crabmeat, picked over for shells and cartilage
Salt and white pepper to taste
French bread cut into bite-size cubes for serving

1. Combine the mayonnaise, sour cream, sherry, and lemon juice in the slow cooker, whisking until smooth. Cover and cook on LOW until the dip is hot throughout, 1 1/2 to 2 hours.

2. Fold in the parsley and crabmeat and season with salt and white pepper. Cover and leave on LOW for another 20 minutes to heat the crab.

3. Set the slow cooker in the entertaining area. Set on LOW, leave the cover off, and dip the bread cubes.

Bagna Cauda

Translating to "hot bath," this olive oil and anchovy mixture is from the mountains of Piedmont, Italy, known for its hearty, tasty, and healthful food. Dip raw seasonal vegetables and grissini (bread sticks) or thin slices of crusty ciabatta or baguette. Pronounced "bahnya cowda," this is a trattoria favorite for groups and is traditionally prepared in an earthenware pot over a candle; the slow cooker is a natural update. Originally, a small pot and fondue fork were placed in front of each person: Dip a vegetable, hold the bread underneath to avoid dripping on yourself, and eat. Extra-virgin olive oil is a must; you want to experience the full flavor of the oil. If you use harder vegetables, such as cauliflower and carrots, be sure to blanch them first for a few minutes in boiling water. The favorite vegetable in Italy for this is the cardoon, an edible thistle that tastes like celery, but serve whatever you have on hand. Accompany with a room-temperature light wine, such as a rosé or fruity red. ○ *Makes about 1¼ cups to serve 6 to 8*

COOKER: Small round
SETTING AND COOK TIME: LOW for 1 to 2 hours

¾ cup extra-virgin olive oil
½ cup (1 stick) unsalted butter or extra-virgin olive oil
1 to 4 cloves garlic, to your taste, smashed flat but left whole
6 to 10 anchovy fillets, to your taste
1 teaspoon red wine vinegar
Small pinch of red pepper flakes
Assorted crudités for serving: red or yellow bell pepper strips, radishes, cucumber slices, blanched carrot sticks, celery sticks, blanched asparagus, small strips of zucchini, thin slices of fennel bulb, scallions, baby romaine or endive leaves, quartered plum tomatoes or whole cherry tomatoes, drained canned artichoke hearts, and/or blanched broccoli or cauliflower florets
Grissini or crusty bread cut into thick fingers for serving

1. Combine the oil, butter, and garlic in the slow cooker.

2. In a marble mortar with a pestle or in a bowl with a fork, mash the anchovy fillets until a paste is formed; add to the oil mixture in the crock and stir until

combined. Cover and cook on LOW until the butter is melted and the anchovies are dissolved, 1 to 2 hours; handle with care, because the oil is very hot.

3. Remove the garlic cloves, especially if they've turned brown, and add the vinegar and red pepper flakes and stir. Arrange the vegetables on a platter or in bowls, and place the grissini in a basket. Set the slow cooker in the entertaining area. Set on LOW for up to 4 hours, leave the cover off, and dip the fresh vegetables and bread. Stir often to keep the anchovies from separating from the oil.

Hot Sausage Dip

(T)his dip came via Columbia, South Carolina, from Beth's aunt, who is a party maven. She sometimes uses a caterer, and other times pulls out her stash of simple foods that are perennially popular. This dip is a total surprise. People will rave. ○ *Makes about 3 cups to serve 8 to 12*

COOKER: Small round
SETTING AND COOK TIME: LOW for 3 to 4 hours

One 12-ounce package breakfast pork sausage meat (such as Jimmy Dean), crumbled
One 10-ounce can stewed tomatoes with chiles (such as Rotel)
One 8-ounce package cream cheese, cut into chunks
Corn chips for serving

1. In a large skillet over medium heat, cook the sausage meat until cooked through and browned, about 10 minutes. Remove to paper towels with a slotted spoon and blot well to soak up any excess fat. Add the stewed tomatoes to the skillet and cook for 1 to 2 minutes. Stir the sausage into the tomatoes.

2. Transfer the mixture to the slow cooker and add the cream cheese, stirring gently. Cover and cook on LOW until the dip is hot throughout and the cheese melted, 3 to 4 hours.

3. Set the slow cooker in the entertaining area. Set on LOW, leave the cover off, and dip the chips.

Caramel Brie

T his recipe always gets raves. Creamy Brie cheese is presented with a thick top coating of sweet caramel. As the party guests cut into the cheese with a cheese spreader, they get some caramel at the same time to spread on crackers or apple slices. Buy the individually wrapped caramels in the candy-aisle bins at the supermarket. ○ *Serves 25 to 30*

COOKER: Small round
SETTING AND COOK TIME: LOW for 1 to 1½ hours

About 4 pounds Brie cheese (two 8-inch wheels, or two 1-kilogram wheels)
15 individually wrapped caramel candies
¾ cup heavy cream or evaporated milk
24 perfect pecan halves, for garnish
Water crackers, sliced French bread, wheatmeal biscuits,
    and/or apple slices for serving

1. Place the Brie on a serving platter or slab of marble suitable for placing on the buffet table. Let the Brie come to room temperature.

2. Unwrap the caramels. Combine the caramels and cream in the slow cooker. Cover and cook on LOW for 1 to 1½ hours to melt the candy; stir with a whisk to smooth the mixture. Add a tablespoon or two more cream if it is too thick; you want the melted caramel to be smooth and as thick as possible, yet still pourable.

3. Unwrap the Brie and, using a rubber spatula, pour the warm caramel sauce onto the center of the cheese round. With a metal spatula and using strokes that go from the center out to the edge, push the caramel out to the edges of the cheese; some of the caramel will drip down the sides. Immediately arrange the pecan halves around the edge of the cheese or in any desired pattern. Let stand for 20 minutes to cool and set the caramel topping, then serve with accompaniments of your choice.

Welsh Rabbit

Welsh rabbit, or rarebit, has no bunny in it. "Rabbit" is an old name for Old English cheddar cheese produced near the Welsh border that was melted and poured over toast. It is a traditional, stick-to-the-ribs British dish and is called *caws pobi* in Welsh. I loved this as a kid (use milk instead of the beer for the young diners) for lunch or dinner. When topped with a poached egg, it is called Golden Buck. This recipe comes from Colonial Williamsburg in Virginia, where it is winter tavern fare, served with mugs of cold ale. Serve this as an appetizer with toast points for dipping. ○ *Serves 4*

COOKER: Medium round

SETTINGS AND COOK TIMES: HIGH for 30 minutes, then LOW for 1½ hours; mustard, beer, and egg added during last 30 minutes

1 cup beer
1 tablespoon butter or margarine
1 pound medium or sharp cheddar cheese, shredded (4 cups)
Dash of Tabasco sauce
Dash of Worcestershire sauce
1 teaspoon dry mustard, such as Colman's
1 large egg, beaten
4 slices toast, crusts trimmed
Hungarian paprika for sprinkling

1. Pour the beer (reserving 2 tablespoons of it in a small bowl) into the slow cooker, add the butter, turn to HIGH, and cook, uncovered, for 30 minutes to evaporate some of the beer and melt the butter.

2. When the beer is hot, add the cheese and the Tabasco and Worcestershire sauces. Reduce the heat to LOW, cover, and cook until the cheese is melted, about 1 hour.

3. Add the mustard to the reserved beer and stir to make a paste, then add the beaten egg. Add the mixture to the slow cooker while stirring constantly with a whisk. Cover and cook for another 30 minutes.

4. Spoon the rabbit over plain or buttered toast, sprinkle with paprika, and serve immediately.

Tomato Fondue

Here's a version of fondue liberally adapted from a recipe by chef John Ash that cuts down on the fat but still provides all the flavor. He uses a goat's-milk Teleme from Redwood Hill Farms for his recipe, but we love regular Teleme or a ball of whole-milk mozzarella, which is easy to find in a good deli and melts wonderfully in the bath of the tomatoes. Serve this with crusty peasant-style bread, which you can use to dip and scoop up the cheesy mixture. ● *Serves 8 to 10*

COOKER: Medium round
SETTING AND COOK TIME: LOW for 2 to 3 hours

2 tablespoons olive oil
¼ cup finely chopped shallots
One 28-ounce can crushed tomatoes with basil, undrained
¾ cup hearty red wine, such as Zinfandel
1 tablespoon finely grated orange zest
1 tablespoon finely chopped fresh Italian parsley
1 tablespoon finely chopped fresh basil
Salt and freshly ground black pepper to taste
One 8-ounce piece Teleme cheese or whole-milk mozzarella cheese
2 French baguettes, thinly sliced

1. In a large skillet, heat the olive oil over medium heat and stir in the shallots; cook, stirring, until soft but not brown. Add the tomatoes and wine, increase the heat slightly, and simmer, uncovered, until the mixture reduces to a light sauce consistency, 5 to 10 minutes. Stir in the orange zest, parsley, and basil, then season with salt and pepper.

2. Pour the mixture into the slow cooker. Place the cheese down into the middle so it is covered with the tomato sauce. Cover and cook on LOW until the cheese is melted, 2 to 3 hours. Stir well.

3. Serve right from the slow cooker. You can dip the bread pieces directly into the sauce, but have cheese spreaders or spoons ready to retrieve the last bit of fondue.

Fondue Neuchâtel

This is the real thing—the traditional recipe! Fondue goes in and out of fashion in this country, but in Europe it is a quintessential winter food for sharing. It was originally cooked communally over an open fire by herdsmen camped out in high alpine meadows. The name comes from the addition of Neuchâtel, a dry, 11 percent alcohol white wine. You can substitute dry Riesling or Champagne. Kirsch, a strong, clear liqueur made from the pits of mountain cherries, is the traditional finishing touch. You can use other clear eaux-de-fruits, such as pear or raspberry brandy. While one used to have to start the fondue on the stovetop, then transfer it to a tabletop chafing dish or *caquelon* (a Swiss earthenware casserole glazed on the inside just for fondue), the whole process is now done beautifully in the slow cooker every step of the way, right up to serving it from the crock and keeping it warm. Long forks or skewers are needed for dipping the bread cubes, but also provide regular forks and small plates for eating. When the fondue is finished, there may be a brown crust on the bottom of the crock. Don't let it burn, but peel it up with a fork and divide among the group to munch on. Keep the bottle of kirsch nearby; often guests will pour a small glass and dip their bread into the fondue, then into the kirsch, a little tradition called *sans souci*— "without care." It is an established ritual to serve hot strong coffee or a brandy after a fondue party. While eating fondue, drink tea or wine, say Julie's friends the Von Kaenels, who are from Neuchâtel, Switzerland. Cold beverages such as water are said to impede digestion of the cheese. ● *Serves 6*

COOKER: Medium round
SETTINGS AND COOK TIMES: HIGH for 30 minutes, then LOW for 1 hour

1 clove garlic, split
1½ cups dry white wine
½ pound Emmental cheese, shredded (2 cups)
½ pound Gruyère cheese, shredded (2 cups)
2½ tablespoons all-purpose flour
3 tablespoons clear fruit brandy, such as kirsch

2 to 3 grindings of freshly ground black pepper
Pinch of freshly grated nutmeg
1 to 2 loaves ciabatta or baguettes, cut into 1-inch cubes

1. Rub the bottom and lower sides of the inside of the crock with the garlic clove, then discard the garlic. Pour the wine into the slow cooker, turn on HIGH, and cook, uncovered, for 30 minutes to evaporate some of the alcohol.

2. Combine the Emmental and Gruyère cheeses in a large bowl and toss with the flour. When the wine is hot, add the cheese slowly, a handful at a time, letting each addition melt before adding the next and stirring to keep lumps from forming. Reduce the heat to LOW, cover, and cook until the cheese is melted, about 1 hour. It will keep on LOW for up to an additional hour before you need to serve it. The melted cheese will be the consistency of a light cream sauce.

3. Stir in the brandy, pepper, and nutmeg right before serving. Set the slow cooker in the entertaining area, set on LOW, leave the cover off, and dip the bread cubes.

Herb Fondue: Omit the nutmeg and add 2 tablespoons chopped fresh Italian parsley and 1 teaspoon minced fresh tarragon or chervil after the cheese is melted.

Shrimp Fondue: Serve 1 pound cold, cooked, peeled, and deveined small to medium-size shrimp with their tails still attached for dipping along with the bread cubes.

Champagne Fondue

Have a leftover bottle of Champagne? Impress your guests with this simple but elegant fondue. Remember to allow about 4 slices of bread per person and, when dipping, to swirl and stir the fondue each time. If the fondue is too thick, add a bit more Champagne. Be sure to leave some crust on each cube of bread, if you can, so that the bread will stay on the fork while dipping. If a guest drops his or her bread into the fondue, there is a penalty: A man must pay for the drinking wine, and a woman pays with a kiss to another diner. Serve with paper-thin strips of prosciutto alongside and more of the same Champagne for drinking.

○ *Serves 6*

COOKER: Medium round

SETTINGS AND COOK TIMES: HIGH for 30 minutes, then LOW for 1 hour

½ clove garlic, split

1½ cups extra-dry Champagne or sparkling wine

1 pound Emmental cheese, shredded (4 cups)

½ pound Gruyère cheese, shredded (2 cups)

1 tablespoon cornstarch or potato starch

1 teaspoon freshly squeezed lemon juice

2 to 3 grindings of freshly ground black pepper

1 to 2 loaves fresh baguette, cut into 1-inch cubes

1. Rub the bottom and lower sides of the inside of the crock with the garlic clove, then discard the garlic. Pour the Champagne into the slow cooker, turn on HIGH, and cook, uncovered, for 30 minutes to evaporate some of the alcohol.

2. Combine the Emmental and Gruyère cheeses in a large bowl and toss with the cornstarch and lemon juice. When the wine is hot, add the cheese slowly, a handful at a time, letting each addition melt before adding the next, and stirring to keep lumps from forming. Reduce the heat to LOW, cover, and cook until the cheese is melted, about 1 hour. It will keep on LOW for up to an additional hour before you need to serve it. The melted cheese will be the consistency of a light cream sauce.

3. Stir in the pepper right before serving. Set the slow cooker in the entertaining area, set on LOW, leave the cover off, and dip the bread cubes.

Buttermilk Fondue

T here is a fabulous saying that goes, "In a country where people eat fondue, there can be no wars," a reference to dunking your bread into a communal pot, relaxing, and chatting amicably between savory bites. This is a delightful nonalcoholic fondue. Use a rich, cultured buttermilk, one with flecks of butter in it if you can find it. This is a substantial fondue that will cure any hunger. ○ *Serves 6*

COOKER: Medium round

SETTINGS AND COOK TIMES: HIGH for 30 minutes, then LOW for 1 hour

½ clove garlic, split

2 cups buttermilk

1 pound Emmental cheese, shredded (4 cups)

¼ pound fresh mozzarella cheese, shredded or cubed

2 tablespoons cornstarch or potato starch

Pinch of salt

¼ teaspoon freshly ground black pepper

Pinch of freshly grated nutmeg

1 to 2 loaves fresh baguette or other crusty country bread, cut into 1-inch cubes

1. Combine the garlic and buttermilk in the slow cooker. Cover and cook on HIGH for 30 minutes while preparing the cheeses.

2. Combine the Emmental and mozzarella cheeses in a large bowl and toss with the cornstarch, salt, pepper, and nutmeg.

3. When the buttermilk is hot, remove and discard the garlic clove and add the cheese slowly, a handful at a time, letting each addition melt before adding the next, and stirring to keep lumps from forming. Reduce the heat to LOW, cover, and cook until the cheese is melted, about 1 hour. It will keep on LOW for up to an additional hour before you need to serve it. The melted cheese will be the consistency of a light cream sauce; if it is too thick, add more buttermilk.

4. Set the slow cooker in the entertaining area, set on LOW, leave the cover off, and dip the bread cubes.

Fondue with Sparkling Apple Cider

This nonalcoholic fondue is made with domestic or imported sparkling apple cider (you could certainly substitute a hard cider, if you like). The cornstarch for coating the cheese is important for keeping the hot mass emulsified, and the lemon juice prevents the cheese from getting stringy. The slow cooker mimics the new electric fondue pots, replacing the more romantic candles and alcohol burners, but the magic of the fire lives on. Serve with potatoes (see variation below) for a wonderful, hearty meal, perhaps accompanied by hot cider to drink while dipping. ● *Serves 6*

COOKER: Medium round

SETTINGS AND COOK TIMES: HIGH for 30 minutes, then LOW for 1 hour

1 clove garlic, split
1½ cups nonalcoholic sparkling apple cider
2 tablespoons freshly squeezed lemon juice
½ pound Emmental cheese, shredded (2 cups)
½ pound Gruyère cheese, shredded (2 cups)
2 to 4 ounces fontina or Brie (rind removed), cubed
1 tablespoon cornstarch or potato starch
2 to 3 grindings of freshly ground black pepper, to your taste
Pinch of Hungarian paprika
1 to 2 loaves ciabatta or baguettes, cut into 1-inch cubes

1. Combine the garlic, cider, and lemon juice in the slow cooker. Cover and cook on HIGH for 30 minutes while preparing the cheeses.

2. Combine the Emmental, Gruyère, and fontina cheeses in a large bowl and toss with the cornstarch. When the cider is hot, remove the garlic clove and add the cheese slowly, a handful at a time, letting each addition melt before adding the next, and stirring to keep lumps from forming. Reduce the heat to LOW, cover, and cook until the cheese is melted, about 1 hour. It will keep on LOW for up to an additional hour before you need to serve it. The melted cheese will be the consistency of a light cream sauce.

3. Stir in the pepper and paprika right before serving. Set the slow cooker in the entertaining area, set on LOW, leave the cover off, and dip the bread cubes.

Potato Fondue: Steam 1 to 2 pounds new potatoes in their skins. Let cool and cut into thick cubes. Arrange on a platter and serve in place of the bread cubes.

Tamari Almonds

B eth has a passion for toasted soy sauce–coated whole almonds. Tamari is the brandy of soy sauces; it is aged in barrels to develop a deep, strong, fermented soy flavor. These nuts are the darling of the health food bins. They can grace a salad or accompany a glass of wine before dinner. ○ *Makes 2 cups to serve 8*

COOKER: Small or medium
SETTINGS AND COOK TIMES: HIGH for 15 minutes, then LOW for 1½ to 2 hours

2 cups (½ pound) whole raw almonds
1 tablespoon almond oil or canola oil
3 tablespoons tamari

1. Combine the nuts, oil, and tamari in the slow cooker and stir with a wooden spoon to coat evenly. Cover and cook on HIGH for 15 minutes, then reduce the heat to LOW and cook, uncovered, stirring occasionally, for 1½ to 2 hours. The nuts will become dry as they toast.

2. Transfer the nuts to a baking sheet lined with parchment paper or aluminum foil and let cool completely. Store at room temperature in an airtight container for up to 3 days.

Malabar Almonds

T hese are really popular and deliciously aromatic nuts, good not only for munching, but also for topping a salad along with a creamy chutney dressing. The curry powder gives a nice punch to the palate. This is adapted from a recipe in *Fine Cooking* magazine. ⚬ *Makes 4 cups to serve 16*

COOKER: Medium round or oval
SETTINGS AND COOK TIMES: LOW for 1½ to 2 hours, then HIGH for 30 minutes to 1 hour

4 cups (1 pound) blanched almonds
2 tablespoons unsalted butter, melted
1 tablespoon Madras curry powder
½ teaspoon ground cinnamon
½ teaspoon ground cumin
¼ teaspoon cayenne pepper
2 teaspoons fine sea salt, or to taste

1. Combine the nuts, melted butter, curry powder, cinnamon, cumin, and cayenne in the slow cooker. Stir with a wooden spoon to coat evenly. Cover and cook on LOW, stirring occasionally, for 1½ to 2 hours.

2. Uncover, turn the setting to HIGH, and cook 30 minutes to 1 hour more.

3. Add the salt and toss with the nuts to distribute evenly. Transfer the nuts to a baking sheet lined with parchment paper or aluminum foil and let cool completely. Store at room temperature in an airtight container for up to 3 days.

Buttery Rosemary Pecan Halves

his is one of Beth's catering staples to set out on the drinks table. Buy the most perfect pecan halves you can find, and the bigger the better. These delicious, savory nuts are a surprise, and addiction is a possibility. Serve warm from the slow cooker, if possible. ❍ *Makes 4 cups to serve 16*

COOKER: Medium round or oval
SETTINGS AND COOK TIMES: HIGH for 15 minutes, then LOW for 1½ to 2 hours

4 cups (1 pound) pecan halves
3 tablespoons unsalted butter, melted
1 tablespoon dried rosemary, crumbled
½ teaspoon cayenne pepper
2 to 3 teaspoons fine sea salt, to your taste

1. Combine the nuts, melted butter, rosemary, and cayenne in the slow cooker. Stir with a wooden spoon to coat evenly. Cover and cook on HIGH for 15 minutes, then reduce the heat to LOW and cook, uncovered, stirring occasionally, for 1½ to 2 hours.

2. Add the salt and toss with the nuts to distribute evenly. Transfer the nuts to a baking sheet lined with parchment paper or aluminum foil and let cool completely. Store at room temperature in an airtight container for up to 3 days.

Maple-Glazed Pecans

W e went nuts when we found out the slow cooker makes wonderful sweet nuts. Whereas in the oven the edges of nuts can get overdone if not carefully watched, there is no such problem in the slow cooker. Toss the nuts to coat with the liquid sugars and let the cooker do the work. These can be eaten out of hand, used as an ingredient in cakes and muffins, or used to garnish ice cream sundaes. ○ *Makes 3 cups to serve 12*

COOKER: Medium round or oval

SETTINGS AND COOK TIMES: HIGH for 45 minutes (add nuts after 30 minutes), then LOW for 1¹/₂ to 2 hours

¾ cup pure maple syrup
3 tablespoons light corn syrup
3 cups (12 ounces) pecan halves

1. Combine the maple syrup and corn syrup in the slow cooker. Cover and set on HIGH for 30 minutes to warm and thin the sweeteners.

2. Add the nuts carefully to avoid splashing and stir with a wooden spoon to coat evenly. Cover and cook on HIGH for another 15 minutes.

3. Reduce the heat to LOW, uncover, and cook, stirring occasionally, for 1½ to 2 hours.

4. Transfer the nuts to a baking sheet lined with parchment paper or aluminum foil and let cool completely. Store at room temperature in an airtight container for up to 3 days.

Spicy Walnuts

uts taste fantastic when flavored with a spicy red chile powder and other savory flavors. Serve these with cheeses, crackers, and wine.

○ *Makes 4 cups to serve 16*

COOKER: Medium round or oval
SETTINGS AND COOK TIMES: HIGH for 15 minutes, then LOW for 1½ to 2 hours

4 cups (1 pound) walnut halves
2 to 3 tablespoons walnut oil
2 tablespoons white Worcestershire sauce
2 ¼ teaspoons red chile powder, preferably New Mexican
½ teaspoon garlic or onion powder
1½ teaspoons coarse sea salt, or to taste

1. Combine the nuts, oil, Worcestershire sauce, chile powder, and garlic powder in the slow cooker. Stir with a wooden spoon to coat evenly. Cover and cook on HIGH for 15 minutes, then reduce the heat to LOW and cook, uncovered, stirring occasionally, for 1½ to 2 hours.

2. Add the salt and toss with the nuts to distribute evenly. Transfer the nuts to a baking sheet lined with parchment paper or aluminum foil and let cool completely. Store at room temperature in an airtight container for up to 3 days.

Walnuts and Ginger

hese nuts are sweet and spicy at the same time. Serve with cheeses, crackers, and wine. ○ *Makes 4 cups to serve 16*

COOKER: Medium round or oval
SETTINGS AND COOK TIMES: HIGH for 15 minutes, then LOW for 1½ to 2 hours

4 cups (1 pound) walnut halves
3 tablespoons unsalted butter, melted
⅓ cup pure maple syrup

Ten ¼-inch-thick slices fresh ginger

1 teaspoon ground coriander

⅓ teaspoon Tabasco sauce or other hot pepper sauce

1 teaspoon coarse sea salt, or to taste

1. Combine the nuts, melted butter, maple syrup, ginger, coriander, and hot sauce in the slow cooker. Stir with a wooden spoon to coat evenly. Cover and cook on HIGH for 15 minutes, then reduce the heat to LOW and cook, uncovered, stirring occasionally, for 1½ to 2 hours.

2. Add the salt and toss with the nuts to distribute evenly. Transfer the nuts to a baking sheet lined with parchment paper or aluminum foil and let cool completely. Store at room temperature in an airtight container for up to 3 days.

Sugared Walnuts

S ugared walnuts are great for munching on their own, or as an addition to your dessert making, such as chopped in a pound cake or arranged as a decoration on top of cakes and puddings. ○ *Makes 4 cups to serve 16*

COOKER: Medium round or oval

SETTINGS AND COOK TIMES: HIGH for 15 minutes, then LOW for 2 hours

4 cups (1 pound) walnut halves

½ cup (1 stick) unsalted butter, melted

⅔ cup confectioners' sugar

1. Combine the walnuts and melted butter in the slow cooker and stir with a wooden spoon to coat evenly. Sprinkle the confectioners' sugar over the nuts through a coarse sieve to eliminate lumps. Cover and cook on HIGH for 15 minutes.

2. Reduce the heat to LOW, uncover, and cook, stirring occasionally, for 2 hours.

3. Transfer to a baking sheet lined with parchment paper or aluminum foil and let cool completely. Store at room temperature in an airtight container for up to 3 days.

Curry Mixed Nuts

hese are simple but effective. You can add more curry powder to taste, but we like it just as presented—with a faint whisper of curry flavor.

○ Makes 3 cups to serve 12

COOKER: Medium round or oval
SETTINGS AND COOK TIMES: HIGH for 15 minutes, then LOW for 1 to 1½ hours

3 cups (¾ pound) salted mixed nuts
1 teaspoon unsalted butter, melted
½ teaspoon curry powder
Salt to taste

1. Combine the nuts, melted butter, and curry powder in the slow cooker. Stir with a wooden spoon to coat evenly. Cover and cook on HIGH for 15 minutes, then reduce the heat to LOW and cook, uncovered, stirring occasionally, for 1 to 1½ hours. The nuts will become dry as they toast.

2. Taste for salt, add some if needed, and toss with the nuts to distribute evenly.

3. Transfer the nuts to a baking sheet lined with parchment paper or aluminum foil and let cool completely. Store at room temperature in an airtight container for up to 3 days.

Retro Party Mix

his is a recipe adapted from Michael Bauer, food editor of the *San Francisco Chronicle*, from an article on retro comfort food. Bauer relates in his story that the staff made a big joke about Chex party mix being so ungourmet and out of fashion; then a gallon of it disappeared within an hour, attacked by mad munchers. It is still great for party guests of all ages. Because of the amount, this must be made in a large cooker. Be sure to use the bacon grease (saved from breakfast or leftover from making a spinach salad) and the margarine; they add flavor and keeping qualities. Some people like to cut back on the salt and toss in a few tablespoons of finely grated Parmesan cheese at the end.

Makes about 20 cups to serve 25

COOKER: Large round or oval
SETTINGS AND COOK TIMES: HIGH for 1 to 1½ hours, then LOW for 20 to 40 minutes

3½ cups Rice Chex cereal
3½ cups Wheat Chex cereal
3½ cups Corn Chex cereal
8 cups Cheerios cereal (about ½ of a 15-ounce box)
3 cups thin pretzel sticks
6 ounces salted Spanish peanuts
3 tablespoons bacon grease, melted
¼ cup (½ stick) margarine, melted
1 tablespoon Tabasco sauce or other hot pepper sauce
2 teaspoons chili powder
1 to 1½ teaspoons fine sea salt, to your taste

1. Coat the inside of the cooker insert with nonstick cooking spray. Combine all the ingredients in the slow cooker and stir to coat evenly with the bacon grease, margarine, and Tabasco sauce. Cook, uncovered, on HIGH for 1 to 1½ hours, stirring often.

2. Reduce the heat to LOW and cook, stirring often, until dry and crisp, 20 to 40 minutes. Transfer the mix to baking sheets lined with parchment paper or aluminum foil and let cool completely. Store at room temperature in a large airtight container for up to 3 days.

The Electric Punch Bowl

The Best Hot Mulled Apple Juice ● 57

Mulled Cider with Cardamom and
Saffron ● 58

"Rum" and Cherry Cider ● 59

Cranberry "Nog" ● 59

Hot Cranberry-Orange Punch ● 60

Hot Spiced Grape Juice ● 61

Hot Apricot Nectar ● 62

Lemongrass Cordial ● 62

Jamaica ● 63

Ponche ● 64

Hot Tomato Virgin Mary ● 65

Baja Tomato Juice ● 66

Spiced Apple and Chamomile Tea ● 66

Ginger-Lemon Tea ● 67

Chai ● 68

Moroccan Mint Tea ● 70

Champurrado ● 71

Hot Eggnog ● 72

Hot Peppermint Milk ● 72

Mexican Coffee with Brandy and
Kahlúa ● 73

Irish Coffee ● 74

Mulled Wine ● 75

Warm Cranberry Zinfandel ● 76

Strawberry–White Wine Punch ● 77

Glögg ● 78

Port Wine Negus ● 79

Spiked Wassail ● 80

Athole Brose ● 81

Hot Buttered Rum ● 82

One of the best uses for your slow cooker, most specifically a large round or oval one, is to make hot drinks for celebrations, especially during the winter holidays. Hot drinks create an ambiance of warm welcome for guests. So whether you are thawing out after a rainy football or soccer game, relaxing après skiing or hiking, or throwing a housewarming or birthday celebration, you'll be sure to find a soul-warming drink here to take the chill off and get the party going.

Hot punches are always better when mixed in advance and allowed to sit over low heat for a few hours to steep and blend. The slow cooker keeps the liquid at a very low simmer, heating the beverage and developing the flavor for the duration of your get-together. People originally made hot drinks, called "possets" and "cups" in days of yore, by thrusting a red-hot poker into a crock of wine. This method is still used by hardy souls with a flair for re-creating the romance of the past, but it is much easier to rely on your slow cooker. Goodbye to guests tramping into the kitchen to serve themselves off the stove out of your stockpot; goodbye to having to deal with a portable burner on the dining room table. The slow cooker as an electric punch bowl is neat and safe (be sure to place it so the cord is not where someone will trip over it).

You can serve any alcoholic spirit, such as rum or brandy, stirred into the concoction, or on the side for spiking each individual mug. For adults, how about a Mexican Coffee with Brandy and Kahlúa (page 73), an old-fashioned heady Swedish Glögg with raisins and blanched almonds floating on top (page 78), or Port Wine Negus (page 79), a bracing, classic brew fragrant with rich ruby port and lemon? How about hot wine lemonade for an afternoon get-together? Make your lemonade as usual, floating slices of fresh lemon on the surface, and simmer in the slow cooker until warm. Then add a nice Sauvignon Blanc, 1 part wine to 3 parts lemonade, and serve hot.

Many people do not want to imbibe the heavy spirits of old and want to be able to serve one beverage to children and adults at large gatherings, so mulled spiced ciders are a wonderful alternative. Try our "Rum" and Cherry Cider (page 59), Hot Cranberry-Orange Punch (page 60), or Mulled Cider with Cardamom and Saffron (page 58). You will never miss the booze. For brunch, our Hot Tomato Virgin Mary (page 65) or Baja Tomato Juice (page 66), almost appetizers in themselves, are perfect with or without the vodka, with the ruffle of a stalk of celery peeking out of the glass. Our teas serve a crowd with no fuss.

Food to serve with your hot punches

should be simple: cookies, salted nuts, or little turkey, chicken, egg salad, or ham sandwiches are ideal flavor mates. If the punch is rich, like our Hot Eggnog (page 72), be sure to keep the appetizers lean, and if it has an ethnic origin, such as Chai (page 68) or Champurrado (page 71), look to serve some complementary food, such as samosas or mango quesadillas.

For all hot drinks, be sure to assemble the proper serving ladle and mugs or heat-proof glassware. Search out heatproof glass mugs, and buy two dozen if you like to entertain a lot. Do not use your every-day drink glasses in case they are not heatproof, in which case they can crack or shatter when filled with hot liquid. For the serving ladle, use a plain or ornate one in silver, stainless steel, or even ceramic. Make sure it is the proper size for your slow cooker, so that it won't slip down into the slow cooker in between guests serving themselves.

The Best Hot Mulled Apple Juice

H ot drinks, originally made with wine and spiced and sweetened with honey, are known as "mulls" or mulled wine. This is a nonalcoholic version of those drinks of centuries ago. You can leave the whole spices loose, as in this version, or wrap them in a cheesecloth bag and remove at serving time.

o Makes about twenty-four 6-ounce servings

COOKER: Large round
SETTING AND COOK TIME: LOW for 4 to 6 hours

1 gallon unfiltered apple juice
1 cup freshly squeezed lemon juice
Five 4-inch cinnamon sticks
2 tablespoons whole cloves
1 lemon, sliced
1 whole nutmeg

1. Combine the apple juice and lemon juice in the slow cooker. Add the cinnamon sticks, cloves, and lemon slices, and grate in the nutmeg. Cover and cook on LOW for 4 to 6 hours.

2. Serve hot, straining out the cinnamon sticks and cloves.

Mulled Cider with Cardamom and Saffron

This is a festive cider to brighten fall and winter gatherings. And it is simplicity itself, with nothing to squeeze or chop! It sounds as though it would be too intensely flavored for children, but surprisingly enough, it's not. Julie has had preschool guests guzzle it down from sippy cups. (For kids, cool it quickly to drinking temperature with an ice cube or two in their cups.) In California, we always make this with Martinelli's still apple cider; choose that or a good-quality, locally made cider.

It's easier than it sounds to halve a nutmeg. Just place it on a cutting board, position the blade of a heavy knife or cleaver at the nutmeg's equator, and press down gently. Do not try to hold the nutmeg while you cut it! The nutmeg should split neatly in two. ○ *Makes about twenty-four 6-ounce servings*

COOKER: Large round
SETTING AND COOK TIME: LOW for 4 to 6 hours

1 gallon apple cider
1 whole nutmeg, split in half
8 whole cloves
Two 3- or 4-inch cinnamon sticks
5 green or white cardamom pods, gently bruised with the
    side of a knife or the bottom of a jar
5 black peppercorns
3 allspice berries
Small pinch of saffron (about 10 threads)

1. Place all the ingredients in the slow cooker. Cover and cook on LOW for 4 to 6 hours.

2. Serve hot, straining out the spices.

"Rum" and Cherry Cider

Beth's friend Sharon Jones spent her high school years in San Diego. On weeknights she would head to a bohemian-style music club on the beach, an establishment so humble that there were no tables and chairs; people just sat on the floor. There was a memorable nonalcoholic rum-and-cherry-flavored cider served, appropriate for the mass of high school students to sip on while local guitar players shared their folk melodies. You will need a bottle of imitation rum flavoring, available near the vanilla extract on your supermarket shelf.

○ *Makes about twenty-four 6-ounce servings*

COOKER: Large round
SETTING AND COOK TIME: LOW for 4 to 6 hours; rum flavoring added during last hour

1 gallon unfiltered apple juice
One 32-ounce bottle cherry juice or cherry cider
Three 4-inch cinnamon sticks
Two to four 1-ounce bottles imitation rum flavoring, to your taste

1. Combine the apple and cherry juices and cinnamon sticks in the slow cooker. Cover and cook on LOW for 3 to 5 hours.

2. Add the rum flavoring, cover, and continue to cook on LOW for another hour.

3. Serve hot, discarding the cinnamon sticks.

Cranberry "Nog"

Beth lived on Skyline Boulevard, overlooking California's Santa Clara Valley, during the 1970s. Her landlord's parents, John and Esther Sills, were eccentric intellectuals and potters from Maine. They would have their many guests, including Zen scholar Alan Watts and the then-mayor of San Francisco, come up the long, winding drive to visit, share a meal on late Sunday afternoons, and discuss the issues of the day. During the winter months, Esther would always have a kettle filled with mulled hot cranberry juice on the stove, with a long-handled ladle hanging on the side and a tray of many different-sized and -shaped hand-thrown pottery mugs from their workshop. Each person could choose his or her own mug. Beth would look into that oversized kettle as she sipped the soothing hot nog, watching the cranberries pop as they heated up.

○ *Makes about twenty-four 6-ounce servings*

COOKER: Large round
SETTING AND COOK TIME: LOW for 4 to 6 hours

1 gallon cranberry juice cocktail
1 cup fresh cranberries, picked over for stems
Six 4-inch cinnamon sticks
1 tablespoon whole cloves
2 lemons, sliced
2 oranges, sliced
½ cup honey, or to taste

1. Place the cranberry juice and cranberries in the slow cooker. Add the cinnamon sticks, cloves, lemon and orange slices, and honey. Cover and cook on LOW for 4 to 6 hours.

2. Serve hot, straining out the spices.

Hot Cranberry-Orange Punch

(T)his is a really special holiday or autumn punch for guests, adults and children alike. You can use fresh or frozen reconstituted orange juice interchangeably. You can also use honey, maple syrup, or brown sugar in place of the granulated sugar. Get ready for people to pass up the wine and drink this instead.

○ *Makes about twenty-four 6-ounce servings*

COOKER: Large round
SETTING AND COOK TIME: LOW for 4 to 6 hours

3 quarts cranberry juice cocktail

1 quart orange juice, fresh or reconstituted frozen

1 cup freshly squeezed lemon juice

1 tablespoon grated orange zest

Four 4-inch cinnamon sticks

2 teaspoons whole cloves

¼ to ½ cup sugar, to your taste

2 oranges, sliced

1. Combine all the ingredients in the slow cooker. Cover and cook on LOW for 4 to 6 hours.

2. Serve hot, straining out the spices.

Hot Spiced Grape Juice

Concord grapes yield a fresh, sweet juice. While grape juice is more often drunk cold on scorching summer afternoons, here is a hot version, redolent with spices, for cold afternoons. In the summer, cool this mixture, then add sparkling water to it and serve over ice. Don't skip the fresh lemon juice; it balances the sweet nature of the grapes. This is a wonderful and just a little bit different drink to serve to friends. ○ *Makes about twelve 6-ounce servings*

COOKER: Medium round
SETTING AND COOK TIME: LOW for 4 to 5 hours

2 quarts purple grape juice

¼ cup freshly squeezed lemon juice

3 strips lemon zest

8 whole cloves

8 allspice berries

3 juniper berries

Two 4-inch cinnamon sticks

2 tablespoons dark raisins

1. Combine the grape and lemon juices in the slow cooker. Place the lemon zest, cloves, allspice, and juniper berries in a small piece of cheesecloth and tie with kitchen twine to make a bag. Add to the juices along with the cinnamon sticks and raisins. Cover and cook on LOW for 4 to 5 hours.

2. Remove the spice bag and cinnamon sticks. Serve hot.

Hot Apricot Nectar

T he thick, unctuous nature of apricot nectar makes for a luscious hot fruit drink. The lemon juice cuts its sweetness and viscosity. Serve with biscotti or shortbread cookies. ○ *Makes about twelve 6-ounce servings*

COOKER: Medium round
SETTING AND COOK TIME: LOW for 2 to 4 hours

1½ quarts apricot nectar
4 cups water
½ cup freshly squeezed lemon juice
Four 4-inch cinnamon sticks
6 whole cloves

1. Combine all the ingredients in the slow cooker. Cover and cook on LOW for 2 to 4 hours.

2. Serve hot, straining out the spices.

Lemongrass Cordial

W ith the popularity of Thai cuisine has come the lemony flavored herb that typifies this style of cooking—lemongrass. *Cymbopogon citratus* is a common herb in Southeast Asian kitchens, often grown in backyard gardens, and looks like grassy tufts of coarse gray-green spring onions. The French, after their long occupation in Indonesia, adopted it as well and call it *citronelle*. The bottom section of the stalk near the root end is the toughest and needs pounding to expose the white heart, which contains a more intense flavor than the upper tender sections. Broken open and simmered, it makes this refreshing hot drink. After steeping, you can toss in a few green tea bags to make a lemongrass–green tea infusion, if you like, which you can serve hot or cold. ❍ *Makes about twelve 6-ounce servings*

COOKER: Medium round
SETTINGS AND COOK TIMES: HIGH until boiling, then LOW for 2 to 4 hours

12 to 14 stalks lemongrass
8 cups water
¼ cup granulated sugar or raw sugar, to taste

1. Place the lemongrass on a cutting board and pound with a mallet until the grass breaks apart. Place the water and lemongrass in the slow cooker. Cover and bring to a boil on HIGH, 45 minutes to 1 hour.

2. Turn the heat to LOW and simmer for 2 to 4 hours.

3. Add the sugar and stir until dissolved. Taste for sugar, adding more if you like a sweeter drink. Discard the lemongrass stems if drinking hot, or leave some in if refrigerating overnight before serving.

4. Serve hot, or let cool, then pour into a large covered container and refrigerate; strain and serve over lots of ice in a tall glass.

Jamaica

A *gua fresca de flor de Jamaica* is a deep red infusion made from the Jamaica flower, more commonly known as hibiscus. In Mexico, there are many street vendors and juice parlors, all of which offer this refreshing drink along with a host of others, such as lime and watermelon juice concoctions. Jamaica flower is the main ingredient in Red Zinger tea bags, made famous by Celestial Seasonings and available nationwide in supermarkets. Jamaica tea can be drunk hot, or chilled and served over ice. It is always made in a glass or highly glazed earthenware container, as the acidic flowers will react with other types of containers, such as enamel, aluminum, or poorly glazed earthenware. The tart tea is often served very sweet, but we use Jacquie McMahan's wonderful recipe, which uses only a bit of sugar and frozen apple juice concentrate. Jamaica flowers are available in bulk from Latin markets. ❍ *Makes about twelve 6-ounce servings*

COOKER: Medium or large round
SETTINGS AND COOK TIMES: HIGH until boiling, then LOW for 2 to 4 hours

4 ounces dried Jamaica flowers
8 cups water
¼ cup sugar or honey, or to taste
One 12-ounce can frozen apple juice concentrate, thawed

1. Place the Jamaica flowers and water in the slow cooker. You can place the flowers in loose, wrap them in 3 cheesecloth bags and tie with kitchen twine, or use a large metal spice ball, as desired. Cover and bring to a boil on HIGH, 45 minutes to 1 hour.

2. Turn the heat to LOW and cook for 2 to 4 hours. Pour through a strainer if using loose flowers, or remove the cheesecloth bags. Add the sugar and apple juice concentrate and stir until dissolved.

3. Serve hot, or let cool, then pour into a large covered container and refrigerate; strain and serve over lots of ice in glasses or mugs.

Ponche

M exico is famous for its homemade *bebidas*, or concocted beverages made from fresh fruits. This punch is a unique blend of tropical fruits, but you could add cherry or orange juice if you like. The fruits dissolve into the water, flavoring it. If you want to add tequila, use a white tequila, which is pale and not aged, for its nice mellow flavor. ❍ *Makes about twelve 6-ounce servings*

COOKER: Medium or large round
SETTING AND COOK TIME: LOW for 6 to 8 hours

2 medium-size apples, peeled, cored, and cut into 8 wedges

¾ cup golden raisins

1 pound guavas, peeled, seeded, and quartered

2 cups peeled and diced fresh pineapple

Three 4-inch pieces raw sugar cane (optional, but nice), cut into strips

1 cup sugar

Three 4-inch cinnamon sticks

8 cups water

Up to 1 ounce per cup silver tequila or white rum (optional)

1. Place the apples, raisins, guavas, pineapple, sugar cane, sugar, and cinnamon sticks in the slow cooker. Add the water and stir. Cover and cook on LOW for 6 to 8 hours; some of the fruits will dissolve.

2. Serve hot, as is or with a jigger of tequila or rum per cup.

Hot Tomato Virgin Mary

ere is our version of the queen of brunch drinks and one of our bracing hot favorites. For traditionalist guests, offer vodka on the side.

○ *Makes about twelve 6-ounce servings*

COOKER: Medium round

SETTING AND COOK TIME: LOW for 3 to 4 hours

4 quarts tomato juice or tomato-vegetable juice, such as V8

2 tablespoons Worcestershire sauce

2 teaspoons hot pepper sauce, or to taste

Celery sticks with leaves for garnish

Lime wedges for garnish

1. Combine the tomato juice and Worcestershire sauce in the slow cooker. Cover and cook on LOW until steamy hot, 3 to 4 hours.

2. Add the hot pepper sauce. Serve hot, ladled into heatproof punch glasses, with a celery stick and lime wedge for each one.

Baja Tomato Juice

T abasco sauce, move over! For this recipe, experiment with one of the zillions of delicious new bottled hot sauces on the market today (even Joe Perry, the guitarist for Aerosmith, has his own brand of hot sauce). Serve this with enchiladas and a green salad with sliced avocado.

○ *Makes about fifteen 6-ounce servings*

COOKER: Medium or large round
SETTING AND COOK TIME: LOW for 3 to 4 hours

1 quart tomato juice
Three 10.5-ounce cans beef consommé
3 cans water, to reconstitute the consommé
1 tablespoon hot pepper sauce, or to taste
1½ teaspoons chili powder
Lemon wedges for garnish

1. Combine the tomato juice, consommé, and water in the slow cooker. Cover and cook on LOW until steamy hot, 3 to 4 hours.

2. Add the hot pepper sauce and chili powder and stir. Serve hot, ladled into heatproof punch glasses, with a lemon wedge for each glass. Keep the bottle of hot sauce on the side for a few more splashes to taste.

Spiced Apple and Chamomile Tea

S piced hot tea drinks are a welcome addition to a winter evening. This looks very festive with the miniature blush-colored Lady apples studded with cloves floating in it. Lady apples can usually be found in the produce section during December. ○ *Makes about twelve 6-ounce servings*

COOKER: Medium or large round
SETTING AND COOK TIME: LOW for 4 to 6 hours

2 quarts unfiltered apple juice

6 cups water

10 chamomile tea bags

Six ½-inch-thick slices fresh ginger

Four 4-inch cinnamon sticks

1 tablespoon whole cloves

8 Lady apples or 4 to 6 very small apples (about 4 ounces each), such as Golden Delicious (see Note)

1. Combine the apple juice, water, and tea bags in the slow cooker. Add the ginger and cinnamon sticks. Press the cloves into the apples and add to the cooker. Cover and cook on LOW for 4 to 6 hours.

2. Serve hot, straining out the spices.

Note: For extra flavor, you can roast the apples, topped with a pat of butter, in a preheated 350°F oven for 20 to 25 minutes, before adding them to the slow cooker.

Ginger-Lemon Tea

The first person Beth watched make ginger-lemon tea was a traveling monk. He scraped the skin off the fresh knob of ginger and sliced it. He added it to a large pan of water and steeped it for a time on the stove. Right before drinking, he added fresh lemon juice and a good dose of honey, which soothes the throat, to get ready to sing *kiirtan*, devotional song compositions that prepare people for meditation. So this is good not only for entertaining, but also for when you have a cold or flu. ○ *Makes about eight 6-ounce servings*

COOKER: Medium round
SETTING AND COOK TIME: LOW for 3½ to 4½ hours

Ten to fourteen ½-inch-thick slices fresh ginger

8 cups water

Juice of 4 to 6 lemons, to your taste

⅓ cup honey or firmly packed light brown sugar, or to taste

1. Bruise the ginger slices with the flat side of a large knife blade or the bottom of a jar. Place in the slow cooker with the water. Cover and cook on LOW for 3 to 4 hours.

2. Stir in the lemon juice and honey. Cover and continue to cook on LOW for another 30 minutes.

3. Serve hot, straining out the ginger.

Chai

When Beth worked at India Joze restaurant in Santa Cruz, California, many years ago, they served a house tea called chai. A local man would arrive at the back door once a week with an oversized white bucket tied to the front of his bicycle, delivering the concentrated brew, the likes of which were really innovative for the time, as the tea was not normally served in American restaurants. It was served at brunch on Sundays with lots of honey and half-and-half. The tea maker was a member of the Yogi Bhajan group. A group from the state of Punjab in India brought along the original tea mixture when their guru came to the United States in the late 1960s, and they used it as a bracing stimulant for spiritual purity. Over the decades it has become known as yogi tea.

The history of chai is a simple, logical evolution of taste. The English colonists brought the tea ritual to India and, with their own panache, locals added elaborate mixtures of spices to the plain Ceylon- or Indian-grown tea leaves, milk, and sugar. The infusion is a euphoria-inducing and healthful concoction blending cardamom, ginger, and long pepper (dried peppercorns still on the vine) with *Camellia sinensis*. Chai tea is now a mainstream phenomenon: Every grocery store carries it in tea bags or already made in bottles, coffee shops offer it as "chai latte" alongside cappuccinos, and there are numerous home recipes in circulation. Here is a simple recipe to make from scratch, although you may certainly just fill your slow cooker with water and add a box of the ready-made chai tea bags or loose masala tea blend available in Indian groceries, both of which taste best with prolonged steeping. ○ *Makes about twenty 6-ounce servings*

COOKER: Medium round

SETTING AND COOK TIME: LOW for 6 to 7 hours; tea added at 4 to 5 hours; sweetened milk added during last hour

16 cups water

Sixteen ½-inch-thick slices fresh ginger

3 teaspoons whole black peppercorns

2 heaping tablespoons green cardamom pods, crushed open

Twelve 4-inch cinnamon sticks

¼ to ⅔ cup loose Darjeeling tea leaves (regular or decaffeinated) or
**   1 dozen Darjeeling tea bags, depending on how strong you like your tea**

1 recipe Sweetened Milk for Chai (recipe follows)

1. Place the water, ginger, peppercorns, cardamom (pods and all), and cinnamon sticks in the slow cooker. Cover and cook on LOW for 4 to 5 hours.

2. Add the tea, cover, and continue to cook on LOW 1 to 2 hours longer. Strain the mixture through two layers of cheesecloth lining a colander and return the mixture to the cooker.

3. Add the sweetened milk to taste, cover, and keep on LOW for another hour, if desired.

4. Serve hot, or cool and refrigerate and serve over ice.

Sweetened Milk for Chai

○ *Makes 7 cups*

6 cups whole milk, half-and-half, or plain soy milk

2 to 3 cups sugar or honey, to your taste

In a large, heavy-bottomed saucepan, heat the milk and sugar together over medium-low heat, stirring, until the sugar dissolves. Do not boil. Remove from the heat and add to the brewed and strained chai, or cool and store in the refrigerator for up to 3 days.

Moroccan Mint Tea

When Beth caters, there is invariably a hostess who requests fresh mint tea Moroccan style, *atay bi nahan*, for after dinner. Posed with the problem of serving several dozen guests from small teapots, here is the perfect answer—the slow cooker. *Atay bi nahan* uses common backyard mint; we use fresh spearmint, which is usually available year-round in the produce department. The essential oils of the *Mentha* plant are concentrated in the leaves, and contact with hot water releases them. The tea is traditionally drunk very sweet, but you can make it less so and add the sugar to taste. You can use granulated sugar cubes if you like, but we prefer raw sugar, which has a bit of molasses still left in it. We like the flavor of Gunpowder green tea, but you can use another type of green tea, if you prefer. ○ *Makes about twenty-four 6-ounce servings*

COOKER: Large round or oval
SETTINGS AND COOK TIMES: HIGH for 1 to 1½ hours, then LOW for 3½ to 6 hours; tea added during last 30 minutes to 2 hours

20 cups water
5 bunches fresh mint, long stems trimmed, but leaves left attached to the stem
20 to 35 raw sugar cubes, to your taste
5 tablespoons loose Chinese Gunpowder green tea leaves or 7 to 8 green tea bags

1. Place the water and mint in the slow cooker, pushing the mint down into the water. Add the sugar cubes. Cover and bring to a boil on HIGH, 1 to 1½ hours.

2. Turn the heat to LOW and simmer for 3 to 4 hours.

3. Wrap the tea in two cheesecloth bags and tie with kitchen twine, or use a metal spice ball. Add to the mint infusion, cover, and continue to cook on LOW for another 30 minutes to 2 hours, depending on when you want to serve the tea and how strong you want it. Discard the tea bags and the mint. Taste for sugar, adding more if you like a sweeter tea.

4. Serve hot. If you wish, rinse a large teapot with hot water, stuff the neck with more fresh mint, and fill with the hot tea out of the cooker to serve, refilling as needed.

Champurrado

C hampurrado is the chocolate version of *atole,* a hot drink of milk thickened with masa harina, the flour used to make corn tortillas. Champurrado is traditionally made in an earthenware pot and is comforting, nourishing, and sustaining, often drunk before long Catholic masses or as a restorative. Low-fat milk is fine, since in Mexico it is often made with half milk and half water. Use a dehydrated masa harina, such as Quaker brand, or a stone-ground organic masa flour. You may substitute two 1½-ounce tablets of Mexican drinking chocolate for the chopped chocolate, if you wish. Dark brown sugar is more similar in taste to *piloncillo,* the little pyramids of raw sugar found in Mexico. Serve this with tamales or for breakfast. ○ *Makes about fifteen 6-ounce servings*

COOKER: Medium round
SETTINGS AND COOK TIMES: HIGH for 20 to 30 minutes, then LOW for 1½ to 2 hours

1 gallon whole or low-fat milk
4 ounces bittersweet chocolate, chopped
1 ⅓ cups firmly packed light or dark brown sugar
1 cup masa harina
7 tablespoons cornstarch
Two 4-inch cinnamon sticks
2½ tablespoons pure vanilla extract
Ground cinnamon for garnish

1. Combine all but 3 cups of the milk with the chocolate and brown sugar in the slow cooker.

2. In a medium-size bowl, whisk together the reserved 3 cups of milk, the masa harina, and the cornstarch. Pour into the cooker and whisk until smooth; add the cinnamon sticks. Cover and simmer on HIGH for 20 to 30 minutes.

3. Turn the heat setting to LOW and cook for 1½ to 2 hours, stirring occasionally. The mixture will thicken and very lightly coat the back of a spoon. At this point you may thin the mixture with a bit more hot milk, if desired.

4. Stir in the vanilla extract. Serve hot, sprinkled with the ground cinnamon.

Hot Eggnog

Y ou don't have to make eggnog from scratch to have a delightful drink that will impress guests. Beth made eggnog like this for many years for catering, and people who would normally pass it by almost dove into the bowl. This is so easy with the slow cooker, since it simmers slowly and never boils. You can double or triple this recipe with no problem in the large cooker. Be sure to have a nutmeg grinder; the top should be nice and thick with the shavings of this sweet, aromatic spice. You may use a milk- or soy milk–based eggnog interchangeably. We like unsweetened whipped cream here, but do sweeten it, if you prefer.

o *Makes about twenty-four 6-ounce servings*

COOKER: Large round
SETTING AND COOK TIME: LOW for 2 to 3 hours

1 gallon store-bought eggnog
1 quart whole milk
1 cup heavy cream, whipped to soft peaks
1 whole nutmeg

1. Combine the eggnog and milk in the slow cooker. Cover and cook on LOW for 2 to 3 hours.

2. When ready to serve, spoon the whipped cream over the surface of the eggnog and heavily dust with grated fresh nutmeg. Serve hot.

Hot Peppermint Milk

A romatic *Mentha x piperita* is the most popular of the cultivated mint family and is known for its lively flavor in syrups and confectionery. Peppermint milk is a variation on soothing peppermint tea, which was a favorite as far back as the Roman times and the Middle Ages, when mint was grown in European monastery gardens. Serve this with chocolate-covered graham crackers or chocolate chip cookies. ○ *Makes about fifteen 6-ounce servings*

COOKER: Small or medium round
SETTING AND COOK TIME: LOW for 2 to 2½ hours

3 quarts whole milk
2 small bunches fresh peppermint leaves, gently crushed
Honey to taste

1. Place the milk and peppermint leaves in the slow cooker, pressing down on the leaves to submerge them. Cover and cook on LOW for 2 to 2½ hours.

2. With a small mesh strainer or spoon, remove the leaves from the infusion. Serve hot, ladled into mugs, with some honey stirred in.

Mexican Coffee with Brandy and Kahlúa

A group of friends, music, maybe some dancing, lots of chatting, and a warming drink incorporating the Mexican flavors of chocolate, almond, cinnamon, orange, and coffee is a combination guaranteed to be a hit. In lieu of the whipped cream, you can float a tablespoon of heavy cream on top.

○ *Makes eight to ten 6-ounce servings*

COOKER: Medium round
SETTING AND COOK TIME: LOW for 2 hours; can be kept on LOW another 1 to 2 hours

8 cups hot or cold freshly brewed coffee
¼ cup chocolate syrup
¼ cup blanched whole almonds
Four 4-inch cinnamon sticks
½ cup brandy
1 cup Kahlúa
Whipped cream for serving
1 orange, cut into 8 rounds, each round slit halfway through, for garnish

1. Combine the coffee, chocolate syrup, almonds, and cinnamon sticks in the slow cooker. Cover and cook on LOW for about 2 hours.

2. Stir in the brandy and Kahlúa and serve immediately, or keep on LOW for 1 to 2 hours. Serve hot, with some whipped cream on top and a slice of orange on the edge of the cup.

Irish Coffee

I rish coffee is perhaps the most famous of all composed coffee drinks. It has been described as a celestial amalgam of liturgy, institution, and celebration in a cup. It was created and made famous at the Buena Vista Café, a bar at the dead end of San Francisco's Fisherman's Wharf, overlooking the bay. Make this for serving along with your dessert buffet or after appetizers at your next cocktail party. Other good excuses include St. Patrick's Day (March 17), St. Bridget's Day (February 1), weddings, and funerals. Use a medium-roast coffee, not dark like French roast or espresso, for this drink. We make the coffee in batches in a drip coffeemaker, or you can make all the coffee at once in a large percolator.

○ *Makes about twenty-four 6-ounce servings*

COOKER: Large round
SETTING AND COOK TIME: LOW for 1 to 2 hours;
   can be kept on LOW another 1 to 2 hours

16 cups hot or cold freshly brewed coffee
⅓ cup sugar
2 to 2½ cups Irish whiskey, to your taste
Whipped cream for serving

1. Combine the coffee and sugar in the slow cooker. Cover and cook on LOW for 1 to 2 hours.

2. Add the whiskey and serve immediately, or keep on LOW for 1 to 2 hours. Serve hot, ladled into a stemmed heatproof glass mug, leaving a full inch below the rim. Top with whipped cream.

Mulled Wine

Mulled wine is a wonderful surprise for guests on a chilly afternoon or evening. Known as *Glühwein*, or "glow wine," it has been a favorite hot drink for centuries, right down to the lemon or orange studded with cloves. For entertaining, it's a breeze, because you make it in advance and need only ladle it into cups or mugs to serve. The wine here is part of an ensemble cast, not the star player, so it doesn't need to be expensive. In fact, this is a great way to use a couple of bottles of wine that are not to your taste for drinking plain. To serve the wine throughout a party, turn the slow cooker to the KEEP WARM or LOW setting. Even if the lid is off for extended periods of time, the wine should stay quite warm. Keep the servings small; because of the brandy, this drink packs a punch.

○ *Makes about twelve 6-ounce servings*

COOKER: Medium or large round or oval
SETTING AND COOK TIME: LOW for 2 to 5 hours

Two 750-milliliter bottles dry red wine
⅔ cup firmly packed light or dark brown sugar
1¼ cups brandy
1 lemon or small orange
6 whole cloves
Two 4-inch cinnamon sticks
1 whole nutmeg, cut in half (see Note)

Combine the wine, brown sugar, and brandy in the slow cooker, stirring to dissolve the sugar. Wash and dry the lemon or orange. Stick the cloves into the fruit and add to the wine, along with the cinnamon sticks and nutmeg. Cover and cook on LOW until the wine is hot, 2 to 5 hours. Serve hot, straining out the spices.

Note: Cutting a nutmeg in half is easier than it might seem. Place it on a cutting board and cut it through its equator with a large, heavy knife. Do not attempt to hold the nutmeg while you cut it!

Warm Cranberry Zinfandel

Beth used to have large parties every year around the holidays, and one feature that was a constant was the big canning kettle on the stove, full of warm red wine and juice. As the evening went on and the supply dwindled, all sorts of different wines and juices would be tossed in to keep the pot going into the wee hours. We love Zinfandel wine, "the" wine of California, for its berry-like richness and deep flavor. Zinfandel was one of the first California wines, the vines from Italy planted in 1850 in Sonoma at what would come to be the Buena Vista Winery by a Hungarian count who has kept the reputation as "the father of California wine." With the slow cooker, guests can stay in the main entertaining area rather than tramping into the kitchen for their cup of hot spiced wine. Remember that hot wine is a dash more potent than when it is served at room temperature.

○ *Makes about twelve 6-ounce servings*

COOKER: Medium or large round or oval
SETTING AND COOK TIME: LOW for 2 to 6 hours

Two 750-milliter bottles Zinfandel
4 cups water
1 quart unsweetened cranberry juice
1½ cups sugar, or to taste
24 whole cloves
24 green cardamom pods
Eight 4-inch cinnamon sticks, broken in half
Zest from 4 oranges, cut off in long strips

Combine the wine, water, cranberry juice, and sugar in the slow cooker. Place the cloves, cardamom pods, and cinnamon sticks in a small piece of cheesecloth and tie with kitchen twine to make a bag. Add to the cooker, along with the orange strips. Cover and cook on LOW until the wine is hot, 2 to 6 hours. Remove the spice bag and serve hot.

Strawberry–White Wine Punch

A fter years of catering, Beth has assembled many excellent hot drinks for a crowd, some wine-based, others not. This one is a favorite all winter long, as it is fruity and light and very different. If you wish this to be nonalcoholic, replace the port with cherry juice and substitute pineapple juice for the white wine.

o Makes about twenty-four 6-ounce servings

COOKER: Large round
SETTING AND COOK TIME: LOW for 5 to 7 hours; wine added at 4 to 5 hours

32 ounces frozen sweetened strawberries, whole or sliced
½ cup sugar
1 cup port
2 limes, sliced
3 sprigs fresh mint
Four 750-milliliter bottles dry white wine

1. Combine the strawberries, sugar, port, limes, and mint in the slow cooker. Cover and cook on LOW for 4 to 5 hours. Strain through two layers of cheesecloth lining a colander and return to the crock (put the lime slices back in or slice another fresh lime and add to the crock).

2. Add the white wine, cover, and continue to cook on LOW for another 1 to 2 hours. Serve hot.

Glögg

A hot winter drink beyond simple mulled wine, Swedish glögg (pronounced glugh) is served at every home in Sweden during Advent and the Christmas holidays. There are, of course, many versions, but this is the original, containing aquavit, the potent, colorless Scandinavian spirit made from potatoes and crushed malt mash whose name translates to "water of life." If you need to substitute vodka for the aquavit, add 2 ounces of caraway seeds to a liter of vodka and keep in the freezer; even your Swedish friends will not know the difference. When you serve your glögg, raise your mug, look your friends in the eye, say "Skål" (pronounced skoal) loud and clear, and sip away.

○ *Makes about twelve 6-ounce servings*

COOKER: Large round
SETTING AND COOK TIME: LOW for 2 to 4 hours

Two 750-milliter **bottles dry red wine**
⅔ **cup port**
⅔ **cup aquavit**
½ cup firmly **packed dark brown sugar**
½ teaspoon **cardamom seeds (removed from 16 pods)**
6 whole cloves
Two 4-inch cinnamon sticks
One 4-inch knob fresh ginger
1 cup golden or dark raisins
⅔ cup blanched **whole almonds, lightly toasted in a 350°F oven**
    for 8 to 10 minutes

1. Combine the wine, port, aquavit, brown sugar, cardamom seeds, cloves, cinnamon sticks, ginger, and raisins in the slow cooker, stirring to dissolve the sugar. Cover and cook on LOW for 2 to 4 hours.

2. Divide the almonds among the serving mugs, ladle in the hot wine, and serve. There should be some whole spices in each serving.

Port Wine Negus

A negus is a hot beverage of wine, lemon, water, and sugar named after an eighteenth-century British colonel who obviously loved his hot wine. This is a drink that could have been served at a royal court in centuries past, and the name *negus*, from Amharic, the language of Ethiopia, also translates as "king of kings." Port is a sweet, fortified, aged wine with a rich, fruity flavor, drunk as an apéritif or dessert wine. While the best ports are from Portugal, the United States now produces many excellent ones; look for the Ficklin, Quady, and Masson brands. The lemon cuts the inherent sweetness of the port. This is usually prepared stovetop in a double boiler to prevent scorching—there is no such problem with the slow cooker. ○ *Makes about twelve 3-ounce servings*

COOKER: Medium round
SETTING AND COOK TIME: LOW for 2 to 4 hours

One 750-milliliter bottle port
1 cup water
Juice and pared rind of 1 lemon (you want attractive long strips of the rind)
1 tablespoon sugar or honey

Place all the ingredients in the slow cooker. Cover and cook on LOW for 2 to 4 hours. Serve hot, and drink slowly, as this is potent stuff.

Spiked Wassail

W assail was traditionally a hot drink made of ale, sherry, sugar, and spices, with pieces of toast and roasted apples floating in it. It is the legendary drink served on the Feast of the Three Kings with an oversized, decorated sweet yeast bread. The word *wassail* is derived from the Anglo-Saxon toast *waes haeil*, or "be whole." On Christmas or Twelfth Night, revelers would carry a large bowl from door to door, asking for it to be filled, a custom known as "wassailing." There are now many versions of wassail, and the palate for hot strong beer is limited, so it has evolved into a spiked juice toddy. The antique French Api apple was probably the apple of choice of the day. It's now called a Lady apple; look for it at Christmas, but any apple will do. ○ *Makes about eighteen 6-ounce servings*

COOKER: Large round
SETTING AND COOK TIME: LOW for 4 to 5 hours

2 quarts unfiltered apple juice or apple cider
1 quart cranberry juice cocktail
¼ cup firmly packed dark brown sugar
12 whole cloves
15 allspice berries
Four 4-inch cinnamon sticks
2 to 6 small firm cooking apples of your choice,
    studded with additional cloves, if you wish
2 cups Calvados

1. Combine the apple juice, cranberry juice, and brown sugar in the slow cooker. Place the cloves, allspice berries, and cinnamon sticks in a small piece of cheesecloth and tie with kitchen twine to make a bag. Add to the juices. Cover and cook on LOW for 4 to 5 hours.

2. Meanwhile, preheat the oven to 375°F. Place the whole apples in a baking pan with a bit of water and bake in the oven until just a bit tender when pierced with a knife, about 45 minutes. Remove from the oven and add the apples to the slow cooker; pour the water from the baking pan into the cooker as well.

3. Remove the spice bag from the wassail and stir in the Calvados. Serve hot.

Athole Brose

Not for the faint of heart or the diet conscious, this is an authentic recipe for a legendary drink from the moors of Scotland. Athole is a small town amid the craggy mountains near Perth, and "brose" is the Scottish word for "brew." Athole Brose is eons old and traditionally served on Christmas, Hogmanay (New Year's Eve), and the day honoring St. Andrew, the patron saint of Scotland. For the true soul-bracing brew, soak 2 cups rolled oats in 4 cups warm water overnight on the counter; strain and mix the resulting oat liquid with the cream (this is really very delicious, and it cuts the richness and potency a lot). This recipe is adapted from an old Dewar's Scotch whisky ad, which recommended Dewar's White Label Scotch as the spirit of choice.

○ Makes about twelve 3-ounce servings

COOKER: Medium round

SETTING AND COOK TIME: LOW for 1¹/₂ to 3 hours;
can be kept on LOW another hour

1 quart heavy cream
2 cups mild honey (preferably heather honey from Scotland)
4 cups Scotch whisky

1. Combine the cream and honey in the slow cooker. Cover and cook on LOW until very hot, 1 to 2 hours, but do not let it boil or try to rush it on a higher heat setting. The honey will melt into the cream.

2. When ready to serve, add the whisky and stir to combine; let mull 20 minutes or so. The brose can stand for 1 hour on LOW. Serve hot, in very small mugs. It can also be cooled and refrigerated, then served chilled.

Hot Buttered Rum

When the air turns cold and the holidays arrive, hot buttered rum appears. Rum is not generally a liquor enjoyed straight up, but it does have the reputation as the world's greatest mixer. It also holds an honored place in the kitchen, and has for hundreds of years. Although rum drinks are often exotic, hot buttered rum is a nice American drink, using pantry staples. Look for a Caribbean brand, as good rum is made on just about every island. You can vary this basic recipe by adding a gallon of unsweetened apple cider and using the large slow cooker. ○ *Makes about twelve 6-ounce servings*

COOKER: Medium round

SETTING AND COOK TIME: LOW for 2½ to 4½ hours; rum added during last 30 minutes

2 cups firmly packed light brown sugar
½ cup (1 stick) unsalted butter
Pinch of salt
½ teaspoon ground nutmeg
8 cups water
4 whole cloves or a few pinches of ground cloves
Three 4-inch cinnamon sticks or a few pinches of ground cinnamon
2 cups amber or dark rum
Extra cinnamon sticks for garnish

1. Combine the brown sugar, butter, salt, nutmeg, and water in the slow cooker. If using the whole cloves and cinnamon sticks, wrap them in a cheesecloth bag, secure with kitchen twine, and place in the cooker. If using the ground spices, add them to the cooker. Cover and cook on LOW for 2 to 4 hours.

2. When ready to serve, add the rum; let mull 20 minutes or so. Serve hot, in small mugs, garnished with cinnamon sticks.

Company Soups from the Slow Cooker

Onion Soup with Champagne, Port, and Camembert o 86

Brandied Red Onion Soup Gratinée o 87

French Vegetable Soup with Pesto o 88

Cream of Root Vegetable Soup Normandy o 89

Asian Cucumber Bisque o 91

Gingered Carrot–Sweet Potato Soup o 93

Monterey Clam Chowder o 94

Homemade Pho with Chicken o 95

Hearty Beef Borscht with Cabbage o 97

Spicy Lentil Soup with Saffron and Cilantro o 98

Black Bean and Pumpkin Soup o 99

Hielem o 100

Split Pea Soup with Ham o 102

Yellow Split Pea Dal with Mango o 103

Soup is one of the easiest dishes to make in a slow cooker. It's practical and economical, so it is easy to see why so many cooks use their slow cookers as soup pots. This is especially true when you are entertaining and need a large amount of food. Soup is simplicity itself but at the same time showcases your ingenuity in the kitchen. Once you have your stock, all you have to do is decide what goes in, taking care to balance the properties of color, texture, and flavor. With a loaf of

fresh French bread and lots of butter and a leafy green salad with a pungent dressing, you have a perfect casual company supper. Or serve your soup in small portions on its own as the elegant first course of a larger meal. There is a soup for every culture and cuisine in the world, giving rise to the saying that "soup has a thousand faces." It embodies the essentials of global cuisine.

Soups are categorized by their thickness: Clear soups are known as broths and consommé; hearty soups filling enough to be a full meal include dense vegetable soups, bean soups, and pureed cream soups. You can specially concoct soup over a few days, taking care to make the stock, or toss it together quickly from what is on hand. You can make it ahead and reheat it, or serve it steaming straight out of the crock with a pretty ladle. With its versatility, you can serve soup as part of an everyday meal, as well as at holidays and special dinner parties. All sorts of breads, from French bread to chewy black bread, biscuits, muffins, corn sticks, and garlic bread, go with soups so nicely.

Soups are the perfect medium in which to practice the principles of what the French (who call their soups *potage* and cook them in a ceramic pot called a *potée*) refer to as *cuisine de marché*, market cookery. We encourage you to use whatever fresh produce is currently available in your market when you create your soups.

Tips for the Best Slow Cooker Soups

- As simple and easy as it is to prepare soups in the slow cooker, it is important not to overcook them to the point of losing the character of the vegetables. You don't want to end up with a flavorless, murky mess. Pay attention to the times recommended.

- Take advantage of the produce-driven market by making soups that change with the seasons. Use fresh ingredients for the best-tasting soups. Soups cook best if all the ingredients are cut to a uniform size so that they cook evenly.

Take the time needed for the ingredients' proper preparation during the chopping stage.

○ During cooking, water or broth should at least cover the solid ingredients for the proper finished consistency. Add boiling liquid to adjust the consistency at any time during the cooking.

○ In figuring how much to make, think about how much you wish to serve each person; is this an appetizer, with about 1 cup soup needed per serving, or a family-style main dish, which can be 2 cups or more per serving?

○ Unless noted, we like the LOW setting best for soups, especially in the new slow cookers where the HIGH creates a rather intense boil. LOW gives a slow simmer with a slight, low boil.

○ Use herbs and spices sparingly, and always taste for the seasonings at the end of cooking before adding more. Slow cookers tend to intensify flavorings.

○ If you like, you can sweat some of the vegetables, such as onions and garlic, in butter or oil on the stovetop before adding them to the crock. This is a nice flavor addition, although optional.

○ To puree soups, either use a handheld immersion blender stick, taking care not to hit the sides of the crock, or transfer the soup in batches to a food processor and pulse. With the immersion blender, you will not have to remove the soup from the crock. Some soups, such

as artichoke and asparagus, are best strained through a coarse metal sieve, because they have tough fibers.

Finishing Touches for Slow Cooker Soups

You can choose to garnish a soup or not. Garnishes can be for visual effect, but can also add another element of flavor and texture that will be stirred into the soup, such as with toasted almonds or a chunky tomato salsa.

○ For thick soups, use croutons (pages 202, 204); grated or shredded cheese, such as Parmesan or cheddar; freshly snipped chives or chopped red or green onions; chopped fresh Italian parsley, watercress, or arugula; edible, unsprayed flower blossoms, such as nasturtiums; thin slices of lemon or lime; shredded meat or poultry; chunky salsa or chopped fresh vegetables; or frizzled (fried) leeks, onions, or shallots.

○ For cream soups, use toasted almonds or pine nuts; freshly snipped chives or chopped green onions; chopped fresh Italian parsley; or dollops of sour cream, crema Mexicana, or crème fraîche (page 90).

○ For clear soups, choose from strips of fresh-made crêpes or croutons (pages 202, 204); dumplings or gnocchi; freshly snipped chives or green onions; chopped fresh Italian parsley; chunks of tofu; slices of avocado; or lemon slices.

Onion Soup with Champagne, Port, and Camembert

This is a hearty, sophisticated version of onion soup thickened with eggs, sans the toast, adapted from a recipe by Malcolm Hebert, a former columnist for the *San Jose Mercury News* and a gourmand of all foods cooked with wine. Serve this with French bread and butter. ○ *Serves 6*

COOKER: Medium or large round or oval
SETTING AND COOK TIME: HIGH for 8 to 9 hours; broth, Champagne, cheese, eggs, and port added during last 20 to 40 minutes

3 tablespoons unsalted butter
4 large white Bermuda onions
3 cups rich beef broth
3 cups dry Champagne, left open for a few hours to go flat
Three 1-inch pieces Camembert cheese, rind removed
3 large eggs
¼ cup port

1. Place the butter in the slow cooker, cover, and cook on HIGH to melt. Peel and thinly slice the onions by hand or in a food processor. Place in the cooker and toss with the butter to coat. Cover and cook on HIGH until the onions are dark brown and caramelized, but not burned, 8 to 9 hours.

2. Add the broth, cover, and heat on HIGH for 15 minutes. Add the Champagne and cheese, cover, and heat for 10 to 30 minutes longer to melt the cheese; stir to mix the cheese into the soup.

3. In a small bowl, beat together the eggs and port. Whisking all the while, ladle some of the hot soup into the egg mixture. Whisking constantly, pour this into the soup and stir until slightly thickened. Cover and cook for 10 minutes. Serve immediately.

Brandied Red Onion Soup Gratinée

O nion soups vary all over the place. In this version, using sweet red onions, a slice of cheese is placed over the rim of the soup bowl and the bowl is set under the broiler. The heat seals the cheese and forms a delightful crust over the soup. You can make the soup one to two days ahead, but serve it the way the chefs in France do, with the toast and cheese placed over it at the very last minute.

o *Serves 6*

COOKER: Medium round
SETTINGS AND COOK TIMES: HIGH for 8 to 9 hours, then LOW for 1 hour

3 tablespoons unsalted butter
3 tablespoons olive oil
3 large red Torpedo (Italian) onions or other red onions, thinly sliced
2 tablespoons all-purpose flour
6 cups rich beef broth
⅓ cup dry white wine
3 to 4 tablespoons brandy or Cognac, to your taste
6 slices French bread, toasted
12 slices mozzarella cheese, cut to fit the tops of the bowls

1. Place the butter and oil in the slow cooker, cover, and set to HIGH to melt the butter. Place the onions in the cooker and toss them with the butter and oil. Cover and cook on HIGH until the onions are dark brown and caramelized, but not burned, 8 to 9 hours.

2. Add the flour and stir for 4 minutes. Add the broth, wine, and brandy. Cover and cook on LOW for 1 hour.

3. Preheat the broiler. Divide the soup among 6 ovenproof soup bowls. Place a slice of toast in each bowl and top with 2 slices of cheese so that the cheese just overlaps the rim of the soup bowl. Place the bowls under the broiler and broil until the cheese seals the bowl and the top becomes slightly brown. Serve immediately.

French Vegetable Soup with Pesto

T here are many variations of *soupe au pistou*, the vegetable soup featuring a floating slice of bread spread with the French version of basil pesto. It is probably one of the most famous country soups of Europe. This is a filling and delightfully low-fat main-course soup. ❂ *Serves 6 to 8*

COOKER: Large round or oval

SETTING AND COOK TIME: LOW for 7 hours; celery, green beans, zucchini, and cabbage added during last hour

2½ quarts water or chicken broth

1 large yellow onion, chopped

2 leeks (white parts only), sliced

One 28-ounce can whole plum tomatoes, undrained and crushed

4 medium-size carrots, halved lengthwise and cut into 1-inch-thick half-moons

1 medium-size acorn squash, peeled, seeded, and cubed

2 large red or white potatoes, peeled and cubed

1 stalk each fresh thyme, basil, and marjoram

¼ bunch fresh Italian parsley

Two 15-ounce cans garbanzo or white beans, rinsed and drained

2 ribs celery, sliced

½ cup chopped celery leaves

¼ pound green beans, ends trimmed and cut into 2-inch lengths

½ pound zucchini, sliced ½ inch thick

⅓ head savoy cabbage, cored and shredded

Salt and freshly ground black pepper to taste

PISTOU BASIL PASTE:

4 cloves garlic, peeled

Leaves from 1 bunch fresh basil (about 2 cups)

¾ cup freshly grated Parmesan cheese

¼ cup olive oil

2 tablespoons crème fraîche, store-bought or homemade (page 90)

LARGE SKILLET CROUTONS:

Six to eight ½- or ¾-inch-thick slices of day-old French bread

2 tablespoons olive oil, or 1 tablespoon olive oil and 1 tablespoon butter

1. Place the water, onion, leeks, tomatoes with their juice, carrots, acorn squash, and potatoes in the slow cooker. Make a bouquet garni by bunching the fresh herbs and parsley together and tying them with kitchen twine. Add the bouquet garni and the beans to the cooker. Cover and cook on LOW until the vegetables are tender, about 6 hours.

2. Meanwhile, to make the pistou, chop the garlic in a food processor. Add the basil and Parmesan. With the motor running, add the olive oil in a stream through the feed tube, and then the crème fraîche. When smooth, transfer to a bowl, cover, and refrigerate until serving time.

3. When the vegetables are tender, add the celery, celery leaves, green beans, zucchini, and cabbage to the slow cooker. Cover and cook for 1 hour.

4. To make the croutons, in a large sauté pan or skillet, heat the 2 tablespoons olive oil or olive oil and butter over medium-high heat. Make sure the oil is distributed evenly. Arrange the slices of bread in the pan, letting the bread soak up the oil. Brown each side about 2 minutes, adding more oil as needed to toast remaining slices. Remove the hot croutons with tongs to a paper towel.

5. Remove the bouquet garni from the slow cooker and season the soup with salt and pepper. To serve, spread the croutons with pistou and place one in the bottom of each shallow soup bowl. Ladle the hot soup over the croutons and serve immediately.

Cream of Root Vegetable Soup Normandy

This is a lovely winter root soup that is pureed after cooking, then blended with tangy crème fraîche for a super-delicious dish. It is basically a potato soup, made with russet potatoes and turnips, a vegetable that looks much like a half-white/half-purple spinning top and that sustained much of provincial Northern Europe for centuries. If you like, you can rinse the greens from the turnips and toss them into the mix to cook as well. Serve this with hot biscuits or French bread. o *Serves 8*

COOKER: Medium or large round or oval
SETTING AND COOK TIME: LOW for 6 to 8 hours; crème fraîche added during last 20 minutes

2 tablespoons unsalted butter, softened

2 large yellow onions, chopped

3 leeks (white parts and 1 inch of the green), sliced ½ inch thick

6 medium-size carrots, sliced ½ inch thick

6 medium-size russet potatoes, peeled and sliced ¼ inch thick

2 large turnips, peeled and sliced ½ inch thick

2 quarts boiling water or chicken broth

Salt and freshly ground black pepper to taste

1½ cups crème fraîche, store-bought or homemade (recipe follows)

1. Rub the bottom half of the inside of the slow cooker insert with the butter. Place the onions, leeks, carrots, potatoes, and turnips in the cooker. Add the boiling water, cover, and cook on LOW until the vegetables are tender, 6 to 8 hours.

2. Using a handheld immersion blender or transferring to a food processor or blender in batches, puree the soup. Season with salt and pepper. Stir in the crème fraîche, cover, and cook on LOW until heated through, about 20 minutes; do not boil. Serve immediately.

Crème Fraîche

There are many ways to make homemade crème fraîche, a thickened cream, but this is the simplest and most successful. It can be used in place of sour cream or heavy cream in recipes. This recipe makes enough for one batch of Cream of Root Vegetable Soup Normandy. It can be doubled or tripled with no problem. Extras will keep in the refrigerator for up to 1 week. ○ *Makes 1½ cups*

1 cup heavy or heavy whipping cream (not ultra-pasteurized, if possible)

⅓ cup full-fat sour cream or buttermilk

2 tablespoons full-fat plain yogurt containing acidophilus cultures

1. In a small bowl, combine the heavy cream, sour cream, and yogurt; whisk until smooth. Leave in the bowl or pour into a clean jar or small crock, preferably sterilized in the dishwasher. Cover with plastic wrap. Let stand at room temperature until thickened, 6 to 8 hours or overnight. Let stand a few hours longer if you want it a bit thicker.

2. Cover and refrigerate until ready to use. It will continue to thicken as it chills.

Asian Cucumber Bisque

Beth saw Chinese cooking teacher extraordinaire Martin Yan prepare this creamy soup on television. It adapted so beautifully to the slow cooker. Silk squash, also called Chinese okra or angled loofah, is found in Chinese markets or in farmers' markets that cater to Asian shoppers. Or you can always use cucumber—we like the long, English cukes for this. Of course, homemade chicken broth is best (make it the day before from our recipe below), but if you are in an Asian market, you can pick up an Asian-style canned chicken broth that is flavored with ginger. ● *Serves 8 to 10*

COOKER: Medium or large round or oval
SETTINGS AND COOK TIMES: HIGH for 30 minutes, then LOW for 5½ to 6½ hours

¼ cup vegetable oil
2 large yellow onions, chopped
2 pounds silk squash, ends trimmed and ridges cut off, or English cucumber, peeled, halved lengthwise, seeds removed, and cut into chunks
⅓ cup long-grain white rice
2 jalapeño chiles, stemmed, seeded, and chopped
Splash of oyster sauce
6 cups chicken broth or 1 recipe Asian Chicken Broth (recipe follows)
One 14-ounce can coconut milk
Salt and white pepper to taste
Chopped fresh cilantro or green onion for garnish (optional)

1. Place the oil, onions, and squash into the slow cooker. Turn the cooker to HIGH and sweat the vegetables for 30 minutes. Add the rice, jalapeños, oyster sauce, and broth to the pot. Cover and cook on LOW for 5 to 6 hours.

2. Using a handheld immersion blender or transferring to a food processor or blender in batches, puree the soup. Add the coconut milk and cook on LOW for 20 minutes, until heated through; do not boil. Season with salt and pepper. Ladle the hot soup into bowls and garnish with cilantro, if desired.

Asian Chicken Broth

This broth, scented with ginger and scallions, is so easy that you will want to make it over and over, as well as keep a stash in the freezer for stir-fries. The secret is chicken wings, which make a phenomenal broth as easy as 1-2-3 in the slow cooker.

○ Makes about 6 cups

COOKER: Medium or large round or oval
SETTINGS AND COOK TIMES: HIGH for 1 hour, then LOW for 8 to 10 hours

3 pounds chicken wings, chopped in half
Five ½-inch-thick diagonal slices fresh ginger
1 bunch green onions, green tops trimmed
½ teaspoon whole black peppercorns
Water to cover (about 6 cups)
Salt to taste (optional)

1. Place the chicken wings, ginger, green onions, and peppercorns in the slow cooker. Add water to cover by 2 to 3 inches. Cover and cook on HIGH for 1 hour. Uncover and skim off the foam from the surface. Cover, reduce the heat setting to LOW, and cook for 8 to 10 hours. If the water cooks down below the level of the ingredients, add a bit more boiling water.

2. Uncover, turn off the cooker, and let the broth cool to lukewarm. Set a large colander lined with cheesecloth or a fine-mesh strainer over a large bowl and pour the broth through to strain. Press down on the vegetables and chicken to extract all the liquid. Discard the vegetables, skin, and bones. Taste the broth and leave unsalted, or add salt if desired. The broth is ready to use and can be refrigerated for up to 2 days. The fat will separate and rise to the top; scoop off with a spoon and discard. Or divide among airtight freezer storage containers, leaving 2 inches at the top to allow for expansion, and freeze for up to 4 months.

Gingered Carrot–Sweet Potato Soup

This soup is a beautiful, brilliant orange color, naturally sweet, good hot or cold, and oh so nutritious. The long cooking time ensures that the soup will puree to a velvety smoothness. When it comes time to garnish and serve the soup, you can be as decadent as you dare. A spoonful of plain yogurt in the center of each bowl will add tang and not disturb the soup's low-fat profile. A touch of crème fraîche or heavy cream—straight from the carton or whipped until softly thickened—will take the soup to a truly elegant level. ○ *Serves 6 to 8*

COOKER: Medium round or oval
SETTING AND COOK TIME: LOW for 9 to 11 hours

1 medium-size to large sweet potato
6 medium-size carrots
1 medium-size to large sweet onion, such as Walla-Walla or Maui
One 1-inch-long piece of fresh ginger
4 cups chicken or vegetable broth
Salt and white pepper to taste
Yogurt; crème fraîche, store-bought or homemade (page 90); or
heavy cream for garnish (optional)

1. Peel the sweet potato and chop into pieces no larger than 1 inch on a side. Peel the carrots and chop into pieces no larger than ¾ inch on a side. Peel the onion and chop into ¾-inch pieces. Use a vegetable peeler or a paring knife to peel the ginger. Mince it finely. Place the sweet potato, carrots, onion, and ginger in the slow cooker and stir to combine. Add the broth. If you are using canned broth, do not add salt or pepper at this point. If you are using unseasoned homemade broth, add ½ teaspoon salt and a dash of white pepper. Cover and cook on LOW until the vegetables are quite tender, 9 to 11 hours.

2. Turn the slow cooker off, uncover, and allow the soup to cool for a few minutes, then puree in a blender or food processor, in batches if necessary, or use an immersion blender right in the crock. You will want to obtain the smoothest puree possible, so let the blender do its work for a few minutes. Check the seasonings and add salt and pepper if necessary. Serve the soup hot or cold, garnished with a spoonful of yogurt, if desired.

Monterey Clam Chowder

Monterey-style clam chowder is a white chowder that is delightful for an autumn soup dinner. Although we use convenient canned clams here, you can also use fresh if you have access to them. To prepare fresh clams for soup, bring 1½ cups of water to a boil in a deep saucepan. Add 3 pints of scrubbed clams, such as littlenecks, and cover. Steam for 8 minutes; the clams should all be open. Discard any clams that do not open. Remove them from the water with a slotted spoon and remove the meat from the shells. Chop and add to the crock, along with their cooking liquid. Serve this warming chowder with oyster crackers and a big vegetable salad. ○ *Serves 10*

COOKER: Large round or oval
SETTINGS AND COOK TIMES: HIGH for 4 to 5 hours, then LOW for 30 minutes

6 slices smoked dry-cured bacon, cut into 3-inch pieces
2 large yellow onions, diced
2 tablespoons all-purpose flour
Eight 6.5-ounce cans baby clams, undrained
2 carrots, diced
2 stalks celery, diced
½ red bell pepper, finely chopped
1½ pounds red potatoes, cubed
6 sprigs fresh Italian parsley
1 bay leaf
1 tablespoon Worcestershire sauce
2 teaspoons dried thyme leaves
8 cups water
2 cups heavy whipping cream
2 cups half-and-half
1 teaspoon salt
½ teaspoon freshly ground black pepper
1 teaspoon Tabasco sauce
¾ cup minced fresh Italian parsley

1. In a medium-size skillet over medium heat, cook the bacon until crisp; remove and drain on a double layer of paper towels and set aside. Add the onion to the drippings and cook until soft, about 5 minutes. Sprinkle with the flour and cook to make a roux, about 2 minutes.

2. Place the clams and their juice, carrots, celery, bell pepper, potatoes, parsley sprigs, bay leaf, Worcestershire, thyme, and water in the slow cooker; add the onions and bacon. Cover and cook on HIGH for 4 to 5 hours. Discard the parsley sprigs.

3. Add the cream and half-and-half. Add the salt, pepper, and Tabasco sauce. Cover and cook on LOW for at least 30 minutes to heat through. Keep warm on LOW, without letting it come to a boil, until serving time. Ladle the hot soup into bowls and top with the minced parsley.

Homemade Pho with Chicken

Pho is the Vietnamese version of Mom's chicken noodle soup. It is a simple, but filling, bowl of shredded meat, rice noodles, and steaming aromatic broth that is incredible for entertaining a group. People just love it. The soup is concocted with fresh chicken poached in chicken broth with toasted whole spices to give it a nice rich flavor. Traditionally, the soup is accompanied by lime wedges and fresh basil, cilantro, and parsley as garnishes. We also like to sprinkle on sliced hot chiles, bean sprouts, and green onion tops. Setting out little plates of garnishes allows each person to build and season his or her individual bowl of pho, adding more along the way if desired. We also suggest you serve hot sauce and hoisin sauce on the side for seasoning. ○ *Serves 12*

COOKER: Large round or oval
SETTING AND COOK TIME: HIGH for 4 to 5 hours

3 bone-in chicken breast halves (2½ to 3 pounds), skin removed
2 bunches green onions, white and green parts separated and
     green parts reserved for garnish
6 cloves garlic, unpeeled and smashed with the side of a knife
½ bunch cilantro sprigs (about 1 cup)

4½ quarts reduced-sodium chicken broth

2 small yellow onions, unpeeled and halved

Three 1- to 2-inch pieces fresh ginger, unpeeled

3 tablespoons Vietnamese fish sauce (*nuoc mam*)

3 whole star-anise pods

6 whole cloves

One 2-inch piece cinnamon stick, broken in half

Pinch of whole fennel seed, lightly crushed

1 bay leaf

18 ounces ¼-inch-wide rice noodles, soaked in cold water for 20 minutes

GARNISHES (CHOOSE WHAT YOU LIKE):

¾ cup fresh cilantro leaves, coarsely chopped

¾ cup fresh Italian parsley, coarsely chopped

3 handfuls mung bean sprouts, rinsed

6 tablespoons Thai basil leaves or Italian basil leaves, shredded

3 tablespoons (or a dozen slices) thinly sliced jalapeño chile, stemmed and seeded

Tops of green onions, sliced into thin strips

3 limes, each cut into 6 wedges

Hoisin sauce

Sriracha red chili hot sauce

Chili garlic paste

1. Place the chicken, white parts of the green onions, garlic, and cilantro into the slow cooker. Add enough broth to fill the crock to just over three-quarters full; if you have any leftover broth, reserve in the refrigerator. Cover and set the heat to HIGH.

2. While the broth is heating, place the onion and ginger on a baking sheet and place under the broiler, about 3 inches under the flame. Char until lightly browned, 8 to 10 minutes, turning halfway through the cooking. Add to the crock, along with the fish sauce. Place the star anise, cloves, and cinnamon stick pieces in a small dry skillet and toast over medium heat, shaking until heated slightly, 3 to 4 minutes; you will smell the aroma as they release their essential oils. Place in a square of cheesecloth with the fennel seeds and bay leaf; tie with kitchen twine and submerge in the broth in the crock. Cover and cook for 4½ to 5 hours, until the soup is steaming and fragrant and the chicken is cooked through.

3. Lift the chicken from the broth with a slotted spoon or tongs and set in a bowl to cool. Using a colander lined with a double layer of cheesecloth, drain the broth into a large heatproof bowl. Discard the vegetables and the spice bag. Return the broth to the crock; cover and keep on LOW.

4. Bring a large pot of water to a boil. Cook the rice noodles according to package directions, until tender but firm (don't overcook or they will be gummy). Drain and rinse under cold water in a colander and set aside.

5. When the chicken is cool enough to handle, pick off the meat and tear into bite-size pieces; return the chicken to the crock. Heat any reserved broth in the microwave and add it to the crock. Divide the noodles among individual bowls, ladle the hot broth over them, and serve immediately, with the garnishes on the side.

Hearty Beef Borscht with Cabbage

There are two kinds of borscht: a cold, brilliantly pink one, so nice in the summer, and a hot, sustaining one that contains a variety of vegetables and is just right for a winter evening. We like this version of hot borscht for its chunky texture, sweetly tangy flavor, and easy preparation. This is a large quantity; for a medium-size slow cooker, you may cut the amounts in half.

o Serves 10 to 12

COOKER: Large round or oval
SETTINGS AND COOK TIMES: HIGH for 1 hour, then LOW for 6 to 7 hours

1 pound lean boneless stewing beef (brisket, chuck, rump, round, or a similar cut)
3 large beets
2 medium-size baking potatoes
1 large red onion
½ small head green cabbage
2 large tomatoes, chopped, or one 14-ounce can chopped tomatoes, undrained
1 teaspoon dillweed
2 teaspoons salt, or to taste
¼ teaspoon freshly ground black pepper, or to taste
Pinch of sugar (optional)
2 tablespoons cider vinegar, or to taste
Cold sour cream for serving

1. Trim as much fat as possible from the beef and cut it into cubes ½ to ¾ inch on a side. Place the beef in the slow cooker.

2. Peel the beets and potatoes and cut into cubes about the same size as the beef. Peel the onion and chop it into ½-inch pieces. Cut the cabbage into wedges, cut out the core, and chop the cabbage into pieces about 1 × ½ inch. Chop the tomatoes. Add the beets, potatoes, onion, cabbage, and tomatoes (with their juice, if using canned) to the slow cooker. Add the dillweed, salt, and pepper. Add enough water so that it covers or almost covers the meat and vegetables. Carefully stir the ingredients to blend them and distribute the seasonings. Cover and cook on HIGH for 1 hour.

3. Turn the heat to LOW and cook until the meat and vegetables are tender, 6 to 7 hours.

4. Before serving, add the sugar, if desired, and vinegar and taste the soup. If necessary, add additional salt, pepper, sugar, or vinegar. Ladle the hot soup into bowls and top with a spoonful of cold sour cream.

Spicy Lentil Soup with Saffron and Cilantro

T his version of lentil soup has a nice Middle Eastern flavor and is just a little bit special for company. Serve in small bowls for a first course, or large ones for a main course with salad and bread. ○ *Serves 8 to 12*

COOKER: Large round or oval
SETTING AND COOK TIME: LOW for 7 to 9 hours

2 tablespoons olive oil
1 medium-size yellow onion, finely chopped
2 ribs celery, chopped
1 medium-size carrot, minced
One 16-ounce can solid-pack whole tomatoes, undrained and chopped
3 cups dried brown lentils, rinsed and picked over
1 teaspoon ground cumin
¾ teaspoon ground coriander

½ teaspoon ground cinnamon

2 tablespoons freshly squeezed lemon juice

Salt and freshly ground black pepper to taste

Large pinch of powdered saffron

⅓ cup packed chopped fresh cilantro

Plain yogurt for serving

1. In a large skillet, heat the olive oil over medium heat. Add the onion, celery, and carrot and cook, stirring a few times, until just softened, about 5 minutes. Place in the slow cooker, along with the tomatoes and their juice, lentils, cumin, coriander, cinnamon, and lemon juice. Add water to come about 3 inches above the vegetables. Cover and cook on LOW for 7 to 9 hours.

2. Season with salt and pepper and stir in the saffron and cilantro. Add water to thin if the soup is too thick. Ladle into serving bowls and serve hot, topped with a dollop of yogurt.

Black Bean and Pumpkin Soup

Beth's friend Connie Rothermel is an innovative and creative cook, especially when it comes to entertaining. A meal at Connie's house is always an adventure, with her wonderful presentation and tasty food. Here is one of her easy-to-assemble, delicious, low-fat soups. Connie uses an excellent dry bouillon, such as Better Than Bouillon, but you can use canned or homemade broth. Use a nice imported sherry vinegar, its smooth taste the result of being fermented in the wooden casks used for sherry wine. Black beans and sherry seem to have a natural affinity. Serve this soup with focaccia or cheese quesadillas. ○ *Serves 8 to 10*

COOKER: Medium round or oval

SETTING AND COOK TIME: LOW for 6 to 7 hours

Three 15-ounce cans black beans, rinsed and drained

One 14.5-ounce can diced tomatoes, drained

1 large yellow onion, chopped

2 large shallots, chopped

3 to 4 cloves garlic, to your taste, crushed

1½ teaspoons ground cumin

4 cups beef broth

One 16-ounce can solid-pack pumpkin

½ cup dry sherry

3 tablespoons sherry vinegar

Salt to taste

Sour cream for garnish

Toasted pumpkin seeds for garnish

1. Place the beans, tomatoes, onion, shallots, garlic, cumin, broth, pumpkin, and sherry in the slow cooker. Stir to combine. Cover and cook on LOW for 6 to 7 hours.

2. Puree the soup in the cooker with a handheld immersion blender or in batches in a food processor or blender. Add the vinegar and stir to combine. Add salt if necessary. Serve hot with a dollop of sour cream and toasted pumpkin seeds sprinkled on top.

Hielem

Hielem is a hearty green chard, noodle, and bean soup with its roots in Tunisia, a North African country with a cuisine similar to that of Morocco, its close neighbor. We love the rich and satisfying combination of butter (lima) beans and garbanzos. The soup is seasoned at the end with harissa—a vibrant chile paste—salt, and pepper. Hielem is what the hand-rolled pasta used in this soup is called, as well as being the name of the soup. You can use dried or fresh angel hair pasta or the thinnest dried egg noodles. This is a great vegetarian soup, thick with tasty cooked greens, when made with vegetable broth. ◦ *Serves 6 to 8*

COOKER: Large round

SETTING AND COOK TIME: LOW for 5 to 6 hours; pasta and Swiss chard added during last 30 minutes to 1 hour

One 15.5-ounce can garbanzo beans, undrained

One 15.5-ounce can butter beans, undrained

½ cup chopped celery leaves

½ cup chopped fresh Italian parsley

⅓ cup tomato paste

4 cups chicken or vegetable broth

2 tablespoons olive oil

1 small yellow onion, chopped

1 rib celery, chopped

½ cup crushed or chopped dried or fresh angel hair pasta or fine egg noodles

1 bunch green Swiss chard leaves and stems, leaves shredded and stems chopped

1 to 2 tablespoons harissa (recipe follows), to your taste

Salt and freshly ground black pepper to taste

Lemon wedges for serving

1. Place the garbanzo and butter beans with their liquid, celery leaves, parsley, tomato paste, and broth in the slow cooker; stir to combine. Cover and turn the setting to LOW.

2. In a small skillet, heat the olive oil over medium heat. Add the onion and celery and cook, stirring a few times, until softened, about 5 minutes; add to the cooker. Cover and cook on LOW for 4 to 5 hours.

3. Stir in the pasta, then pack in the Swiss chard; it will cook down. Cover and cook until the pasta and chard stems are tender to the bite, 30 minutes to 1 hour longer on LOW or 10 to 15 minutes on HIGH.

4. Stir in the harissa and season with salt and pepper. Serve hot with lemon wedges.

Harissa

This savory-hot condiment native to North African cuisine is traditionally used to flavor meats. Because it is a homemade concoction, there are as many versions as there are cooks. This version uses fresh chiles and mint leaves, while others use dried New Mexican red chiles and garlic. Use harissa as a flavoring in soups and stews, in couscous water before making the couscous, or thinned with water to make a dip for French bread. Only a small amount is needed to flavor an entire dish. ○ *Makes 1 cup*

2 small fresh hot red peppers, seeded and chopped into a few pieces

3 tablespoons torn fresh mint leaves

1 teaspoon ground coriander

1 teaspoon ground cumin

¼ teaspoon cayenne pepper

¼ teaspoon salt

⅔ cup olive oil

Place the peppers, mint, coriander, cumin, cayenne, and salt in a food processor and process into a paste. Drizzle in some oil just to bind. Place the paste in a jar or small plastic container and cover with the oil. Store in the refrigerator for up to 1 month.

Split Pea Soup with Ham

H ere is the best split pea soup ever made with a leftover ham bone. It is good for lunch or supper on a cold rainy weekend, and it also freezes well. Split pea soup instantly brings back memories for us of large family meals around the table. It becomes very thick when chilled in the refrigerator, but as it is re-heated, it will slowly melt. If it is still too thick, thin it with a bit of water or broth. Serve with rye or French bread and butter, some nice white cheddar cheese, and chunks of fresh apples. You will have a feast. ✺ *Serves 8 to 12*

COOKER: Large round or oval

SETTING AND COOK TIME: LOW for 13 to 15 hours; meat shredded and bay leaves, thyme, salt, and pepper added at 12 hours

3 cups dried green split peas, rinsed and picked over

10 cups water or chicken broth

1 ham bone or 2 meaty ham hocks, rinsed

2 medium-size yellow onions, diced

3 large carrots, diced

2 ribs celery with leaves, diced

2 bay leaves

½ teaspoon dried thyme or 1½ teaspoons chopped fresh thyme

Salt and freshly ground black pepper to taste

1. Place the split peas in the slow cooker along with the water, ham bone, onions, carrots, and celery. Stir to combine. Cover and cook on LOW until the peas are completely tender, about 12 hours.

2. Skim off any scum that comes to the top. Remove the ham bone, let it cool a bit, then strip off the meat. Discard all fat and bone. Shred the meat and return it to the soup. Add the bay leaves and thyme and season with salt and pepper. Cover and simmer on LOW 1 to 3 hours longer.

3. Puree the soup in the cooker using an immersion blender, or in batches using a blender or food processor. Add more salt and pepper if necessary. Serve hot.

Yellow Split Pea Dal with Mango

Beth loves yellow split peas and makes a number of soups with them. Here, they are prepared in the style of a thick Indian dal, a soup that is high in protein and inexpensive to make. On the advice of her friend Dada Shamitananda, a monk who teaches yoga and Indian cooking classes, we have included some chopped green mango (which adds a touch of sour just like vinegar does), added near the end of cooking along with the spices. The mango should have a uniform green skin, be firm, and have pale flesh; while ripe mangoes are sweet and soft, unripe mangoes are firm and astringent. The spices need to be toasted to bring out their full flavor, so fry them quickly in a bit of butter before adding them to the soup. As with many traditional Indian vegetarian dishes, note that this one uses no onions or garlic in its preparation. Don't skip the cold plain yogurt and ripe mango garnish; they make the soup. ○ *Serves 6 to 8*

COOKER: Medium or large round or oval
SETTING AND COOK TIME: LOW for 8 to 10 hours; toasted spices and mango added at 6 to 7 hours

2 cups dried yellow split peas, rinsed and picked over
6½ cups water
10 whole cloves
One 4-inch cinnamon stick
3 tablespoons unsalted butter
2 teaspoons ground cumin
1 teaspoon ground turmeric

½ teaspoon brown mustard seeds

½ teaspoon ground coriander

¼ teaspoon cayenne pepper

¼ teaspoon ground ginger

1 large green (unripe) mango (optional), peeled, pitted, and chopped

1½ teaspoons salt, or more to taste

4 cups cooked basmati rice

1½ cups plain yogurt, for serving

1 large ripe mango (about 14 ounces), peeled, pitted, and chopped, for serving

1. Place the split peas, water, cloves, and cinnamon stick in the slow cooker. Cover and cook on LOW for 6 to 7 hours.

2. Remove the cloves and cinnamon stick. Add boiling water to thin if the soup is too thick.

3. In a medium-size skillet, melt the butter over medium heat. Add the cumin, turmeric, mustard seeds, coriander, cayenne, and ginger; cook 1 to 2 minutes, stirring constantly, just to heat and gently toast the spices. Stir the spice mixture and green mango, if using, into the cooked dal. Cover and cook on LOW 2 to 3 hours longer.

4. Stir in the salt. Serve in bowls poured over the rice and top with yogurt and chopped ripe mango.

Slow Cooker Savory Sauces

Mole Poblano Sauce ○ 107

Ancho Chile Sauce ○ 108

Red Wine Barbecue Sauce ○ 109

Our Basic KC Barbecue Sauce ○ 110

Chinese-Style Barbecue Sauce ○ 111

Tequila and Pineapple Barbecue
Sauce ○ 112

Yellow Bell Pepper Sauce with
Thyme ○ 113

Thai Peanut Sauce ○ 114

Garnet Cumberland Sauce ○ 115

Old-Fashioned Mint Sauce ○ 116

Indian Tomato Sauce ○ 117

Creole Tomato Sauce with Shrimp ○ 118

Country Tomato Sauce with Roasted
Vegetables ○ 119

Family-Style Winter Tomato Sauce ○ 120

Beefy Tomato Sauce with Sausage
and Fennel ○ 121

Fresh Herb and Cream Sauce ○ 122

Salsa Alfredo ○ 123

Herbed Chèvre Sauce ○ 124

Sauces are the cornerstone of so many cuisines, and they can certainly make a dish something special. Sauces have become so much a staple that it is easy to identify sauce creations and their locality of origin just by name: mole, marinara, curry, béarnaise, Mornay, roux. Each classic sauce has evolved into what it is today through being influenced by available ingredients, an important element, and local eating habits. The French, the source of most of the simple techniques used in sauce preparation today, christened sauces *la poésie de la cuisine*, or "poetry of the kitchen," for their delicate flavors.

Sauces as we know them were probably originally invented in medieval times to dispel the monotony of serving the same dishes day after day and to disguise spoilage. Today they are flavor enhancements, and sometimes the primary focus of a dish, especially where pasta is concerned. The modern cook is able to whip up dishes with an international flair just by knowing a few good sauces.

Although many sauces are made in the pan *alla momento*, slow cooker sauces come together quickly, then simmer for hours without fuss. Flavored with a medley of seasonal, dried, and canned ingredients, these easy sauces beckon even the most novice cook. The classic Mexican, Italian, and barbecue sauces are especially nice prepared on their own in the crock, since they make the most of the long, all-day slow-cooking process, and there seems to be no end to their regional variety. We wanted a collection to show variety in flavor, as in so many tomato sauces, and texture. Although barbecue sauces are known as a finishing sauce in grill cookery, slow-cooking uses the sauce for the entire cooking time.

After you have made your sauces on the stovetop, you can use a slow cooker on the KEEP WARM setting to hold your sauce for about 2 hours before serving in place of a double boiler. Please do not use the LOW setting, which is a cooking setting that is too high for just warming.

Mole Poblano Sauce

M̲ole poblano sauce is a Mexican tomato and dried red chile–based sauce with a dash of chocolate added for depth of flavor rather than for sweetness. It has a deep brick-red hue from the dried chiles and is a great sauce to pour over chicken, pork tenderloin, or rabbit. Look for dried ancho and pasilla chiles in a Mexican market or the Hispanic section of a large supermarket. They are sold in clear plastic packets. Break off the stem and shake out the seeds before using them; for extra heat, leave some seeds in. ● *Makes about 4 cups*

COOKER: Medium round
SETTING AND COOK TIME: LOW for 3 to 5 hours

¼ cup olive oil
½ cup finely chopped yellow onion
3 cloves garlic, minced
One 14.5-ounce can chopped tomatoes, undrained, or 5 ripe plum tomatoes, peeled, seeds squeezed out, and cut into chunks
2 tablespoons tomato paste
2 dried ancho chiles, stemmed, seeded, and torn into chunks
2 dried pasilla negro chiles, stemmed, seeded, and torn into chunks
2 ounces semisweet chocolate, chopped, or 2½ tablespoons semisweet chocolate chips
1½ teaspoons sesame seeds
1 heaping tablespoon slivered almonds
2 cups chicken broth
Salt to taste

1. In a medium-size skillet over medium heat, heat 2 tablespoons of the oil, then cook the onion and garlic, stirring, until softened, about 5 minutes. Transfer to the slow cooker and add the remaining 2 tablespoons oil, the tomatoes and their juice, tomato paste, ancho chiles, pasilla chiles, chocolate, sesame seeds, almonds, and broth. Stir to combine, then cover and simmer on LOW for 3 to 5 hours.

2. Puree the sauce in the slow cooker using a handheld immersion blender, or transfer it in batches to a blender or food processor and puree. Season with salt. The sauce will keep in the refrigerator in an airtight container for 5 to 7 days.

Ancho Chile Sauce

T his is a delicious all-purpose tomato sauce for any type of Mexican cooking—with huevos rancheros and enchiladas, over chicken or rabbit, and in casseroles. There are a few steps before it all goes into the cooker, including roasting the garlic and grinding the chiles, but the effort is worth it for the flavor it creates. The dried smoked ancho chile is a deep red and has an underlying taste like raisins or prunes. This is a sauce Beth learned when she took a class from Ed Brown, author of the Tassajara cookbooks. Brown made three tomato sauces, all from canned tomatoes but each with different spices, to show how the sauce was totally different each time. ○ *Makes about 4 cups*

COOKER: Medium round
SETTING AND COOK TIME: LOW for 5 to 6 hours

1 large head garlic, base cut off
Olive oil
2 dried ancho chiles
One 28-ounce can tomato puree
One 14.5-ounce can chopped tomatoes, undrained
2 tablespoons tomato paste
Scant ½ teaspoon dried Mexican or regular oregano
1 tablespoon balsamic or cider vinegar
Pinch of sugar
Salt to taste

1. Preheat the oven to 350°F. Place the garlic on a baking sheet or in a gratin dish and brush it with olive oil. Bake until soft, about 30 minutes. Remove and let cool.

2. Meanwhile, place the chiles on a baking sheet and bake until puffy, about 3 minutes. Let cool, then cut open and remove the stem and seeds; grind the chiles in a small food processor or coffee mill to make 2 to 3 tablespoons of powder.

3. Place the chile powder, tomato puree, chopped tomatoes with their juice, tomato paste, and oregano in the slow cooker. Squeeze the garlic out of its skins into the crock. Puree the sauce right in the crock using a handheld immersion blender, or transfer it in batches to a blender or food processor and puree, then return to the crock. Cover and simmer on LOW for 5 to 6 hours.

4. Stir in the vinegar and sugar, then season with salt. The sauce will keep in the refrigerator in an airtight container for 5 to 7 days, or in the freezer for up to 1 month.

Red Wine Barbecue Sauce

T his is our plain ol' all-purpose barbecue sauce, unadulterated and straight-forward, from our first book. It is tangy from the red wine and lemon juice. It is so popular and tasty that we present it again here, scaled up to make a large amount. ○ *Makes 9 cups*

COOKER: Medium or large round or oval
SETTING AND COOK TIME: LOW for 5 to 8 hours

1 cup olive oil
3 large yellow onions, chopped
1½ cups dry red wine
1 cup apple cider vinegar
6 cups ketchup
1 cup freshly squeezed lemon juice
¾ cup firmly packed light or dark brown sugar
9 tablespoons Worcestershire sauce
3 tablespoons soy sauce
4 teaspoons chili powder
3 tablespoons paprika

1. Heat the oil in a large skillet over medium heat; add the onions and sauté until limp, 5 to 7 minutes. Add the wine and vinegar and bring to a boil. Transfer the contents of the skillet to the slow cooker and add the ketchup, lemon juice, brown sugar, Worcestershire sauce, soy sauce, chili powder, and paprika.

2. Cover and cook on LOW for 5 to 8 hours. If the sauce is not thick enough for you, remove the cover, turn the setting to HIGH, and cook for up to 30 minutes longer, until it reaches the desired consistency. Puree the sauce in the crock with an immersion blender, or transfer it in batches to a blender or food processor and puree. Cool, then transfer to an airtight container and refrigerate for up to 2 months.

Our Basic KC Barbecue Sauce

H ere is a simple version of Kansas City–style sauce—tomatoey, tangy, thick, pungent, and sweet—similar to bottled sauces in the store. We like this sauce because it goes together very quickly with simple ingredients.

o *Makes about 4 cups*

COOKER: Medium round or oval
SETTING AND COOK TIME: LOW for 5 to 8 hours

¼ **cup olive oil**
1 large yellow onion, chopped
4 cloves garlic, minced
One 32-ounce can tomato puree
½ **cup bottled chili sauce**
½ **cup honey**
¼ **cup soy sauce**
2 tablespoons Worcestershire sauce
1 tablespoon Dijon mustard

1. Heat the oil in a medium-size skillet over medium heat; add the onion and garlic and sauté until limp, about 5 minutes. Transfer the contents of the skillet to the slow cooker and add the tomato puree, chili sauce, honey, soy sauce, Worcestershire sauce, and mustard.

2. Cover and cook on LOW for 5 to 8 hours. If the sauce is not thick enough for you, remove the cover, turn the setting to HIGH, and cook for up to 30 minutes longer, until it reaches the desired consistency. Puree in the crock with an immersion blender, or transfer it in batches to a blender or food processor and puree. Cool, then transfer to an airtight container and refrigerate for up to 2 months.

Chinese-Style Barbecue Sauce

Here is another very easy barbecue sauce to whip up from a basic pantry. It is high in sugar, so expect a nice sticky glaze to result. The flavors are wonderful on pork spareribs. ○ *Makes about 8 cups*

COOKER: Medium or large round or oval
SETTING AND COOK TIME: LOW for 5 to 6 hours

1 cup (2 sticks) unsalted butter
3 large yellow onions, chopped
6 cloves garlic, minced
1 cup unseasoned rice vinegar
6 cups canned tomato puree
2 cups firmly packed light brown sugar
¾ cup soy sauce
9 tablespoons Worcestershire sauce
⅓ cup chili paste with garlic

1. Melt the butter in a large skillet over medium heat; add the onions and garlic and sauté until limp, 5 to 7 minutes. Add the vinegar and bring to a boil. Transfer the contents of the skillet to the slow cooker and add the tomato puree, brown sugar, soy sauce, Worcestershire sauce, and chili paste.

2. Cover and cook on LOW for 5 to 6 hours. If the sauce is not thick enough for you, remove the cover, turn the setting to HIGH, and cook for up to 30 minutes longer, until it reaches the desired consistency. Puree in the crock with an immersion blender, or transfer it in batches to a blender or food processor and puree. Cool, then transfer to an airtight container and refrigerate for up to 2 months.

Tequila and Pineapple Barbecue Sauce

W hen our friend Nancyjo Riekse, a caterer, told us about using tequila in sauces, at first we hesitated, thinking it might be too strong. But with the renaissance of good-quality tequilas, we found the flavor complex and appealing. Some recipes even call for a specific type of tequila. For this recipe, use a silver or plata tequila, also known as white or blanco, which is unaged and has a nice agave nectar flavor. A bit more complex is the reposado, which is aged in oak barrels for three months. ● *Makes about 3½ cups*

COOKER: Medium round or oval
SETTINGS AND COOK TIMES: HIGH for 1 hour, then LOW for about 2 hours

Two 6-ounce cans tomato paste
Two 12-ounce cans frozen pineapple juice concentrate, thawed
1¼ cups silver tequila
2 shallots, very finely minced
1 cup apricot jam
¼ cup freshly squeezed lemon juice
3 tablespoons balsamic vinegar
2 tablespoons minced or pureed canned chipotle chiles in adobo sauce
Splash of hot pepper sauce, such as Tabasco

1. Combine the tomato paste, pineapple juice, tequila, shallots, jam, lemon juice, vinegar, and chiles in the slow cooker. Cover and cook on HIGH for 1 hour to bring to a simmer, keeping the cover open slightly to allow for some evaporation. Turn the cooker to LOW and cook until thick, about 2 more hours.

2. If the sauce is not thick enough for you, remove the lid, turn the cooker back to HIGH, and cook for up to 30 minutes longer, until it reaches the desired consistency. Add the hot pepper sauce, then taste and add more, if desired. Let cool, then transfer to an airtight container and refrigerate for up to 2 weeks.

Although barbecue sauces are known as finishing sauces in grill cookery, slow-cooking uses the sauce for the entire cooking time, allowing the sauces to meld right into the meat. The marinades and mops used to keep the meat juicy on the grill are simply not necessary in the slow cooker. Do use a dry rub, though, and marinate your meat for an hour or two, if you like, before coating with a sauce to cook.

Yellow Bell Pepper Sauce with Thyme

This is a delicious and simple summer sauce. After Beth's friend Mary Cantori spent a week at the Rancho La Puerta Spa, just over the border from San Diego in Baja California, she came back with lots of practical, yummy vegetarian dishes; this is one of them. Serve it with stuffed vegetables, fish, or poultry, or even over cheese enchiladas or pasta. ○ *Makes about 5½ cups*

COOKER: Medium round
SETTING AND COOK TIME: LOW for 4 to 6 hours

4 large yellow bell peppers, seeded and cut into chunks
3 cups vegetable broth
2 small white onions, chopped
4 sprigs fresh thyme, tied together with kitchen twine
Salt and freshly ground black pepper to taste

1. Place the peppers, broth, onions, and thyme in the slow cooker. Cover and simmer on LOW until the peppers are tender, 4 to 6 hours.

2. Remove the thyme and discard. Use a handheld immersion blender to puree the sauce right in the crock, or transfer it in batches to a blender or food processor and puree. Season with salt and pepper. The sauce will keep in the refrigerator in an airtight container for 5 to 7 days, or in the freezer for up to 1 month.

Red Bell Pepper Sauce with Saffron: Substitute red bell peppers for the yellow peppers and a small pinch of saffron threads for the thyme.

Thai Peanut Sauce

T hai spicy peanut sauce is served in a lot of restaurants nowadays, and it is a versatile vegetarian sauce that tastes good with shrimp or chicken, as a dip, or over steamed vegetables, pan-fried tofu, or cooked white rice with chopped fresh cilantro and minced green onions. There are many versions, but the best ones are made with traditional ingredients. Thai red curry paste, a combination that contains onions, ginger, hot red chiles, lime, and cilantro, is available in Asian markets, as are the palm sugar, fish sauce, and tamarind paste. If you use vegetable broth, this will keep indefinitely in the refrigerator.

Makes about 4 cups

COOKER: Medium round

SETTING AND COOK TIME: LOW for 1½ to 2½ hours

One 15-ounce can unsweetened coconut milk

2 cups vegetable or chicken broth

3 to 4 tablespoons Thai red curry paste, to your taste

1 cup smooth peanut butter

1 tablespoon grated fresh ginger

2 tablespoons light brown sugar or palm sugar (also sold as jaggery)

2 tablespoons Thai or Vietnamese fish sauce or soy sauce

Juice of 1 lime

1 tablespoon tamarind paste

Salt to taste

1. Combine the coconut milk, broth, curry paste, peanut butter, ginger, and brown sugar in the slow cooker. Cover and simmer on LOW until thickened and hot, 1½ to 2½ hours.

2. Add the fish sauce, lime juice, and tamarind paste; stir until dissolved. Season with salt. If the sauce is too thick, thin it with more coconut milk; if too thin, stir in more peanut butter, a tablespoon at a time. Serve hot or at room temperature. The sauce will keep in an airtight container in the refrigerator indefinitely if made with vegetable broth, and for 5 to 7 days if made with chicken broth.

Garnet Cumberland Sauce

I f you are familiar with British cuisine (before the era of the Naked Chef and Nigella), you will probably have come in contact with Cumberland sauce, a luscious sweet-spicy sauce served with ham, turkey, and especially game. Beth was given this recipe as a gift by one of her British-born catering clients, and it has not only graced many a table, but it also makes a fabulous food gift.

○ *Makes about 1½ cups*

COOKER: Small round
SETTING AND COOK TIME: LOW for 1½ to 2 hours

Peel of 2 large oranges, removed in strips with a vegetable peeler
1 cup red currant jelly
½ cup port
½ cup freshly squeezed orange juice
¼ cup freshly squeezed lemon juice
4 teaspoons Dijon mustard
2 teaspoons white Worcestershire sauce
½ teaspoon sweet Hungarian paprika
½ teaspoon ground ginger
2 tablespoons plus 1 teaspoon cornstarch

1. In a food processor, drop the orange peel through the feed tube, pulsing to grind. Add all of the remaining ingredients and process for 1 minute.

2. Transfer the mixture to the slow cooker. Cover and cook on LOW until very hot, slightly thickened, and clear, 1½ to 2 hours, stirring occasionally if you happen to be nearby. The sauce can sit for 1 hour on LOW or KEEP WARM before serving. It will keep in the refrigerator in an airtight container for up to 1 month.

Old-Fashioned Mint Sauce

This mint sauce was the predecessor to mint jelly. Use a really nice vinegar from a specialty food store; it will be a dominant flavor in the sauce. Serve with lamb and roasted vegetables and potatoes. This is best made in a 1½- to 3-quart slow cooker. ● *Makes about 2 cups*

COOKER: Small or medium round or oval
SETTING AND COOK TIME: HIGH for 1 hour

1 cup water
¾ cup white wine vinegar or champagne vinegar
¾ cup confectioners' sugar
1 bunch fresh spearmint (5 to 10 large sprigs)
Pinch of salt

1. Place the water, vinegar, and confectioners' sugar in the slow cooker. Cover and cook on HIGH until at a good rolling boil, about 45 minutes.

2. Remove the lid and let the liquid evaporate a bit while you remove the spearmint leaves from their stems and finely chop them. Add the mint and salt to the cooker, cover, and cook until the leaves are limp, 5 to 10 minutes. Serve warm. The sauce will keep in the refrigerator in an airtight container for several days, but the mint will lose some of its fresh flavor.

Indian Tomato Sauce

T his is a zesty all-purpose tomato sauce, sometimes called a gravy, for any type of Indian food; it goes nicely with fried stuffed pastries such as samosas and fritters, over rice, over vegetables, over meatloaf or grain patties, or in casseroles. It is particularly delicious with eggplant. We like to toss in a few tablespoons of cilantro at the end, which adds a fresh taste. ○ *Makes about 4 cups*

COOKER: Medium round
SETTING AND COOK TIME: LOW for 5 to 6 hours

2 tablespoons olive oil
1 tablespoon unsalted butter
One 1-inch piece fresh ginger, cut into 4 slices
½ teaspoon ground cumin
One 28-ounce can tomato puree
½ cup vegetable or chicken broth
1 jalapeño chile
½ teaspoon cayenne pepper
Pinch of ground turmeric
Pinch of light or dark brown sugar
3 tablespoons chopped fresh cilantro or Italian parsley
Salt and freshly ground black pepper to taste

1. Place the olive oil and butter in a small skillet over medium heat. When the butter has melted, add the ginger and cumin and cook until sizzling, no more than 1 minute; immediately remove from the heat.

2. Place the tomato puree and broth in the slow cooker. Add the ginger and cumin with their butter and oil, along with the jalapeño, cayenne, turmeric, and brown sugar; stir to combine. Cover and simmer on LOW for 5 to 6 hours.

3. Remove and discard the ginger slices and jalapeño (you may chop the chile and return it to the sauce, if you like), then stir in the cilantro and season with salt and pepper. Serve warm. The sauce will keep in the refrigerator in an airtight container for 5 to 7 days, or in the freezer for up to 1 month (if freezing, do not add the cilantro until serving time).

Creole Tomato Sauce with Shrimp

Here is a completely different rendition of tomato sauce, right down to the Tabasco and the shrimp. This is adapted from Renee Shephard and Fran Raboff's *Recipes from a Kitchen Garden* (Ten Speed Press, 1987). Serve it over long-grain white or brown rice, garnished with lots of chopped parsley. We like it over pecan brown rice. ○ *Makes about 6 cups*

COOKER: Medium or large round or oval

SETTINGS AND COOK TIMES: LOW for 6 to 8 hours; turned to HIGH and shrimp added during last 10 minutes

1 tablespoon unsalted butter

3 tablespoons olive oil

¼ cup all-purpose flour

1 large yellow onion, chopped

3 ribs celery, diced

1 medium-size red bell pepper, seeded and diced

Two 28-ounce cans chopped tomatoes, undrained

One 6-ounce can tomato paste

½ teaspoon dried thyme

1 bay leaf

½ teaspoon Tabasco sauce

Pinch of red pepper flakes

Pinch of light brown sugar

1 cup chicken broth

Pinch of cayenne pepper

Salt and freshly ground black pepper to taste

2 pounds medium-size raw shrimp, peeled and deveined

Chopped fresh parsley for garnish

1. In a medium-size skillet, melt the butter in 1 tablespoon of the oil over medium heat; add the flour and cook, stirring constantly, until it turns golden brown. Scrape onto a plate. Add the remaining 2 tablespoons oil to the skillet and cook the onion, celery, and bell pepper, stirring, until softened, about 5 minutes.

2. Transfer the vegetable mixture to the slow cooker. Add the tomatoes and their juice, tomato paste, thyme, bay leaf, Tabasco sauce, red pepper flakes, brown sugar, broth, and flour mixture, and stir to combine. Cover and simmer on LOW for 6 to 8 hours.

3. Remove the bay leaf. Add the cayenne and season with salt and black pepper. Add the shrimp and turn the heat setting to HIGH. Cover and cook until the shrimp are pink, firm, and curled, 8 to 12 minutes depending on their size. Test one to be sure it is cooked through. Sprinkle with parsley and serve hot.

Country Tomato Sauce with Roasted Vegetables

T his recipe comes from Beth's bread-baking friend Bunny Dimmel. Although the addition of the pork chop may sound unusual, it is an old Italian cooking trick to make the sauce richer. Bunny uses her mortar and pestle to grind up the oregano and basil to enhance their flavors. This sauce is gloriously thick and smooth, punctuated with tasty roasted vegetables that are cooked first on HIGH before making the sauce on LOW. Serve it over spaghetti or penne with crusty bread and a salad of greens, ripe olives, and tomato wedges dressed with olive oil and balsamic vinegar. ❍ *Makes about 6 cups*

COOKER: Large round or oval
SETTINGS AND COOK TIMES: HIGH for 1 to 1½ hours, then LOW for 8½ to 10½ hours

2 medium-size yellow onions, cut into 8 wedges
2 medium-size red bell peppers, seeded and cut into 16 strips
One 6- to 8-ounce lean bone-in pork chop
6 cloves garlic
2 tablespoons olive oil
Two 28-ounce cans tomato sauce
Two 12-ounce cans tomato paste
1½ cups water
2 teaspoons each dried oregano and basil, crumbled or ground in a mortar and pestle
Salt and freshly ground black pepper to taste

1. Place the onions, bell peppers, pork chop, and garlic cloves in the slow cooker; toss with the olive oil. Cover and cook on HIGH for 1 to 1½ hours.

2. Meanwhile, in a large mixing bowl, whisk together the tomato sauce, tomato paste, and water. After the allotted time, add the tomato mixture to the cooker. Submerge the pork chop in the sauce. Cover and cook on LOW for 8 to 10 hours.

3. Stir in the oregano and basil and season with salt and pepper. Cover and cook on LOW for about 30 minutes longer.

4. Remove the pork chop, chop or shred the meat, and return it to the sauce. Serve immediately. The sauce will keep in the refrigerator in an airtight container for up to 5 days, or in the freezer for up to 2 months.

Family-Style Winter Tomato Sauce

his pot of fabulous winy tomato sauce simmers all day. Because of the amount it makes, you must use a large slow cooker. But that's okay, because it is also a long-lasting sauce: It will keep in the freezer for up to 3 months. Serve this over penne, ziti, or shells, or use it in lasagna or baked pasta dishes. It is extremely versatile. ○ *Makes 18 cups*

COOKER: Large round or oval
SETTING AND COOK TIME: LOW for 8 to 10 hours;
seasonings added at 6 to 7 hours

Six 28-ounce cans diced plum tomatoes, undrained
1½ cups dry red wine, such as Zinfandel
¾ cup olive oil
6 cloves garlic, or to your taste, minced
1 tablespoon sugar
⅓ cup shredded fresh basil
1 tablespoon dried oregano
1 tablespoon salt
2 teaspoons red pepper flakes
1 teaspoon chili powder
Freshly ground black pepper to taste

1. Place the tomatoes and their juice, wine, oil, garlic, and sugar in the slow cooker; stir to combine. Cover and cook on LOW for 6 to 7 hours.

2. Add the basil, oregano, salt, red pepper flakes, and chili powder; stir to combine. Cover and cook for another 2 to 3 hours.

3. Use a handheld immersion blender to puree the sauce in the crock, or transfer it in batches to a food processor or blender and puree. Depending on your preference, you may leave it a bit chunky or make it very smooth. Season with pepper and serve hot.

Beefy Tomato Sauce with Sausage and Fennel

The addition of fennel-spiced sausage meat makes for delicious eating over penne, rigatoni, spaghetti, fettuccine, or even rice! This sauce is thick and rich. If you do not smell the fennel in the sausage, crush ½ teaspoon fennel seed in your mortar and pestle and add it to the crock. We love this sauce!

○ *Makes about 8 cups*

COOKER: Medium round or oval
SETTING AND COOK TIME: LOW for 8 to 9 hours

1 pound lean ground beef
¾ pound sweet Italian sausage with fennel, removed from casings
1 medium-size yellow onion, chopped
1 shallot, minced
2 medium-size carrots, finely chopped
1 medium-size bell pepper of any color, seeded and chopped
¼ cup dry red wine
One 28-ounce can crushed tomatoes
One 8-ounce can tomato sauce
One 6-ounce can tomato paste
1 tablespoon light brown sugar or raw sugar
1 tablespoon dried mixed Italian herbs
½ teaspoon fennel seed (optional), crushed
Salt and freshly ground black pepper to taste

1. In a large skillet over high heat, cook the beef and sausage together; allow the beef to brown lightly and cook the sausage until no longer pink, breaking up any clumps of meat and mixing them together well. Drain off and discard the fat and transfer the meat to the slow cooker.

2. Add the onion, shallot, carrots, and bell pepper to the skillet, reduce the heat to medium, and cook, stirring a few times, until the onion and shallot are softened, about 5 minutes. Add the wine and cook for 1 minute, scraping up any browned bits stuck to the pan, then transfer to the crock. Add the crushed tomatoes, tomato sauce, tomato paste, sugar, herbs, and fennel seed, if using; stir to combine. Cover and cook on LOW for 8 to 9 hours.

3. Season with salt and pepper and serve hot. The sauce will keep in the refrigerator in an airtight container for up to 4 days, or in the freezer for up to 1 month.

Fresh Herb and Cream Sauce

S erved over fettuccine, this sauce makes an elegant but easy first course or a dinner if served with salad and steamed vegetables. The herbs *must* be absolutely fresh, otherwise do not make it. We usually have the greatest proportion of herbs (more than half) be basil and parsley, then we add the other, stronger, herbs in small amounts. ● *Makes 2 cups*

COOKER: Small round
SETTING AND COOK TIME: LOW for 1$\frac{1}{2}$ to 2 hours

2 cups heavy cream
$\frac{1}{2}$ cup minced fresh herbs (any combination of basil, Italian parsley, chervil, oregano, savory, tarragon, dill, chive, thyme, lovage, and/or marjoram)
Salt and freshly ground black pepper to taste

1. Place the cream and herbs in the slow cooker. Cover and cook on LOW until very hot and bubbly, 1$\frac{1}{2}$ to 2 hours.

2. Season with salt and pepper and serve hot. You may keep the sauce on the KEEP WARM or LOW setting for up to 1 hour before serving.

Salsa Alfredo

Next to marinara sauce, creamy white Alfredo sauce is the all-time favorite with pasta lovers. It is not light in calories, but a little of this sauce goes a long way; this recipe coats a full pound of fettuccine. ○ *Makes 1½ cups*

COOKER: Small round
SETTING AND COOK TIME: LOW for 1 to 1½ hours

6 tablespoons (¾ stick) unsalted butter, cut into pieces
1 cup heavy cream
½ cup freshly grated Parmesan cheese, plus more for sprinkling
Ground nutmeg to taste
Salt and freshly ground black pepper to taste

1. Place the butter and cream in the slow cooker. Cover and simmer on LOW until hot, 1 to 1½ hours.

2. Stir with a whisk. Sprinkle in the cheese and nutmeg and season with salt and pepper. Serve hot. You may keep the sauce on LOW or KEEP WARM for up to 1 hour before serving. The sauce will keep in the refrigerator in an airtight container for up to 2 days.

Herbed Chèvre Sauce

T his luscious, gently tart sauce is perfect for dressing up any type of plain steamed vegetable, such as broccoli, cauliflower, green beans, zucchini, and even spinach, as well as roasted meat or poultry. We find the cheese has plenty of salt, but add a dash if you feel it needs it. ○ *Makes 2 cups*

COOKER: Small round
SETTING AND COOK TIME: LOW for 1½ to 2 hours

1 cup heavy cream
1 tablespoon walnut or other nut oil
6 ounces chèvre, such as Chabis or Montrachet, crumbled
2 tablespoons chopped fresh basil
2 tablespoons chopped fresh Italian parsley
2 tablespoons chopped fresh chives
Pinch of ground white pepper, or to taste

1. Place the cream, oil, and chèvre in the slow cooker. Cover and cook on LOW until very hot and the cheese is melted, 1 to 1½ hours.

2. Sprinkle in the basil, parsley, chives, and pepper; stir to combine. Cover and let simmer 20 minutes longer. Serve hot. The sauce can be made up to 1 day ahead and reheated before serving.

Slow-Cooked Vegetables

Slow-Steamed Artichokes ○ 129

Braised Fresh Shell Beans ○ 130

Crock-Baked Beets ○ 131

Red Cabbage with Red Wine, Apricots,
and Honey ○ 132

Carrots Glazed with Marmalade, Brown
Sugar, and Butter ○ 132

Celery Victor ○ 133

Raja Rellenos ○ 134

Corn in Cream ○ 136

Crock-Roasted Fresh Corn on
the Cob ○ 137

Nancyjo's Tofu and Corn Posole ○ 138

Eggplant Caponata ○ 139

Braised Belgian Endive ○ 140

Roasted Garlic ○ 141

Italian-Style Braised Green Beans ○ 142

Braised Leeks ○ 143

Mushrooms Forestière on Toast ○ 143

Rosemary-Balsamic Onions ○ 145

Ragoût of Peas and Artichokes with
Tarragon ○ 146

Braised Peas with Lettuce ○ 147

New Potatoes with Fresh Lemon-Herb
Butter ○ 148

Potatoes and Fennel ○ 149

Twice-Crocked Stuffed Potatoes with
Macadamia Nuts ○ 150

Scalloped Potatoes ○ 151

Mashed Potato Casserole ○ 152

Good Old-Fashioned Mashed
Potatoes ○ 152

Blue Cheese–Sour Cream Mashers o 154

Mashed Potatoes and Carrots with Crisp Bacon and Chives o 155

Cider-Braised Turnips o 156

Candied Yams with Apples and Cranberries o 156

Tortino di Zucchini o 157

Vegetable Curry o 158

Chinese Vegetable Hot Pot o 160

Braised Spring Vegetables o 161

Ragoût of Baby Vegetables o 162

Of all foods, vegetables are the trickiest to cook in the slow cooker because of their wide variety in textures and cooking times. Generally, the key to success with vegetables in the slow cooker is to remember that they will cook a lot faster than meat or bean stews, so you will not be cooking all day. They still utilize the French-style braising method, where there is close contact between the vegetable and its cooking liquid. The vegetables also cook slowly in their own steam. Please pay close attention to our recommended cooking times; they vary widely. The best braised vegetables are those with a lot of cellulose, which allows them to retain their flavor essence even when soft and mushy. Roots, tubers, and winter squashes are really stars in the slow cooker, but, surprisingly, long-cooked greens and green beans are excellent as well. Artichokes and beets come out perfectly. Be sure to try making your own fresh stewed tomatoes and roasted garlic.

Each type of vegetable cooks a little differently than any of the others, but we have assembled what we consider a really nice cornucopia of vegetable recipes, both simple braises of a single vegetable and vegetable stews, to appeal to a wide range of palates. We also looked for practical recipes that are still special enough to serve to guests.

The following list of vegetables is meant to be a guide for the cook. The vegetables are grouped by like characteristics, with simple instructions for preparing them for the slow cooker. We did not put in cooking times, because those vary depending on quantity, the size of the pieces, how much you fill the slow cooker, and whether the vegetable is to be simply braised or fully submerged in liquid, like a stew. Denser vegetables, such as roots, tubers, and winter squash, will always take longer to cook than, say, peas and leafy greens. Also take into account the age of the vegetable: Fresh baby vegetables cook a lot faster than do end-of-season, tougher ones. Often we start with some root vegetables and add the more tender veggies toward the end of cooking, to keep the texture consistent.

As always, we encourage you to be adventurous: Rinse, pare, and trim as needed, and then cut into wedges, quarters, cubes, julienne, thick or thin segments, or diagonal or straight slices (just keep pieces uniform in size). Use our recipes as a starting point for your own creations. If you are slicing or julienning a lot of vegetables, use a food processor or a mandoline. Mix and match your vegetable combinations, then serve the delicious results straight out of the cooker with their cooking juices, or drizzle with a flavorful oil and vinegar, compound butter, or special sauce.

Roots and Tubers

- Carrots: Trim tips and ends, peel if desired, and cut into chunks, coins, or dice. Leave baby carrots whole.

- Beets: Trim ends and peel. Leave whole (babies can have some of the stem left on) or cut into slices or quarters.

- Parsnips: Same as carrots.

- Potatoes (russet or Idaho bakers, red or white boilers, baby creamer new potatoes, purple potatoes, Yukon gold): Scrub whole potatoes in their jackets or peel, as desired. Cook whole, quartered, diced, or sliced.

- Turnips and rutabagas: Same as potatoes.

- Jerusalem artichokes and celeriac: Same as potatoes.

- Daikon radish: Same as carrots.

- Water chestnuts: Peel and slice.

- Yams and sweet potatoes: Cut off ends and peel. Cut into chunks or slices.

Winter Squashes

- Acorn, chayote (cut in half and remove seeds), blue hubbard, butternut, turban, pumpkin, sweet dumpling, golden nugget, kabocha, spaghetti: Small squashes can be cooked whole (peel, halve, and clean out seeds and fibers after steaming). Large squashes are best halved or cut into chunks (peel, cut in half lengthwise, and clean out seeds and fibers before steaming).

Thistles

- Artichokes: Trim stems and pull off lowest leaves. Use a large cleaver to cut about 1 inch from top of leaves, and use scissors to trim spines off any outer leaves.

- Cardoons: Discard outer ribs, and trim spines and string if tough. Cut off stalk end and cut ribs like celery.

Leafy Greens and Stalks

- Asparagus: Trim or snap off thick end of the stalk, and peel. Leave the stalks whole or cut into diagonal chunks. Serve loose, or tie into bundles with scallion or chive greens before cooking.

- Celery: Cut off stalk end and leaf end. Cut stalks into chunks. Leave hearts whole. Use the leaves in soups and stews.

- Fennel: Cut off stalk end and frond end. Cut into halves or quarters, then chop.

- Swiss chard, spinach, bok choy, arugula, beet greens, collard greens, dandelion, broccoli rabe, mustard greens, kale, sorrel, Belgian endive (leave whole), radicchio, fiddleheads, watercress, grape leaves: A standard bunch of greens will feed two to four people. Greens, especially chard and kale, are often used for wrapping a filling.

Vegetables That Are Fruits

- Sweet bell peppers (green, red, yellow, orange): Cut in half and remove stems, seeds, and ribs. Cut into slices, strips, or chunks.

- Tomatoes (salad, plum, cherry, green): Leave whole, cut in half, or mash.

- Green tomatoes: Cut into halves or quarters.

- Tomatillos: Remove the papery coating and cut into halves or quarters.

- Japanese or baby eggplant: Leave skin on; remove stem end and cut into halves or quarters.

- Mild chile peppers (Anaheim, Big Jim, poblanos): Remove stems and seeds if desired.

Cabbages and Onions

- Red onions, yellow onions, white boiling onions, baby pearl onions: Cut off both ends and peel off papery outer layers. Cook whole, quartered, or chopped.

- Broccoli and cauliflower: Trim off thick ends of stalks. Cut whole heads into florets. Peel broccoli stalk and cut into strips.

- Brussels sprouts: Leave whole or cut into halves or quarters.

- Cabbage (green, red, napa, savoy): Cut off the stem end section, and cut into quarters or coarsely shred. Tie quarters with kitchen twine to retain shape and aid in easy removal.

- Leeks and spring onions: Wash thoroughly, cut off roots and tops, and split stalks in half.

Beans, Pods, and Seeds

- Green beans, haricots verts, Chinese long beans, yellow wax beans: Cut or snap ends off. Leave whole or cut into pieces.

- Peas: Remove shells or use snow peas or sugar snap peas; peel off the string from the stem end.

- Butter beans, fava beans, fresh lima beans: Remove shells.

- Edamame (soybeans in the pod): Leave as is.

- Mung bean sprouts: Leave as is.

- Okra: Use whole or cut into slices.

- Corn on the cob (yellow or white): Shuck and steam whole or break into pieces.

Summer Squashes

Summer squashes are the most difficult vegetable to cook in the slow cooker, because overcooking happens quickly and turns them into a mushy soup. Pay close attention and use short cooking times.

- Zucchini, pattypan, yellow crookneck: Trim stems and ends. Cut into chunks, coins, dice, or long quarters.

Slow-Steamed Artichokes

T he oval slow cooker has the best shape for cooking whole artichokes, because they can sit in one layer. If you only have a round cooker, buy artichokes of a comparable size and fit them tightly side by side in the cooker. You may need to make two layers. o *Serves 8 to 10*

COOKER: Medium or large round or oval
SETTING AND COOK TIME: LOW for 6 to 7 hours

8 to 10 large artichokes
2 cups water
¼ cup olive oil
1 lemon, sliced
4 cloves garlic or 2 thick slices onion

1. For each artichoke, cut the stem flush with the bottom of the artichoke so it can stand flat. Cut off the top 1 inch and, with kitchen shears, snip off the tip of each exposed leaf. Arrange with stem end down and packed together, standing up in the slow cooker; add the water, oil, lemon slices, and garlic.

2. Cover and cook on LOW for 6 to 7 hours, until a leaf is very tender and separates with no resistance when pulled off. Remove the artichokes from the cooker with tongs. Serve hot or at room temperature, or wrap in plastic and chill to serve cold.

Braised Fresh Shell Beans

We decided to put the fresh shell beans here with the vegetables rather than with the dried beans. They are a rarity in regular supermarkets, but they are in their glory in the summer at regional farmers' markets and roadside produce stands. Freshly picked, the beans, still in their long pods, are a real treat for vegetable lovers. You may use any type of fresh bean you come across, from lima and cranberry to white beans, in this recipe. The small beans cook in only 1½ hours; the large beans take 3 to 4 hours. Serve with some of your favorite extra-virgin olive oil for drizzling and fresh French or Italian bread. ○ *Serves 12*

COOKER: Medium round or oval
SETTING AND COOK TIME: HIGH for 1½ to 4 hours

⅓ cup olive oil
4 shallots, minced
6 pounds fresh shell beans, shelled (you will have 1 to 1½ cups per pound
   of beans, depending on the size)
2 cups water, vegetable broth, or chicken broth
Salt and freshly ground black pepper to taste
2 tablespoons fresh chopped herbs, such as thyme, parsley, marjoram, and/or basil
2 to 3 teaspoons red or white balsamic vinegar

In a small skillet, warm the olive oil over medium heat and cook the shallots until soft. Place in the slow cooker and add the beans and water. Cover and cook on HIGH for 1½ to 4 hours, depending on the size of the bean. Season with salt and pepper and stir in the herbs and vinegar. Serve immediately, or refrigerate and serve cold.

Crock-Baked Beets

Wrapping beets in foil before roasting them is one of the best-kept secrets of the vegetable world; the beets cook beautifully and come out tender and silky. The timing will vary somewhat; small beets will cook more quickly. In addition, if you fill the cooker with beets, plan on additional cooking time. If you are serving company and want to do the messy prep work ahead of time, you can trim and peel the beets while they are raw. Cut each beet into wedges, add salt, pepper, and a dab of butter, and wrap tightly in aluminum foil. (Surprisingly, cut beets cook in about the same amount of time as whole ones.) This way, the beets will be ready to serve right out of the slow cooker. Serve the beets whole, cut into wedges, or mashed. They are good hot, with butter, salt, and pepper. To serve them cold, toss them with a vinaigrette before refrigerating them. ○ *Serves 12*

COOKER: Large round or oval
SETTING AND COOK TIME: HIGH for 4 to 6 hours

6 small or 3 large bunches of beets (12 to 30 beets depending on the size), scrubbed
Olive oil

1. Prepare each whole beet by leaving the root end intact and trimming the stem to a 1-inch stub to prevent bleeding. Place each beet on a piece of foil and sprinkle with some olive oil. Wrap each whole beet in foil and pile them in the slow cooker. If your beets are small, wrap 3 together.

2. Cover and cook on HIGH for 4 to 6 hours, depending on the size of the beets. (To check for doneness, pierce a beet with the tip of a sharp knife through the foil. When the knife goes in with no resistance, the beet is done.) The more beets in the cooker, the longer the cook time will be. Remove the beets from the cooker with tongs, unwrap, and, when cool enough to handle, slip off the skins with the help of a paring knife.

3. Leave whole if small, or slice or cut into chunks if large. Serve immediately, or refrigerate and serve cold.

Red Cabbage with Red Wine, Apricots, and Honey

This is a pretty braise of cabbage and dried fruit, sweeter than ones made with green cabbage and vinegar. Peasant dishes like these can also contain some chopped ham and goose fat, a favorite cooking flavor in France and central Germany. Serve with roasted poultry, pork, or sausages, steamed vegetables, and dense pumpernickel bread, especially during the winter holidays. ○ *Serves 8 to 10*

COOKER: Medium or large round or oval
SETTING AND COOK TIME: LOW for 5 to 6 hours

1 to 2 medium-size heads red cabbage, cored and shredded (12 to 14 cups)
1¼ cups chopped dried apricots
½ cup dry red wine, such as Merlot or Syrah
¼ cup honey
3 tablespoons freshly squeezed lemon juice
Salt to taste

1. Place the cabbage and apricots in the slow cooker and stir to mix. Combine the wine, honey, and lemon juice in a small bowl; pour over the cabbage and toss to coat. Cover and cook on LOW until the cabbage is tender, 5 to 6 hours.

2. Season with salt. Serve hot, or cover with plastic wrap and refrigerate to serve cold.

Carrots Glazed with Marmalade, Brown Sugar, and Butter

Who doesn't love candied carrots? They are a boon to the busy cook who has a group to feed. Fill the slow cooker with the convenient bagged baby carrots, or cut regular carrots into thick strips or coins. We keep backup jars of orange marmalade in the cupboard because it is so useful for cooking and making glazes.

○ *Serves 12*

COOKER: Medium round

SETTING AND COOK TIME: LOW for 4½ to 6 hours

Two 32-ounce packages baby carrots
1⅓ cups orange marmalade
⅓ cup firmly packed light or dark brown sugar
6 tablespoons (¾ stick) unsalted butter, melted
¼ cup water
Salt and freshly ground black pepper to taste

1. Combine the carrots, marmalade, brown sugar, butter, and water in the slow cooker; toss to coat the carrots completely. Cover and cook on LOW until the carrots are tender when pierced with the tip of a knife, 4½ to 6 hours. The time will vary with the thickness of the carrots, so be sure to check at 4½ hours.

2. Season with salt and pepper, stir gently, and serve hot.

Celery Victor

C elery Victor is one of those unabashedly old-fashioned dishes for company that have come and gone in fashion, but we think it's a classic. A dish you would order for luncheon in a grand hotel dining room, it is named after its creator, Chef Victor Hirtzler, former chef at the St. Francis Hotel in San Francisco. Although celery is often eaten raw or used in combination with other vegetables, here it is cooked and the star of the dish. This originally was garnished with chopped tomato and hard-boiled egg, but here we keep it nice and simple with a mustard vinaigrette. This is best made in an oval cooker so that the long celery hearts have all the room they need to cook perfectly. Use the leftover broth for soup, or drink it; it is delicious. Serve with grilled, broiled, or roasted meats, ham, or poultry. ○ *Serves 6*

COOKER: Medium oval

SETTINGS AND COOK TIMES: HIGH for 30 minutes, then LOW for 1½ hours
(cooked celery then needs to chill for at least 4 hours)

3 large bunches celery

1½ to 2 cups chicken broth

Herb bouquet of 2 sprigs fresh Italian parsley and some celery tops from the outer stalks with leaves, tied together with kitchen twine

Salt and freshly ground black pepper to taste

3 tablespoons white wine vinegar or champagne vinegar

1 tablespoon Dijon mustard

⅓ cup olive oil

2 tablespoons minced fresh chives

1. Remove the outer stalks of the celery, leaving a center heart at least 2 inches wide; leave the tops and leaves in place. Cut each heart in half lengthwise and trim the root end, but leave the heart held together. Trim off the very top leaves and reserve for garnish. Place the celery hearts in the slow cooker in a single layer and add the broth just to cover. Toss in the herb bouquet and add a dash of salt and pepper. Cover and cook on HIGH for 30 minutes.

2. Reduce the heat setting to LOW and cook until the celery is tender when pierced with the tip of a knife, about 1½ hours. Cut and discard the kitchen twine. Let the celery cool in the liquid, then transfer to a serving dish and chill in a single layer in the refrigerator for at least 4 hours and up to overnight.

3. Before serving, whisk together 3 to 4 tablespoons of the cold celery broth, the vinegar, mustard, and oil. Remove the celery from the broth with a slotted spoon, divide among 6 plates, drizzle with a spoonful of the mustard sauce, and serve with the reserved chopped celery leaves and the chives sprinkled over the top.

Raja Rellenos

R*elleno* is the Spanish word for "stuffed," and *raja* is the word for "chile strip." The traditional way to prepare this favorite Mexican dish is to stuff rich cheese into roasted whole chiles, then fry them. Here, the process is stripped of the messy preparation as well as some of the fat. Cotija is a white, crumbly Mexican cheese; it's milder than feta, though still a bit salty. If you are sensitive to salt, break the cheese into 3 or 4 large chunks and rinse under cool water, patting dry with paper towels before grating. If you can't find cotija, use asadero, a mild white Mexican cheese that melts easily; Monterey Jack is another good substitute. For a heartier dish, you can sprinkle the cheese layer with shredded cooked chicken or turkey, black beans, or corn. This is a lovely brunch or supper dish, served with a stack of hot tortillas and a crisp green salad. For a more substantial meal, offer it with beans and Mexican red rice. ○ *Serves 6 to 8*

COOKER: Medium or large, oval preferred
SETTING AND COOK TIME: HIGH for 2½ to 3 hours

Two 7-ounce cans roasted whole green chiles, drained, or
   8 large poblano or Anaheim chiles
½ pound cheddar cheese, finely shredded
½ pound cotija cheese, finely shredded
2 cups prepared salsa of your choice
4 large eggs, beaten
2 tablespoons all-purpose flour
¾ cup evaporated milk

1. Coat the inside of the crock with nonstick cooking spray. If using canned chiles, rinse them inside and out and pat dry on paper towels; cut into thick strips. If using fresh chiles, char over a flame, under the broiler, or on the surface of a grill until the skin is blackened. Place in a closed paper bag for 10 minutes to loosen the skins. Peel off the skins under cold running water. Slit each chile, remove the seeds, cut off the stem end, and cut into thick strips.

2. In a large bowl, toss together the cheddar and cotija cheeses.

3. Spread ½ cup of the salsa in the crock. Layer in one-fourth of the chile strips. Sprinkle with one-third of the cheese mixture. Repeat the chile and cheese layers, ending with chiles. Pour the remaining 1½ cups salsa over the chiles.

4. In a blender or food processor, or in a medium-size bowl with a whisk, combine the eggs, flour, and milk, mixing until smooth. Pour into the slow cooker, covering the top of the salsa. Cover and cook on HIGH until the casserole looks set, 2½ to 3 hours, taking care not to let the casserole burn around the edges. Serve hot.

Corn in Cream

Here is a really old recipe from *The Gourmet Cookbook* (Gourmet Distributing Corp., 1957), when Earle McAusland was the publisher of *Gourmet* magazine. The recipe gave no specific amounts, but said only to "fill a buttered earthenware casserole with corn, salt, and pepper, and add the cream to cover." The corn absorbs the cream as it cooks. This is really delicious and very, very simple. You can add 1 to 2 teaspoons chopped fresh herbs, such as basil, if you like. If you have a large group of diners, just fill a medium-size crock up to three-quarters full of corn kernels and cook it a bit longer on the HIGH setting. Serve this with any kind of roasted meat. ○ *Serves 8 to 10*

COOKER: Small round
SETTING AND COOK TIME: HIGH for 1¹⁄₂ to 2 hours

1 to 2 tablespoons unsalted butter, softened
8 to 9 ears fresh white or yellow corn, kernels cut from the cob
Salt and freshly ground black pepper to taste
2 cups hot heavy cream

Coat the bottom of the crock and a few inches up the sides with the butter. Place the corn in the slow cooker and season with salt and pepper. Pour in the hot cream; it will come up level with the corn (you may not use all the cream if the ears were small). Cover and cook on HIGH until the mixture is as thick as you want and the corn is cooked, about 1½ hours. If you want it thicker, remove the lid and let it cook 15 to 30 minutes longer. Serve straight from the crock in small bowls.

Crock-Roasted Fresh Corn on the Cob

The best corn to eat is either just picked or just purchased from a roadside produce stand that's next to a farm. As soon as corn is picked, the sugar in the kernels begins to turn into starch, so supermarket corn on the cob will take longer to cook and be a bit tougher after cooking, because it is usually a few days old. If you must store fresh corn, be sure to refrigerate it until ready to cook. We think you will be surprised what a nice job the slow cooker does with corn on the cob (and no big pot of boiling water to hassle with), even though it needs an extended amount of time. After cooking, you can leave the corn in the crock on KEEP WARM until serving time. For this recipe, be sure to get corn still in its fresh green husk. o *Serves 4 to 8*

COOKER: Medium or large round
SETTING AND COOK TIME: HIGH for 1 to 2 hours

4 to 8 ears fresh yellow or white corn in the husks
½ to ¾ cup water
Butter for serving

1. Carefully pull back the husk from each ear, but leave it attached at the stem end. Remove the silk from each ear and rinse under cold running water. If the ear is too long to fit upright in your slow cooker, trim off the top. Fold the outer husk back up around the corn and tie the top with a bit of kitchen twine or a strip of husk leaf. Trim the stems flat so that the ears can stand upright in the slow cooker (do not stack them horizontally).

2. Arrange the ears with the stem ends down and packed together, standing up in the cooker; add the water (½ cup for the medium-size cooker; ¾ cup for the large cooker). Cover and cook on HIGH until the corn is very tender (pull back the husk and pierce with the tip of a knife to check), 1 to 2 hours, depending on the age of the corn.

3. Remove the corn from the cooker with tongs, remove the husks, and slather with butter. Eat immediately.

Nancyjo's Tofu and Corn Posole

During the testing of the recipes in this book, caterer Nancyjo Rieske decided to make a version of our traditional posole without the pork and hominy for her vegetarian clients. She used lots of corn kernels and tofu instead of the meat. It ended up a wonderful and creative variation and a great dish to serve vegetarian diners. Don't forget all the garnishes; they make the dish really special. ○ *Serves 8*

COOKER: Medium round

SETTING AND COOK TIME: LOW for 4 to 5 hours; cilantro, salt, and pepper added during last hour

One 12-ounce package extra-firm tofu, cut into ½-inch cubes

2 medium-size yellow onions, chopped

4 cups frozen or fresh corn kernels, thawed if necessary

Two 7-ounce cans diced roasted green chiles, drained

8 cups vegetable or chicken broth

6 to 8 cloves garlic, crushed

2 tablespoons chili powder

4 teaspoons crumbled dried oregano

1 teaspoon ground cumin

½ cup minced fresh cilantro

1 teaspoon salt, or to taste

Freshly ground black pepper to taste

FOR SERVING:

Flour tortillas

Shredded iceberg lettuce

Sliced radishes

Chopped green onions (white parts and some of the green)

Diced avocado

Toasted pumpkin seeds

Chunky tomato salsa

Chopped fresh cilantro leaves

Lime wedges

1. Place the tofu, onions, corn, chiles, broth, garlic, chili powder, oregano, and cumin in the slow cooker. Cover and cook on LOW for 4 to 5 hours. During the last hour, add the cilantro, salt, and pepper.

2. Serve hot in shallow soup bowls with warm flour tortillas and your choice of garnishes available in separate bowls.

Eggplant Caponata

C aponata is an eggplant stew that is usually eaten as an appetizer or side dish. It is a nice surprise during a salad course for a casual dinner party. It is also very convenient, as well as tasty, because it can be made a few days ahead and will taste even better after a few days. Caponata is made throughout Italy, but you can identify Sicilian versions because they contain celery. Serve at room temperature with French or Italian bread.

⊙ *Makes about 5 cups to serve 10 to 12*

COOKER: Medium round or oval
SETTING AND COOK TIME: LOW for 6 to 7 hours

3 to 4 small eggplants (about 1½ pounds), left unpeeled and cubed
Salt to sweat the eggplant
6 tablespoons olive oil
2 medium-size onions, chopped
2 ribs celery, chopped
One 28-ounce can chopped stewed tomatoes, undrained
3 tablespoons tomato paste
2 tablespoons red wine vinegar
Salt and freshly ground black pepper to taste
1 cup pitted black olives of your choice, chopped, or two 4-ounce cans
    sliced black olives, drained
¼ cup nonpareil capers, rinsed and drained
2 tablespoons chopped fresh basil

1. Place the eggplant in a colander over a plate and sprinkle with some salt; let stand at room temperature for 1 hour to sweat and remove bitterness (you can skip this step if using Japanese eggplants). Rinse under cold running water and drain well. Pat dry with paper towels.

2. Pour 3 tablespoons of the olive oil into the slow cooker. Place the eggplant in the crock and toss with the oil; you can drizzle with more oil, if desired. Add the onions and celery in a layer on top of the eggplant. In a medium-size bowl, combine the tomatoes, the remaining 3 tablespoons olive oil, the tomato paste, vinegar, and salt and pepper. Pour into the crock, cover, and cook on LOW until the eggplant is tender, 6 to 7 hours.

3. Stir in the olives, capers, and basil. Serve warm or at room temperature, or let cool, transfer to an airtight container, and refrigerate overnight or for up to 1 week.

Braised Belgian Endive

E ndive, also called chicory, succory, or witloof, is a stunningly beautiful vegetable. In the same family as the frizzy lettuces, it is a fat, compact spike of overlapping leaves that are pale green at their tips. Growing endive is an art in Belgium; trenches covered in light soil keep the spears protected from light until just before harvesting, hence their pale white color except for the tips. Endive is usually eaten raw in salads, but it is an elegant cooked vegetable as well. Look for endive from late October until March; the early-season offerings are the sweetest, just in time for Thanksgiving. The inherent bitterness is concentrated in the root, so you can bore a cone-shaped piece out of the center of the root if you wish, keeping the leaves intact. Serve this with grilled, broiled, or roasted meats, ham, or poultry. ○ *Serves 6*

COOKER: Medium round or oval
SETTING AND COOK TIME: LOW for 4 to 5 hours

3 tablespoons unsalted butter, softened
12 Belgian endives, each tied with kitchen twine
½ cup water
1 tablespoon freshly squeezed lemon juice
Chopped fresh Italian parsley for garnish

1. Smear the bottom of the crock with the butter in a thick layer. Place the endives in the slow cooker, in a single layer if possible, and add the water and lemon juice. Cover and cook on LOW until the endives are tender when pierced with the tip of a knife, 4 to 5 hours.

2. Cut and discard the kitchen twine. Serve immediately, sprinkled with the parsley, or let cool in the cooking liquid, then remove and refrigerate for at least 4 hours or up to overnight. Sprinkle with the parsley before serving chilled or at room temperature.

Roasted Garlic

R oasted garlic is a supporting actor in so many wonderful dishes, as well as a star in its own right. Roasting garlic heads whole changes the character of the cloves completely, from crisp, white, and tongue-burningly pungent to creamy, brown, and sweet, with just a hint of the garlic punch they pack when raw. We love roasted garlic spread on crusty bread instead of butter, or tossed with steamed green beans or asparagus. Try it smeared over the dough as a first layer on pizza or pureed in dips, dressings, or earthy mashed potatoes. Use roasted cloves instead of raw cloves in stovetop sautés or in our slow cooker braises, simply adding them along with the liquid. **o** *1 head serves 2 to 4 as a spread*

COOKER: Small, medium, or large round
SETTING AND COOK TIME: LOW for 5 hours

2 or more heads garlic
2 or more teaspoons extra-virgin olive oil
Fresh or dried herbs of your choice, such as rosemary,
**   thyme, oregano, or marjoram (optional)**

1. Remove the loose outer, papery layers from the garlic heads. Place the heads, in pairs, on squares of aluminum foil large enough to enclose them. Over each pair of garlic heads, drizzle 2 teaspoons olive oil. If desired, add one or more herbs. If using dried herbs, crumble a pinch of the herb between your fingers over the garlic. If using fresh herbs, place small sprigs in each packet. Fold the foil around the

garlic and herbs, sealing the edges tightly. Place the packets in the slow cooker. Cover and cook on LOW until the garlic is very tender (squeeze a head with your fingers to check the degree of softness), about 5 hours.

2. To use the cloves, cut the heads of garlic in half, or simply cut off the pointed end of each head. Squeeze out the cloves. To serve with bread, break the heads into sections and offer one section to each person; diners can squeeze the soft cloves out of their skins. The roasted garlic will keep, in an airtight container in the refrigerator, for up to 3 days.

Italian-Style Braised Green Beans

From one of our favorite food writers, Janet Fletcher, comes this Mediterranean version of green beans, which is perfect for the slow cooker because none of the liquid evaporates, but, rather, is absorbed into the beans. Serve this as a side dish or, as Janet suggests, over a pound of cooked fresh fettuccine with Parmesan or Asiago cheese sprinkled over the top. ❍ *Serves 8 to 10*

COOKER: Medium round or oval
SETTING AND COOK TIME: LOW for 6 to 7 hours

3 pounds fresh green beans, ends trimmed
3 cups peeled, seeded, and chopped fresh tomatoes or drained canned chopped tomatoes
½ cup olive oil
4 to 6 cloves garlic, to your taste, minced
1 teaspoon fennel seeds, crushed in a mortar
½ teaspoon red pepper flakes
Salt to taste
5 to 6 cups chicken or vegetable broth

1. Place the beans, tomatoes, oil, garlic, fennel, and red pepper in the slow cooker. Add a bit of salt and the broth just to cover the beans. Cover and cook on LOW until the beans are soft, 6 to 7 hours, depending on the size and age of the beans.

2. Some of the liquid should be absorbed by the beans. If not, uncover, turn the cooker to HIGH for a few minutes, and boil it off. Serve immediately.

Braised Leeks

An elegant member of the onion family, leeks are sold in bunches with their greens still attached. The greens are cut off before cooking, because they are very tough, although they are a good addition when making stock. You can also freeze the leftover cooking broth for use in making stock. Remember that leeks must be halved and rinsed carefully to remove the sandy grit trapped in the layers; otherwise, you will have an unappetizing dish. Serve these with grilled, broiled, or baked meats or poultry, or poached salmon. They are also good sprinkled with some shredded Swiss cheese and browned under the broiler, or served with sour cream or a vinaigrette. ○ *Serves 6*

COOKER: Medium or large round or oval
SETTING AND COOK TIME: HIGH for 1½ to 2 hours

8 medium-size to large leeks
⅔ cup chicken broth
2 tablespoons unsalted butter, cut into pieces

1. Rinse the leeks under cool running water. Halve them lengthwise, peeling off the tough outer layer and cutting off about 2 inches of the green tops. Rinse them again to remove all sand.

2. Place the leeks in the slow cooker, add the broth, and dot with the butter. Cover and cook on HIGH until tender, 1½ to 2 hours. Serve warm, or let cool in the broth, then remove and refrigerate for 4 hours or up to overnight, and serve cold.

Mushrooms Forestière on Toast

This is an opportunity to use the wonderful bounty of dried and fresh mushrooms now offered in most supermarket produce departments. You will have a good amount of liquid from the mushrooms; we like it with cream added, so the flavorful juices soak into the toast nicely. If it is too much liquid for your sensibility, then pour some off and freeze for adding to stock, or remove the lid and cook on HIGH at the end of the cooking time to evaporate some of the liquid. Remember to check the mushrooms at 3½ hours to gauge their degree of doneness to suit your palate; some people like their mushrooms distinct and barely cooked, while others like them a bit mushy. Do serve with the sprinkling of parsley and chives; they are an integral part of the dish. Serve this with a big salad tossed with vinaigrette, and cheese and fruit. ○ *Serves 8*

COOKER: Large round or oval
SETTING AND COOK TIME: HIGH for 4 to 5 hours; cream and tomatoes added during last 30 minutes

1 ounce dried mushrooms of your choice
Boiling water to cover
¼ cup olive oil
½ cup (1 stick) unsalted butter
4 to 6 medium-size shallots, to your taste, chopped
3 pounds assorted fresh mushrooms (such as white, brown, oyster, shiitake, portobello, and cremini; if using shiitake or portobellos, discard stems), thickly sliced
6 tablespoons dry white wine
1 cup heavy cream
2 large fresh plum tomatoes, peeled, seeded, and diced
2 tablespoons freshly squeezed lemon juice
Salt and freshly ground black pepper to taste
16 slices white, French, sourdough, or whole wheat bread, toasted
½ cup minced fresh Italian parsley, for garnish
½ cup minced fresh chives, for garnish

1. Place the dried mushrooms in a bowl and cover with boiling water. Let stand at room temperature until softened, 30 minutes to 1 hour. Strain through a coffee filter, reserving the liquid.

2. Place the oil, butter, shallots, and fresh and dried mushrooms in the slow cooker; toss to distribute the shallots evenly. Add the wine and ¼ cup of the strained mushroom liquid. Cover and cook on HIGH until the mushrooms are tender, 3½ to 4½ hours.

3. Stir in the cream, tomatoes, and lemon juice. Cover and continue to cook on HIGH for 30 minutes longer. Season with salt and pepper.

4. To serve, place 2 pieces of toast on each plate. Spoon the mushroom stew over the toast, then sprinkle with the parsley and chives. Serve immediately.

Rosemary-Balsamic Onions

oo often, onions are thought of only as a flavoring aromatic, not as something worth eating in their own right. That's really too bad, especially now that new research is demonstrating some health benefits from eating onions. Here is one delicious way to put more onions on your plate. This high-flavor, low-calorie side dish is really nice at Thanksgiving, when everyone wants something light to balance out the many heavy foods on the menu, but we enjoy it all year. If you are lucky enough to find sweet onions such as Walla Wallas, Vidalias, Mauis, or Texas Sweets, you will have a special treat. ○ *Serves 6 to 8*

COOKER: Medium or large round
SETTING AND COOK TIME: HIGH for 2 to 2½ hours

4 medium-size yellow onions
4 tablespoons balsamic vinegar
1½ tablespoons extra-virgin olive oil
3 sprigs fresh rosemary or ½ teaspoon dried
Salt and freshly ground black pepper to taste

1. Wash the onions, paying special attention to the root ends. Cut the onions in half the long way (through the root end) and peel them. Trim the pointed end, but do not trim the root end (that's what will keep the cooked onions together).

2. Place the onions in the slow cooker, cut sides up. Drizzle in the vinegar and olive oil. Tuck fresh rosemary in among the onions, or sprinkle on dried rosemary. Sprinkle very lightly with salt and pepper. Cover and cook on HIGH until the onions are very tender when pierced with a sharp knife, 2 to 2½ hours.

3. Use a slotted spoon to carefully transfer the onions to a serving platter. Pour the liquid from the crock over the onions. Serve hot or at room temperature.

Ragoût of Peas and Artichokes with Tarragon

his simple side dish made with frozen peas and frozen artichoke hearts tastes like a whole lot more. Serve with pan-fried fish or roasted chicken dishes. This can be kept on the KEEP WARM setting and served as part of a buffet. ○ *Serves 8*

COOKER: Medium round
SETTINGS AND COOK TIMES: HIGH for 30 minutes, then LOW for 3 to 3 1/2 hours

Two 10-ounce packages frozen artichoke hearts, thawed
Two 12-ounce packages frozen petite peas, thawed
2 medium-size white boiling onions, chopped
1/4 cup (1/2 stick) unsalted butter, cut into pieces
2 long strips lemon peel
1/2 teaspoon dried tarragon
1/4 cup chicken broth or water
Salt and freshly ground black pepper to taste

1. Coat the inside of the crock with nonstick cooking spray.

2. Combine the artichoke hearts, peas, onions, and butter in the slow cooker. Add the lemon peel and tarragon, then the broth. Cover and cook on HIGH for 30 minutes to get the pot heated up.

3. Reduce the heat setting to LOW and cook until the vegetables are tender, 3 to 3 1/2 hours. Season with salt and pepper and serve hot from the crock.

Braised Peas with Lettuce

T he French have a unique method for preparing those large, tough peas that tend to show up at the end of the season, slow-cooking them under a blanket of lettuce, where they stay nice and green. Don't worry if they look a bit wrinkled after cooking; they will taste delicious. This is particularly good with chicken dishes. ○ *Serves 8*

COOKER: Medium round
SETTINGS AND COOK TIMES: HIGH for 30 minutes, then LOW for 2 to 3 hours

1 medium-size head Boston lettuce, outer leaves removed
1 sprig fresh thyme, savory, or mint
8 white boiling onions (16 if they are really tiny), peeled
½ cup (1 stick) unsalted butter, softened
½ teaspoon sugar
½ teaspoon salt
½ teaspoon ground white pepper
3½ to 4 pounds fresh peas in the pod (5 to 6 cups shelled peas of a uniform size),
    or two 12-ounce packages frozen garden peas (not petites), thawed
¼ cup water

1. Coat the inside of the crock with nonstick cooking spray. Line the bottom and sides of the crock with the outer lettuce leaves. Reserve some leaves for the top. Open the lettuce heart, place the herb sprig inside, and tie with kitchen twine. Place in the slow cooker and add the onions.

2. In a small bowl, mash together the butter, sugar, salt, and pepper. Place in a large bowl along with the peas and, with your hands, gently squeeze the butter into the mass of peas; it is okay if some peas are bruised, but try not to crush any. Pack the peas around the heart of lettuce in the crock and top with more lettuce leaves. Add the water. Cover and cook on HIGH for 30 minutes to get the pot heated up.

3. Reduce the heat setting to LOW and cook until the peas are tender, 2 to 3 hours. At 2 hours, lift the cover to check their progress. At the end of the cooking time, remove and discard the lettuce. Serve the peas hot from the crock.

New Potatoes with Fresh Lemon-Herb Butter

We love new potatoes for entertaining, and here they get to languish with butter, lemon, and herbs poured all over them. There is a general rule of slow cookers: Don't lift the lid or too much heat will escape. Well, it's pretty hard to check if the food's done if you don't lift the lid, so just be discreet; poke the potatoes quickly and resist the urge to do it too often. Serve these at a fancy dinner or piled in a pretty serving bowl on a buffet table. ○ *Serves 10 to 12*

COOKER: Large round or oval
SETTING AND COOK TIME: HIGH for 3 to 3½ hours

3 to 3½ pounds small new potatoes
½ cup water
½ cup (1 stick) unsalted butter or margarine
¼ cup chopped fresh Italian parsley
3 tablespoons freshly squeezed lemon juice
3 tablespoons chopped fresh chives
3 tablespoons chopped fresh dill
Salt and freshly ground black pepper to taste

1. Place the potatoes in the slow cooker with the water. Cover and cook on HIGH until tender when pierced with a sharp knife, 3 to 3½ hours.

2. In a small saucepan on the stovetop or in a small bowl in the microwave, heat the butter with the parsley, lemon juice, chives, and dill; you are not cooking this, just melting the butter and warming the herbs. Pour the butter mixture over the hot potatoes in the crock and toss to coat evenly. Season with salt and pepper. Serve immediately.

Potatoes and Fennel

F ennel is a vegetable that is crunchy like celery but with an anise-like taste; it is a very popular ingredient for entertaining because it has a special flavor and complements both fish and meats very nicely. People tend to either love it or hate it. Slice both of the vegetables the same thickness for even cooking.

○ *Serves 10*

COOKER: Medium or large round or oval
SETTING AND COOK TIME: HIGH for 3 to 3 $1/2$ hours

3 pounds new red or white potatoes, left unpeeled and sliced
3 pounds fennel bulbs (1 large or 2 small), stalks trimmed away, cut in half,
    and sliced (retain some fronds)
1 $1/3$ cups vegetable or chicken broth
Salt and freshly ground black pepper to taste
$1/3$ cup olive oil or unsalted butter, melted

1. Coat the inside of the crock with nonstick cooking spray or brush with olive oil. Place half of the potatoes in the slow cooker, then top with half the fennel; layer in the remaining potatoes and fennel. You can chop some of the fennel fronds and sprinkle them on top of the potatoes, if you like. Add the broth. Cover and cook on HIGH until the potatoes are tender when pierced with a sharp knife, 3 to 3½ hours.

2. Season with salt and pepper, drizzle with the olive oil, and serve immediately.

Twice-Crocked Stuffed Potatoes with Macadamia Nuts

Although macadamia nuts are a luxury, we like to incorporate them into party fare. Many people avoid them because they think the nut is high in fat, but, just for the record, they have the "good," heart-smart kind of fat. Be sure to buy unsalted nuts. Don't dry the potatoes after washing them, but, rather, put them into the slow cooker still wet. ○ *Serves 6 to 12*

COOKER: Medium or large round or oval
SETTINGS AND COOK TIMES: HIGH for 4 to 6 hours, or LOW for 6 to 8 hours; then HIGH for 45 to 60 minutes

6 large Idaho or russet baking potatoes, left unpeeled
1 cup heavy cream
½ cup chopped unsalted macadamia nuts
¼ cup thinly sliced green onions
Salt and ground white pepper to taste
1 cup shredded Swiss cheese (about 4 ounces)

1. Wash the potatoes. Prick each dripping-wet potato with a fork or the tip of a sharp knife and place in the slow cooker; do not add water. Cover and cook on HIGH for 4 to 6 hours, or on LOW for 6 to 8 hours (pierce with the tip of a knife to check for doneness).

2. Remove the potatoes from the cooker with tongs and cut in half. Scoop out the center of each half with a large spoon, leaving enough potato to keep the shell intact. Place the flesh in a large bowl and add the cream; beat until smooth with a fork, electric mixer, or potato masher. You want the mixture to be quite thick. Stir in the nuts and green onions and season with salt and pepper. Spoon the filling back into the shells, mounding each. Place each half back in the slow cooker, setting them in a single layer touching each other, and sprinkle with the cheese. Cover and cook on HIGH for 45 to 60 minutes.

3. Remove carefully from the cooker with tongs and serve immediately.

Scalloped Potatoes

A scalloped dish, the most famous being made with potatoes, tips off the cook that the ingredients will be layered and then held together with a creamy milk-based sauce. Is there anyone who does not like scalloped potatoes? This really works best in an oval cooker, giving the potatoes a lot of surface area to mimic an oval or rectangular casserole. Serve these right out of the cooker with a long-handled silver-plated serving spoon. ○ *Serves 6*

COOKER: Medium oval or large oval or round
SETTING AND COOK TIME: LOW for 5 1/2 to 6 hours

6 medium-size russet potatoes, peeled and sliced 1/4 inch thick
1 teaspoon salt, or to taste
1/2 teaspoon freshly ground black pepper
1 medium-size yellow onion, sliced 1/4 inch thick
2 cups shredded cheddar cheese (about 1/2 pound)
1/4 cup chopped celery leaves
2 tablespoons unsalted butter or margarine, melted
1/4 cup all-purpose flour
One 13-ounce can evaporated milk
1 1/2 tablespoons minced fresh Italian parsley

1. Coat the inside of the crock with nonstick cooking spray. Layer the potato slices, salt, pepper, onion, and cheese in the slow cooker.

2. In a food processor, combine the celery leaves, butter, flour, and evaporated milk; process until smooth. Pour into the crock. Cover and cook on LOW until the potatoes are tender and piping hot, 5 1/2 to 6 hours.

3. Sprinkle with the parsley and serve immediately.

Mashed Potato Casserole

This casserole pops up every winter holiday season because of its yummy richness and ease of preparation for a group. This can be prepped through the end of step 1 up to a day ahead, covered with plastic wrap, and refrigerated before popping it into the slow cooker to cook the next day. ○ *Serves 12*

COOKER: Medium or large round or oval
SETTING AND COOK TIME: LOW for 5 to 6 hours

5 pounds baking potatoes, such as russet or Idaho, peeled and quartered
One 8-ounce package cream cheese, cut into chunks and softened
¼ cup (½ stick) unsalted butter
1 cup sour cream
½ cup hot whole milk
1¼ teaspoons salt
½ teaspoon ground white pepper

1. In a large saucepan, cover the potatoes with salted cold water by 1 inch and simmer until tender, about 20 minutes. Drain and return to the pan. While still warm, add the cream cheese and butter; whip with an electric mixer until smooth. Beat in the sour cream, milk, salt, and pepper.

2. Transfer to the slow cooker. Cover and cook on LOW for 5 to 6 hours. Serve hot.

Good Old-Fashioned Mashed Potatoes

There are many ways to prepare mashed potatoes these days, but nothing satisfies like the real thing. Russet baking potatoes make for fluffy mashed, while yellow-fleshed Yukon golds make sweeter and creamier mashed, and the white- or red-skinned new potatoes make a denser mashed. You can multiply this recipe as many times as needed. ○ *Serves 6*

COOKER: Small, medium, or large round, depending on the amount of potatoes (use medium if making the volume below)

SETTING AND COOK TIME: KEEP WARM or LOW for 4 to 5 hours

2 pounds potatoes, peeled and cut into chunks

3 to 4 tablespoons salted or unsalted butter, cut into pieces

⅔ cup hot whole milk or half-and-half

Pinch of salt

1. Place the potatoes in a saucepan and cover with cold water. Bring to a boil, then reduce the heat to a simmer and cook until fork tender, 15 to 20 minutes. Drain well and return to the pan on the stovetop to evaporate any extra water, if necessary. Pass through a food mill or mash with a potato masher. Stir or mash or beat in the butter, milk, and salt until fluffy. Do not use a food processor.

2. Lightly coat the inside of the crock with butter or nonstick cooking spray and spoon in the mashed potatoes. If you like, press a pat of butter into the top. Cover and keep on KEEP WARM or LOW for 4 to 5 hours. Serve at the table right from the crock.

• • Keeping Mashed Potatoes Warm in the Slow Cooker • •

Have you run out of room on the stovetop, or are you trying to make a number of dishes way before guests arrive? Let the slow cooker help, especially with mashed potatoes. "My favorite slow cooker trick is to make the mashed potatoes on the morning of Thanksgiving," says cooking teacher Judith Dunbar-Hines. "The main thing is that you don't have to be rushing around with those boiling, mashing tricks just at the last minute. Put them in the crock and let them wait until it's time to serve. I brush the inside of the pot with melted butter, add the potatoes, add a little butter on top, and leave it on LOW. If they aren't made with broth, you can keep them warm safely for 4 to 5 hours. I can't tell you how delighted I was at the frantic end of the meal prep, when all the guests were arriving, because the potatoes were already done and ready and waiting." We fold a few thicknesses of paper towels and place them under the lid while the potatoes keep warm to absorb any excess moisture.

Blue Cheese–Sour Cream Mashers

Blue cheese and potatoes are one of those surprisingly successful culinary marriages. This is a very special version of mashed potatoes. You'll want to season the potatoes with freshly ground pepper, but because blue cheese is fairly salty on its own, you probably won't need any additional salt. You can multiply this recipe as many times as needed. ○ *Serves 6*

COOKER: Small, medium, or large round, depending on the amount of potatoes (use medium if making the volume below)
SETTING AND COOK TIME: KEEP WARM or LOW for 4 to 5 hours

2 pounds potatoes, peeled and cut into chunks
3 to 4 tablespoons salted or unsalted butter, cut into pieces
1 cup sour cream
¼ cup hot whole milk or half-and-half
¼ cup to ½ cup crumbled blue cheese
Freshly ground black pepper to taste

1. Place the potatoes in a saucepan and cover with cold water. Bring to a boil, then reduce to a simmer and cook until tender, 15 to 20 minutes. Drain well and return to the pan on the stovetop to evaporate any extra water, if necessary. Pass through a food mill or mash with a potato masher. Stir or mash or beat in the butter, sour cream, and milk until fluffy. Do not use a food processor. Gently fold in the blue cheese and pepper.

2. Lightly coat the inside of the crock with butter or nonstick cooking spray and spoon in the mashed potatoes. If you like, press a pat of butter into the top. Cover and keep on KEEP WARM or LOW for 4 to 5 hours. Serve at the table right from the crock.

Mashed Potatoes and Carrots with Crisp Bacon and Chives

This combination of equal parts potatoes and carrots is just divine. Do make this dish during the winter holidays. You can multiply this recipe as many times as needed. ◦ *Serves 6*

COOKER: Medium or large round or oval, depending on the amount of potatoes (use medium if making the volume below)

SETTING AND COOK TIME: KEEP WARM or LOW for 4 to 5 hours

1 pound Yukon gold or russet potatoes, peeled and cut into 2-inch cubes

1 pound carrots, cut into 1-inch cubes

¼ cup (½ stick) unsalted butter

2 teaspoons cider vinegar

Salt and freshly ground black pepper to taste

¼ pound sliced bacon, fried until crisp, drained, and chopped

2 tablespoons chopped fresh chives

1. Place the potatoes and carrots in a saucepan and cover with cold water. Bring to a boil, then reduce to a simmer and cook until tender, 15 to 20 minutes. Drain well and return to the pan on the stovetop to evaporate any extra water, if necessary. Pass through a food mill or mash with a potato masher. Stir or mash or beat in the butter, vinegar, salt, and pepper until fluffy. Do not use a food processor.

2. Coat the inside of the crock with butter or nonstick cooking spray and spoon in the mashed potatoes and carrots. Sprinkle the bacon and chives on top. Cover and keep on KEEP WARM or LOW for 4 to 5 hours. Serve at the table right from the crock.

Cider-Braised Turnips

W hen fall hits and fresh, unfiltered sweet cider is in the refrigerated section of the supermarket, make this simple vegetable dish. You cook the turnips, then mash them to serve. It is adapted from a wonderful book, *America's Best Slow Cooker Recipes* (Robert Rose, 2000) by Donna-Marie Pye, who has also done a recipe booklet for the Rival Company. The flavor combination of the cider with the turnips is memorable and perfect for the winter holiday table.

○ *Serves 4 to 6*

COOKER: Medium round
SETTING AND COOK TIME: HIGH for 4 to 6 hours

2 pounds turnips, peeled and cut into chunks
2 cups unfiltered apple cider
3 tablespoons unsalted butter
1 tablespoon light or dark brown sugar or pure maple syrup
¼ teaspoon ground nutmeg
Salt and freshly ground black pepper to taste

1. Place the turnips and cider in the slow cooker. Cover and cook on HIGH until tender and the cider is evaporated, 4 to 6 hours.

2. Turn off the cooker and remove the cover. Add the butter, brown sugar, and nutmeg and mash the turnips with a fork, potato masher, immersion blender, or handheld electric mixer, taking care not to hit the sides of the crock. Season with salt and pepper and serve hot. This can stay on LOW or KEEP WARM for up to 1 hour before serving.

Candied Yams with Apples and Cranberries

T his holiday casserole is less cloying than the traditional version, with the tart, fresh cranberries offsetting the sweetness of the yams and apples. This is a must with roast turkey or baked ham. ○ *Serves 6 to 8*

2 pounds yams, peeled and sliced ½ inch thick

2 medium-size tart cooking apples, such as Fuji or pippin, peeled, cored,
    quartered, and sliced ½ inch thick

One 12-ounce bag fresh cranberries, rinsed and picked over for stems

¾ cup firmly packed light brown sugar

1 teaspoon ground cinnamon

¼ teaspoon ground nutmeg

½ cup unfiltered apple or pear juice

3 tablespoons unsalted butter, cut into bits

1. Coat the inside of the crock with butter or nonstick cooking spray. Alternate slices of the yams and apples in the crock, in overlapping layers. Sprinkle with the cranberries. Combine the brown sugar, cinnamon, and nutmeg in a small bowl; sprinkle over the cranberries. Drizzle with the apple juice and dot with the butter.

2. Cover and cook on LOW until the yams are tender when pierced with the tip of a knife, 6 to 7 hours. Serve hot from the crock.

Tortino di Zucchini

Try layering zucchini with some country bread into a baked omelet of sorts for Sunday brunch or supper. You can omit the Canadian bacon if you want to make it a vegetable tortino. Serve with a green salad. ❍ *Serves 6*

COOKER: Medium round
SETTING AND COOK TIME: HIGH for 3 to 3½ hours

3 tablespoons unsalted butter

1 medium-size yellow onion, chopped

½ cup slivered Canadian bacon

3 to 4 medium-size zucchini, sliced ½ inch thick on the diagonal,
    to make about 2 heaping cups

Eight 1-inch-thick slices country bread, crusts removed and cut into fingers

1 cup shredded medium-sharp cheddar or fontina cheese (about 3 ounces)

Two 13-ounce cans evaporated milk

3 large eggs

3 tablespoons freshly grated Parmesan cheese

2 tablespoons minced fresh chives

2 tablespoons minced fresh Italian parsley

1. Melt the butter in a large skillet over medium heat. When it foams, add the onion and cook, stirring a few times, until softened, about 5 minutes. Add the Canadian bacon and cook for a few minutes. Push to the side of the pan and add the zucchini; stir just to brown a bit; do not cook until really soft.

2. Coat the inside of the crock with nonstick cooking spray. Arrange one-third of the bread over the bottom of the crock; you can push to mold the bread to the shape of the crock, but have the pieces touching each other to make a solid layer on the bottom. Spoon in a layer of half of the vegetable mixture, and then one-third of the cheddar cheese. Make another layer of bread, then add the rest of the vegetable mixture, and the second third of the cheddar cheese. Top with the rest of the bread and cheddar.

3. In a medium-size bowl, thoroughly whisk together the milk, eggs, Parmesan, chives, and parsley; pour over the bread in the cooker. Cover and cook on HIGH until the custard is set, 3 to 3½ hours. An instant-read thermometer inserted into the center should register 190°F.

4. Let the tortino rest, covered, in the turned-off cooker for 15 minutes before serving hot.

Vegetable Curry

There are literally thousands of variations on curried dishes. This is a simple vegetarian meal of vegetables and beans, and is wonderful served with steamed plain basmati rice, a hot-sweet peach or mango chutney, yogurt salad with cucumbers, and a flatbread like chapatis. The combination of coconut, spices, tomatoes, and green beans is a traditional one in Indian cooking. Be sure to cut the cauliflower into uniformly sized pieces, because the success of the dish is the slow braising and you want all the vegetables to be cooked to the same tenderness. ○ *Serves 8*

COOKER: Medium or large round or oval

SETTING AND COOK TIME: LOW for 5½ to 6½ hours; zucchini and green beans added halfway through cooking time; tofu added during last 30 minutes

2 small heads cauliflower, broken into florets

4 large carrots, sliced ½ inch thick

6 medium-size new white potatoes, diced

Two 15-ounce cans garbanzo beans, drained and rinsed

One 28-ounce can chopped tomatoes, undrained

2½ cups unsweetened coconut milk

5 tablespoons olive oil or sesame oil

2 medium-size yellow onions (optional), diced

2 tablespoons ground coriander

4 teaspoons ground cumin

2 teaspoons ground turmeric

2 tablespoons grated fresh ginger

2 small jalapeño chiles, seeded and minced

6 medium-size zucchini, thickly sliced

½ pound fresh green beans, ends trimmed and cut into 1-inch pieces

Two 14-ounce blocks firm tofu (optional), cubed

Salt and freshly ground black pepper to taste

Plain yogurt for serving

About ½ cup chopped fresh cilantro, for garnish

1. Place the cauliflower, carrots, potatoes, garbanzo beans, tomatoes, and coconut milk in the slow cooker.

2. In a large skillet, heat the oil over medium heat and cook the onion, if using, stirring a few times, until softened, about 5 minutes. Add the coriander, cumin, turmeric, ginger, and jalapeños; sauté 1 minute and add the mixture to the crock. Cover and cook on LOW for 5½ to 6½ hours, until the vegetables are just tender and still hold their shape. About halfway through cooking, add the zucchini and green beans. If using the tofu, add it during the last 30 minutes of cooking. Season with salt and pepper. Serve hot, with a dollop of yogurt and fresh cilantro sprinkled on top.

Chinese Vegetable Hot Pot

T his vegetable stew is adapted from Rick Rodgers's *The Slow Cooker Ready and Waiting Cookbook* (William Morrow, 1992), still one of the best cookbooks in the genre. Traditionally, this would be made in a ceramic Chinese sand pot, which is glazed on the inside and rough like raw clay on the outside, with wire reinforcement. Fresh water chestnuts are easily found in Chinese markets and specialty produce markets. Serve this with cooked rice noodles or steamed long-grain white rice. ● *Serves 6 to 8*

COOKER: Medium or large round or oval

SETTING AND COOK TIME: LOW for 6 to 7 hours; tofu, cabbage, and snow peas added during last hour

8 cups vegetable or chicken broth

1 large or 2 small white onions or 4 young leeks, sliced ½ inch thick

4 ribs celery, sliced 1 inch thick on the diagonal

3 medium-large carrots or parsnips, peeled and sliced ½ inch thick

2 medium-size red bell peppers, seeded and sliced into strips

One 8-ounce can water chestnuts, drained and sliced, or ½ cup peeled and sliced fresh water chestnuts

8 Chinese dried black mushrooms, rinsed

A few thick slices fresh ginger, to your taste

3 cloves garlic, crushed with the flat side of a knife

3 tablespoons soy sauce or tamari, plus more for drizzling

¼ teaspoon red pepper flakes, or more to taste

One 14-ounce block soft or firm tofu, drained and cut into 1-inch cubes

About 3 packed cups chopped napa cabbage or Chinese flowering cabbage

3 ounces fresh or frozen snow peas, thawed if necessary and strings removed

⅓ cup minced fresh cilantro leaves, for garnish

Coarsely chopped green onions (white parts and some of the green) for garnish

1. Pour the broth into the slow cooker. Add the onion, celery, carrots, bell peppers, water chestnuts, mushrooms, ginger, garlic, soy sauce, and red pepper. Cover and cook on LOW for 6 to 7 hours. At 5 to 6 hours, add the tofu, cabbage, and snow peas.

2. To serve, ladle into soup bowls and top with the cilantro and green onions. Have a cruet of soy sauce or tamari on the table for drizzling.

Braised Spring Vegetables

Tender spring vegetables have a clean, fresh taste. We flavor them with tarragon, the *estragon* or "little dragon" of the herb world; with the vinegar, we have the distinctive flavor combination of the famous béarnaise sauce of French cookery. Serve this with buttered toast, made from a really delicious homemade or crusty bread, cut into triangles, or buttered egg noodles. ○ *Serves 8*

COOKER: Medium or large round or oval
SETTING AND COOK TIME: LOW for 4 to 4½ hours

4 pounds medium-thick asparagus, tough bottoms snapped off and cut into 1-inch pieces
4 large leeks (white parts only), cut in half lengthwise, rinsed well, and sliced
2 large yellow or green bell peppers, seeded and cut into thin strips
2 large red bell peppers, seeded and cut into thin strips
2 pounds fresh peas, shelled, or 2 cups frozen petite peas, thawed
⅔ cup vegetable or chicken broth
⅓ cup plus 2 tablespoons red or white wine vinegar
1 tablespoon dried tarragon, crushed, or 2½ teaspoons minced fresh tarragon
A few outer leaves from a head of Boston-type lettuce (optional)
6 tablespoons extra-virgin olive oil

1. Place the asparagus, leeks, yellow and red bell peppers, peas, broth, ⅓ cup of the vinegar, and 1½ teaspoons of the tarragon in the slow cooker. Cover with a layer of lettuce leaves, if desired. Cover and cook on LOW until the asparagus is tender but still slightly crisp, 4 to 4½ hours.

2. Drain and freeze the broth for later use in stock, if desired. Mix together the remaining 2 tablespoons vinegar, the remaining 1½ teaspoons tarragon, and the olive oil. Drizzle over the vegetables and serve immediately, warm, or refrigerate for at least 4 hours and up to overnight and serve chilled.

Ragoût of Baby Vegetables

 A ragoût is a thick stew, sometimes made with meat or game, but here with vegetables of the season. Serve it with steamed basmati rice and a simple roasted meat. ● *Serves 8*

COOKER: Large round or oval

SETTINGS AND COOK TIMES: LOW for 4½ to 5 hours, asparagus and peas added during last 30 minutes to 1 hour; HIGH for 10 minutes

30 baby white boiling onions, peeled, or two 16-ounce bags frozen baby onions, thawed

Two 16-ounce bags baby carrots

24 medium-size new red or white potatoes, cut in half

4 bunches (16 to 20) baby turnips, with 1 inch of stem intact and left whole

1 cup vegetable or chicken broth

2 tablespoons minced fresh marjoram or summer savory

⅓ cup chopped fresh Italian parsley

2 pounds fresh asparagus, tough bottoms trimmed

4 pounds fresh peas, shelled (5½ to 6 cups), or 6 cups frozen petite peas, thawed

½ cup (1 stick) unsalted butter, cut into pieces

1. Place the onions, carrots, potatoes, turnips, and broth in the slow cooker. Cover and cook on LOW for 4 hours.

2. Add the marjoram, parsley, asparagus, and peas. Cover and continue to cook on LOW until the vegetables are tender, another 30 to 60 minutes.

3. Remove the lid and turn the cooker to HIGH. Add the butter and cook for 10 minutes to reduce slightly. Serve hot.

Slow-Cooked Grains and Stuffings

Risotto Milanese o 165

Risotto Verde o 166

Pumpkin-Sage Risotto o 168

Shrimp Risotto with Parsley and
Basil o 170

Risotto with Asparagus and
Arugula o 171

Mushroom-Gorgonzola Risotto
in Radicchio Wraps with
Balsamic Syrup o 172

Wild Rice with Dried Apricots,
Cherries, and Pecans o 173

Orange-Walnut Wild Rice o 175

Wild Rice with Coconut and
Raisins o 176

Green Chile Grits o 177

Double Corn Spoonbread o 178

Arizona Vegetable and Herb Bread
Stuffing o 179

Mushroom-Chard Whole Wheat
Bread Stuffing o 181

Thanksgiving Sausage Bread
Pudding o 182

Cornbread Stuffing with
Bacon, Chestnuts, and Dried
Cherries o 184

Prosciutto, Parmesan, and Pine Nut
Holiday Stuffing o 185

Grains cook up beautifully moist and fluffy in the slow cooker, with no worrying about whether you're using too much liquid or overcooking them to mush. Here we offer you some of our favorite first-course and side-dish grains for entertaining.

One of the nice surprises with the slow cooker is that you can make a great risotto in it without any stirring and without spending a minute watching over it. Risotto is a unique rice dish with a consistency that is likened more to a sauce than a pilaf. Pearly Italian Arborio rice is used exclusively for risotto, because it has a lot of surface starch. The rice becomes creamy during cooking, very much like a savory rice pudding. The center remains a bit toothy; if you have never had risotto before, you might think your rice is not quite cooked. It is traditionally a first course in Italian meals, not an accompaniment like American rice, except when paired with osso buco. We like it with all types of beef stews.

Risotto has a reputation as a very time-consuming rice dish to make because of all the stirring and adding of boiling stock in small portions. In the slow cooker, you can make really fabulous risotto, braised at a gentle, steady, low boil. Do watch the time closely in the slow cooker so that it doesn't overcook. Risotto is best served immediately (it thickens dramatically as it stands at room temperature), but in a pinch, it will keep on the KEEP WARM setting for up to an hour. A warm shallow soup bowl is nice for serving, along with a soup spoon, although correct etiquette calls for a fork.

And yes, you can prepare regular rice successfully in the slow cooker, but you can't reach for just any type of rice on the shelf. Converted rice, the familiar orange box of Uncle Ben's, is the kind to use. Converted rice has been steamed before hulling, which makes for a firmer grain. That firmness is what allows it to stand up to long, slow-cooking without getting sticky or gummy. Actually, the slow cooker is a wonderful solution for those times when you want to serve rice to a large group. You can start the slow cooker well ahead of time and know that your rice will be hot and ready when you want it to be. Often we call for other rices in recipes, such as wild rice, when we are looking for a particular consistency or flavor, so please follow our suggestions carefully.

One of the most surprising foods to prepare in the slow cooker is bread stuffing. Instead of stuffing the turkey, many food purists and food professionals now cook the stuffing outside the bird. However, casserole-cooked stuffing was always too dry for us, but it turns out that's not the case in the slow cooker. It comes out beautifully, like a moist, dense soufflé.

While the turkey fills the oven at your next holiday feast, let the stuffing cook to perfection on the counter in the slow cooker. The main advantage of the slow cooker is that, unlike your stove, it can be left unattended for hours as you take care of last-minute shopping or cleaning.

Risotto Milanese

R isotto Milanese, or risotto with saffron, is one of the trademark dishes of Italian cuisine. It is usually eaten as a first course out of a shallow bowl and washed down with a nice Chianti. We recommend using saffron threads instead of powdered saffron, which is really a lot more potent; you want a faint saffron flavor, nothing overstated or overpowering. Serve as a side dish to Osso Buco (page 332), wonderful Italian braised veal shanks, and carbonata, Milanese beef stew. Traditionally, this risotto is served with shavings of white truffles or a drizzle of truffle oil as a garnish. ○ *Serves 6 to 8*

COOKER: Medium or large round or oval
SETTING AND COOK TIME: HIGH for 2 to 2½ hours

6 cups chicken broth (or two 15-ounce cans chicken broth plus water to equal 6 cups)
Pinch of saffron threads
2 tablespoons olive oil
¼ cup (½ stick) unsalted butter
1 medium-size yellow onion, chopped
2 cups Arborio, Vialone nano, or Carnaroli rice
⅔ cup freshly grated Parmesan cheese, plus more for serving
Salt to taste

1. Heat 1 cup of the broth and crush the saffron into it; let stand for 15 minutes.

2. In a small skillet over medium heat, warm the oil and 2 tablespoons of the butter together, then add the onion and cook, stirring, until softened, 2 to 3 minutes. Add the rice, stirring for a few minutes, until it turns from translucent to opaque (do not brown). Scrape the mixture into the slow cooker using a heatproof rubber

spatula. Add the saffron broth and the remaining chicken broth. Cover and cook on HIGH for 2 to 2½ hours. The risotto should be only a bit liquid, and the rice should be *al dente*, tender with just a touch of tooth resistance.

3. Add the remaining 2 tablespoons butter, cover, and wait a minute for it to soften. Stir in the cheese and add salt if desired. Serve immediately, spooned into bowls, with more Parmesan for sprinkling. Risotto will keep on the KEEP WARM setting for an hour or so.

Risotto Verde

S ave this green risotto for a special occasion—it is thick with green onions, parsley, spinach, and basil. Usually even the thought of making a large batch of risotto is out of the question; it is just too time-consuming. But this is a large-quantity risotto, and it is as easy as making it for two: There is no watching, no stirring, no boiling over. This risotto will keep on the KEEP WARM setting for an hour or so, so you can serve it at a buffet right out of the cooker, or keep it warm in the kitchen until you are ready to serve. ○ *Serves 12*

COOKER: Large round or oval
SETTING AND COOK TIME: HIGH for 2 to 2½ hours

¾ **cup (1½ sticks) unsalted butter**
¾ **cup finely chopped green onions**
3½ **cups Arborio, Vialone nano, or Carnaroli rice**
¾ **cup finely chopped fresh Italian parsley**
12 **ounces fresh spinach, coarsely chopped**
10½ **cups hot chicken broth or light vegetable broth**
1½ **teaspoons salt**
6 **tablespoons chopped fresh basil**
2 **cups freshly grated Parmigiano-Reggiano cheese**

1. In a large sauté pan over medium heat, melt 6 tablespoons of the butter. Add the green onions and cook until soft, 1 minute. Add the rice and stir to coat the grains, 1 to 2 minutes. Add the parsley and spinach and cook until wilted, 1 minute. Scrape the mixture into the slow cooker and add the broth and salt.

2. Cover and cook on HIGH for 2 to 2½ hours, until all the liquid is absorbed, but the rice is still moist. Stir in the remaining 6 tablespoons butter in pieces, the basil, and 1 cup of grated cheese. Serve hot, passing the remaining 1 cup grated cheese on the side.

•• Risotto Know-How ••

There are distinct steps to making risotto: cooking the onion and rice, adding the stock and other ingredients, and then adding the butter and cheese to finish, known as "creaming."

1. Risotto must be made by first sautéing chopped onion in butter (or half butter and half olive oil), then the rice. Place pieces of butter in a sauté pan over medium-high heat on the stovetop. Butter is traditional for sautéing the onion, but these days a bit of olive oil is added, and maybe some pancetta. The butter will melt in about 1 to 2 minutes. Add the chopped onion, leek, or shallot; cook until soft and any liquid they exude evaporates. If using wine, add and cook to evaporate off the alcohol, 1 to 2 minutes.

2. Add the measured amount of rice to the hot butter and onion; stir with a wooden spoon. The rice will gradually heat up and gently sizzle. Stir occasionally and gently to coat all the grains. Give the rice a full 1 to 2 minutes to cook. This precooks the outer coating of the rice to keep the grains separate while slowly absorbing and cooking in the aromatic stock.

3. Scrape the hot rice mixture into the crock with a heatproof rubber spatula. Add the stock (never water), if using, and any other ingredients as specified in the recipe. Stir a few times. Cover and cook on the HIGH heat setting. You may open the slow cooker once or twice to stir gently, but this is optional. Use a light stock, such as chicken, duck, or veal. You will have three to four times the amount of liquid to rice and there will be less evaporation with the cover closed than when you cook on the stovetop. You don't have to fuss about the exact amount. You just add all the stock at once (with no preheating of the stock). But the stock is really important. Without the stock, the risotto just won't taste right. Never add wine at the end; it will taste too bitter and the alcohol will not be cooked off, affecting the delicate taste of your risotto.

4. Check the rice for tenderness at 2 hours, and at that point either continue cooking or turn off the machine. With a plastic or wooden spoon, stir the risotto a few times, adding the butter and cheese, or cream. The bit of butter swirled in at the end of cooking is very traditional, but optional. The risotto can keep on the KEEP WARM setting for about an hour before serving. Serve immediately in shallow soup bowls with more Parmesan cheese for sprinkling (use as much as you like) and the pepper grinder.

Pumpkin-Sage Risotto

B eth met Eda of Daylight Farms in Half Moon Bay, California, when Beth did a story on special eating pumpkins for a harvest article. There are many varieties of pumpkin winter squash, each more delicious than the last. Pumpkin makes excellent risotto in this recipe, adapted from one by Eda; it is left in chunks so you can discern it as a vegetable. Italians are sticklers for the right cheese: Parmigiano-Reggiano. Buy a chunk of imported, even just a little bit, if you can, otherwise domestic Parmesan is okay. You can use Pecorino Romano sheep's-milk cheese in place of the Parmesan (it is quite a bit stronger), Asiago (poor man's Parmesan), or a Parmesan-Romano combination, if you like. We like it shredded as well as finely grated. ○ *Serves 10 to 12*

COOKER: Large round or oval
SETTING AND COOK TIME: HIGH for 2½ hours; pumpkin added during last 30 minutes

1 small pumpkin (2½ pounds), peeled, seeded, and cut into 1-inch cubes
3 tablespoons extra-virgin olive oil
Salt and freshly ground black pepper to taste
3 tablespoons unsalted butter
½ cup chopped shallots
1 to 2 cloves garlic, finely chopped
3 cups Arborio, Vialone nano, or Carnaroli rice
1½ cups dry white wine, such as Pinot Grigio
9 cups low-sodium chicken broth
¾ cup freshly grated Parmigiano-Reggiano or other Parmesan cheese, plus more for serving
2 to 3 tablespoons chopped fresh sage

1. Position a rack in the top third of the oven and preheat to 400°F. Spread the pumpkin on a baking sheet and toss with 1½ tablespoons of the oil. Season lightly with salt and pepper. Bake until tender, about 35 minutes. Remove from the oven and cover with aluminum foil to keep warm.

2. Heat the butter and remaining 1½ tablespoons oil together in a heavy-bottomed Dutch oven or flameproof casserole over medium heat. Add the shallots and garlic and cook, stirring, until softened, 3 to 4 minutes. Add the rice and cook, stirring, until it turns from translucent to opaque (do not brown), about 2 minutes. Add the wine, increase the heat to HIGH, and cook until almost evaporated, about 2 minutes. Scrape the mixture into the slow cooker using a heatproof rubber spatula. Add the broth, cover, and cook on HIGH for 2 hours.

3. Add the pumpkin, cover, and cook until all the liquid is absorbed but the rice is still moist, another 30 minutes.

4. Stir in the cheese and season with salt and pepper, if necessary. Serve immediately, spooned into bowls and sprinkled with the sage. Risotto will keep on the KEEP WARM setting for an hour or so.

· · What Type of Rice for Risotto? · ·

Arborio medium-grain rice is labeled *fino* or *superfino* and is the right size grain for risotto. Lesser grades are labeled *fino, semifino*, and *commune*, and are fine to use in soups. Lundberg Family Farms of California has a domestic California Arborio on the market that the company spent 10 years developing. RiceSelect offers a Texas Arborio (called risotto rice), and there is another domestic brand called CalRiso. All can be substituted cup for cup for their imported Italian cousins, making lovely, less expensive risottos, although gourmets insist the Italian rices make the most authentic risottos. A 500-gram bag, a little over 1 pound, yields about 2 cups of raw rice.

There is a little family of Italian medium-grain rices grown for risotto that include Carnaroli and Vialone nano along with the Arborio. Carnaroli is grown alongside Arborio in Piedmont and Lombardy. The newest hybrid of Italian Carnaroli is just starting to be exported from Argentina by Lotus Foods and is considered equal, even superior, to Arborio. In Venice and Verona, Vialone nano is cooked until *all'onde*, or "wavy," which is a bit looser in texture than other risotto recipes; it is easily available now through Williams-Sonoma. Although each rice has its own subtle, distinct flavor, you can use them interchangeably in risotto recipes.

Shrimp Risotto with Parsley and Basil

Risotto is a natural base for plump shrimp. Do not let this risotto sit on the KEEP WARM setting; with the shrimp, you need to eat it as soon as it is cooked. ○ *Serves 6*

COOKER: Medium round
SETTING AND COOK TIME: HIGH for 2½ to 3 hours; shrimp added during last 20 minutes

6 cups chicken broth
1½ pounds medium-size shrimp, peeled and deveined, tails attached and shells reserved
Pinch of saffron threads
1 tablespoon olive oil
2 tablespoons unsalted butter
3 small white boiling onions, chopped
2 cups Arborio, Vialone nano, or Carnaroli rice
½ cup dry white wine
½ cup freshly grated Parmesan cheese, plus more for serving
3 tablespoons minced fresh Italian parsley
2 to 3 tablespoons minced fresh basil, to your taste

1. Combine 1 cup of the broth and the reserved shrimp shells in a small saucepan. Bring to a boil, then simmer until the shells turn pink, about 15 minutes. Strain and crush the saffron into the broth.

2. In a small skillet over medium heat, warm the oil and butter together and cook the onions, stirring, until softened, 3 to 4 minutes. Add the rice, stirring, for a few minutes, until it turns from translucent to opaque (do not brown), about 2 minutes. Add the wine and reduce slightly. Scrape the mixture into the slow cooker using a heatproof rubber spatula. Add the shrimp shell broth and the remaining 5 cups chicken broth. Cover and cook on HIGH for 2 to 2½ hours. The risotto should be only a bit liquid and the rice should be *al dente*, tender with just a touch of tooth resistance.

3. Add the shrimp (just throw it on top of the rice), cover, and continue to cook on HIGH until pink, about 20 minutes.

4. Stir in the cheese, parsley, and basil and serve immediately, spooned into bowls, with more Parmesan for sprinkling.

Risotto with Asparagus and Arugula

 his springtime risotto is a study in flavor and color contrasts: mild asparagus with sharp arugula; green vegetables with white rice. ○ *Serves 8*

COOKER: Medium round
SETTING AND COOK TIME: HIGH for 2 to 2½ hours;
    arugula added during last 15 minutes

2 tablespoons olive oil
¼ cup (½ stick) unsalted butter
⅔ cup chopped shallots
2 cups Arborio, Vialone nano, or Carnaroli rice
6 cups chicken broth (or two 15-ounce cans low-sodium chicken broth plus
    water to equal 6 cups)
2 pounds asparagus spears, ends trimmed and cut on the diagonal into
    1½-inch pieces
2 loosely packed cups arugula leaves, large leaves cut into 1½-inch ribbons
⅔ cup freshly grated Parmesan cheese, plus more for serving
Salt and freshly ground black pepper to taste

1. In a small skillet over medium heat, warm the oil and 2 tablespoons of the butter together. Add the shallots and cook, stirring, until softened, 3 to 4 minutes. Add the rice, stirring, until it turns from translucent to opaque (do not brown), about 2 minutes. Scrape the mixture into the slow cooker using a heatproof rubber spatula. Add the broth and asparagus pieces, cover, and cook on HIGH for 2 to 2¼ hours. The risotto should be only a bit liquid and the rice should be *al dente*, tender with just a touch of tooth resistance.

2. Stir in the arugula, cover, and continue to cook on HIGH until it is wilted, about 15 minutes more. Add the remaining 2 tablespoons butter and cover for about 1 minute to allow the butter to soften. Stir in the butter and cheese and season with salt and pepper. Serve immediately, spooned into bowls, with more Parmesan for sprinkling.

Mushroom-Gorgonzola Risotto in Radicchio Wraps with Balsamic Syrup

R adicchio has a definite sharp flavor that melds so nicely with the rich Gorgonzola and sautéed mushrooms in this risotto to make a splendid party dish. You can serve it as a vegetable side or first course or as part of a buffet. The risotto is a snap in the slow cooker, and the assembly is easy. Purchase the best balsamic vinegar you can afford; it has a marvelous taste when reduced with the honey. If you have any risotto left over, just refrigerate overnight, then the next day form into patties, coat with bread crumbs, and fry the patties in olive oil for a risotto pancake. ○ *Serves 8*

COOKER: Medium or large round or oval
SETTING AND COOK TIME: HIGH for 2 to 2½ hours

7 tablespoons unsalted butter
1 medium-size yellow onion, diced
1 bay leaf
1 teaspoon chopped fresh thyme leaves
1 teaspoon chopped fresh marjoram leaves
1½ cups Arborio rice
½ cup dry white wine
4½ cups hot vegetable or chicken broth
½ pound cremini mushrooms, sliced
½ pound baby portobello mushrooms, sliced
½ pound white mushrooms, sliced
16 outer leaves from 2 to 3 large round heads radicchio
1 cup crumbled Gorgonzola cheese
Salt and freshly ground black or white pepper to taste

BALSAMIC SYRUP:
1 cup balsamic vinegar
4 tablespoons honey

1. In a large sauté pan over medium-high heat, melt 3 tablespoons of the butter. Cook the onion, bay leaf, thyme, and marjoram until the onions are translucent, about 5 minutes. Add the rice and sauté for 2 minutes. Add the wine and cook to evaporate some of the alcohol, 1 to 2 minutes. Scrape the mixture into the slow cooker and add the hot broth.

2. Add the remaining 4 tablespoons butter to the pan and, when melted, add the sliced cremini, portobello, and white mushrooms. Sauté for 8 to 10 minutes over medium-high heat until they brown a bit (they do not need to be completely cooked through). Scrape the mushrooms into the crock and stir to combine. Cover and cook on HIGH for 2 to 2½ hours.

3. While the risotto is cooking, immerse the radicchio leaves in an ice bath for 20 minutes to soften them and mellow their flavor. Transfer to towels to dry.

4. To make the balsamic syrup, place the vinegar and honey in a medium-size sauté pan. Over medium-high heat, bring to a boil, then reduce the heat and simmer until the mixture has reduced to a syrupy consistency, about 10 minutes. Remove from the heat and set aside to cool.

5. When the risotto is done, stir in the Gorgonzola and season with salt and pepper. The risotto will keep on the KEEP WARM setting for an hour or so, until you are ready to assemble the wraps.

6. Lay the radicchio leaves out flat on a clean work surface. Put a few tablespoons of the mushroom risotto in the center of a leaf, fold the two outer sides into the center, then roll up like a burrito to encase the filling. Place with the folded side down on a serving platter. Repeat with the remaining leaves. When all the wraps are done, drizzle with the balsamic syrup. Serve immediately, or cover with plastic wrap and let stand no longer than 2 hours to serve at room temperature.

Wild Rice with Dried Apricots, Cherries, and Pecans

Wild rice, the folkloric state grain of Minnesota, is known as the "gourmet or epicurean grain." It is the only grain native to North America and grows in the lakes and shallow moving waters (18 inches to 3 feet maximum) fed by melting ice that lace the Great Lakes along the American-Canadian border (western Ontario, eastern Manitoba, Wisconsin, and Minnesota). Some wild rice is still harvested in the old way by native tribespeople, who balance in traditional birch bark racing canoes sewn together with spruce roots that are so light they float like corks. The rice is traditionally harvested by beating the rice spikes with flexible forked flails fashioned from saplings, the legal method of harvesting on public waters. Hand-gathered lake rice, always labeled with its place of origin, is quite expensive, but cultivated rice is very affordable, though less assertive in flavor. Hand-gathered rice is distinctly matte, while paddy-grown rice is a very shiny sable black, the result of being left out to cure in the weather longer. Hand-harvested rice is parched immediately over open fires, giving it a variety of distinctly matte colors, from ruddy red-brown, deep chocolate, and tan to a subtle gray-green. Each brand of wild rice has its own particular taste, so if you have experienced a brand that was too husky or bitter for your palate, experiment with others, or use it in combination with other rices for a milder overall taste.

○ Serves 12 to 16

COOKER: Medium round
SETTING AND COOK TIME: LOW for 4½ to 6 hours

2 cups converted white rice (such as Uncle Ben's)
2 cups wild rice, rinsed until the water is clear and drained
Two 15-ounce cans low-sodium vegetable or chicken broth
1 cup hot water
½ cup dry sherry
4 medium-size shallots, finely chopped
Freshly ground black pepper to taste
½ cup chopped dried apricots
½ cup dried cherries
½ cup pecans, toasted in a dry skillet over medium heat until fragrant

1. In the slow cooker, combine the white and wild rices, broth, water, sherry, shallots, and pepper. Cover and cook on LOW until the rices are tender but not mushy, 4½ to 6 hours. Do not remove the lid to check before the rice has cooked for at least 4 hours. The rice can keep on KEEP WARM for up to 2 hours.

2. Gently stir in the apricots, cherries, and pecans. Serve immediately.

Orange-Walnut Wild Rice

 Here we make good use of one of the many commercial brands of wild and white mixed rices, like those packed by Uncle Ben's, spiking it with citrus flavor. Wild rice melds well with all types of nuts. ○ *Serves 6*

COOKER: Medium round
SETTING AND COOK TIME: LOW for 4½ to 6 hours

1½ cups packaged wild and white rice mix
3 cups vegetable or chicken broth
3 tablespoons grated orange zest or 1 tablespoon dried orange peel
3 tablespoons freshly squeezed orange juice
¼ teaspoon salt
1 tablespoon unsalted butter
½ cup chopped walnuts, toasted in a 350°F oven until lightly browned
3 tablespoons chopped fresh chives
⅓ cup packed chopped fresh Italian parsley leaves

1. Briefly rinse the wild rice mix in a strainer under cold running water. Combine the rice, broth, orange zest, orange juice, salt, and butter in the slow cooker. Cover and cook on LOW until the kernels are open and tender, but not mushy, 4½ to 6 hours. Do not remove the lid to check before the rice has cooked for at least 4 hours.

2. Gently stir in the walnuts, chives, and parsley. Serve immediately.

Wild Rice with Coconut and Raisins

M ost coconut rices are made with canned coconut milk added to the cooking water. Here, smoky-rich wild rice is cooked with toasted unsweetened coconut to make a luscious, fresh-tasting rice that goes well with all manner of poultry dishes (it is fantastic with turkey). You want a rice grain that swells to three to four times its raw size and splits slightly down the side to show a gray-white interior. If it splits and curls like a butterfly, it is overcooked, and you should adjust your timing the next time. Use this rice to make a stir-fry with the leftovers the next day, because it is so good. ○ *Serves 10*

COOKER: Medium round
SETTING AND COOK TIME: LOW for 4 to 5 hours

3 tablespoons unsalted butter or coconut oil
⅔ cup shredded unsweetened coconut
2 cups wild rice, rinsed and drained
¾ cup dark raisins
4 cups hot vegetable broth or chicken broth
1 teaspoon salt, or to taste

1. Heat the butter in a small sauté pan over medium heat and add the coconut; cook until just light brown, 10 to 20 seconds only.

2. Place the rice, raisins, broth, and salt in the slow cooker; add the coconut and stir to combine. Cover and cook on LOW for 4 to 5 hours, until the kernels are open and tender, but not mushy. Do not remove the lid to check before the rice has cooked for at least 3½ hours. Turn off the cooker and let the rice stand for 10 minutes, covered, then fluff with a fork. Serve immediately.

Green Chile Grits

T he mild flavor of cornmeal grits is deliciously enhanced when seasoned with chiles. This dish is great served fresh out of the slow cooker alongside grilled chicken or pork. Or you can refrigerate it until firm, pan-fry it, and serve it alongside omelets. ○ *Serves 6 to 8*

COOKER: Medium round
SETTING AND COOK TIME: HIGH for 3 to 3 1/2 hours, or LOW for 7 to 9 hours

2 cups stone-ground cornmeal grits
6 cups water
1/2 teaspoon paprika
1/2 to 1 teaspoon salt
4 ounces canned, chopped, mild green chiles
1 jalapeño chile, seeded and minced
1 pinch cayenne pepper or red chile powder

1. Combine all the ingredients in the slow cooker. Cover and cook on HIGH for 3 to 3½ hours, or LOW for 7 to 9 hours, stirring occasionally. If cooking on HIGH, check for consistency when stirring, adding ¼ to ½ cup boiling water to thin it if it gets too thick.

2. Serve immediately, or refrigerate the mixture in a buttered loaf pan for a few hours or overnight, covered with plastic wrap. Unmold, slice into ½-inch-thick pieces, and fry in butter until browned, turning once.

Double Corn Spoonbread

S poonbread is a soul-satisfying Southern specialty served with savory foods much like mashed potatoes. The cooked cornmeal mush is called "batter bread" as well as spoonbread and may contain cooked rice, hominy, different cheeses, and vegetables, as in this recipe. Scoop this piping hot right out of the cooker onto plates. ○ *Serves 6*

COOKER: Medium round
SETTING AND COOK TIME: HIGH for 3 to 3 1/2 hours

3 cups whole or low-fat milk
1/2 cup medium-ground yellow cornmeal
1 1/4 teaspoons salt
1/4 cup (1/2 stick) unsalted butter, cut into pieces
2 cups fresh yellow or white corn kernels or frozen petit corn, thawed
1 teaspoon hot pepper sauce, such as Tabasco
1 tablespoon baking powder
6 large eggs
1 cup shredded cheddar cheese (about 4 ounces)

1. Place the milk, cornmeal, and salt in a large saucepan. Whisking constantly to prevent lumps, heat to boiling. Reduce the heat to a simmer and cook for 1 minute, until thickened. Stir in the butter until melted, then stir in the corn and hot pepper sauce. Sprinkle with the baking powder and whisk in the eggs until completely smooth. Fold in the cheese.

2. Spray the inside of the crock with a nonstick vegetable cooking spray. Pour in the spoonbread batter. Cover and cook on HIGH for 3 to 3½ hours, until the spoonbread looks set but is not quite firm. Serve immediately.

Arizona Vegetable and Herb Bread Stuffing

Beth's friend of many decades, Johanna Miller, spends her Thanksgiving holidays with friends in Arizona. One year they made this stuffing in the slow cooker, and Johanna was amazed at how delicious it was. This is a very moist stuffing mixture with lots of herbs. ○ *Serves 8 to 10*

COOKER: Large round or oval
SETTINGS AND COOK TIMES: HIGH for 1 hour, then LOW for 4 to 5 hours

¾ cup (1½ sticks) unsalted butter or margarine
2 medium-size yellow onions, chopped
2 cups chopped celery
1 pound fresh white mushrooms, sliced
12½ cups packed stale white bread cubes (about 2 pounds bread)
¼ cup chopped fresh Italian parsley
1½ teaspoons poultry seasoning
1½ teaspoons salt
2 teaspoons crumbled dried sage or 2 tablespoons chopped fresh sage
1 teaspoon crumbled dried thyme or 2 teaspoons chopped fresh thyme
½ teaspoon dried marjoram or savory or 1½ teaspoons chopped fresh marjoram or savory
½ teaspoon freshly ground black pepper
2 to 3 cups chicken or turkey broth, to your taste
2 large eggs, beaten, or ½ cup liquid egg substitute (optional)

1. Melt the butter in a large skillet over medium heat. Liberally brush the inside of the crock with some of the melted butter, then cook the onions, celery, and mushrooms in the skillet until soft, 15 minutes.

2. Place the bread in a large bowl, add the parsley, poultry seasoning, salt, sage, thyme, marjoram, and pepper, and toss to combine. Pour the sautéed vegetables over the bread cubes and mix together.

3. In a large measuring cup, beat together the broth and the eggs, if using. Pour enough broth over the stuffing to moisten it evenly. Pack the stuffing lightly into the slow cooker. Cover and cook on HIGH for 1 hour.

4. Reduce the heat to LOW and cook until puffy and nicely browned around the edges, 4 to 5 hours. The stuffing can sit in the crock, covered, on KEEP WARM for 2 to 3 hours before serving. Serve hot, right out of the crock.

Tips for Good Slow Cooker Stuffings

- A 1-pound loaf of bread will yield about 8 cups of cubed bread, a 1½-pound loaf will yield about 10 cups of cubed bread, and a 2-pound loaf will yield about 12 cups of cubed bread. White bread will give a lighter-texture stuffing than whole wheat or whole grain. You can use anything from French bread to focaccia. Around the holidays, small bakeries will often bag their day-old bread, in delightful combinations, for use in stuffings; keep an eye out for them. If you use cornbread, make it the day before and leave it out. You can use packaged stuffing mix, if desired.

- Don't use fresh bread in these recipes, because it doesn't soak up enough liquid. You can use fresh bread cubed and dried in the oven, day-old bread cut into cubes and air-dried overnight, or a package of seasoned commercial stuffing mix. If you are using really stale bread, you need to soak it in chicken broth or milk to soften it a bit.

- Never use raw meats, especially pork products or oysters, in stuffings. Loose pork sausage or any type of raw sausage must be cooked completely, whether sautéed, baked, boiled, or grilled, before adding it to the stuffing mix.

- Adding leafy vegetables, such as Swiss chard or parsley, lightens the texture of a stuffing.

- We give a guideline for the amount of liquid needed to moisten the recipes, but you can add more or less, depending on how moist or crumbly you like your stuffing.

- Spoon the stuffing loosely into the crock, rather than packing it in, to allow room for the stuffing to expand as it heats up.

- You will serve about ½ to 1 cup of prepared stuffing per person. Take into account your love of leftovers when deciding how much to make.

- Let unused portions come to room temperature, then transfer to an airtight storage container and refrigerate for up to 3 days.

Mushroom-Chard Whole Wheat Bread Stuffing

This stuffing can be served alongside your holiday turkey, or as an extravagantly delicious, nutritious main dish. In fact, it was created to be just that, by Julie's brother-in-law, a vegetarian, one Thanksgiving several years ago. If you use fresh shiitake mushrooms, you'll find that their flavor is subtler than the dried ones. ○ *Serves 8 to 10*

COOKER: Large round or oval
SETTING AND COOK TIME: LOW for 5 to 6 hours

6 medium-size dried or fresh shiitake mushrooms
2 tablespoons olive oil
2 tablespoons unsalted butter
2 large onions, coarsely chopped
2 cups celery, coarsely chopped
½ pound cremini or white mushrooms, thinly sliced
¾ teaspoon ground cumin
¾ teaspoon ground coriander
Pinch of ground cloves
1 teaspoon salt
¼ teaspoon freshly ground black pepper
1 pound stale whole wheat bread, cut into ½-inch cubes (crusts included)
6 ounces pecans, coarsely chopped and toasted in a 350°F oven until fragrant
4 ounces hazelnuts, crushed or chopped and toasted in a 350°F oven until fragrant
1 bunch red Swiss chard, stems included, blanched in boiling water for 1 minute, leaves sliced into ½-inch-wide ribbons and stems coarsely chopped
1 to 2 cups vegetable broth, to your taste

1. If you are using dried shiitake mushrooms, place them in a small bowl and add hot tap water just to cover. Allow them to soak until softened, about 1 hour. Alternatively, place them in a small microwave-safe container, add water just to cover, and cover tightly with plastic wrap; microwave on HIGH for 2 minutes. Allow to cool until you can handle them; drain. Whether using fresh or dried mushrooms, discard the stems and slice the caps thinly.

2. In a large nonstick skillet, heat the oil and butter together over medium-high heat. When the butter has melted, add the onions and celery and cook, stirring occasionally, until translucent, 7 to 10 minutes. Add the cremini and shiitake mushrooms and stir for a minute or two. Add the cumin, coriander, cloves, salt, and pepper and cook, stirring, until the mushrooms are a bit browned, about 5 minutes. Remove from the heat.

3. Place the bread cubes in a large bowl. Add the pecans, hazelnuts, and Swiss chard and toss to combine. Add the mushroom mixture and mix well. Add about 1 cup of the broth and toss to coat evenly. Add more broth as needed until all of the bread is very lightly moistened throughout. Taste and adjust the seasonings, if needed.

4. Coat the inside of the crock with oil, butter, or nonstick cooking spray. Pack the stuffing lightly into the slow cooker. Cover and cook on LOW until puffy and brown around the edges, 5 to 6 hours. The stuffing can sit in the crock, covered, on KEEP WARM for 2 to 3 hours before serving. Serve hot, right out of the crock.

Thanksgiving Sausage Bread Pudding

(T) his is our moistest stuffing, and it conveniently uses prepackaged stuffing mix, just in case that is what you are in the mood for. It should be eaten within a half hour of being done because of the sausage mixture. ● *Serves 8*

COOKER: Medium oval or large round
SETTINGS AND COOK TIMES: HIGH for 1 hour, then LOW for 4 to 5 hours

½ **pound mild pork sausage, casings removed**
3 **tablespoons unsalted butter or margarine**
1 **medium-size yellow onion, chopped**
2 **cups chopped celery, including leaves**
1 **large bell pepper of any color, seeded and chopped**
4 **ounces baby bok choy, sliced into ½-inch-thick ribbons**
½ **cup chopped zucchini**
½ **pound fresh mushrooms, sliced**
One 8-**ounce package dry herb stuffing mix (4 cups)**
1 **cup chopped fresh Italian parsley**

1 teaspoon poultry seasoning

½ teaspoon salt

¼ teaspoon freshly ground black or white pepper

Pinch of cayenne pepper or New Mexican red chile powder

1 cup condensed beef consommé

½ cup Madeira

4 large eggs, beaten, or 1 cup liquid egg substitute

1. Coat the inside of the crock with butter, oil, or nonstick cooking spray. In a large skillet over medium heat, crumble the sausage and cook until browned and cooked through. Remove to a large bowl. Melt the butter in the same skillet, then cook the onion, celery, bell pepper, bok choy, zucchini, and mushrooms, stirring occasionally, until soft, about 15 minutes.

2. Add the stuffing mix to the sausage in the bowl, along with the parsley, poultry seasoning, salt, pepper, and cayenne; toss to combine. Pour the sautéed vegetables over the stuffing mix and mix together.

3. In a large measuring cup, beat the consommé, Madeira, and eggs together. Pour over the bread and mix to moisten evenly. Pack the stuffing lightly into the slow cooker. Cover and cook on HIGH for 1 hour.

4. Reduce the heat to LOW and cook until puffy and nicely browned around the edges, 4 to 5 hours. The stuffing can sit in the crock, covered, on KEEP WARM for ½ hour before serving. Serve hot, right out of the crock.

Cornbread Stuffing with Bacon, Chestnuts, and Dried Cherries

T his recipe is adapted from one that appeared in a Williams-Sonoma Christmas mail-order catalog. Chestnuts appear around Christmas and are a favorite starchy nut to add to stuffings. Use canned or jarred peeled and steamed chestnuts; they are convenient and delicious. ● *Serves 8 to 10*

COOKER: Medium round or oval
SETTINGS AND COOK TIMES: HIGH for 1 hour, then LOW for 4 to 5 hours

8 to 10 cups crumbled cornbread or three 7-ounce packages
    commercial cornbread stuffing mix
2 tablespoons olive oil
8 strips pork or turkey bacon, chopped
2 medium-size yellow onions, chopped
2 ribs celery, chopped
1 large carrot or parsnip, chopped
¼ cup chopped fresh Italian parsley
2 tablespoons chopped fresh sage
1 teaspoon poultry seasoning
Salt and freshly ground black or white pepper to taste
One 14- to 16-ounce can or jar whole chestnuts, drained
1 heaping cup dried sweet or tart cherries
3 cups chicken or turkey broth
1 large egg, beaten, or ¼ cup liquid egg substitute (optional)

1. Preheat the oven to 350°F. If using fresh cornbread, place the crumbled cornbread on a baking sheet and dry in the oven for 15 to 20 minutes. Set aside in a large bowl.

2. Heat the oil in a large skillet over medium heat and cook the bacon, stirring, until crisp; transfer to paper towels to drain. Add the onions, celery, and carrot to the skillet and cook, stirring a few times, until softened, about 5 minutes. Add the parsley, sage, and poultry seasoning, season with salt and pepper, and toss to combine. Pour the sautéed vegetables, bacon, chestnuts, and cherries over the cornbread and mix together.

3. In a large measuring cup, beat together the broth and the egg, if using. Pour in enough broth to moisten the cornbread mixture evenly. Pack the stuffing lightly into the slow cooker. Cover and cook on HIGH for 1 hour.

4. Reduce the heat to LOW and cook until puffy and nicely browned around the edges, 4 to 5 hours. The stuffing can sit in the crock, covered, on KEEP WARM for 2 to 3 hours before serving. Serve hot, right out of the crock.

Prosciutto, Parmesan, and Pine Nut Holiday Stuffing

H ere is a wonderful twist on traditional stuffing. Look for attractive, medium-size leeks, usually sold in a bunch of three. This is a recipe loosely adapted from one in Lunds and Byerly's supermarket FoodE Recipe Binder, their in-house collection of fabulous recipes. ○ *Serves 8 to 10*

COOKER: Medium round or oval
SETTINGS AND COOK TIMES: HIGH for 1 hour, then LOW for 4 to 5 hours

6 tablespoons (¾ stick) unsalted butter
3 medium-size leeks, halved, rinsed, and white parts sliced crosswise
2 ribs celery with leaves, chopped
Two 8-ounce packages herb stuffing mix
1¾ cups grated Parmesan cheese
¼ cup chopped fresh flat-leaf parsley
1½ tablespoons chopped fresh sage
4 ounces finely sliced prosciutto, coarsely chopped
½ cup pine nuts, toasted in a dry skillet until golden
1 cup dried cranberries
Two 14.5-ounce cans chicken broth
1 large egg (optional), beaten

1. Heat the butter in a medium-size skillet over medium heat and cook the leeks and celery until soft, about 5 minutes.

2. In a large bowl, combine the stuffing mix, Parmesan, parsley, sage, prosciutto, pine nuts, and cranberries. Add the cooked leeks and celery.

3. In a large measuring cup, beat together the broth and egg, if using. Pour enough broth into the bowl to moisten the bread mixture evenly. Pack the stuffing lightly into the slow cooker. Cover and cook on HIGH for 1 hour.

4. Reduce the heat to LOW and cook until puffy and nicely brown around the edges, 4 to 5 hours. The stuffing can sit in the crock, covered, on KEEP WARM for 2 to 3 hours before serving. Serve hot right out of the crock.

Not from the Slow Cooker Accompaniments

Basmati Rice o 188

Jasmine Rice o 189

Calrose Rice o 189

Short-Grain Brown Rice o 190

Saffron Rice o 190

Pullao with Indian Spices o 191

Victoria's Armenian Rice and Vermicelli Pilaf o 191

Orange Rice o 192

Basic Wild Rice o 193

Couscous o 193

Basic Bulgur o 194

Gorgonzola Polenta o 194

Slow Cooker Cornmeal Dumplings o 195

Gnocchi alla Romana o 196

Spaetzle o 197

German Potato Dumplings o 198

Matzo Balls o 199

Oven-Roasted Potatoes o 200

Oven-Roasted Spaghetti Squash o 200

Caesar Salad o 201

Salad of Greens with Goat Cheese o 203

While the slow cooker is bubbling away all day with the entrée, usually all you will need to do as host is plan a salad or vegetable and a starchy side dish to accompany the one-pot meal, and a feast is born. Here are a few of our very favorite simple side dishes, all made using conventional methods, such as the oven or stovetop. We have also included a sampling of dumplings, which are always a nice extra touch for hearty old-fashioned stews.

Basmati Rice

Basmati—rich tasting, aromatic, and flavorful—is the queen of rices. It is sold under many brand names. Look for Tilda, Pari, and Dehra Dun, all of which note on the label that they have been aged. Basmati must be rinsed thoroughly to clean off the collected debris from packaging and processing. This rice is good with poultry, beef, lamb, or vegetable stews. ○ *Serves 6 to 8*

> 2 cups white basmati rice, rinsed until the water runs clear
> 4 cups cold water
> Pinch of salt
> 2 teaspoons to 2 tablespoons unsalted butter, to your taste
> 2 teaspoons freshly squeezed lime juice (optional)

1. Place the drained rice and cold water in a medium-size heavy saucepan and let it soak for 10 to 15 minutes.

2. Bring the water and rice to a rolling boil, uncovered, over high heat. Add the salt, butter, and lime juice, if using. Stir and reduce the heat to low. Cover and cook for 15 to 20 minutes, until all the liquid is absorbed.

3. Remove the covered pan from the heat and let stand for 10 minutes without removing the lid. Remove the lid and fluff the rice gently with a fork. Serve hot.

Jasmine Rice

 This rice can also be cooked in a rice cooker using these same proportions. ◦ *Serves 6 to 8*

2 cups jasmine rice, rinsed until the water runs clear
3 cups cold water

1. Place the drained rice and cold water in a large, heavy saucepan. Bring the water and rice to a rolling boil, uncovered, over high heat. Stir and reduce the heat to low. Cover the pan tightly and cook for 20 minutes, until all the liquid is absorbed.

2. Remove the covered pan from the heat and let stand for 10 minutes without removing the lid. Remove the lid and fluff the rice gently with a fork. Serve hot.

Calrose Rice

Calrose is the trade name for California-grown, medium-grain white rice. It is also known as Japanese-style rice, because it is a bit sticky and the type of rice served with Japanese cuisine, perfect for balancing on chopsticks. In terms of having a bland, clean taste, this rice is one of the best in the world. It is a delicious simple side dish with butter and salt. Although Calrose rice is inexpensive, some premium brands of Japanese-style rice that we also love include Nishiki and Tamaki Gold. ◦ *Serves 6 to 8*

2 cups white medium-grain rice, rinsed until the water runs clear
3 cups cold water
½ teaspoon salt

1. Place the drained rice, cold water, and salt in a large, heavy saucepan. Bring the water and rice to a rolling boil, uncovered, over high heat. Stir and reduce the heat to low. Cover the pan tightly and cook for 20 minutes, until all the liquid is absorbed and the rice is tender.

2. Remove the covered pan from the heat and let stand for 5 minutes without removing the lid. Remove the lid and fluff the rice gently with a fork. Serve hot.

Short-Grain Brown Rice

Beth learned to make this brown rice from her friend Andrew Whitfield. Up to that time, it seemed never to cook right for her. The secret? Never lift the lid to peek. These are the proportions to use when preparing Wehani red rice as well. ● *Serves 6 to 8*

3¾ cups water
2 cups short-grain brown rice

In a medium-size heavy saucepan, bring the water to a rolling boil over high heat. Add the brown rice and return to a rolling boil. Cover tightly, reduce the heat to the lowest setting, and simmer for exactly 1 hour, taking care not to lift the lid before that time, until the rice is tender and all the liquid has been absorbed. Serve immediately.

Saffron Rice

Saffron rice is so delicate and versatile that it goes with just about every stew, curry, and roast we make. ● *Serves 6 to 8*

4 cups chicken broth
2 cups long-grain white rice or basmati rice, rinsed until the water runs clear
Pinch of salt (optional)
2 tablespoons unsalted butter
Pinch of saffron threads or ¼ teaspoon ground turmeric

1. Bring the broth to a boil in a medium-size heavy saucepan. Add the rice, the salt, if using, the butter, and the saffron. Stir. Reduce the heat to the lowest setting, cover tightly, and simmer until all the liquid is absorbed, 20 to 25 minutes.

2. Remove from the heat and let stand for 10 minutes, covered. Serve hot.

Pullao with Indian Spices

 Serve this unique and subtly flavored rice with meat and vegetable curries. ◦ *Serves 6*

¼ cup (½ stick) unsalted butter
One 3-inch cinnamon stick
5 green cardamom pods
1½ cups basmati rice, rinsed until the water runs clear
½ teaspoon salt
3 cups water
⅓ cup unsalted dry-roasted cashews (optional), coarsely chopped

1. Melt the butter in a medium-size heavy saucepan over medium heat. Add the cinnamon, cardamom, and rice and cook, stirring, for a few minutes to heat through and coat with the butter. Add the salt and water and bring to a rolling boil over high heat. Reduce the heat to low, cover, and simmer until all the water is absorbed and the rice grains are separate, 20 to 25 minutes.

2. Remove from the heat and let stand for 10 minutes, covered. Stir in the cashews, if using. Serve immediately.

Victoria's Armenian Rice and Vermicelli Pilaf

This is a basic pilaf of rice with vermicelli noodles from food writer Victoria Wise's family. It's a dish she remembers from when she was a child growing up in the Sacramento area. Other than the simple flourishes of pepper and a pat or two of butter at the end, no trimmings are necessary. ◦ *Serves 8 to 12*

3 tablespoons unsalted butter, plus 2 to 3 pats to finish the dish
1 cup broken-up vermicelli, fine egg noodles, or fideos nests
2 cups long-grain white rice
5 cups water
Freshly ground black pepper to taste

1. Melt the 3 tablespoons butter in a medium-size heavy saucepan over medium-high heat. Add the vermicelli and stir until it begins to turn golden, about 1½ minutes. Add the rice and continue to stir until well coated and translucent, about 2 minutes. Add the water and bring to a boil. Reduce the heat to low, cover, and simmer without lifting the lid for 20 minutes, at which point the rice should be cooked through.

2. Sprinkle pepper over the rice and place 2 or 3 pats of butter on top. Cover and set aside, off the heat, for 10 to 30 minutes.

3. When ready to eat, use two forks to fluff the rice and mix in the pepper and butter. Serve immediately.

Orange Rice

 erve this with chicken dishes, rabbit, or vegetable curry. If using the basmati rice, use only 1 cup of water. ○ *Serves 4 to 6*

3 tablespoons unsalted butter
¾ cup diced celery
1 small white boiling onion, minced
1¼ cups water
¾ cup freshly squeezed orange juice
Grated zest of 1 small orange
Pinch of salt
Pinch of dried thyme
1 cup long-grain white or basmati rice, rinsed until the water runs clear

1. Melt the butter in a medium-size heavy saucepan over medium heat. Add the celery and onion and cook, stirring, for a few minutes to soften. Add the water, orange juice, orange zest, salt, thyme, and rice. Bring to a rolling boil over high heat. Reduce the heat to low, cover, and simmer until all the water is absorbed and the rice grains are separate, 20 to 25 minutes.

2. Let stand for 10 minutes, covered, then serve hot.

Basic Wild Rice

Serve this nutty, chewy grain with your favorite poultry dishes. ○ *Serves 6*

2½ cups water, vegetable broth, or chicken broth
1 cup wild rice, rinsed until the water runs clear
½ to 1 teaspoon salt, to your taste

Bring the water to a rolling boil in a medium-size heavy saucepan. Add the wild rice and salt and return to a boil, uncovered, then cover, reduce the heat to low, and simmer until all the water is absorbed and the rice grains are separate, about 45 minutes. Fluff with a fork and serve hot.

Couscous

Couscous is the Moroccan version of pasta, made from finely sieved semolina. Serve this with lamb tagine or vegetable or chicken stews.

○ *Serves 6 to 8*

2 cups water, vegetable broth, or chicken broth
6 tablespoons (¾ stick) unsalted butter or ¼ cup olive oil or sesame oil
½ teaspoon salt
2 cups couscous

1. Bring the water, butter, and salt to a rolling boil in a medium-size saucepan. Pour in the couscous and quickly stir to prevent lumping.

2. Cover, remove from the heat, and let stand until all the liquid is absorbed, about 10 minutes. Fluff with a fork before serving.

Basic Bulgur

Bulgur is simply cracked wheat, and it cooks up into one of the most delicious and satisfying starchy side dishes to serve with your stews and ragoûts. Serve it just like you would brown rice. ○ *Serves 6 to 8*

¼ cup (½ stick) unsalted butter
2 cups bulgur wheat
4 cups water, vegetable broth, or chicken broth
Pinch of salt

1. In a medium-size heavy saucepan, melt the butter over medium heat. Add the bulgur and stir for a few minutes to heat and coat with the butter.

2. Add the water and salt and bring to a boil. Cover, reduce the heat to medium-low, and simmer until all the water is absorbed and the grains are separate, about 15 minutes. Fluff with a fork before serving.

Gorgonzola Polenta

Here is a delicious polenta, enriched with two cheeses, to serve alongside your stews. ○ *Serves 4 to 8*

4 cups water, chicken broth, or vegetable broth
1 cup coarse cornmeal
¼ cup freshly grated Parmesan or Pecorino Romano cheese
2 tablespoons chopped fresh Italian parsley
Salt and freshly ground black pepper to taste
4 ounces Gorgonzola cheese (preferably Gorgonzola dolce), cut into serving-size cubes

1. In a large, heavy saucepan, bring the water to a boil. Stir in the cornmeal slowly, to prevent lumps. Reduce the heat to low and, with a wooden spoon, stir regularly to prevent the polenta from burning. Continue to stir and cook until the polenta is tender but still has a little texture, 10 to 15 minutes.

2. Stir in the Parmesan and parsley and season with salt and pepper. If it is too thick, stir in a little more broth. Spoon the polenta into large, shallow bowls and make a well in the center. Place a portion of Gorgonzola in the center of each and serve hot.

Slow Cooker Cornmeal Dumplings

Since cornmeal contains no gluten-forming proteins to hold it together, it is mixed here with some regular flour. You can use either stone-ground cornmeal or the degerminated kind you'll find in supermarkets. These are great with poultry stews. ○ *Serves 6*

1 cup all-purpose flour
½ cup fine- or medium-grind yellow or white cornmeal, or masa harina
1½ teaspoons baking powder
½ teaspoon salt
3 tablespoons margarine or solid vegetable shortening
1 large egg
½ to ⅔ cup cold whole milk, as needed

1. In a medium-size bowl, combine the flour, cornmeal, baking powder, and salt. Cut in the margarine with a fork until the mixture is crumbly. Stir in the egg and ½ cup of the milk and blend until a lumpy, thick, soft dough forms, adding the remaining milk if necessary. Do not overmix.

2. Using an oversized spoon, scoop out some dough and drop immediately on top of the finished simmering stew in the slow cooker, taking care to place the dumplings on top of something solid rather than directly into the liquid, so that they can steam nicely. Cover and cook on HIGH until the dumplings are cooked through, 25 to 30 minutes. Pierce the dumplings with a toothpick, bamboo skewer, or metal cake tester; it should come out clean. Serve immediately.

Dumplings

Large or small, shaped into balls, disks, or sausages, dumplings go into finished soups or stews to steam, or into a pot of boiling water to be cooked. They are then eaten as a dinner side or as a main dish, like noodles, with butter or gravy. Some of the dumpling recipes on these pages are designed to be cooked on top of the finished stew in your slow cooker; others need to be cooked on the stovetop or in the oven.

Gnocchi alla Romana

G nocchi (pronounced NYOH-kee), a substantial and filling comfort food, can be made from flour, semolina, or potatoes. Gnocchi are teardrop shaped if formed by hand or a flat round shape if cut out with a biscuit cutter. They are at their simple best when served with butter and grated Parmesan cheese but are also exquisite with veal or beef stews. Try to find semolina that looks like finely ground cornmeal. ○ *Serves 6*

3 cups whole milk

⅔ cup semolina flour

½ teaspoon salt

2 tablespoons unsalted butter

1 large egg

1¼ cups freshly grated Parmesan cheese

2 tablespoons unsalted butter, melted, mixed with
   2 tablespoons olive oil, for drizzling

1. Grease a large baking sheet with a 1-inch rim with olive oil.

2. Combine the milk, semolina, and salt in a large, heavy saucepan. Bring to a boil and stir with a whisk to prevent lumps. Reduce the heat to medium-low and simmer, stirring constantly, until thick, 5 to 8 minutes, switching to a wooden spoon when the whisk becomes clogged.

3. Remove from the heat and immediately beat the butter, egg, and ⅔ cup of the Parmesan into the hot mixture. With a large spatula, spread the gnocchi onto the prepared baking sheet in an even ½- to ¾-inch-thick layer. Refrigerate, uncovered, until firm, at least 1 hour. If keeping longer, cover with plastic wrap.

4. Preheat the oven to 400°F. Butter a shallow 9 × 13-inch baking dish.

5. Using a 2-inch round biscuit cutter, cut out rounds close together to keep scraps to a minimum. Arrange the rounds in overlapping rows in the prepared baking dish. Drizzle with the butter–olive oil mixture and sprinkle with the remaining Parmesan. Bake in the center of the oven until brown and heated through, 20 to 30 minutes. Serve hot.

Spaetzle

S oft spaetzle (which means "little sparrows") dumplings are served as a side dish like noodles or rice and are delicious with beef, veal, or pork stews. This is a real peasant food, served from Alsace to Hungary and southern Germany. If you love these, invest in a spaetzle maker, which looks like a hand grater. Using one is much easier than cutting them by hand. ○ *Serves 6*

3 cups all-purpose flour

1 teaspoon salt

3 large eggs

⅔ to 1 cup cold whole or low-fat milk or water, as needed

3 tablespoons unsalted butter

2 tablespoons light sour cream

1. In a large bowl, combine the flour and salt. Make a well and add the eggs and milk to the center. Blend well with a wooden spoon until evenly moistened; the dough will be very thick and moist. If you use ⅔ cup milk, you will have a firm dough; if you use a bit more, it will be softer. Cover with plastic wrap and let rest at room temperature for 30 to 45 minutes.

2. Preheat the oven to 350°F.

3. In a large stockpot, bring a generous amount of salted water to a rapid boil. If using a spaetzle maker, place it over the boiling water; it will rest on the rim of the pot. Place the dough into the hopper and slide the carriage back and forth, dropping pear-shaped bits of dough into the water. If shaping the spaetzle by hand, place the dough on a wet cutting board and rest it, carefully, on the rim of the pot. Using a damp paring knife or soup spoon, cut off little irregular portions the width of a pencil and about ½ inch long at the edge of the board and let them fall into the boiling water.

4. Simmer, uncovered, until the spaetzle float back up to the surface, 1 to 2 minutes. Remove with a fine-mesh strainer or slotted spoon, shake off the excess water, and place in a shallow casserole.

5. Toss with the butter and sour cream to keep them from sticking together. Bake for 8 to 10 minutes. Serve immediately. Or you may cover and refrigerate for up to 8 hours; reheat for 12 to 15 minutes before serving.

German Potato Dumplings

P otato dumplings are the largest in the dumpling family, usually the size of a woman's fist. Potato dumplings are good with all types of roasted meats and game sauced with rich gravies, as well as beef stews, wurst, and sauerkraut. Plan on serving 1 to 2 per person; they will be devoured. ○ *Serves 8 to 10*

2½ pounds russet potatoes, unpeeled
9 ounces potato flour (not potato starch flour) or
    1 to 1¼ cups unbleached all-purpose flour
1 large egg, lightly beaten
1 teaspoon salt
1 very small white boiling onion, finely minced
¼ cup (½ stick) unsalted butter
1 cup dry bread crumbs
Chopped fresh Italian parsley for garnish

1. Place the potatoes in a large, deep saucepan and cover with cold water. Bring to a boil, reduce to a rolling simmer, and cook until tender when pierced with a knife, 30 to 40 minutes. Drain and let cool to room temperature (you can reserve the potato liquid for use in bread or the dumplings; it will keep for a day refrigerated). Slit the skins open on each potato. Refrigerate the potatoes, covered, overnight.

2. Bring a large deep saucepan filled with salted water to a rolling boil over high heat. Flour a baking sheet. Preheat the oven to the lowest setting and place a large shallow baking dish in it to warm.

3. Peel the potatoes. Rice or grate the potatoes into a large bowl. Add the potato flour or 1 cup of the all-purpose flour, the egg, salt, and onion. Knead the mixture to form a soft dough ball that is just past sticky, adding 1 tablespoon or so more flour, if necessary. Pull off pieces of dough and make 4-inch balls (a heaping ¼ cup, about the size of a tennis ball); place on the prepared baking sheet for transporting to the stove. You will make about 14 dumplings.

4. With a slotted spoon, slip the dumplings into the boiling water. Keeping the water at a gentle rolling boil, simmer the dumplings, uncovered. The dumplings will sink, then float; cook for 3 to 4 minutes after they come to the surface. They will be compact looking and firm in the center. Remove with a slotted spoon to drain, then place in the warmed baking dish. Cover by tenting with aluminum foil.

5. In a small skillet, melt the butter over medium heat. Add the bread crumbs and quickly brown, stirring. Sprinkle the mixture over the dumplings and roll them to coat. Sprinkle with the parsley. Keep warm in a low oven for up to 2 hours before serving. If there are any leftovers, reheat the next day in the microwave.

Matzo Balls

What is real chicken soup without matzo balls, also known as knaidlach, made from matzo meal? Whip up a batch of these and add them to your simple chicken or vegetable soups. If you do not keep kosher—and are not cooking for someone who is—feel free to use butter instead of margarine or another fat.

○ *Serves 4 to 6*

3 tablespoons rendered chicken fat; unsalted margarine,
    melted and cooled; or vegetable oil
3 large eggs, slightly beaten
¾ cup matzo meal
1 teaspoon salt
1 tablespoon finely minced fresh Italian parsley (optional)

1. In a medium-size bowl, combine the chicken fat and eggs. Add the matzo meal, salt, and parsley, if using. Blend well with a fork until evenly moistened. Cover with plastic wrap and refrigerate for 1 hour.

2. In a large stockpot, bring a generous amount of salted water to a rapid boil. Divide the dough into 10 equal portions. Shape into balls by rolling the dough with your hands, using some water to moisten them, if necessary. Drop them into the boiling water, reduce the heat to medium-low, cover, and simmer for 45 minutes. Remove with a slotted spoon and place in the soup. If necessary, you can place the cooked matzo balls in a single layer in a covered container and refrigerate for up to 24 hours before adding them to the soup.

Oven-Roasted Potatoes

While we have nice potato recipes made in the slow cooker elsewhere in this book, if your cooker is bubbling away with a stew or roast and you want to serve it with potatoes, these can be prepared quickly in the oven. ❍ *Serves 6*

1½ pounds small red or white potatoes, cut in half or quartered

¼ cup olive oil

1 teaspoon salt

Freshly ground black pepper to taste

1 to 2 tablespoons chopped fresh herbs, such as thyme, savory,
    marjoram, or rosemary, to your taste

1. Preheat the oven to 450°F.

2. On a sheet pan or in a shallow gratin dish, toss the potatoes with the oil, salt, pepper, and herbs. Roast until browned, about 30 minutes, turning over with a metal spatula once or twice during the roasting for even browning. Serve hot.

Oven-Roasted Spaghetti Squash

Spaghetti squash looks like pasta, but it is most emphatically a vegetable. It is a fabulous accompaniment to all manner of beef, turkey, and game stews. ❍ *Serves 6 to 8*

One 2- to 3-pound spaghetti squash

¼ cup (½ stick) unsalted butter, softened

¼ cup honey (optional)

Salt and freshly ground black pepper to taste

1. Preheat the oven to 350°F.

2. Cut the squash in half lengthwise and scoop out the seeds. Butter the cavities, drizzle with the honey, if using, and season with salt and pepper. Place on a baking sheet and cover loosely with aluminum foil. Bake in the center of the oven until the squash is tender, about 45 minutes.

3. Remove from the oven and pull out the flesh with a fork. It will look like long strands of spaghetti. Serve hot in a mound alongside your stew.

Caesar Salad

C aesar salad is a premier salad for company. The original Caesar salad was created by Italian chef and restaurateur Caesar Cardini in Tijuana, Baja California, in the 1920s. It took Hollywood diners by storm and has been a mainstay in restaurants and on dinner tables ever since. Although lots of people have an aversion to anchovies, when this dressing is made properly, you never know they're there (use within a day for the subtlest flavor). You can rub the salad bowl with garlic, but we prefer it in the dressing. We also like this version because there is no raw egg in the dressing (the original version had the egg gently coddled before tossing it with the greens tableside). When you garnish this famous salad with your own croutons, it further boosts the already incredible flavor. ○ *Serves 6*

12 cups torn romaine lettuce
Four ¾-inch-thick slices French or sourdough bread
Melted butter or olive oil for drizzling
2 to 3 cloves garlic, crushed

CAESAR DRESSING:
2 cloves garlic
One 2-ounce can flat anchovy fillets in olive oil
3 tablespoons freshly squeezed lemon juice
1 teaspoon Dijon mustard
½ cup extra-virgin olive oil
¼ cup grated Parmesan cheese

Freshly ground black pepper to taste
One 4-ounce block Parmesan cheese, for shaving

1. Place the romaine lettuce in a large salad bowl. Cover and refrigerate until ready to serve.

2. Preheat the oven to 375°F.

3. Cut the sliced bread into large cubes; you will have 3 to 4 cups. Place on an ungreased baking sheet. Drizzle the bread cubes with melted butter and bake for 15 to 20 minutes, stirring about every 5 minutes to keep from burning. Remove from the oven when just golden and drizzle with more melted butter. Toss the croutons with the crushed garlic while they are hot. Set aside to cool to room temperature.

4. To make the dressing, in the work bowl of a food processor, drop the garlic through the feed tube with the motor running to chop. Stop the machine and add the anchovies. Process until smooth. Add the lemon juice and mustard. Add the olive oil through the feed tube, drizzling it in and processing the mixture until just thick. Add the grated Parmesan cheese, pulsing a few times to blend. Transfer to a covered container and refrigerate until ready to serve.

5. Bring to the table the bowl of greens, the dressing, the croutons, a pepper mill, the block of Parmesan, and a cheese slicer. Grind the pepper over the greens, then toss with the dressing, coating all the leaves. Add the croutons and toss to distribute. Serve at once, covering the top of each salad with some shaved Parmesan.

•• To Serve with Your Slow-Cooked Meals: Salads ••

With many of our recipes, we give serving suggestions. But often, since the meal is an all-in-one-pot wonder, all that you need in addition is a bit of bread and a nice green salad. Well, we know how easy it is to get into a rut and make the same salad and the same dressing all the time. The salads and dressings on pages 201 to 208 will help you break out of the salad doldrums.

There are two distinctly different types of salads for entertaining. One is a plated dinner salad, either a simple mixture of tossed greens or a more elaborate composed salad, either of which you have portioned out in the kitchen before serving. The other is a buffet salad served in a large bowl or from a large platter with enough to serve the entire party, each person helping him- or herself. In either case, freshly washed greens and herbs and refreshing, but more substantial foods such as cucumbers, root vegetables, and tomatoes all come into play.

Salad of Greens with Goat Cheese

Once upon a time, an architecture student ate at a small, local hangout and helped in the kitchen one day when the staff was shorthanded. He ended up working in the kitchen, helped owner Alice Waters create a legendary food scene, and, in the process, became a chef. The man is Jeremiah Tower, one of the most lauded chefs on the West Coast of the past three decades, and the restaurant was Chez Panisse in Berkeley, California. Before he owned his own restaurants, Tower taught cooking classes in San Francisco. This salad is one of his most famous creations and the signature plated salad of a new generation of foodies, made with a domestic cheese (little known at the time) called chèvre, from Laura Chenel in Marin County. The salad we share here comes from a faded recipe on his letterhead from one of those classes long ago. This composed salad has had many transmutations through its popular life, but this is the original, and it is as fabulous and fresh as it was on the day it was created. ❍ *Serves 8*

VINAIGRETTE:
1 cup olive oil or walnut oil
¼ cup champagne vinegar
Salt and freshly ground black pepper to taste

CROUTONS:
Eight ½-inch-thick slices French bread,
    each piece cut in half on the diagonal
4 cloves garlic

CHEESE ROUNDS:
1 cup olive oil
1 cup coarse fresh bread crumbs
Eight 1-ounce rounds firm Crottin goat cheese, or 2 logs
    Montrachet cheese, each log cut into 8 rounds

SALAD:
10 to 12 heaping cups mixed salad greens (such as endive,
    chicory, sorrel, baby dandelion, watercress, arugula,
    celery leaves, baby hearts of romaine)

1. To make the dressing, in a small bowl, combine the oil, vinegar, salt, and pepper. Set aside.

2. To make the croutons, rub the slices of bread with the whole cloves of garlic on both sides; discard the garlic. Set aside.

3. To make the cheese rounds, pour ¾ cup of the olive oil into a small, shallow dish. Place the bread crumbs on a plate. Dip the rounds of cheese first into the oil, then into the bread crumbs, coating both sides. Heat the remaining ¼ cup olive oil in a medium-size skillet over medium heat. Place the coated rounds of cheese in a single layer in the skillet and cook until golden on the bottom; carefully turn with a metal spatula to brown the other side, 1 to 2 minutes. Remove to a plate.

4. To prepare the salad, place the greens in a large bowl and toss with the dressing. Divide among 8 salad plates. Place a warm cheese round (or 2, if using Montrachet) in the center of each plate of greens. Quickly place the bread slices in the hot oil remaining in the skillet and brown them on both sides. Tuck 2 croutons onto each plate of salad. Serve immediately.

·· About Salad Dressings ··

Finding new recipes for salad dressings has got to be one of the most difficult tasks in the food world; you have to notice one in a food magazine or have a great one at someone's house. So here we give a little extra to our readers: our favorite tried-and-true salad dressings to pour over your simple pile of greens. Beth originally compiled these as a gift for her catering clients who loved all the different dressings and vinaigrettes she served. These homemade dressings will last for 5 to 7 days in the refrigerator in a covered container.

Vinaigrettes are basically a combination of oil and vinegar. To make any of the vinaigrettes here, place your vinegar and any other flavor ingredients in a small bowl. In a slow, steady stream, add the oil, using a wire whisk to beat until the mixture is combined. Use immediately, let stand at room temperature for up to 2 hours to blend the flavors, or refrigerate for up to 1 week. You can also mix vinaigrettes with an immersion blender or food processor, or just simply shake them together in a screw-top jar.

Lemon-Chive Vinaigrette

This is a delight on seasonal greens. ❍ Makes about ²/₃ cup

2 to 4 tablespoons freshly squeezed lemon juice, such as Eureka or Meyer, to your taste
1 tablespoon minced fresh chives
1 teaspoon Dijon mustard (optional)
½ cup olive oil
Salt and freshly ground black or white pepper to taste

In a small bowl, combine the lemon juice, chives, and mustard. Slowly drizzle in the olive oil, whisking to combine thoroughly. Add salt and pepper.

Walnut Vinaigrette

This is good on a salad of Bibb lettuce, watercress, shredded Swiss cheese, and toasted walnuts. ❍ Makes about ³/₄ cup

2 tablespoons red wine vinegar
2 tablespoons red wine or port
½ cup walnut oil
Salt and freshly ground black or white pepper to taste

In a small bowl, mix the vinegar and red wine. Slowly drizzle in the walnut oil, whisking to combine thoroughly. Add salt and pepper.

Shallot Vinaigrette

This is very nice drizzled on rice, bean, and pasta salads. ○ Makes about 1 cup

⅓ cup white wine vinegar or champagne vinegar
¼ cup Dijon mustard
1 shallot, minced
¾ cup olive oil
Salt and freshly ground black or white pepper to taste

In a small bowl, mix the vinegar, mustard, and shallot. Slowly drizzle in the olive oil, whisking to combine thoroughly. Add salt and pepper.

Blueberry Vinaigrette

Try this on a spring salad of Bibb lettuce or warm steamed asparagus. ○ Makes about 1 cup

⅓ cup blueberry vinegar
¼ cup fresh blueberries, picked over for stems
⅓ cup olive oil
Salt and freshly ground black or white pepper to taste

In a small bowl, mix the vinegar and blueberries. Slowly drizzle in the olive oil, whisking to combine thoroughly. Add salt and pepper.

Cranberry Vinaigrette

This is good on a winter salad of Bibb lettuce, watercress, endive, and any type of toasted nut. If you like it creamy, whisk in ⅓ cup heavy cream along with the oil.

○ Makes about ⅔ cup

2 tablespoons cranberry juice, sweetened or unsweetened
1 tablespoon cider vinegar
2 teaspoons pure maple syrup or honey
½ teaspoon Dijon mustard
½ cup walnut oil or olive oil
Salt and freshly ground black or white pepper to taste

In a small bowl, mix together the cranberry juice, vinegar, maple syrup, and mustard. Slowly drizzle in the walnut oil, whisking to combine thoroughly. Add salt and pepper.

Basil Vinaigrette

This is great on all kinds of lettuces or over sliced tomatoes. ◉ Makes about ¾ cup

2 tablespoons white or red wine vinegar
⅓ cup olive oil
1 teaspoon Dijon or coarse-grained mustard
1 clove garlic, crushed
3 to 4 tablespoons chopped fresh basil, to your taste
Salt and freshly ground black or white pepper to taste

Place all of the ingredients in a blender and blend until smooth.

Margarita Mayonnaise Dressing

This is fabulous on sliced raw tomatoes, mixed with chicken salad, or over steamed vegetables like cauliflower. ◉ Makes about 1½ cups

1½ cups mayonnaise
2 tablespoons freshly squeezed lime juice
1½ tablespoons orange liqueur, such as Cointreau
1½ teaspoons gold tequila
Freshly ground black pepper to taste

Place all of the ingredients in a medium-size bowl and whisk to combine. Or you may add all of the ingredients to a small food processor and pulse a few times to combine.

Simple Creamy Curry Dressing

Serve this over a pile of butter lettuce leaves or mixed with chicken, turkey, or shrimp salad. ◉ Makes about 1 cup

½ cup sour cream
½ cup mayonnaise
1 tablespoon mango chutney
Juice of ½ lime
1 teaspoon hot curry powder
Freshly ground black pepper to taste

Place all of the ingredients in a small bowl and whisk to combine. Or you may add all of the ingredients to a small food processor and pulse a few times to combine.

Thousand Island Dressing

Pour this over a wedge of iceberg lettuce or a chef's salad topped with chopped hard-boiled egg. ○ Makes about 2 cups

1½ cups mayonnaise (low-fat is okay)

½ cup prepared chili sauce

2 tablespoons minced fresh Italian parsley

1 tablespoon freshly squeezed lemon juice

1 tablespoon ketchup

Dash of Tabasco or other hot pepper sauce

Freshly ground black pepper to taste

Place all of the ingredients in a medium-size bowl and whisk to combine. Or you may add all of the ingredients to a small food processor and pulse a few times to combine.

The New-Fashioned
Bean and Chili Pot

Slow Cooker Pot of Beans ● 214

Cuban Black Beans ● 215

Julie's Hummus ● 217

New Year's Black-Eyed Peas ● 220

Fresh Fava Beans with Tomatoes and
Saffron ● 221

Braised Flageolets with Herbs ● 223

Red Bean Stew and Rice ● 224

Christmas Limas with Greens ● 225

Slow Cooker Cassoulet ● 226

Hickory Barbecued Pinto Beans ● 228

Indian Baked Beans ● 229

Calico Bean Bake ● 230

Gringo Chili for a Crowd ● 231

Pinto Bean Chili with Mexican
Sausage ● 232

Elizabeth Taylor's Chili ● 234

Turkey Chili with White Beans ● 235

Roasted Vegetable White Bean
Chili ● 237

Chili Colorado ● 242

Chili con Carne ● 244

Prune Chili ● 245

When you are feeding a crowd and you need to pay attention to economy, a small amount of beans will make a pot of chili, a casserole, or a stew, or even top a large salad. The slow cooker, developed originally from an existing electric bean pot, is the most efficient way to cook all types of dried beans and legumes. There is minimal evaporation during the cooking, just like in the old potbelly-shaped brown and cream clay bean pot that went into the oven or the fire embers.

Although it is easiest to reach for canned beans, which we do for the sake of convenience and speed in many recipes, do also take the time to make beans from scratch and enjoy their delicious nature.

The term *bean* refers not only to regular beans but also to legumes and peas, known as pulses. A legume is technically the edible seed inside a pod. There are a vast variety from which to choose, each with its own size, appearance, and texture. Beans can be consumed in both fresh and dried form. During summer months you may come across fresh beans—always called fresh shell beans—especially at your farmers' market. Fresh beans will always cook much faster than dried beans and need no soaking.

Once you embrace the world of dried beans, you will be amazed at the veritable cornucopia of shapes, colors, and sizes available and their wide range of flavors and textures. We have plenty to choose from, including old favorites such as pinto beans, black-eyed peas, and black beans, as well as "new'" heirlooms, such as cranberry beans, chestnut-flavored Christmas limas, and the lesser-used cooked beans such as limas and soybeans.

It is time to look at beans as a special main dish, suitable to serve to guests: Southwestern bean chilis and saltines; pinto bean and cheese burritos, now as American as pot roast; Italian cannellini beans nestled in a bed of hot polenta or piled on bruschetta; Cuban *moros y cristianos*, black beans with white rice; the complex *feijoada* black bean stew of Brazil; the gingery, spicy dals of India; chickpeas and lentils, the Moroccan farmer's breakfast; pinquitos, the small pink beans that are the soul of the Santa Maria outdoor barbecue; and Louisiana red beans and rice. For special parties, we give a delicious shortened version of French cassoulet, hearty baked beans and meat made in the French style, with the addition of duck legs, a dinner party classic. Also, we make a pot full of flageolets, the classic accompaniment to lamb, for company and holiday dinners.

Beans have a reputation of being hard to cook. We demystify that and give simple directions for the best slow cooker beans.

The cooking time definitely depends on what size the bean is (in general, small beans take longer to cook), the age of the bean (the older the bean, the more water it needs to rehydrate), and how long it has been pre-soaked. As one of our testers wrote about the flexible nature of cooking beans: "Cook until tender, anywhere from 4 to 8 hours on HIGH, depending on your slow cooker and the phase of the moon. If you're going to be out of the house, put the pot on LOW, and make sure you've got an extra 2 inches of liquid in it. Cook for 8 to 10 hours, bringing it to HIGH whenever you get back to the house."

We have included tips for cooking and soaking beans, as well as a cooking time chart. The rule of thumb is to have three times the amount of liquid as there are beans, which translates to 2 to 3 inches of liquid above the beans. You can always use more water (3 quarts of water to a pound of beans is not unusual), then drain the excess liquid later. We also like to add acidic ingredients—such as tomatoes, vinegar, or lemon juice—toward the end of cooking, to avoid toughening the beans' skins. Always be sure to add the salt near the end of the cooking time or at serving time; if you add it in the beginning, the beans will never get tender. The bean mantra is "soak, simmer, then flavor." Store your stash of cooked beans in the refrigerator for up to 3 days, or freeze for up to 2 months. Frozen beans can be defrosted quickly in the microwave in 1-cup increments, or even added frozen to a bubbling pot of soup.

For most cooks, chili is the first dish they make in their new slow cookers, and it is great party fare, as well as being a simple dinner or lunch for the kids. Chili is a wildly popular dish all over the country, and it is also one of the premier reasons to own a slow cooker. Our collection of recipes includes Elizabeth Taylor's Chili (page 234), which was airlifted over from Chasen's restaurant in Beverly Hills to Rome when she was working on the set of *Cleopatra* in the early 1960s. A glamorous star, but her had-to-have food was a humble chili! We have adapted it here for the slow cooker.

While chili purists will debate, often heatedly, whether beans belong in a chili or not, we love 'em in ours. Chili smacks of the colorful, fiery, nutritious, festive, and addictive qualities that characterize Mexican cuisine, but it is not a Mexican food. It is pure Americana. And we have gone ahead and used every type of meat and bean, and even roasted vegetables, to make all sorts of wonderful chilis.

The traditional bean for chili is the pinto, also called the frijol bean or Mexican red bean, a faintly streaked reddish brown and pink bean grown in the Southwest. Translating from the Spanish to "painted," the pinto is a variety of the *Phaseolus vulgaris* family that includes kidney beans, pink beans, and navy beans, also used to make chili. Today's chili makers do not limit themselves; there are chilis made with black turtle beans, Great Northerns, black-eyed peas, anasazi beans, cannellini white kidneys, dappled black and white appaloosas, giant pintos, and the mottled brown and cream

Jacob's cattle. In any of our recipes, you can substitute one of these more exotic American-grown varieties to vary the flavor of your chili. And mixing two or three different varieties is also popular, especially in vegetarian versions.

Beef and/or pork are the standard meats in most chili recipes, but sometimes different types of sausages or crumbled sausage meat and salt pork appear. Today, "white chilis" made with chicken and turkey are popular. Some recipes, from as far away as Morocco, call simply for lamb, water, chiles, and spices. The Navajo make their

•• Slow Cooker Bean Cooking Time Chart ••

While beans are often categorized by whether they were first grown in the Old or New Worlds, we like how chef and food doyenne Madeleine Kamman denotes them: by color. It is the best way to remember the individual beans.

The white varieties, all very different in appearance, include garbanzos (also called chickpeas or cecis), small plump navy beans, pea beans, soldier beans, plain white beans (known as haricots), Great Northerns, black-eyed peas, yellow-eyed peas, cannellini, and butter beans. They take the longest time to cook and need a long soaking time.

The rose-pink to red-black varieties include red kidneys, small pink (a small kidney) and red beans, black or turtle beans (*frijoles negros*), black runners, pintos (nicknamed the Mexican strawberry because of its mottled coloring) and their hybrids like rattlesnake and appaloosa beans, and cranberry beans, the traditional New England bean for succotash and rarely used outside of that region. All the beans have a light to dark reddish color and can be speckled.

The green varieties include all types of large and baby limas and both *flageolet verts* and *flageolet blancs* (the most expensive bean, imported from France and Belgium). For all beans, the lighter the color, the more delicate the flavor is; the darker the color, the more sweet, robust, and earthy.

The following instructions are based on 1 to 2 cups of beans or legumes with at least 3 inches of water to cover. Beans can also be cooked in broth or vegetable stock, which tastes especially nice if the beans will be eaten as a side dish. The beans should always be completely covered with liquid throughout the entire cooking time. Beans are done when tender and most of the cooking liquid has been absorbed, although if you are making a dish to eat with a spoon, such as Tuscan beans, they can remain soupy. Always check your beans toward the end of the cooking time and add more boiling water if they look too dry. If the beans are to be used in another dish, such as chili, soup, vegetable stew, or a cassoulet, you will cook them *al dente* rather than totally soft.

The following chart tells approximately how long to cook various kinds of dried beans on HIGH in the slow cooker. These times are meant to be used as guidelines, because variables

chili with lamb, red chiles, and hominy.

American-style chili is characterized by a flavor and color combination of spicy-hot red chile powder and Southwestern herbs like oregano and cumin, sometimes even with accents of cinnamon and cloves. For a mild chili, there are just pinches of this and that. For the chili heads, there is plenty of everything, plus hot sauce, jalapeños, some pure red chile powder, and cayenne pepper. Remember that the quality of your chili powder will affect the overall flavor of your finished chili dramatically, so search out one you like. Some

such as hard or soft water, the mineral composition of the soil where the beans were grown, and the age of the beans will slightly affect cooking times. Remember that beans and legumes always take slightly longer to cook at higher altitudes. Pre-soak all beans, except split peas and the various kinds of lentils. Pre-soaking not only rehydrates the beans and makes for a more even cooking process, but it also leeches off some of the compounds that make beans hard to digest (note the foamy water that is poured off).

Type of Dried Bean	Cook Time on HIGH Setting/Pre-soaked
Black beans (turtle beans)	3 hours
Black-eyed peas	3½ hours
Cannellini beans	3 hours
Fava beans	2½ hours
Flageolets	3½ to 4 hours
Garbanzo beans (chickpeas)	3½ to 4 hours
Great Northern beans	2½ hours
Kidney beans, red	3 hours
Lentils, brown	1½ hours (firm-tender for salads)
Lentils, brown	2 hours (completely tender for soup)
Lentils, green	2 hours
Lentils, red	1½ hours
Lima beans, baby or small	2½ hours
Lima beans, large	2 hours
Navy beans	2½ to 3 hours
Pink beans, small (pinquito)	3½ hours
Pinto beans	3 hours
Red beans, small	2½ hours
Soybeans	4 hours
Split peas, green or yellow	2½ hours
White beans, small	3 hours

are a blend of dried ground chiles, cumin, garlic salt, oregano, and even some flour. We also like to use pure chile powders, which are simply ground chiles, to pack a pure chile flavor.

Although chilis are most often served with warm corn or flour tortillas, other equally delicious accompaniments are biscuits, sopaipillas (little fried bread triangles), and, of course, all manner of cornbreads, cornsticks, and cornmeal muffins, a natural pairing.

Slow Cooker Pot of Beans

Dried beans are the kind of good and good-for-you food that doesn't get much publicity. They're not flashy, but they're one of the best bargains in the supermarket, in terms of both money and nutrition. And if you use your slow cooker, they're a bargain in the effort department as well. If you have ever nervously timed beans in a hissing pressure cooker or laboriously scraped burned beans from a pot that got too hot on the bottom (perhaps that even happened before the beans on top were cooked!), we've got a little secret to tell you: The slow cooker is the way to go. Unlike the pressure cooker, you don't need to-the-minute timing. Unlike the stovetop, there is almost no risk of burning your beans, as long as you follow our simple directions. ○ *Serves 10 to 14*

COOKER: Large round or oval
SETTING AND COOK TIME: See Slow Cooker Bean Cooking Time Chart (page 213)

2 pounds dried beans
About 16 cups water
1 bouquet garni (optional), consisting of two 4-inch-long pieces celery tied with a sprig fresh
    rosemary, sage, or thyme
Coarse or fine sea salt to taste
Shredded cheese of your choice (optional)

1. Place the beans in a colander and rinse under running water; pick over for damaged beans or small stones. Place in a 5- or 6-quart cooker (there must be plenty of room for them to bubble without spilling over) and cover with cold water. Soak for 6 to 12 hours. Drain.

2. Add the fresh water and the bouquet garni, if using, to the beans in the crock. Make sure the beans are covered by a few inches of water, adding more as needed. Cover and cook on HIGH. The beans must be covered with liquid at all times to cook properly. The water will cook into a liquid similar in color to whatever bean you are cooking; it is called bean liquor. When the beans are done, they will be tender yet hold their shape and not fall apart. Discard the bouquet garni. Leave the beans whole, or gently mash a portion of the beans in the pot, which will thicken them nicely.

3. Serve the beans immediately in soup bowls, topped with a sprinkling of sea salt and shredded cheese, if desired. Or let stand in the cooker for 1 hour, uncovered, then drain and use in another recipe or transfer with their liquor to an airtight container and refrigerate for up to 5 days.

Cuban Black Beans

T hese beans are divine and are considered comfort food. We just load up the slow cooker, but you can sauté the onion and garlic first, if you like. The beans will be rather soupy in consistency. Black beans are known to be easy to digest, so feel free to eat a giant bowl. Serve with white rice and lots of chopped cilantro. ● *Makes about 7 cups to serve 6 to 8*

COOKER: Large round
SETTINGS AND COOK TIMES: HIGH for 4 to 6 hours; or HIGH for about 2 hours, then LOW for 6 to 7 hours

1 pound black or turtle beans
1 medium-size yellow onion, finely chopped
2 to 3 cloves garlic, to your taste, chopped
Pinch of ground cumin
1 bay leaf, 1 sprig fresh epazote or savory, or 1 tablespoon dried epazote
¼ cup olive oil
10 to 12 cups water, as needed
One ¾-pound ham hock or smoked turkey wing
Salt and freshly ground black pepper to taste
Tabasco sauce to taste

·· Tips for Cooking Dried Beans in the Slow Cooker ··

We cooked dozens of pots of plain beans. We tried pre-soaking and not pre-soaking. We cooked on LOW and on HIGH. We used different sizes and shapes of slow cookers. Here's what we think are the best practices for slow-cooking beans.

1. Do pre-soak dried beans before cooking in the slow cooker. (The exceptions are the same as for stovetop bean cookery: lentils and split peas.) Although it is possible to slow-cook unsoaked beans, we found that cooking times are much more predictable if the beans have been soaked beforehand. Soak the beans in cold water for 6 hours or overnight, or use the quick-soak method: Bring the beans to a boil on the stove in a large pot with plenty of water. Boil for 2 minutes, then cover the pot and remove from the heat. Let stand for 1 hour. Drain the beans and cook them as indicated in the recipe, or follow our chart on page 213.

2. Cook beans on HIGH. We found that beans cook more evenly on the HIGH heat setting of a slow cooker.

3. Use either a medium-size or a large slow cooker. Use either a round or an oval-shaped slow cooker. Most small slow cookers don't have a HIGH setting, so we don't recommend them for bean cooking. In addition, they are too small for anything more than ½ cup of dry beans. We found that the shape of a slow cooker doesn't matter. Round and oval cookers performed equally well.

4. For general proportions, with 1 cup of pre-soaked beans, use 4 cups of water or broth. For 2 cups of pre-soaked beans, use 6 cups of water or broth. Cooking times will vary some-what based on the moisture level of the beans and the amount of beans, so be sure to check 30 to 60 minutes or so before the end of the cooking time in case you need to add some boiling water. The ultimate test? Bite into one.

5. Do not add salt until after the beans are cooked; salt added at the beginning toughens them, and they will not absorb water properly during the cooking process.

6. You can store your cooked beans in their liquor (flavored cooking water) and serve as a soup, or drain in a colander, scooping out the beans with a slotted spoon.

1. Place the beans in a colander and rinse under cold running water; pick over for damaged beans and small stones. Place in a 5- or 6-quart slow cooker (there must be plenty of room for them to bubble without spilling over) and cover with cold water by 3 inches; soak for 6 to 12 hours. Drain.

2. Add the onion, garlic, cumin, bay leaf, olive oil, and enough of the water to the beans in the crock to cover by 2 inches. Add the ham hock, nestling it down into the liquid. Cover and cook on HIGH for 4 to 6 hours, or on HIGH for about 2 hours, then on LOW for 6 to 7 hours. When done, the beans will be nice and tender. At the end of cooking you will have plenty of liquid left in the crock.

3. Remove the bay leaf or herb sprig and discard. Remove the ham hock; cut off the meat and return the meat to the beans. Add salt, pepper, and Tabasco sauce and serve hot.

Julie's Hummus

Hummus is a mashed puree of chickpeas, olive oil, and lemon juice that is immensely popular in the Middle East. The traditional way to serve hummus is to spread it on a plate and drizzle it with flavorful olive oil. That's fine for spreading it on bread, but if you are going to dip veggies into the hummus, it's more practical to pile it into a bowl. We also like to garnish our hummus with sesame seeds. Toast them in a small skillet over medium-high heat just until they are warm and fragrant, but not burned, 1 to 2 minutes. ❍ *Makes 4 cups to serve 16*

COOKER: Medium or large round or oval
SETTING AND COOK TIME: HIGH for 3 1/2 to 4 hours

1 cup dried chickpeas
5 cups water
1/3 cup tahini
1/4 cup freshly squeezed lemon juice
1/4 cup extra-virgin olive oil
2 cloves garlic
1 teaspoon salt, or to taste
1/2 teaspoon ground cumin

¼ teaspoon freshly ground black pepper

Dash of cayenne pepper

1 tablespoon sesame seeds for garnish (optional), toasted

1 teaspoon to 1 tablespoon extra-virgin olive oil, for garnish (optional), to your taste

1. Place the chickpeas in a colander and rinse under cold running water. Pick over for any damaged beans and small stones. Transfer to the slow cooker along with water to cover by 3 inches. Soak for 6 to 12 hours.

2. Drain, add the 5 cups water, cover, and cook on HIGH until the beans are quite tender and the transparent skin that covers each bean slips off easily, 3½ to 4 hours.

3. Drain, reserving the cooking liquid. Place the beans in a blender or food processor with ½ cup of the cooking liquid, the tahini, lemon juice, olive oil, garlic, salt, cumin, black pepper, and cayenne pepper. Process until quite smooth. If you are going to use it as a dip, you want a texture like that of guacamole. If you are going to use it as a sandwich spread, it can be a bit thicker. Add more of the cooking liquid, if needed, mixing after each addition, until the desired consistency is reached. Taste and adjust the seasonings, adding more lemon juice, salt, cumin, black pepper, and/or cayenne, if desired. Serve immediately, or refrigerate in an airtight container for up to 1 week. When ready to serve, sprinkle with sesame seeds and drizzle with olive oil, if desired.

·· More Hummus ··

Once you've mastered the basic hummus, try something new. Here are a couple of flavorful varieties to enjoy.

Hummus with Tofu and Roasted Vegetables

○ Makes 3 cups to serve 12

4 cloves garlic

1 medium-size red bell pepper, seeded and quartered

1 medium-size yellow onion, cut in half

3 tablespoons extra-virgin olive oil

3 cups chickpeas cooked according to Slow Cooker Pot of Beans (page 214), drained and liquid reserved

Juice of 1 lemon

¼ cup tahini

Pinch of cayenne pepper

4 ounces soft tofu, drained if necessary

Salt to taste

1. Preheat the oven to 375°F.

2. Place the garlic, pepper, and onion in a small heavy roasting pan, tucking the garlic under the pepper quarters and laying the onion halves face down in the pan. Drizzle with 1 tablespoon of the olive oil and roast until soft when pierced with the tip of a knife, about 40 minutes. When cool, remove and reserve the garlic and finely chop the vegetables.

3. In a food processor, pulse the cooked chickpeas to mash them. Add the roasted garlic, lemon juice, tahini, the remaining 2 tablespoons olive oil, and the cayenne pepper and, with the machine running, slowly add ¼ cup of the reserved chickpea liquid and the tofu, processing until you get a fluffy, smooth consistency. Season with salt to taste and adjust the consistency of the mixture by adding more bean liquor, if necessary. Fold in the chopped pepper and onion. Scrape into a serving bowl and serve immediately, or refrigerate in an airtight container for up to 5 days.

Chipotle Hummus from The Prado in Balboa Park

⊙ Makes 4 cups to serve 16

3 cups chickpeas cooked according to Slow Cooker Pot of Beans (page 214), drained

2 cloves garlic

Juice of 1 small lemon

Juice of 1 lime

1½ tablespoons canned chipotle chiles in adobo sauce

⅓ cup tahini

¼ cup loosely packed fresh cilantro leaves

Pinch of cayenne pepper

½ cup extra-virgin olive oil, or more if needed

Salt to taste

In a food processor, pulse the cooked chickpeas to mash them. Add the garlic, lemon and lime juices, chipotles with adobo sauce, tahini, cilantro, and cayenne pepper and, with the machine running, slowly add the olive oil until you get a fluffy, smooth consistency. Season with salt and adjust the consistency with more oil, if necessary. Scrape into a serving bowl and serve immediately, or refrigerate in an airtight container for up to 4 days.

•• How Many Dried Beans Are Equivalent
to a 15-Ounce Can of Beans? ••

Depending on the type of bean cooked, 1 cup of dried beans cooked with 3 to 4 cups of water will yield about 3 cups of cooked beans. This is slightly less than two 15- or 16-ounce cans of beans—each can contains about 1¾ cups of beans. One pound of raw dried beans (approximately 2⅓ cups) will yield about 6 to 7 cups of cooked beans.

New Year's Black-Eyed Peas

This recipe is adapted from Darra Goldstein's very special book *The Winter Vegetarian* (Harper Perennial, 1996). Black-eyed peas are a Southern staple, and eating them on New Year's Day supposedly brings good luck. Serve plain in bowls with a nice side salad of oranges and olives in a sherry vinaigrette. Or serve them as part of a New Year's brunch buffet. For an additional Southern touch, add hot biscuits. ◦ *Serves 12*

COOKER: Large round
SETTING AND COOK TIME: HIGH for 3½ to 5 hours; tomatoes added at 2½ hours

2 pounds dried black-eyed peas
8 cups hot water
3 large yellow onions, finely chopped
1 cup dark molasses
Two 28-ounce cans stewed tomatoes, undrained
½ teaspoon dried oregano
A few dashes of Tabasco sauce
Salt and freshly ground black pepper to taste

1. Place the beans in a colander and rinse under cold running water; pick over for damaged beans and small stones. Place in a 5- to 6-quart slow cooker (there must be plenty of room for them to bubble without spilling over) and cover with 3 inches of cold water; soak for 6 to 12 hours. Drain the beans and return them to the crock.

2. Add the hot water, onions, and molasses to the crock. Cover and cook on HIGH for 2½ hours, then stir in the tomatoes and their juices.

3. Cover and continue to cook on HIGH for another 1 to 2½ hours. The beans should be covered with liquid at all times to cook properly. When done, they will be tender and hold their shape.

4. Stir in the oregano and Tabasco sauce and season with salt and pepper. Serve hot for a main dish or at room temperature as an appetizer. This will keep, stored in an airtight container in the refrigerator, for up to 5 days.

Fresh Fava Beans with Tomatoes and Saffron

Oversized pods of fresh fava beans, also known as broad beans or horse beans, appear in the spring through early summer and grace many restaurant menus. You can buy them small or very large, each with a different texture and flavor according to size. Sort of a cross between a vegetable and a true bean, they have an inedible tough skin, so they need to be blanched first to remove it. People adore fava beans for their unique flavor, which has been described as almost grassy. They are an integral part of homey Mediterranean cooking, hailing back to the time of the Romans; the name derives from the Latin word *faba*, meaning "bean." You can also make this dish with dried fava beans. Using the Slow Cooker Pot of Beans recipe (page 214), soak overnight, cook until firm-tender, 2 to 2½ hours, and then continue with this recipe. ○ *Serves 6 to 8*

COOKER: Medium or large round
SETTING AND COOK TIME: HIGH for 2 to 3 hours; favas added at 1½ to 2 hours

4 pounds medium-size fresh fava beans, shelled (3 to 4 cups)
3 tablespoons olive oil
2 small shallots, finely chopped
2 jarred roasted red peppers, patted dry and chopped
One 28-ounce can crushed tomatoes

3 tablespoons tomato paste

¼ cup white wine

¼ teaspoon crushed saffron threads

1 pound penne pasta

A few dashes of Tabasco sauce

Salt and freshly ground black pepper to taste

Shredded Parmesan or Asiago cheese for sprinkling

1. Bring a large pot of salted water to a boil. Add the shelled favas and boil 30 seconds to 1 minute. Drain and rinse under cold running water. With a sharp knife or your fingernail, slit open the bean's outer skin and squeeze; the bean will slip out from inside the skin.

2. In a small skillet over medium heat, heat the olive oil, then cook the shallots, stirring, until softened, about 5 minutes. Add to the slow cooker, along with the peppers, tomatoes, tomato paste, wine, and saffron. Cover and cook on HIGH for 1½ to 2 hours, then add the favas.

3. Cover and continue to cook on HIGH for another 20 minutes to 1 hour, depending on the age of the favas, until very tender. While the favas finish cooking, cook the pasta according to the package directions.

4. Season the beans with Tabasco sauce, salt, and black pepper. Serve hot over the pasta with lots of cheese for sprinkling.

Braised Flageolets with Herbs

Dried flageolets are known as the royalty of beans. They are accessible and rare at the same time, and have a delightful fragrance and taste. They are harvested while immature, hence their lovely, muted sage green color. They are a traditional side dish to roast leg of lamb. They were once only imported, but many dedicated American bean growers now also grow them. If you see them, grab them. If you like creamy beans, add ½ cup cream at the end of the cooking— it transforms the beans into pure elegance. ○ *Serves 12 to 15*

COOKER: Large round or oval
SETTING AND COOK TIME: HIGH for 4 to 4½ hours

2 pounds dried *flageolets verts*
¼ cup olive oil
4 large shallots, diced
2 large carrots, diced
2 large ribs celery, diced
2 cloves garlic, quartered
6 sprigs fresh thyme or tarragon
2 bay leaves
4 cups beef or lamb broth
6 to 8 cups hot water
Sea salt and freshly ground black pepper to taste

1. Place the beans in a colander and rinse under cold running water; pick over for damaged beans and small stones. Place in a 5- to 6-quart slow cooker (there must be plenty of room for them to bubble without spilling over) and cover with 3 inches of cold water; soak for 6 to 12 hours. Drain and return to the crock.

2. Heat the oil in a small skillet over medium heat and cook the shallots, stirring, until softened, about 5 minutes. Add to the slow cooker along with the carrots, celery, garlic, thyme, bay leaves, broth, and 6 cups of the hot water. Cover and cook on HIGH for 4 to 4½ hours. The beans should be covered with liquid at all times to cook properly. Add extra hot water as needed so that the beans are not dry. When done, the beans will be tender. Discard the bay leaf and season with salt and pepper. Serve hot.

Red Bean Stew and Rice

Red beans and white rice are a New Orleans specialty. Spicy andouille sausage is traditional, but you can substitute kielbasa, if you like. Serve with cornbread. ○ *Serves 6 to 8*

COOKER: Large round or oval
SETTING AND COOK TIME: LOW for 9 to 10 hours

1 pound dried small red beans
11 cups water
2 whole fresh jalapeño chiles, stems removed
½ pound andouille sausage, chopped
1 pound cooked ham, chopped
4 cloves garlic, chopped
1 small yellow or white onion, chopped
2 to 3 teaspoons salt, to your taste
½ teaspoon dried oregano
½ teaspoon ground cumin
4½ to 6 cups cooked long-grain white rice

1. Place the beans in a colander and rinse under cold running water; pick over for damaged beans and small stones. Place in a 5- or 6-quart cooker (there must be plenty of room for them to bubble without spilling over) and cover with 3 inches of cold water; soak for 6 to 12 hours. Drain and return to the crock.

2. Add the water, chiles, andouille sausage, ham, garlic, and onion to the crock. Cover and cook on LOW for 9 to 10 hours. The beans should be covered with liquid at all times to cook into a thick gravy. When done, they will be tender and hold their shape.

3. Toward the end of the cooking time, add the salt, oregano, and cumin. Serve the hot beans in soup bowls, over mounds of hot rice.

Christmas Limas with Greens

We love Christmas limas, with their meaty texture and chestnut-like flavor. They are an heirloom bean now becoming more widely available. You can find them in markets that carry an assortment of artisan beans. You can also buy them online from Phipps Country Store & Farm in Pescadero, California (650-879-0787), at www.phippscountry.com, or from Rancho Gordo in Napa, California, at www.ranchogordo.com. ○ *Serves 6 to 8*

COOKER: Large round or oval
SETTING AND COOK TIME: HIGH for 6 to 7 hours

1 pound dried Christmas lima beans
3 cups hot water
2 beef, chicken, or vegetable bouillon cubes
⅓ cup olive oil
2 small yellow onions, quartered
2 cloves garlic
2 sprigs fresh thyme
2 fresh sage leaves
1 to 2 cups baby spinach leaves or arugula
Fine sea salt and freshly ground black pepper to taste
Extra-virgin olive oil for drizzling

1. Place the beans in a colander and rinse under cold running water; pick over for damaged beans and small stones. Place in a 5- or 6-quart slow cooker (there must be plenty of room for them to bubble without spilling over) and cover with 3 inches of cold water. Soak for 12 hours. Drain well and return to the slow cooker.

2. Cover the beans by 2 inches with fresh water. Cover and cook on HIGH for 3 hours; the beans will be parcooked. Drain again and rinse.

3. Add the 3 cups of hot water, the bouillon cubes, olive oil, onions, garlic, thyme, and sage to the beans in the slow cooker. Cover and cook on HIGH for 3 to 4 hours. The beans should be covered with liquid at all times. When done, they will be tender and hold their shape. Discard the garlic cloves and whole herbs.

4. Add the spinach; cover for 5 minutes to wilt. Season with salt and pepper, then serve immediately, drizzled with olive oil.

Slow Cooker Cassoulet

Cassoulet is a dish that typifies French home and bistro cooking and has somewhat of a legendary status among gourmands. It is comfort food to Francophiles, and Beth's Parisian friend Caroline would have her father ship cans of it to the United States while she lived here. Traditionally, cassoulet is a dish of stewed haricot beans with *confit d'oie* (preserved salted cooked goose) native to the Languedoc and Pyrenees, an area that uses a lot of goose, as well as duck, in recipes. The casserole is so common that it has a baking dish of the same name. This version, a poor man's cassoulet, is adapted from Mark Bittman, cookbook author and food columnist for the *New York Times*. It is simplified a lot from the original, which takes umpteen steps to prepare, but is definitely delicious just the same. It is excellent winter food; serve it with a simple salad with a red wine vinegar and olive oil vinaigrette and a dry red wine. ○ *Serves 8 to 10*

COOKER: Large oval

SETTING AND COOK TIME: HIGH for 5 to 6 hours;
    finishing in a 400°F oven for 15 minutes is optional

1 pound dried small white beans, such as pea or navy, or *flageolets verts*

8 sweet Italian sausages (about 1½ pounds)

4 duck legs

8 cloves garlic, crushed

2 medium-size yellow onions, chopped

4 medium-size carrots, cut into chunks

4 cups chopped fresh tomatoes or two
    14.5-ounce cans chopped plum tomatoes, undrained

6 to 8 sprigs fresh thyme or 1 teaspoon dried thyme

1 bay leaf

½ pound slab bacon or salt pork, in 1 piece

2 pounds boneless pork shoulder, trimmed of any fat, cut into
    1½-inch cubes, and tossed in a bit of flour

Chicken or vegetable broth, or water, or a mixture, as
    needed to cover by several inches

Salt and freshly ground black pepper to taste

1½ cups plain fresh bread crumbs tossed with

    2 tablespoons olive oil (optional)

Chopped fresh Italian parsley for garnish

1. Place the beans in a colander and rinse under cold running water; pick over for damaged beans and small stones. Place in a 5- or 6-quart slow cooker (there must be plenty of room for them to bubble without spilling over) and cover with cold water; soak for 6 to 12 hours. Drain.

2. In a large skillet over medium-high heat, brown the sausages and duck legs on all sides, cooking in batches, if necessary.

3. Add the garlic, onions, carrots, tomatoes, thyme, and bay leaf to the beans in the slow cooker. Nestle in the slab bacon and sprinkle with the pork cubes. Lay the sausages and duck legs on top and push into the beans a bit. Add broth to cover by 2 inches. Cover and cook on HIGH until the beans and meats are tender and cooked through, 5 to 6 hours.

4. When done, season with salt and pepper. If you like, remove the cassoulet from the slow cooker and transfer to a deep casserole; cover with the bread crumbs and bake in a preheated 400°F oven until they brown, about 15 minutes. (You can also just toast the crumbs quickly in a hot skillet, then sprinkle each portion with them.) Garnish with parsley and serve hot.

Hickory Barbecued Pinto Beans

 This is a spicy and quick version of baked beans that is great for outdoor gatherings. ● *Serves 6 to 8*

COOKER: Medium or large round or oval
SETTING AND COOK TIME: HIGH for 5½ to 6½ hours

1 pound dried pinto beans
8 cups hot water
2 medium-size yellow onions, chopped
1 tablespoon chili powder
¾ cup hickory-flavored barbecue sauce
½ cup ketchup
3 tablespoons light or dark brown sugar
1½ tablespoons Dijon mustard
¾ teaspoon ground ginger
A few dashes of hot pepper sauce or pinch of cayenne pepper
Salt to taste

1. Place the beans in a colander and rinse under cold running water; pick over for damaged beans and small stones. Place in a 5- or 6-quart slow cooker (there must be plenty of room for them to bubble without spilling over) and cover with cold water by 3 inches; soak for 6 to 12 hours. Drain and return to the crock.

2. Add the hot water, onions, and chili powder to the slow cooker. Cover and cook on HIGH for 3½ hours. The beans need to be covered with liquid at all times to cook properly. When done, they will be tender and still hold their shape.

3. Drain off all the cooking liquid, then stir in the barbecue sauce, ketchup, brown sugar, mustard, ginger, and hot pepper sauce. Cover and cook on HIGH for another 2 to 3 hours. Season with salt and serve hot.

Indian Baked Beans

These are the Southwestern equivalent of Boston baked beans, hearty like their Eastern cousins yet redolent of oregano, the herb so beloved in Southwestern cooking. Depending on the age of your beans, you may need to add a bit more boiling water during cooking. These are nice as a side dish to fajitas; or serve as a main dish with white rice and cornbread. ○ *Serves 8 to 10*

COOKER: Large round or oval
SETTINGS AND COOK TIMES: HIGH for 2½ hours to parcook the beans,
    then HIGH to bring to a boil and LOW for 10 to 14 hours

1 pound dried pinto beans
6 to 8 slices bacon, cut into 2-inch lengths
1 large yellow onion, chopped
2 ribs celery, chopped
One 16-ounce can stewed tomatoes
⅓ cup firmly packed light brown sugar
3 tablespoons cider vinegar
1½ teaspoons salt, or to taste
½ teaspoon dried oregano

1. Rinse the beans in a colander under cold running water; pick over for damaged beans and small stones. Place in the slow cooker and cover with 3 inches of cold water. Soak overnight. Drain and return to the crock.

2. Cover the beans with fresh water by 3 inches. Cover and cook on HIGH for 2½ hours, until still undercooked but tender. Do not drain.

3. Meanwhile, in a small skillet over medium-high heat, brown the bacon pieces. Remove and drain on paper towels. Remove all but 2 tablespoons of the drippings, then add the onion and celery and cook, stirring, until softened, about 5 minutes.

4. Add the onion and celery, bacon, stewed tomatoes, brown sugar, vinegar, salt, and oregano to the beans in the slow cooker; stir to mix well. The liquid should cover the beans by ½ inch, otherwise, add some boiling water. Cover and cook on HIGH to bring to a boil, then reduce the heat to LOW and cook until the beans are soft, thick, and bubbling, 10 to 14 hours. Serve hot.

Calico Bean Bake

We have no idea when or where the term *calico* became associated with this baked bean dish, but perhaps it is because there is a mixture of canned beans and the resulting dish looks a bit speckled. Beth got the recipe from her boyfriend's mom in the 1970s, and it became her favorite bean dish. It's a snap to assemble. The frozen limas are frozen fresh beans; the canned butter beans are cooked dried limas. They each have a different taste. This is a staple for barbecues and potluck buffets and is fantastic served cold the next day. ○ *Serves 10 to 12*

COOKER: Medium or large round or oval
SETTING AND COOK TIME: LOW for 6 to 8 hours

6 strips lean smoky bacon
1 medium-size yellow onion, finely chopped
1 clove garlic, minced
One 27-ounce can brick-oven baked pork and beans
One 16-ounce can red kidney beans, rinsed and drained
One 15.5-ounce can butter lima beans, drained
One 10-ounce package frozen baby lima beans, thawed
One 16-ounce can chickpeas, rinsed and drained
¾ cup ketchup
⅓ cup firmly packed light brown sugar
3 tablespoons cider vinegar
2 teaspoons Dijon mustard

1. In a medium-size skillet over medium heat, cook the bacon to render some of the fat, but leave it soft. Drain on paper towels. Remove all but 2 tablespoons of the drippings and then cook the onion, stirring, until softened, about 5 minutes. Add the garlic and cook for 30 seconds to 1 minute.

2. Combine all the beans in the slow cooker and add the ketchup, brown sugar, vinegar, and mustard. Add the onion mixture and stir to combine. Lay the bacon strips over the top, pressing them into the beans. Cover and cook on LOW for 6 to 8 hours. Serve hot, at room temperature, or cold.

Gringo Chili for a Crowd

Sometimes you need a really good meat and kidney bean chili to make for a crowd. Here it is, as basic and American as it can be, based on a recipe attributed to Polly Bergen, an actress popular in the '50s and '60s. It was probably served at many a Hollywood buffet. Serve right out of the crock with hot long-grain white rice, warm flour tortillas, and, of course, the myriad wonderful toppings in individual bowls, letting guests do their own thing. ○ *Serves 12 to 16*

COOKER: Large round or oval
SETTING AND COOK TIME: LOW for 9 to 12 hours

2 tablespoons olive oil
4 pounds lean ground beef or chuck
3 cloves garlic, minced
6 large yellow onions, chopped
4 medium-size green bell peppers, seeded and chopped
3 ribs celery, chopped
Four 15-ounce cans red kidney beans, rinsed and drained
Three 28-ounce cans whole tomatoes, undrained
Two 6-ounce cans tomato paste
¼ cup chili powder or New Mexican red chile powder, or to taste
3 pinches of cayenne pepper
3 whole cloves
1 bay leaf
3 tablespoons red wine vinegar
Salt to taste

FOR SERVING:
Shredded sharp cheddar cheese
Shredded sharp Monterey Jack cheese
Shredded iceberg lettuce
Sliced black olives
Strips of roasted green chile peppers
Chopped tomatoes
Sliced radishes
Sour cream

Guacamole or chopped avocado

Chopped fresh cilantro

Lime wedges

1. In a very large skillet over medium-high heat, heat the olive oil, then cook the ground beef and garlic until the meat is no longer pink, breaking up any clumps, about 8 minutes; drain off the fat. You may have to do this in two or more batches. Place the beef in the slow cooker. Add the onions and bell peppers to the skillet and cook, stirring, until tender; add to the cooker. Add the celery, kidney beans, tomatoes with their juices, tomato paste, chili powder, cayenne pepper, cloves, bay leaf, and vinegar to the cooker and stir to combine.

2. Cover and cook on LOW for 9 to 12 hours, stirring occasionally. During the last hour, season with salt. If the chili is too thin, leave the lid off and cook a bit longer; if it is too thick, add a splash of red wine. The longer you let it simmer, the better it gets. Serve with the topping choices on the side.

Pinto Bean Chili with Mexican Sausage

P into beans make a delicious chili, although when they are available we use other beans like Desert Pebble, Buckskins, or rattlesnakes. Although we used canned beans here, you can use freshly cooked pinto beans, made the day before, as well. Use a traditional sausage such as chorizo, or substitute a spicy turkey sausage, just being sure to cook it thoroughly before adding it to the chili. Serve in shallow soup bowls or dinner plates with a rim, passing the delicious, colorful accompaniments to guests. Serve with fresh, warm flour tortillas.

○ *Serves 12*

COOKER: Large round or oval

SETTING AND COOK TIME: LOW for 9 to 12 hours

2 tablespoons olive oil

1 pound fresh chorizo sausage

2 large white onions, chopped

3 cloves garlic, minced

3 tablespoons ancho chile powder, or to taste

1 tablespoon ground cumin

2 teaspoons ground coriander

Three 28-ounce cans whole tomatoes, undrained

Two 6-ounce cans tomato paste

3 medium-size yellow or red bell peppers, seeded and chopped

1 bay leaf

Four 15-ounce cans pinto beans, rinsed and drained

Salt to taste

Red pepper flakes to taste

¼ cup chopped fresh cilantro

FOR SERVING:

Shredded sharp cheddar cheese

Grated *queso fresco*

Diced seeded tomatoes

Minced scallions

Minced red onion

Sour cream

Chopped fresh cilantro

Lime wedges

1. In a very large skillet over medium-high heat, heat the olive oil, then cook the sausage until the meat is no longer pink, about 15 minutes. Drain on paper towels and, when cool, thinly slice.

2. Add the onions and garlic to the skillet and cook, stirring, until tender; add the chile powder, cumin, and coriander, stirring and taking care not to burn. Add the whole tomatoes with their juices and swish around to combine with all the spices, then pour everything into the slow cooker. Add the tomato paste, bell peppers, bay leaf, and beans to the cooker and stir to combine. Add the sausage slices.

3. Cover and cook on LOW for 9 to 12 hours, stirring occasionally. During the last hour, season with salt and red pepper flakes, and add the cilantro. If the chili is too thin, leave the lid off and cook a bit longer. The longer you let it simmer, the better it gets. Serve with the topping choices on the side.

Elizabeth Taylor's Chili

This is the recipe served at the Beverly Hills Hotel. On any day of the week you can stroll in there, just like a celebrity, and have this for lunch. Elizabeth Taylor made this chili famous when she was working on the set of *Cleopatra* in Rome in the early 1960s. She had gallons flown over regularly from the famous Beverly Hills restaurant Chasen's, which was reported in the movie magazines of the time as really quite outrageous. Chasen's is gone now, but its chili remains. For this chili, you will be roasting a triangle tip in the oven and cooking the beans from scratch first, so plan accordingly (you can skip the roast, if you like, and just make it with the ground meats). This is a no-garlic chili but it is fairly hot—you can cut back on the chili powder, if you like. ○ *Serves 10 to 12*

COOKER: Large round or oval
SETTINGS AND COOK TIMES: HIGH for 2 to 2½ hours, then LOW for 7 to 8 hours; salt, pepper, beef, and cheese added during last 30 minutes

½ pound dried red kidney beans, picked over, soaked overnight in cold water to cover, and drained
One 1½-pound triangle tip beef roast (also called tri-tip)
2 tablespoons olive oil
1 medium-size yellow onion, diced
1 medium-size red onion, diced
1 pound lean ground beef or chuck
1 pound ground pork
5 large ripe tomatoes, cut in half, seeded, and chopped
1 cup dry red wine
One 8-ounce can tomato sauce
6 tablespoons chili powder, or to taste
3 pinches of cayenne pepper
Salt and freshly ground black pepper to taste
1 cup shredded cheddar cheese

FOR SERVING:
Shredded cheddar cheese
Sour cream
Chopped green onions (white parts and some of the green)

1. Place the drained, soaked beans in the slow cooker and add enough water to cover by 3 inches. Cover and cook on HIGH until tender but not mushy, 2 to 2½ hours. Drain. (This can be done the night before.)

2. Meanwhile, preheat the oven to 425°F. Place the triangle tip on a roasting pan and roast until an instant-read meat thermometer inserted in the thickest part registers 120°F, 35 to 40 minutes. Remove from the oven and let cool completely. Cut the meat into 2 × ½-inch strips. (This can be done the night before.)

3. In a large skillet over medium-high heat, heat the olive oil and cook the yellow and red onions, stirring, until softened, about 5 minutes; place in the slow cooker. Add the ground beef and pork to the skillet and cook until no longer pink, breaking up any clumps, about 8 minutes; drain off the fat. Transfer to the slow cooker, add the kidney beans, tomatoes, wine, tomato sauce, chili powder, and cayenne pepper, and stir to combine.

4. Cover and cook on LOW for 7 to 8 to hours. During the last 30 minutes, season with salt and black pepper. Add the triangle tip strips and cheddar, stir, cover, and let the cheese melt and the meat heat through, about 30 minutes.

5. Serve the chili in bowls with additional cheddar cheese, sour cream, and chopped green onions.

Turkey Chili with White Beans

T his is a light chili, made with turkey instead of beef. It has lots of beans and a hint of cocoa, like a mole. Look for either the baby white beans, which are like navy beans, or cannellini beans, also known as white kidney beans. Serve this with hunks of French bread or cornsticks. ○ *Serves 12*

COOKER: Medium or large round or oval
SETTING AND COOK TIME: LOW for 6 to 9 hours;
    beans and salt added during last hour

4 tablespoons olive oil

3 large yellow onions, chopped

3 pounds ground dark turkey meat

4 to 6 tablespoons chili powder, to your taste

2½ teaspoons dried oregano

2½ teaspoons ground cumin

2 bay leaves

2 tablespoons unsweetened cocoa powder or ¼ of 1 round Ibarra sweet Mexican drinking chocolate tablet

½ teaspoon ground cinnamon

Two 28-ounce cans whole tomatoes, undrained

Two 8-ounce cans tomato sauce

6 cups beef broth

Six 15-ounce cans small white beans or cannellini beans, or a combination, rinsed and drained

Salt to taste

FOR SERVING:

Chopped red onion

Chopped fresh cilantro

Shredded Monterey Jack cheese

Sour cream

1. In a large skillet over medium-high heat, heat the olive oil and cook the onions, stirring, until tender. Add the turkey and cook, stirring, until no longer pink, about 10 minutes. Transfer to the slow cooker and stir in the chili powder, oregano, cumin, bay leaves, cocoa powder, cinnamon, tomatoes with their juices, tomato sauce, and broth. Break up the tomatoes with a spoon or spatula. Cover and cook on LOW for 6 to 9 hours, stirring occasionally, if possible. During the last hour, add the beans and salt. The longer you let it simmer, the better it gets, within reason, of course.

2. Serve the chili in bowls with the toppings on the side in little bowls.

Roasted Vegetable White Bean Chili

H ere is a nice vegetarian chili that will really impress. The roasted vegetables make it so tasty, and one of our favorite chiles, the ancho, adds richness and body. Whole ancho chiles (which are dried poblanos) are widely available in supermarkets in 3- to 4-ounce cellophane packages. They look almost heart-shaped and are a deep brownish red color and slightly wrinkled. If you use only one ancho chile, the chili will be very mild; we usually use two. This recipe is adapted from *366 Delicious Ways to Serve Rice, Beans, and Grains* by Andrea Chesman (Plume, 1998). ● *Serves 12*

COOKER: Large round or oval

SETTINGS AND COOK TIMES: HIGH for 2 to 2½ hours, then LOW for 5 to 6 hours; season with salt and pepper during last hour

2 pounds dried Great Northern beans, picked over, soaked overnight
   in cold water, and drained

4 quarts water

2 dried whole ancho chiles, or to your taste

2 large heads garlic

2 large red onions, slivered

4 medium-size red or yellow bell peppers, seeded and cut into strips

24 tomatillos, husked and quartered

⅓ cup olive oil

4 teaspoons ground cumin

2 teaspoons chili powder or New Mexican red chile powder

White wine, vegetable broth, or water, if needed

Salt and freshly ground black pepper to taste

Toast Soldiers for serving (recipe follows)

FOR SERVING:

6 ounces goat cheese, crumbled

¾ cup minced fresh cilantro

¾ cup loosely packed arugula leaves, chopped if large

2 limes, cut into wedges

1. Place the drained, soaked beans, water, and ancho chiles in the slow cooker. Cover and cook on HIGH until tender but not mushy, 2 to 2½ hours. The chiles will rehydrate. Do not drain. (You can do this the night before.)

2. Meanwhile, preheat the oven to 400°F. Place the garlic, onions, bell peppers, and tomatillos in an oiled ceramic baking dish; toss with the olive oil to coat. Bake until browned and tender, 30 to 45 minutes. (This can also be done the night before.)

3. Remove the ancho chiles from the beans. Wearing plastic or rubber gloves, remove and discard the stems, seeds, and membranes. Scrape the flesh off the skin, chop the flesh if it is firm, and return it to the slow cooker with the cooked beans. Cut the heads of garlic in half and squeeze the pulp into the slow cooker. Add the rest of the roasted vegetables to the cooker, along with the cumin and chili powder. If the chili is dry, add a bit of wine. (This can also be done the night before.)

4. Cover and cook on LOW for 5 to 6 hours. During the last hour, season with salt and black pepper.

5. Serve the chili in bowls topped with the goat cheese, then the cilantro and arugula in a fluffy pile on top and lime wedges on the side to squeeze over the top. Serve with Toast Soldiers alongside.

Toast Soldiers

○ *Makes 24 toasts*

6 long, slender baguettes (½ pound each), cut lengthwise into quarters with a serrated knife
About 1⅓ cups olive oil

1. Preheat the oven to 400°F. Line 2 large baking sheets with parchment paper or aluminum foil.

2. Place the baguette quarters side by side on the baking sheets with some space in between. With a clean pastry brush, brush the olive oil on all sides of the wedges. Bake until the edges just begin to turn golden, 8 to 12 minutes; the baguette will still be soft inside. You may have to rotate the inside wedges to the outside and vice versa at about 5 minutes for even browning. Serve warm from the oven or at room temperature.

Cornbreads to Serve with Chili and Bean Dishes

Chili or beans and cornbread are a traditional pairing, probably stemming from the old West/Southwest chuckwagon and Mexican rancho cooking popular from California to Texas. There are lots of pan cornbreads, cornsticks, and muffins from which to choose, and, because they are quick breads, they are made in a flash in your oven while your chili or beans slow-cook. All cornbreads freeze well, but really taste best hot from the oven. These breads and muffins can all be frozen in plastic freezer bags for up to 1 month, then reheated before serving.

Pumpkin Cornmeal Muffins

These muffins are wonderful with black bean chilis or ribs. They have a hint of molasses that adds to their satisfying quality. ☉ Makes 12 muffins

1 cup unbleached all-purpose flour

1 cup fine- or medium-ground yellow cornmeal, preferably stone ground

2 teaspoons baking powder

1 teaspoon pumpkin pie spice blend

½ teaspoon baking soda

½ teaspoon salt

¼ cup (½ stick) unsalted butter or margarine, melted

1 large egg

¼ cup honey

¼ cup light molasses

¾ cup buttermilk

½ cup pumpkin puree

1. Preheat the oven to 375°F. Grease 12 cups of a standard muffin tin.

2. Combine the flour, cornmeal, baking powder, spice blend, baking soda, and salt in a large bowl.

3. In a medium-size bowl, beat together the melted butter, egg, honey, molasses, buttermilk, and pumpkin puree. Mix into the dry ingredients until just combined. Take care not to overmix. The batter will be lumpy.

4. Spoon the batter into the prepared pan, filling the cups almost to the top. Bake until golden around the edges, the tops are dry, and a cake tester inserted into the center comes out clean, about 20 minutes. Let stand 10 minutes on a wire rack before turning the muffins out of the cups to cool. Serve hot, warm, or at room temperature.

Chile Cornsticks

A basket of cornsticks elicits ohhhs and ahhhs at parties; they look so special and are a traditional accompaniment to chili. If you don't have a cornstick pan, you can make this recipe in a muffin pan. ☉ Makes 18 cornsticks

1¼ cups unbleached all-purpose flour
¾ cup yellow cornmeal, preferably stone ground
3 tablespoons sugar
2½ teaspoons baking powder
½ teaspoon salt
1 cup whole or low-fat milk
6 tablespoons (¾ stick) unsalted butter, melted
1 large egg
1 cup fresh or thawed frozen baby white or yellow corn kernels
4 tablespoons chopped green chiles

1. Preheat the oven to 425°F. Grease a cornstick pan (you will be making about 18 cornsticks, so use a second pan or plan to reuse one pan). Place the pan in the oven to heat up.

2. In a large mixing bowl, combine the flour, cornmeal, sugar, baking powder, and salt. Make a well in the center of the dry ingredients and add the milk, butter, and egg. Stir with a large spatula until just combined. Stir in the corn and green chiles.

3. Spoon the batter into the prepared cornstick pan, filling the batter even with the top of the pan. Bake for 12 to 18 minutes, until golden around the edges, firm to the touch, and a toothpick inserted into the center comes out clean. Unmold and serve hot.

Honey Cornbread with Apricots

This unusual cornbread is wonderful with vegetarian chilis. If you use canned apricots, pat them dry with paper towels before folding them into the batter. Instead of the apricots, you can use 1½ cups fresh raspberries or blueberries. ☉ Makes one 9-inch square cornbread

1⅔ cups unbleached all-purpose flour
1⅓ cups fine-ground yellow cornmeal, preferably stone ground
1 tablespoon plus 1 teaspoon baking powder
1 teaspoon salt
3 large eggs
1½ cups buttermilk
½ cup corn or canola oil

½ cup honey

5 whole fresh or canned apricots, pitted and chopped (about 1½ cups)

1. Preheat the oven to 400°F (375°F if using a glass baking dish). Coat a 9-inch square baking dish with nonstick cooking spray.

2. Combine the flour, cornmeal, baking powder, and salt in a large bowl.

3. In a medium-size bowl, beat together the eggs, buttermilk, oil, and honey. Mix into the dry ingredients until just combined. Take care not to overmix. The batter will be lumpy. Fold in the chopped apricots.

4. Pour the batter into the prepared pan. Bake until golden around the edges and a cake tester inserted into the center comes out clean, 25 to 35 minutes. Let stand 10 minutes on a wire rack before cutting into squares to serve warm.

Sour Cream Cornmeal Muffins

This is a wonderful muffin to serve with all sorts of chilis, soups, or ribs. The recipe is easy and foolproof. ○ Makes 12 standard-size, 24 mini, or 6 oversized muffins

1 cup unbleached all-purpose flour

1 cup fine- or medium-ground yellow cornmeal, preferably stone ground

¼ cup sugar

2 teaspoons baking powder

½ teaspoon baking soda

½ teaspoon salt

¼ cup olive oil

2 large eggs

1 cup sour cream

1. Preheat the oven to 400°F. Grease 12 cups of a standard muffin tin, 24 cups of a mini-muffin tin, or 6 cups of an oversized muffin tin.

2. Combine the flour, cornmeal, sugar, baking powder, baking soda, and salt in a large bowl.

3. In a medium-size bowl, stir together the oil, eggs, and sour cream. Mix into the dry ingredients until just combined. Take care not to overmix. The batter will be lumpy.

4. Spoon the batter into the prepared pan, filling the cups almost to the top. Bake until golden around the edges, the tops are dry, and a cake tester inserted into the center comes out clean, 18 to 23 minutes for standard muffins, 10 to 14 minutes for mini-muffins, and 25 to 30 minutes for oversized muffins. Let stand 5 minutes on a wire rack before turning out of the cups to cool. Serve hot, warm, or at room temperature.

Chili Colorado

olorado is a Spanish word meaning "red." Like many foods from the Southwest, this beef in red chile sauce is deeply flavored but not necessarily hot. Making red chile sauce is easy enough, once you have located pure ground chile in the Mexican food section of your market. Ground chile is quite different from the chili powders you'll find shelved with the spices; those have other spices added and are not suitable for chile sauce. The heat of this dish will depend on the heat of the chile powder you start with: If you want a milder result, choose a variety of ground chile marked "mild." But you don't have to make your own sauce. Ever since a former housemate of Julie's introduced her to the excellent Las Palmas brand of canned red chile sauce, Julie has made it a pantry staple. Sometimes labeled "red chile sauce'" and sometimes labeled "enchilada sauce," Las Palmas comes in mild, medium, and hot.

Chili colorado is wonderful eaten as a stew with warm, buttered tortillas, crusty bread, or even a stack of saltines. Or let chili colorado serve as the basis for the best burritos, tacos, or enchiladas you have ever made. ● *Serves 6*

COOKER: Medium or large round or oval
SETTING AND COOK TIME: LOW for 5 to 7 hours

2 tablespoons vegetable oil
2 pounds lean stewing beef, trimmed of fat and cut into 1- to 1½-inch cubes
¼ cup water
3 to 4 cups Red Chile Sauce (recipe follows) or one
    28-ounce can Las Palmas red chile sauce

1. In a large, heavy skillet, heat the oil over medium-high heat. Pat the beef cubes dry with paper towels. Add half the beef to the skillet and allow to brown well on all sides, about 5 minutes. As the beef browns, remove it with a slotted spoon to the slow cooker. Repeat with the remaining beef. Pour off the fat from the pan.

2. Return the pan to the heat, add the water, and bring to a boil, scraping up any browned bits stuck to the pan. Pour into the crock. Add the chile sauce to the skillet, bring to a boil, and pour it into the crock. Cover and cook on LOW for 5 to 7 hours. Serve hot.

Red Chile Beef Stew: Add 4 or 5 medium-size russet potatoes, peeled and cut into 2-inch chunks, to the crock before you add the beef.

Red Chile Sauce

This is the real thing—no tomatoes. It's the basic red sauce of New Mexico, where chiles are proudly grown and consumed in great quantities. A building block of countless dishes, it is used by the spoonful as a condiment or by the cup in everything from huevos rancheros to enchiladas. Be sure to buy pure ground red chile powder, which is often found in plastic pouches in the Mexican food section, not chili powder, which is sold with the spices. You can also look for the large whole, dried red New Mexico chile pods. Wash them, cut them open, discard the stems, remove the seeds and veins (unless you want really hot chile sauce), let the pods dry completely, and then grind them very finely in the blender, taking care not to let the chile dust get into your eyes or nose. ❍ *Makes about 4 cups*

¼ **cup vegetable oil**
2 cloves garlic, put through a garlic press or very finely minced
¼ **cup all-purpose flour**
1 cup red chile powder, mild, medium, or hot, to your taste
4 cups water
Salt to taste

In a large skillet or Dutch oven, heat the oil over medium-high heat. Add the garlic and cook, stirring, for 1 or 2 minutes; do not let the garlic brown. Stir in the flour. Reduce the heat to medium and add the chile powder; chile burns very easily, so keep stirring. Stir in the water. Raise the heat to medium-high and let the sauce come to a simmer. Season with salt. The sauce is ready to use as is, but if you want a thicker sauce, let it simmer for 10 to 15 minutes. The sauce will keep in an airtight container in the refrigerator for 1 week, or frozen for up to 3 months.

Chili con Carne

C *hili con carne* translates to "chili with meat"—no beans, no onions, no tomatoes—and it is the original beef chili, with a legend attached that nuns in a convent in Mexico invented it. Here, we have adapted food writer Elaine Corn's recipe for Texas chili from her book *As American as Apple Pie* (Prima Publishing, 2002). It calls for round steak cut into small cubes or the extra-coarse grind of round or chuck known as "chili grind." A good butcher will grind it for you if you cannot find it in your supermarket case, or else you can grind your own beef using the grinder attachment in a KitchenAid stand mixer or in a food processor. Serve this with cornbread. ○ *Serves 8 to 10*

COOKER: Medium or large round or oval

SETTING AND COOK TIME: LOW for 7 to 9 hours;
    salt and masa harina added during last hour

2 tablespoons olive oil

3 pounds boneless beef round steak, trimmed of excess fat and
    cut into ¼-inch cubes, or chili-grind beef

3 cloves garlic, finely chopped

6 tablespoons chili powder, or to your taste

1 teaspoon cayenne pepper or 2 tablespoons New Mexican
    red chile powder, or to your taste

1 tablespoon ground cumin

1 tablespoon dried oregano

1 tablespoon hot pepper sauce, such as Tabasco sauce

6 cups water, or more to cover

Salt to taste

3 tablespoons masa harina

FOR SERVING:

Saltine crackers

Shredded longhorn cheese

Diced onion

Chopped fresh jalapeño chiles or canned jalapeño chiles en escabèche

1. In a very large, heavy skillet over medium-high heat, heat the oil, then brown the meat until no longer pink, about 8 minutes; drain off the fat. Place in the slow cooker, then add the garlic, chili powder, cayenne, cumin, oregano, hot pepper sauce, and enough water to cover by 1 inch, and stir to combine. Cover and cook on LOW for 6 to 8 hours, stirring occasionally, if possible.

2. During the last hour, season with salt. Mix the masa harina with some cold water to make a paste; stir it in, cover, and cook until thick. The longer you let the chili simmer, the better it gets, within reason, of course.

3. Serve with lots of crumbled saltines, shredded cheese, diced onion, and chopped jalapeños.

Prune Chili

T his is a no-bean chili with the secret ingredient of prunes added for sweetness and as a thickening agent. Although you may think that meat and prunes in a spicy broth is a unique blending, one taste of this thick chili and you will know how excellent a marriage it is. This recipe is adapted for the slow cooker. The original was the winner in one of the cooking categories at the annual Prune Festival in Yuba City in California's Central Valley in the late 1980s. Serve with Honey Cornbread with Apricots (page 240) or Pumpkin Cornmeal Muffins (page 239). ● *Serves 10 to 12*

COOKER: Large round or oval
SETTING AND COOK TIME: LOW for 8 to 9 hours

1 tablespoon olive oil
3 pounds beef sirloin tip, trimmed of fat and cut into ½-inch cubes
½ pound sweet Italian sausage, casings removed
1 medium-size yellow onion, finely chopped
5 cloves garlic, minced
One 14.5-ounce can beef broth
One 15-ounce can tomato sauce
One 12-ounce package pitted prunes, diced
1 to 2 jalapeño chiles, to your taste, seeded and diced

1 tablespoon hot or sweet paprika

1 teaspoon crumbled dried oregano

3 cups water

3 tablespoons New Mexican red chile powder

2 tablespoons California chile powder

2 tablespoons ground cumin

FOR SERVING:

Shredded cheddar cheese

Sliced green onions

Diced fresh tomatoes

1. In a large skillet over medium-high heat, heat the oil, then brown the beef cubes in batches and transfer to the slow cooker. Cook the crumbled sausage meat in the skillet until no pink remains, about 4 minutes, and add to the cooker. Add the onion, garlic, broth, tomato sauce, prunes, jalapeño, paprika, and oregano to the cooker and stir to combine. In a medium-size bowl, combine the water, both chile powders, and the cumin; whisk to combine to prevent lumps and pour into the cooker. Cover and cook on LOW for 8 or 9 hours.

2. Serve the chili hot and sprinkle with lots of shredded cheese, sliced green onions, and diced tomatoes.

Poultry, Game Birds, and Rabbit

Chicken Mole Enchilada Casserole ○ 251

Chicken in Champagne ○ 252

Honey-Mustard Chicken ○ 253

Chicken Marsala ○ 254

Brandied Chicken with Hazelnuts ○ 255

Chicken with Mango and Coconut ○ 257

Coq au Cabernet ○ 258

Chicken with Orange Sauce ○ 259

Country Captain ○ 261

Crème de Cassis Chicken ○ 262

Chicken with Glazed Walnuts and
Grand Marnier ○ 264

Spicy Turmeric Chicken ○ 266

Chicken Thighs with Garlic and
Sparkling Wine ○ 267

Barbecued Chicken Wings
for a Crowd ○ 271

Sujata's Curried Chicken Wings ○ 273

Crocked Buffalo Chicken Wings ○ 274

Garlic and Lime Chicken Wings with
Chipotle Mayonnaise ○ 275

Plum Sauce Chicken Wings ○ 277

Old-Fashioned Turkey Breast with
Pan Gravy ○ 278

Rolled Turkey Breast with
Prosciutto ○ 280

Turkey Legs with Mandarins ○ 282

Cold Poached Turkey Tenderloins with
Chutney-Yogurt Sauce ○ 283

White Meatloaf ○ 284

Duck Breasts à l'Orange ○ 286

Braised Pheasant with Mushrooms in
Riesling ○ 288

Pheasant with Apple-Shallot
Cream ○ 290

Braised Rabbit with Prunes and
Green Olives ○ 291

Stewed Rabbit with Red Wine and
Wild Mushrooms ○ 293

At noon you find out you are having eight guests at your house for dinner. There is barely time to shop, much less prepare and set the table. What do you serve? Poultry, of course. Not everyone likes fish and so many do not eat red meat, but everyone likes chicken and turkey, even duck breast. When cooking for a large group with a variety of eating habits and tastes, you can depend on chicken or turkey to shine as the star of the meal. In addition to being popular, they are nutritious and low in fat, and very economical for a crowd. In short, poultry is a food par excellence for dinner parties and buffets.

Because it is so mild tasting, poultry lends itself to seemingly endless flavor combinations. Every world cuisine has poultry of some type in its repertoire. In this chapter, we have a number of very easy entertaining dishes made with poultry pieces, especially boneless breasts, because they are so convenient and easy to serve and eat. Try our Chicken with Mango and Coconut (page 257) or the Chicken with Glazed Walnuts and Grand Marnier (page 264). A few hours in the cooker and you have a homemade, hot, impressive entrée. We favor turkey and duck breasts as well as chicken, which are superb for crowds.

From rich poultry broths that simmer all day to elegant party fare like chicken with liqueur-spiked sauces, the slow cooker is a great way to cook chicken, turkey, Cornish game hen, rabbit, pheasant, and duck. We admit we didn't always see it that way! In fact, we made all of the classic mistakes when we began to experiment with poultry in our slow cookers. We cooked it too long, ruining the flavor and turning the texture practically to sawdust. We didn't take the time to brown chicken pieces first and ended up with unappetizingly pale slow-cooked poultry. We used too much liquid and drowned it. But we finally learned.

There are exceptions to every rule, including the guidelines that follow here, but in general, this is what we learned after slow-cooking dozens upon dozens of poultry dishes: Unless you are making soup, broth, or a poached dish, you should use very little liquid—much less liquid than you would use in stovetop or oven cooking. Generally speaking, ½ to ¾ cup of liquid is enough. If you are cooking whole chickens or ducks, an oval cooker is nice, because it will cradle a whole bird nicely, but you can still get delicious results in a round cooker. We use plenty of boneless breasts and thighs in our recipes, because they cook on high heat for a short time and end up creating a great slow cooker meal. We also love duck breasts; they are low in fat and cook as easily as chicken, and they make an impressive dish for company.

At the supermarket or butcher shop, the poultry is grouped by species: chicken, turkey, game hens, duck, and other game, such as pheasant. (You'll often find rabbit near the poultry end of the meat case as well.) Poultry can be fresh or frozen, and it is available whole, as pieces, ground, or boned into roasts. All are suitable for cooking in the slow cooker (except for whole turkey). Figure on about ½ pound of meat per serving with the bones, and 4 to 6 ounces per serving for boneless poultry.

Turkey is available whole, in parts such as drumsticks, wings, and thighs, ground, as bone-in and boneless breast roasts, and as halved or whole breasts, all of which are good for slow-cooking except for the whole turkey, which is too large to fit in the cooker and is best done by traditional means. Count on 1 pound of meat with bones per person.

Commercial farm-raised game birds, such as duck, squab, quail, and pheasant, are available now throughout the year in supermarkets and butcher shops, not just from seasonal hunting in fields and forests, opening new frontiers for home cooks. Although the flavor is a bit more robust than chicken and turkey, it is much milder than the leaner wild counterparts. Every species is a bit different, and the flavor of farm-raised game also varies based on the sex, size, and diet of the animal, as well as the geographic area it is from. Some game is gently aged to tenderize it, and you might wish to use a marinade as well. Because most farm-raised game is very lean, it would typically need some fat to cook, but in the slow cooker, the naturally moist braising process eliminates the barding and basting associated with this type of cooking. Duck, squab, and quail are often sold frozen; pheasant is usually available fresh from September to February due to its growing patterns, and it is also available frozen year-round. Butcher shops are the best places to shop for game. All are sold whole, with the exception of duck, so for many recipes you will need to ask the butcher to cut them into pieces if you do not want to do it yourself.

Slow Cooker Poultry Pointers

Slow-cooking is an excellent method for thoroughly cooking poultry of all types, but there are rules for cooking it safely, so please read the following section carefully.

- Use all fresh poultry within 2 to 3 days of purchase, and freeze it for 9 to 10 months maximum. Thaw poultry in the refrigerator in its original wrapping with a plate underneath in case of dripping; it is important that poultry remain cold while thawing. For a whole bird, estimate 24 hours of thawing time per 5 pounds; parts will thaw in half a day. The sell-by date stamped on the package indicates the date 7 days after the bird was processed, and it is the cutoff date for sale. Refrigerated, the bird will still be good. If you have any doubt, ask the butcher how fresh the bird is and when it should be cooked by. Never buy frozen poultry that has frozen liquid in the package, which is an indication that it has been either frozen after sitting for a while or partially thawed and then refrozen.

- Because poultry may carry potentially harmful organisms or bacteria, take care when handling it. Thoroughly rinse and dry the poultry before working with it. Wash your hands, work surfaces, and utensils with hot soapy water before and after handling. Poultry is always cooked completely through (and never eaten raw), and is never served rare like beef and lamb.

- Never use room-temperature poultry; it will reach the correct temperature as the slow cooker heats up. Unless a recipe specifically calls for it, never place frozen poultry directly into the slow cooker.

- Poultry pieces cook more efficiently than large pieces or a whole bird. Boneless pieces, such as breast and thighs, cook the fastest, with bone-in pieces taking longer to cook. Please add extra time, 1 to 2 hours, if substituting bone-in poultry for boneless in any recipe, or follow the time guidelines in a recipe designed for the type of poultry you are using.

- Since the slow cooker takes a while to reach a safe bacteria-killing temperature, use poultry directly from the refrigerator and get the cooker turned on quickly. Please note the danger zone for bacterial growth in poultry is between 40° and 140°F. The heating rate for a slow cooker is 3 to 4 hours on the LOW setting to get the contents up to a safe food temperature of 140° to 165°F; it will then increase to over 200°F by 6 hours. The same temperatures will be reached in half the time on the HIGH setting. We recommend not lifting the lid for the first 3 to 4 hours to allow the heat to come to the proper cooking temperature as fast as possible.

- Poultry should be cooked throughout but still be juicy, and the juices should run clear when it is done. Although all poultry has both white and dark meat, when properly cooked there will be no trace of pink in either when pierced with a fork at the thickest point. Poultry is done when the internal temperature reaches about 170°F on an instant-read thermometer. Refrigerate cooked poultry within 2 hours of cooking.

Chicken Mole Enchilada Casserole

Mole poblano is one of Mexico's most famous dishes. Dark brown in color, with a toasty, smoky, sweet-hot flavor deepened with the addition of nuts and bitter chocolate, the sauce is unmistakable and unforgettable. Making it from scratch can be a major undertaking, but, fortunately, you don't have to do that to eat mole at home. Simply look for mole pastes or concentrates in the Mexican food section of your supermarket. Several brands are sold in the United States. Doña Maria is one brand we like; you simply mix it with chicken broth or water and you're ready to go! ○ *Serves 8*

COOKER: Medium or large round or oval
SETTING AND COOK TIME: HIGH for 2 hours, or LOW for 4 to 5 hours

¾ cup mole concentrate (see headnote)

3 cups chicken broth

1 tablespoon vegetable oil

1 large yellow onion, chopped

1 dozen soft corn tortillas, each one cut into 4 strips lengthwise

2½ to 3 cups cooked skinless, boneless chicken cut into ¾-inch pieces

2 cups regular or low-fat sour cream

½ pound *queso fresco* or feta cheese (if you are using feta, rinse it well under
   cold water to remove excess salt before using), crumbled

2 tablespoons sesame seeds or slivered almonds, toasted in a dry skillet
   over medium heat until fragrant

1. In a large measuring cup or medium-size bowl, stir together the mole concentrate and broth until smooth. This is your mole sauce.

2. In a large skillet, heat the oil over medium-high heat, then add the onion and cook, stirring, until softened, about 5 minutes. Set aside.

3. Pour about ½ cup of the mole sauce into the slow cooker; tilt to spread it around. Layer 12 of the tortilla strips on top of the sauce. Pour on about one-fourth of the remaining mole sauce. Layer on one-third of the sautéed onion. Layer on one-third of the chicken. Use a spoon to dollop on one-fourth of the sour cream. Sprinkle on one-fourth of the crumbled cheese. Continue to build the casserole the same way, making two more layers (you will use up all of the onion and chicken). Finish the casserole with the remaining tortilla strips, mole sauce, sour cream, and cheese.

4. Sprinkle the sesame seeds over the top. Cover and cook on HIGH for 2 hours, or LOW for 4 hours. The casserole will begin to brown around the edges, but do not allow it to burn.

5. Let cool for a few minutes before cutting into squares or wedges to serve.

Chicken in Champagne

B eth used to serve this dish to her fussiest catering clients. It is simple and tastes like the best restaurant dish. Use any type of dry Champagne you like. You will only use ½ cup, so you can serve the rest of the bottle as an apéritif. Serve over long-grain white or basmati rice or orzo. ○ *Serves 8*

COOKER: Medium or large round or oval
SETTING AND COOK TIME: HIGH for 2½ to 3 hours

1 large yellow onion, cut in half and sliced into half-moons
3 shallots, sliced
1½ pounds fresh white mushrooms, quartered
8 boneless, skinless chicken breast halves, or 2½ to 3 pounds boneless chicken thighs,
 or a combination, trimmed of fat
½ cup dry Champagne or sparkling wine
⅔ cup crème fraîche, store-bought or homemade (page 90)
Salt and freshly ground black pepper to taste

1. Layer the onion, shallots, mushrooms, and chicken in the slow cooker. Pour the Champagne over the top. Cover and cook on HIGH until the chicken is tender and cooked through, 2½ to 3 hours. The chicken will make some of its own juice as well.

2. Transfer the chicken to a warm platter. Leave the cooker on HIGH, add the crème fraîche to the vegetables, and whisk until smooth. Season with salt and pepper. Let cook a few minutes until hot. Pour the sauce and vegetables over the chicken and serve immediately, or place the chicken back in the cooker and serve directly out of the crock.

Honey-Mustard Chicken

For this easy and quick recipe, from Julie's friend Batia Rabec, you will need to search out the little yellow-and-green boxes of Knorr Dijonne Entrée Mix. This is one convenience product that really delivers! Serve this with rice, pasta, or mashed potatoes to soak up the delicious sauce. ○ *Serves 12*

COOKER: Large round or oval
SETTINGS AND COOK TIMES: HIGH for 2½ hours, then LOW for 1 hour

3 tablespoons unsalted butter
12 boneless chicken breast halves, with skin on
One 1.7-ounce package Knorr Dijonne Entrée Mix
1½ cups dry white wine
⅔ cup heavy cream
⅔ cup honey
Salt and freshly ground black pepper to taste

1. Melt the butter in a large skillet over medium-high heat. When it foams, add as many pieces of the chicken, skin side down, as will fit in a single layer without crowding, and cook until deep golden brown on both sides, 5 to 7 minutes per side. Remove to a plate while you cook the remaining chicken.

2. Transfer the chicken to the slow cooker. Sprinkle on the Knorr Dijonne mix and pour in the wine. Cover and cook on HIGH for 2½ hours.

3. Pour the cream and the honey over the chicken. Cover, turn the cooker to LOW, and cook for 1 hour.

4. Sample the sauce and add salt and pepper if necessary. Serve hot.

Chicken Marsala

Here is a classic: chicken in a creamy sauce of Marsala wine and mushrooms. Marsala is a fortified wine that is Italian in origin, though it is now made domestically, too. You want a dry Marsala for this recipe, which comes from Batia Rabec. Julie and Batia tested it at a dinner party featuring several of Batia's elegant slow cooker creations. Everyone loved this recipe! Look for dried porcini mushrooms in little cellophane packets in the produce or deli section of your supermarket. ● *Serves 8*

COOKER: Large round
SETTING AND COOK TIME: HIGH for 4 to 5 hours

About 1 ounce dried porcini mushrooms
1 cup all-purpose flour
8 boneless chicken breast halves, with skin on
3 tablespoons unsalted butter
10 cloves garlic
2 teaspoons salt, plus more to taste
¼ teaspoon freshly ground black pepper, plus more to taste
1 cup dry Marsala
4 tablespoons cornstarch
⅔ cup whole or low-fat milk
6 tablespoons heavy cream

1. Place the mushrooms in a heatproof cup or small bowl. Add boiling water to cover and let soak while you proceed with the recipe.

2. Place the flour on a shallow plate or a pie plate. One piece at a time, dredge the chicken in the flour, coating both sides and shaking off any excess.

3. Melt the butter in a large skillet over medium-high heat. When it foams, add as many pieces of the chicken, skin side down, as will fit in a single layer without crowding, and cook until deep golden brown on both sides, 5 to 7 minutes per side. When you turn the first batch of chicken over, add 5 of the garlic cloves; brown the garlic but do not let it burn. Transfer the browned chicken and garlic to the slow cooker and repeat with the remaining chicken and garlic. Sprinkle with the salt and pepper.

4. Add the Marsala to the skillet and bring to a boil, scraping up any browned bits stuck to the pan. Pour the liquid over the chicken. Remove the mushrooms from their soaking liquid and distribute them over the chicken. Pour the mushroom soaking liquid through a fine-mesh strainer or coffee filter to remove any grit, and add the liquid to the cooker. Cover and cook on HIGH for 4 to 5 hours.

5. Preheat the oven to 375°F. With a slotted spoon, transfer the chicken and garlic (if you wish to serve the garlic) to a shallow baking dish. Place in the oven to keep warm while you finish the sauce.

6. In a small bowl, stir the cornstarch into the milk to make a smooth slurry. Pour the sauce from the cooker into a small saucepan. Stir in the cream and bring to a boil over high heat. Add the slurry and cook at a boil, stirring, until it thickens, 3 to 4 minutes. Season with salt and pepper. Serve the warm chicken with the sauce poured on top or on the side.

Brandied Chicken with Hazelnuts

When Batia Rabec and Julie got ready to make this in a whirlwind of slow cooker cooking one day, they did not feel like roasting hazelnuts or peeling tiny onions. Batia's well-stocked neighborhood market came to the rescue, with canned crisply roasted hazelnuts and a bag of frozen tiny onions. If you are not so lucky, you can roast the hazelnuts by tossing them with a bit of oil and salt and baking them at 350°F on a cookie sheet until they are fragrant and lightly browned, about 10 minutes. To peel tiny onions, drop them into boiling water and blanch for 1 minute or less. Remove to a colander and slit the skins. They should then slip right off between your fingers. This recipe also calls for the brandy in the skillet to be flamed, which isn't hard and really adds to the flavor of the sauce. If you are nervous about this step, you may skip it. Just add the brandy to the chicken in the skillet, bring it to a boil, and cook for a minute or two before removing the chicken to the cooker. If you are going to flame the brandy, be sure to use a skillet that does *not* have a nonstick coating; cast iron or stainless steel works well. This is especially nice served over couscous. ○ *Serves 8*

COOKER: Large round or oval

SETTING AND COOK TIME: HIGH for 4 hours; onions added during last 30 minutes

3 tablespoons unsalted butter
8 boneless chicken breast halves, with skin on
2 teaspoons salt
¼ teaspoon freshly ground black pepper, or more to taste
1 cup brandy
2 bags (about 20 ounces) frozen tiny boiling onions, defrosted
⅔ cup roasted, salted, chopped hazelnuts

1. Melt the butter in a large skillet (not a nonstick one) over medium-high heat. When it foams, add as many pieces of the chicken, skin side down, as will fit in a single layer without crowding, and cook until deep golden brown on both sides, 5 to 7 minutes per side. As the chicken is browned, use a slotted spoon to transfer it to the slow cooker, sprinkling salt and pepper over the pieces as you go.

2. When the final pieces of chicken have browned but are still in the skillet, add the brandy to the skillet and bring it to a boil. Being careful of long sleeves and dangling hair, touch a long lit match to the liquid in the pan and turn off the stove. The liquid will catch fire and burn for about 30 seconds, then the flames will extinguish themselves. With a slotted spoon, transfer the chicken to the slow cooker. Bring the brandy back to a boil, scraping up any browned bits stuck to the pan. Pour the liquid over the chicken. Cover and cook on HIGH for 3½ hours.

3. Stir in the onions. Cover and continue to cook on HIGH for another 30 minutes.

4. Serve the chicken with the sauce, sprinkled with the hazelnuts.

Chicken with Mango and Coconut

This super-easy idea is another great brainstorm from Julie's friend Batia Rabec, a certified genius when it comes to slow cooker chicken. It makes use of a convenience product to which we are now addicted: A Taste of Thai Chicken and Rice Dinner Seasoning. If you can't find this magic little packet in your supermarket, you can buy it online at www.atasteofthai.com. We like Chaokoh brand coconut milk and Philippine brand dried mangoes. Serve this hot over steamed white or brown jasmine rice. ● *Serves 12*

COOKER: Large round or oval
SETTING AND COOK TIME: HIGH for 2 ¼ hours

3 pounds boneless, skinless chicken breast halves, cut into strips about
    1 inch wide and 4 inches long
Two 13.5-ounce cans unsweetened coconut milk
6 tablespoons sweetened or unsweetened dried shredded coconut
½ cup triple sec or other orange-flavored liqueur
1.75-ounce package of A Taste of Thai Chicken and Rice Dinner Seasoning
1½ cups chopped dried mango

1. Place the chicken strips in the slow cooker. Without shaking them, open the cans of coconut milk. Carefully spoon off the top third of the liquid in each can and add it to the chicken. This thick portion on the top is coconut cream; reserve the remaining coconut milk for another purpose.

2. Add the shredded coconut, triple sec, and Thai seasoning to the slow cooker. Stir well to mix and coat the chicken. Add the mango and stir again. Cover and cook on HIGH for 2¼ hours. Serve hot.

Coq au Cabernet

B atia Rabec's version of this French classic features a cream-thickened sauce, which, while certainly not traditional, is truly delicious. Look for dried porcini mushrooms in little cellophane packets hanging on the wall in the produce or deli section of your supermarket. Sometimes they are sold in bulk, and if that is the case, don't let the per-pound price scare you. A single ounce is all you need to add a deep woodsy flavor to this special dish. Rice or noodles are nice alongside the chicken; you definitely want something that can soak up the creamy, aromatic sauce. ○ *Serves 8*

COOKER: Large round or oval
SETTING AND COOK TIME: HIGH for 5 hours

About 1 ounce dried porcini mushrooms
1 cup all-purpose flour
8 boneless chicken breast halves, with skin on
3 tablespoons unsalted butter
2 teaspoons salt
¼ teaspoon freshly ground black pepper
1 teaspoon dried oregano or 4 teaspoons chopped fresh oregano
12 cloves garlic
4 bay leaves
2 teaspoons Dijon mustard
1½ cups Cabernet Sauvignon
4 tablespoons cornstarch
⅔ cup whole or low-fat milk
6 tablespoons heavy cream

1. Place the mushrooms in a heatproof cup or small bowl, add boiling water to cover, and let soak while you proceed with the recipe.

2. Place the flour on a shallow plate or a pie plate. One piece at a time, dredge the chicken in the flour, coating both sides and shaking off any excess.

3. Melt the butter in a large skillet over medium-high heat. When it foams, add as many pieces of the chicken, skin side down, as will fit in a single layer without crowding, and cook until deep golden brown on both sides, 5 to 7 minutes per side. As the chicken pieces are browned, use a slotted spoon to transfer them to the slow cooker, sprinkling with the salt, pepper, and oregano as you go. Add the garlic to the skillet; brown it, but do not let it burn. Transfer the garlic to the slow cooker.

4. Remove the mushrooms from their soaking liquid and distribute them over the chicken. Pour the soaking liquid through a fine-mesh strainer or coffee filter and add the liquid to the cooker. Tuck the bay leaves in among the chicken pieces. Stir the mustard into the wine and pour it over the chicken. Cover and cook on HIGH for 5 hours.

5. Preheat the oven to 375° F. With a slotted spoon, transfer the chicken and garlic (if you wish to serve the garlic) to a shallow baking dish and keep warm in the oven while you finish the sauce.

6. Stir the cornstarch into the milk to make a smooth slurry. Pour the sauce from the cooker through a fine-mesh strainer into a small saucepan, bring to a boil over high heat, and let boil for a minute or two to reduce it slightly. Stir in the cream, then add the slurry and cook, stirring, until the sauce thickens, 4 to 6 minutes. Spoon a little bit of sauce onto each plate and top it with a piece of chicken and a clove or two of garlic. Spoon more sauce over the chicken and serve hot.

Chicken with Orange Sauce

When Julie and Batia Rabec served a lineup of slow cooker dishes at a tasting party, this won first place because of its true orange flavor, which comes from three sources: Cointreau, orange zest, and orange juice. If you are nervous about flaming the Cointreau, you may skip this step. Just add it to the chicken in the skillet, bring it to a boil, and cook for a minute or two before removing the chicken to the slow cooker. If you are going to flame the Cointreau, be sure to use a skillet that does *not* have a nonstick coating; cast-iron or stainless steel works well. o *Serves 8*

COOKER: Large round or oval
SETTING AND COOK TIME: HIGH for 3 to 4 hours

3 tablespoons unsalted butter

8 boneless chicken breast halves, with skin on

2 teaspoons salt

¼ teaspoon freshly ground black pepper

⅔ cup Cointreau or other orange-flavored liqueur

Juice and grated zest of 4 oranges

4 tablespoons cornstarch

⅔ cup whole or low-fat milk

6 tablespoons heavy cream

1. Melt the butter in a large skillet (not a nonstick one) over medium-high heat. When it foams, add as many pieces of the chicken, skin side down, as will fit in a single layer without crowding, and cook until deep golden brown on both sides, 5 to 7 minutes per side. As the chicken is browned, use a slotted spoon to transfer it to the slow cooker, sprinkling with the salt and pepper as you go. When the final pieces of chicken are in the pan, add the Cointreau and bring it to a boil. Being careful of long sleeves and dangling hair, touch a long lit match to the liquid in the pan and turn off the stove. The liquid will catch fire and burn for about 30 seconds, then the flames will extinguish themselves. With a slotted spoon, transfer the chicken to the slow cooker. Bring the Cointreau back to a boil, scraping up any browned bits stuck to the pan. Pour the liquid over the chicken, along with the orange juice, then sprinkle with the orange zest. Cover and cook on HIGH for 3 to 4 hours.

2. Preheat the oven to 375°F. With a slotted spoon, transfer the chicken to a shallow baking dish and place in the oven to keep warm while you finish the sauce.

3. Stir the cornstarch into the milk to make a smooth slurry. Pour the sauce from the cooker into a small saucepan. Stir in the cream and bring to a boil over high heat. Add the slurry and cook, stirring, until it thickens, 3 to 4 minutes. Taste for salt. Serve the chicken hot with the sauce poured over the top or on the side.

Country Captain

S o, of course, you are going to include a recipe for Country Captain," said our literary agent, referring to one of her and her husband's favorite old-time chicken stews (it was also a favorite of Franklin Delano Roosevelt, served at the Little White House in Warm Springs, Georgia). Country Captain is a tomato-based chicken curry that is especially popular, even beloved, in the Deep South and Georgia. It is included in every Southern Junior League cookbook. Beth's friend Qui, now in her nineties, who had a summer home in Georgia during the 1940s and 1950s, speaks lyrically of being served Country Captain. Legend holds that one of the myriad British sea captains delivering spices to the South in the 1800s introduced the recipe for use with the Indian spices he brought. It is a favorite party dish and is often served with bowls of garnishes such as shredded coconut, finely chopped green apple, diced bananas, and chopped green onions, but just a big bowl of toasted almonds is also traditional. This version is garnished with almonds and has fresh mango added with the tomatoes, courtesy of the *Cook's Illustrated* test kitchen; it makes this stew special but can be omitted. Be certain to use Madras-style hot curry powder to achieve the authentic taste of the dish. ○ *Serves 6*

COOKER: Large round or oval
SETTING AND COOK TIME: HIGH for 4½ to 5 hours; mango added at 2 to 2½ hours

8 bone-in chicken thighs, with skin on
1 teaspoon salt, or more to taste
⅛ teaspoon freshly ground black pepper, or more to taste
1 tablespoon vegetable oil
1 large onion, chopped
1 cup seeded and chopped green bell pepper
1 tablespoon Madras-style curry powder
2 teaspoons sweet paprika
⅛ teaspoon cayenne pepper
One 14.5-ounce can diced tomatoes, undrained
One 15-ounce can tomato sauce

¾ cup chicken broth

1 bay leaf

Pinch of dried thyme

½ cup dark raisins or dried currants

1 firm, ripe fresh mango, peeled, pitted, and diced

½ cup slivered almonds

Hot steamed Carolina long-grain white rice or basmati rice for serving

1. Season the chicken liberally with the salt and pepper. Heat the oil in a large skillet over medium-high heat; add the chicken, skin side down, and cook until deep golden brown on both sides, 5 to 7 minutes per side. Transfer to a plate and set aside. Remove all but a spoonful of drippings from the pan, add the onion and green pepper, and cook, stirring, until softened but not browned, about 5 minutes. Add the curry powder, paprika, and cayenne and cook, stirring, just until fragrant, no more than 1 minute. Add the tomatoes with their juices, tomato sauce, and broth, and bring to a boil, stirring to distribute the spices. Stir in the bay leaf, thyme, and raisins.

2. Remove the skin from the chicken thighs and place the thighs in the slow cooker. Pour the tomato mixture over the chicken. Cover and cook on HIGH for 2 to 2½ hours.

3. Stir in the mango, cover, and continue to cook on HIGH until the chicken is tender and cooked through, another 2½ hours.

4. Preheat the oven to 350°F. Place the almonds on a baking sheet and toast until golden brown, about 7 minutes.

5. To serve, place some hot rice on a plate, top with some chicken and sauce, then sprinkle each serving with a few of the almonds.

Crème de Cassis Chicken

P oultry dishes that sport a sauce that is just a tad sweet seem somehow festive and are always a big success at parties. Crème de cassis is a sweetish liqueur created in Dijon, France, and is made from black currants, so it's only fitting to slip a few dried currants into the sauce as well. Be sure to note that once a bottle of cassis is opened, it has a shelf life of only 4 to 8 months, as opposed to other liqueurs that will stay potent in flavor indefinitely. ○ *Serves 8*

COOKER: Large round or oval
SETTING AND COOK TIME: HIGH for 4½ to 5 hours; heavy cream and currants added during last hour

1 cup all-purpose flour
12 bone-in chicken thighs, with skin on
3 tablespoons unsalted butter
2 teaspoons salt, or more to taste
¼ teaspoon freshly ground black pepper, or more to taste
10 cloves garlic
1 cup crème de cassis
⅓ cup dried currants
⅔ cup heavy cream

1. Place the flour on a shallow plate or a pie plate. One piece at a time, dredge the chicken in the flour, coating both sides and shaking off any excess.

2. Melt the butter in a large skillet over medium-high heat. When it foams, add as many pieces of the chicken, skin side down, as will fit in a single layer without crowding, and cook until deep golden brown on both sides, 5 to 7 minutes per side. As the chicken pieces are browned, use a slotted spoon to transfer them to the crock, sprinkling with the salt and pepper as you go. When you have turned the final pieces of chicken, add the garlic; brown it but do not let it burn. Transfer the chicken and garlic with a slotted spoon to the slow cooker. Pour the crème de cassis over the chicken. Cover and cook on HIGH for 3½ to 4 hours.

3. Sprinkle the currants over the chicken and pour the cream over the top, lifting the topmost pieces of chicken to allow the cream to flow underneath. Cover and continue to cook on HIGH until the chicken is tender and cooked through, another hour. Serve the chicken hot, topped with the currant cream sauce.

Chicken with Glazed Walnuts and Grand Marnier

This recipe is from Julie's friend Batia Rabec, a fabulous home cook and dedicated slow cooker user. Batia loves to entertain and, in her hands, the humble slow cooker turns out truly elegant party fare. Batia appreciates the way in which the slow cooker allows her to cook for a party over two days: You can do the messy part of this dish (the sautéing) the day before the event and refrigerate the chicken, garlic, onions, and peppers right in the crockery insert. The next day, add the salt, pepper, and Grand Marnier and start the slow-cooking. Grand Marnier is a combination of Cognac and bitter oranges grown in Haiti. In the United States, you will find Grand Marnier Cordon Rouge, or "Red Ribbon," with a red sash around the neck of the bottle. The flavor is not sweet and it is welcome in the kitchen for what it does to humble ingredients. If you find glazed walnuts in your grocery or specialty food store, by all means use those. If you want to make them, see the recipe on page 265. o *Serves 8*

COOKER: Large round or oval
SETTING AND COOK TIME: HIGH for 4½ to 5 hours

1 cup all-purpose flour
12 bone-in chicken thighs, with skin on
3 tablespoons unsalted butter
8 cloves garlic
2 large onions, cut in half and sliced into half-moons
2 cups thin strips red bell pepper
2 teaspoons salt, or more to taste
¼ teaspoon freshly ground black pepper, or more to taste
1 cup Grand Marnier
⅔ cup glazed walnut halves (recipe follows)

1. Place the flour on a shallow plate or a pie plate. One piece at a time, dredge the chicken in the flour, coating both sides and shaking off any excess.

2. Melt the butter in a large skillet over medium-high heat. When it foams, add as many pieces of the chicken, skin side down, as will fit in a single layer without crowding, and cook until deep golden brown on both sides, 5 to 7 minutes per side. As the chicken pieces are browned, use a slotted spoon to transfer them to a plate. After all the chicken is browned, add the garlic to the skillet; brown it but do not let it burn. Transfer the garlic to a small plate. Add the onion and red pepper to the pan and cook, stirring, until softened but not browned, about 5 minutes.

3. Using a slotted spoon, transfer the onion and pepper to the slow cooker. Place the chicken on top, skin side up. Tuck the garlic in among the chicken pieces. Sprinkle with the salt and pepper; pour over the Grand Marnier. Cover and cook on HIGH until the chicken is tender and cooked through, 4½ to 5 hours.

4. To serve, distribute the onion and pepper among the plates. Top with the chicken and sprinkle each serving with a few of the glazed walnuts.

Glazed Walnuts

These are a flavorful addition to this chicken recipe, and they are wonderful as a salad topping or as a snack with drinks. ○ *Makes ⅔ cup*

⅔ cup walnut halves and pieces
1½ tablespoons sugar
⅛ teaspoon cinnamon
Pinch of salt
Pinch of freshly ground black pepper
Dash of cayenne pepper

Have a clean plate ready near the stove. Place the walnuts in a small, heavy non-stick skillet. Sprinkle on the sugar and spices. Cook over medium heat, stirring constantly with a wooden spoon, until the sugar melts, 3 to 5 minutes. Almost all of the sugar will cling to the walnuts. Immediately dump out the walnuts onto the plate to cool. If you leave them in the hot skillet even a moment too long, they will burn. These can be made a day ahead and stored at room temperature until needed.

Spicy Turmeric Chicken

This recipe from Laura Quemada is adapted from Madhur Jaffrey's *Indian Cooking* (Barron's, 2003). "The original recipe called for a 3-hour marinating period and then baking the chicken in the oven. I found that basting the chicken with the marinade, then throwing the whole thing in the slow cooker, works wonderfully well," says Laura. "When I make this dish, my measurements are approximate, depending on the size of the bird and how spicy or lemony or garlicky I want the bird to taste. I serve an Indian vegetable with this, but I think steamed peas or green beans would be nice. The Mexican in me likes the chicken wrapped in a tortilla the next day. According to Ms. Jaffrey, the chicken has a very red look from the combination of paprika and chile powder or cayenne pepper. You can adjust the quantities of either for more or less heat." Just keep the total to no less than 1½ tablespoons. Serve this over rice. ○ *Serves 6*

COOKER: Medium oval or large round or oval
SETTING AND COOK TIME: HIGH for 4 to 5 hours, or LOW for 7 to 9 hours

TURMERIC MARINADE:
1 tablespoon ground cumin
1 tablespoon paprika
1 tablespoon ground turmeric
1½ teaspoons red chile powder or ½ to 1 teaspoon cayenne pepper, to your taste
1 to 1½ teaspoons freshly ground black pepper, to your taste
2½ teaspoons salt
2 to 3 cloves garlic, to your taste, mashed to a paste
6 tablespoons freshly squeezed lemon juice

One 4- to 4½-pound broiler/fryer chicken, skinned and trimmed of excess fat

1. Coat the inside of the crock with nonstick cooking spray.

2. To make the marinade, combine the marinade ingredients in a small bowl or a small food processor. Be warned: The turmeric leaves a yellow stain behind, so use glass or stainless steel implements if you do not want your dishes yellowed. Please also note that this dish will stain a light-colored crock.

3. Wash and dry the chicken thoroughly. Reserve the giblets and neck for another use. Cut off any lumps of fat. Using your hand, apply the marinade generously all over and inside the bird. Your hand will stain yellow, so use a disposable plastic glove, if desired (get one at your supermarket deli). Place the chicken in the slow cooker (with no liquid). Cover and cook on HIGH for 4 to 5 hours, or on LOW for 7 to 9 hours, depending on the size of the bird and the cooker, until the meat pulls easily away from the bones and an instant-read thermometer inserted into the thickest part of the thigh reads 180°F. The cooking juices can be reduced or served as is. Serve hot.

Chicken Thighs with Garlic and Sparkling Wine

T his is wonderful party fare, perfect for a birthday or any occasion when you might want to open a few bottles of bubbly. Choose a delicious domestic or imported sparkling wine for this dish; obviously, it doesn't have to be Dom Perignon. If you have a special champagne stopper, you can refrigerate the unused portion in the bottle until evening and it will still be fine for drinking. This is also a good recipe to have in your files for after a celebration, to use up leftover sparkling wine. This is another contribution from Batia Rabec. ○ *Serves 6*

COOKER: Medium or large round or oval
SETTING AND COOK TIME: HIGH for 4 to 4½ hours; cream added during last hour, and dish requires a final 20 minutes in the oven

¾ cup all-purpose flour

6 boneless chicken thighs, with skin on

3 tablespoons unsalted butter

1 cup chopped yellow onion

6 cloves garlic, chopped

1 teaspoon salt

⅛ teaspoon freshly ground black pepper, or more to taste

½ cup dry sparkling wine or Champagne

½ cup heavy cream

1. Place the flour on a shallow plate or a pie plate. One piece at a time, dredge the chicken in the flour, coating both sides and shaking off any excess.

2. Melt the butter in a large skillet over medium-high heat. When it foams, add the chicken, skin side down, and cook until deep golden brown on both sides, 5 to 7 minutes per side. Remove with a slotted spoon to a plate. Add the onion and garlic to the pan and cook, stirring, until softened but not browned, about 5 minutes.

3. Using a slotted spoon, transfer the onion and garlic to the slow cooker. Place the chicken on top, skin side up. Sprinkle with the salt and pepper; pour over the sparkling wine. Cover and cook on HIGH for 3 to 3½ hours.

4. Stir in the cream, cover, and continue to cook on HIGH until the chicken is tender and cooked through, for 1 hour more.

5. Preheat the oven to 400°F. Transfer the chicken to a shallow baking dish, pour the sauce over the chicken, and bake for 20 minutes. Serve hot.

•• Slow Cooker Poached Eggs ••

Poached eggs are so nice on toast and so easy to produce in the slow cooker. Use an oval cooker if you have one, because you can cook a larger number of eggs at one time. It is okay to put the custard cups directly on the bottom of the cooker, because the heat comes from around the sides instead of just from the bottom, as in a saucepan.

COOKER: Medium or large round or oval
SETTING AND COOK TIME: HIGH for 30 to 45 minutes; eggs
   added during last 12 to 15 minutes

Pyrex custard cups (1 per egg)
1 to 2 large eggs per person

1. Pour about ½ inch of the hottest possible tap water into the slow cooker. Cover and cook on HIGH for 20 to 30 minutes.

2. Coat as many custard cups as will fit in your cooker in a single layer with cooking spray. Break 1 egg into each cup. Place the cups in the cooker. Cover and cook on HIGH for 12 to 15 minutes. You can test them by pressing each egg yolk gently with a spoon. When the white is firm but the yolk is still soft, they are done. If you need to keep one batch of eggs

warm while cooking more, ease them out of the cups with the edge of a spoon and place them in a bowl of very warm salted water while you poach the rest of the eggs. Drain the eggs on a clean tea towel before serving.

Eggs Benedict

The French have an encyclopedia of ways to serve all manner of composed egg dishes, with eggs Benedict being just one. This is a great centerpiece for an elegant brunch. This recipe provides for half of an English muffin and one egg per person; double the proportions if you want to serve two eggs per person. ○ Serves 6

3 English muffins, fork-split to make 6 halves, or 6 oversized biscuits, split
6 slices Canadian bacon, grilled or pan-fried for a few minutes, or smoked turkey
6 Slow Cooker Poached Eggs (opposite)
1 recipe Hollandaise Sauce (recipe follows)

Toast the English muffins or warm the biscuits in the oven. Arrange one on each serving plate. Cover each with a slice of Canadian bacon, then a poached egg. Pour over some hollandaise and serve immediately while still hot.

Hollandaise Sauce

This is the real thing. And once you have prepared and tasted this version of hollandaise, you will never balk at preparing it again. The sour cream stabilizes the delicate sauce without any loss of flavor. It is a snap to make in the food processor. ○ Makes $1^2/_3$ cups

4 large egg yolks
1 tablespoon freshly squeezed lemon juice
Dash of salt and ground white pepper
1 cup (2 sticks) unsalted butter, melted and hot
$1/_3$ cup sour cream (low-fat is okay)

Place the yolks, lemon juice, salt, and pepper in a food processor; process 15 seconds to combine. With the motor running, add the hot melted butter in a slow, steady stream, drop by drop at first, then dribbling it in, until the sauce is creamy and emulsified. Add the sour cream and pulse a few times to combine. Pour into a deep container that can stand in a water bath until serving.

Jacquie's Southwest-Style Poached Eggs with Chipotle Gravy

This version of Mexican-style poached eggs from food writer Jacqueline Higuera McMahan is sauced with a picante chipotle gravy and served on a square of cornbread. Prepare the gravy (it makes 2½ cups) and cornbread first. Then, while the bread is cooling, poach the eggs. For this recipe, you will poach 6 to 12 eggs, that is, 1 to 2 eggs per person, depending on what else you are serving. ◦ Serves 6

CHIPOTLE GRAVY:
1 to 2 dried chipotle or mora chiles, rinsed and soaked in
    boiling water to cover for at least 1 hour
2 to 4 tablespoons water or chicken broth
1 tablespoon unsalted butter
1 tablespoon olive oil
1 large shallot, minced
2 tablespoons all-purpose flour
1 teaspoon dried thyme
½ teaspoon dried sage, crumbled
1 cup whole or low-fat milk
⅔ cup chicken broth
¼ cup heavy cream
1 teaspoon salt

1 recipe Vanilla Pan de Maiz (page 391)
6 to 12 Slow Cooker Poached Eggs (page 268)

1. To make the gravy, puree the softened chiles in a food processor with the water or broth. Set aside.

2. Melt the butter with the oil in a medium-size saucepan over medium heat. Add the shallot and cook, stirring, until softened. Add the flour and cook, stirring, until lightly browned, about 1 minute. Add the thyme and sage, then slowly whisk in the milk and broth. Simmer until thickened, about 5 minutes, then stir in the cream. Let simmer until thickened and slightly reduced, about 15 minutes. Stir in 2 teaspoons of the chile puree and the salt and let simmer 5 minutes longer. Taste and add more chile puree as desired; remember, it's spicy. Keep warm until serving, or refrigerate overnight and reheat before serving.

3. To assemble, place a square of the vanilla cornbread on a plate, top with 1 or 2 poached eggs, and ladle some hot chipotle gravy over all. Serve immediately.

Barbecued Chicken Wings for a Crowd

he BBQ Queens, Karen Adler and Judith Fertig, usually cook these in a smoker, but they're also mighty tasty made in the slow cooker. Hot, spicy, and smoky, these chicken wings make a great appetizer for a party.

○ *Serves 8 as a main dish, 20 as an appetizer*

COOKER: Large round or oval
SETTING AND COOK TIME: LOW for 4 hours

1½ cups BBQ Queens' Barbecue Spice (recipe follows) or other barbecue spice mixture
5 pounds chicken wings, cut at joints, with bony wing tips reserved for stock or discarded
2 cups tomato-based barbecue sauce, store-bought or homemade (page 110)

1. Place the barbecue spice in a large paper bag or a pan, then toss the chicken wings in the spice mixture. Coat the inside of the crock with nonstick cooking spray. Arrange the wings in the slow cooker.

2. Cover and cook on LOW for 2 hours, then pour the barbecue sauce over the wings. Stir to blend until evenly coated, and cook for another 2 hours or until the wings are tender. Serve hot or warm.

BBQ Queens' Barbecue Spice

This spice mixture gives you a sweet (from the celery seeds) and hot (from the pepper) one-two punch with a savory undertone from the garlic powder and onion salt. This is adapted from a recipe in Karen Adler and Judith Fertig's cookbook, *The BBQ Queens' Big Book of Barbecue* (The Harvard Common Press, 2005). ○ *Makes 2 cups*

½ cup black pepper
½ cup sweet Hungarian paprika
¼ cup garlic powder
¼ cup onion salt
3 tablespoons dry mustard
3 tablespoons celery seed
3 tablespoons chili powder

Combine all the ingredients in a large glass jar with a tight-fitting lid. Secure the lid and shake to blend. This will keep in the cupboard for several months.

•• Wing It ••

Chicken wings are no longer a culinary afterthought. They are the ultimate fun finger food—perfect for party snacks, picnics, buffets, or casual suppers. Chicken wings went modern with the media blitz of being hacked into pieces, deep-fried, and served in the Anchor Bar in Buffalo, New York, with blue cheese dip. Wings adapt to all sorts of ethnic flavors of their marinades and sauces: Indian, Chinese, American, Greek, Moroccan, and even Mexican mole. If you are baking or frying chicken wings, there is no reason not to cook them whole, and let the diners disjoint them. If you are using your slow cooker, however, your cooking space is somewhat limited, so it's really best to disjoint the wings and cook only the first two sections. (Also, whole wings tend to tangle in the slow cooker, which can be frustrating when you are trying to stir them to distribute the seasoning evenly.)

A chicken wing is made up of three sections, called joints: The first one is sometimes called a mini drumstick, and that's exactly what it looks like. It's the meatiest part of the wing, with a single center bone. The middle wing joint has two slender bones and a somewhat more modest amount of very flavorful meat. The third joint is the wing tip; its best use is in the stock pot, where its bony character will add flavor and thickness to your chicken soups.

To disjoint a chicken wing, place it on a cutting board. Bend one of the joints open against the board and use a sharp knife to cut right through the joint. When you find just the right spot to cut, your knife will slide right through. It won't take you long to get the hang of it. Cut through the other joint in the same manner, then use your knife to trim off any large hanging flaps of skin. Drop the wing tips into a sturdy plastic bag and freeze them for stock.

Thanks to new marketing strategies by the poultry industry, it's now easier than ever to serve chicken wings. At the fresh meat counter, you may be able to find packages of so-called mini-drumsticks, the first wing joints only. In warehouse stores and large supermarkets, you can buy large bags of frozen first and second wing joints. These are often called party wings or drumettes and are especially convenient because they are frozen individually, which allows you to remove only the quantity you need. Place them in a separate plastic bag and thaw them in the refrigerator overnight. If you are in a hurry, place them in a plastic bag in a sink full of cold water.

Sujata's Curried Chicken Wings

Beth went to high school with a man who changed his name and became the artist Sage Gentle Wing, a Tibetan mask dancer. Sage studied with the beloved Indian dance team of Asoka and Sujata, who did bit-part movie work in Hollywood in the 1940s in exotic dance scenes. Beth was thrilled to find this appetizer in the *Los Angeles Times California Cookbook* (Harry N. Abrams, 1981). Sujata served these wings at a party at the Pacificulture-Asia Museum in Pasadena decades ago, before Asoka and Sujata retired from performing and public life. They are spicy and fabulous. Make the curry paste first; it keeps in the refrigerator for weeks. This needs to marinate overnight, so plan accordingly.

○ Serves 4 as a main dish, 10 as an appetizer

COOKER: Large round or oval
SETTING AND COOK TIME: HIGH for 3 to 4 hours

SUJATA'S CURRY PASTE:
¼ cup ground coriander
1 tablespoon ground cumin
1 tablespoon ground turmeric
½ teaspoon chili powder
2 teaspoons brown mustard seeds, crushed with a mortar and pestle
½ teaspoon ground cloves
½ teaspoon ground cardamom
½ teaspoon ground cinnamon
3 tablespoons cider vinegar
2 to 3 tablespoons water, as needed

4 pounds chicken wings, cut at joints, with bony wing tips reserved
    for stock or discarded, or 3 pounds chicken drumettes
1 teaspoon fine sea salt
1 tablespoon Asian sesame oil

1. To make the curry paste, combine all the spices in a small bowl. Mix in the vinegar, then drizzle in the water and stir to make a loose paste.

2. Rinse the wings and pat dry. Place in a large bowl and sprinkle with the salt. Mix together the curry paste and the sesame oil; toss with the wings until evenly coated. Cover and refrigerate overnight to marinate.

3. Coat the inside of the crock with nonstick cooking spray. Arrange the wings in the slow cooker. Cover and cook on HIGH for 3 to 4 hours. If possible, stir gently halfway through cooking with a wooden spoon, bringing the wings on the top to the bottom to coat with sauce. Serve hot or warm.

Crocked Buffalo Chicken Wings

B uffalo chicken wings, the most famous chicken wings in the world, were originally a pub recipe published in the *Buffalo News* in western New York. They are cut at the joints (discarding the tip) and are usually deep-fried; here they are crock-cooked. The spicy chicken paired with the tangy, cold dipping sauce is still culinary juxtaposition at its best. It is positively addictive. Be sure to serve the celery sticks alongside. ○ *Serves 4 as a main dish, 10 as an appetizer*

COOKER: Medium or large round or oval
SETTING AND COOK TIME: HIGH for 3 to 4 hours

4 pounds chicken wings, cut at joints, with bony wing tips reserved for
   stock or discarded, or 3 pounds chicken drumettes
1 tablespoon canola or olive oil
¼ cup freshly squeezed lemon juice
¼ cup cider vinegar
3 tablespoons Worcestershire sauce
½ to 1 bottle (2 to 5 ounces) Louisiana hot pepper sauce, to your taste
2 tablespoons honey

BLUE CHEESE DIP:
1 cup mayonnaise
½ cup sour cream
1 clove garlic, crushed, or ½ teaspoon garlic powder
2 teaspoons white wine vinegar or champagne vinegar
A squeeze of fresh lemon juice

A few grinds of black pepper

1 to 2 green onions (white parts only), finely chopped

1 cup crumbled blue cheese (4 ounces)

1 bunch celery, ends trimmed and cut into long sticks, for dipping

1. Coat the inside of the crock with nonstick cooking spray. Rinse the wings and pat dry.

2. Heat the oil in a large, heavy skillet over medium-high heat. In batches, if necessary, brown the wings nicely, 3 to 5 minutes per side. As they brown, transfer them to the slow cooker.

3. Combine the lemon juice, vinegar, Worcestershire sauce, hot pepper sauce, and honey in a small bowl, and whisk to combine. Pour over the wings, and stir to coat evenly. Cover and cook on HIGH for 3 to 4 hours. If possible, stir gently halfway through cooking with a wooden spoon, bringing the wings on the top to the bottom to coat with sauce.

4. To make the blue cheese dip, combine all the ingredients in a small bowl and whisk until smooth; cover and refrigerate until ready to serve.

5. Serve the wings hot or warm, with the blue cheese dip and celery sticks.

Garlic and Lime Chicken Wings with Chipotle Mayonnaise

his is adapted from a recipe from one of our favorite cooking magazines, *Cooking Pleasures*. It is a different type of marinade for wings, as it contains no sugar or honey. The chipotle mayonnaise for dipping is really tasty, so don't skip it. ○ *Serves 4 as a main dish, 10 as an appetizer*

COOKER: Medium or large round or oval
SETTING AND COOK TIME: HIGH for 3 to 4 hours

4 pounds chicken wings, cut at joints, with bony wing tips reserved for
  stock or discarded, or 3 pounds chicken drumettes

LIME MARINADE:

2 teaspoons cumin seeds

⅔ cup freshly squeezed lime juice (from 5 to 6 limes)

⅓ cup olive oil

Grated zest of 2 limes

6 cloves garlic, finely minced

2 teaspoons crumbled dried marjoram or Mexican oregano

1½ teaspoons salt

CHIPOTLE MAYONNAISE:

1 cup mayonnaise

½ cup sour cream

2 to 3 canned chipotle chiles in adobo sauce, to your taste, finely chopped,
   plus 1 tablespoon of the sauce

1 tablespoon Dijon mustard

1. Rinse the wings and pat dry.

2. To make the marinade, place the cumin seeds in a small skillet and toast over medium heat until golden and fragrant, shaking the pan to assure even toasting. Remove from the skillet and crush in a mortar with a pestle. Combine the crushed cumin seeds with the remaining marinade ingredients in a large shallow bowl and whisk to combine. Add the wings, in a single layer if possible, so they sit in the marinade. Cover and refrigerate for about 4 hours.

3. Coat the inside of the crock with nonstick cooking spray. Heat a large, heavy skillet over medium-high heat. Lift the chicken out of the marinade, reserving the marinade, and brown it nicely in the hot skillet, 3 to 5 minutes per side, in batches if necessary. As the wings brown, transfer them to the slow cooker. Pour over the reserved marinade. Cover and cook on HIGH for 3 to 4 hours. If possible, stir gently halfway through cooking with a wooden spoon, bringing the wings on the top to the bottom to coat with sauce.

4. To make the chipotle mayonnaise, combine all the ingredients in a small bowl and whisk until smooth, or pulse a few times in a food processor for a smoother sauce; cover and refrigerate until ready to serve.

5. Serve the wings hot or warm, with the chipotle mayonnaise for dipping.

Plum Sauce Chicken Wings

W e love thick and sticky Asian plum sauce, whether it is used for dipping or glazing. This recipe has a dash of five-spice powder, which is a pungent mixture of cinnamon, fennel seed, star anise, cloves, and Szechuan peppercorns. Consider it the Chinese version of chili powder.

○ *Serves 4 as a main dish, 10 as an appetizer*

COOKER: Large round or oval
SETTING AND COOK TIME: HIGH for 3 to 4 hours

4 pounds chicken wings, cut at joints, with bony wing tips reserved for
    stock or discarded, or 3 pounds chicken drumettes
1 tablespoon Asian sesame oil
1¼ to 1½ cups Asian plum sauce, to your taste
2 tablespoons unsalted butter, melted, or Asian sesame oil
2 tablespoons orange juice concentrate or pineapple juice concentrate, thawed
½ teaspoon Chinese five-spice powder

1. Coat the inside of the crock with nonstick cooking spray. Rinse the wings and pat dry.

2. Heat the oil in a large, heavy skillet over medium-high heat. In batches, if necessary, brown the wings nicely, 3 to 5 minutes per side. As they brown, transfer them to the slow cooker.

3. Combine the plum sauce, butter, orange juice concentrate, and five-spice powder in a medium-size bowl and whisk to combine. Pour over the wings and stir to coat evenly. Cover and cook on HIGH for 3 to 4 hours. If possible, stir gently halfway through cooking with a wooden spoon, bringing the wings on the top to the bottom to coat with sauce. Serve hot or warm.

Old-Fashioned Turkey Breast
with Pan Gravy

C ooking turkey in a slow cooker is so easy it is almost what we would call a no-brainer: Load up the crock with the ingredients and turn it on. Turkey is lean and tasty and no longer needs to be relegated to Thanksgiving. Here, we cook the breast in a simple braising liquid, which keeps it moist, and serve it with flavorful gravy made from the juices. If you have a second slow cooker, consider making a stuffing (pages 179–185) for a festive accompaniment. ⊙ *Serves 8*

COOKER: Medium or large round or oval
SETTING AND COOK TIME: HIGH for 5 to 7 hours; turkey breast added after first hour

One 15.5-ounce can chicken broth
2¼ cups water
2 ribs celery, cut into large pieces
1 medium-size onion, coarsely chopped
¼ cup (½ stick) unsalted butter, cut into pieces
1 teaspoon salt-free dried mixed-herb seasoning, such as
 Mrs. Dash or other salt-free blend
One 5- to 6-pound bone-in whole turkey breast, rinsed and patted dry
¼ cup instant flour, such as Wondra
2 to 3 tablespoons Madeira, to your taste
Salt and freshly ground black pepper to taste

1. Combine the broth, 2 cups of the water, the celery, onion, butter, and herb seasoning in the slow cooker. Cover and cook on HIGH until it simmers, about 1 hour.

2. Add the turkey, skin side down, cover, and continue to cook on HIGH for an additional 4½ to 6 hours. Turkey is done when an instant-read thermometer inserted into the center registers 170° to 180°F.

3. When the turkey is cooked, transfer it to a platter, cover with aluminum foil, and let stand for 10 minutes before carving.

4. Meanwhile, to prepare the gravy, strain the liquid left in the cooker through a cheesecloth-lined colander; press to squeeze the juice from the vegetables and discard the vegetables. Skim off the fat with a spoon. Pour the liquid into a large nonstick skillet and bring to a boil over high heat. In a small bowl, whisk together the flour, the remaining ¼ cup water, and the Madeira until the flour dissolves. Pour this slurry into the hot broth, stirring constantly until the gravy is thick and bubbly. Add salt and pepper. Serve with the hot sliced turkey.

•• Homemade Bread: Sweet Potato Dinner Rolls ••

Hand-formed homemade rolls add a very nice touch to a holiday meal. If you like, bake these at 300°F for 15 minutes, until cooked through but not browned. Cool, then store in the freezer for up to 1 month. When ready to serve, defrost in the bag and bake as directed below. ◐ Makes 2½ dozen rolls

1 package (scant 1 tablespoon) active dry yeast or 2 teaspoons instant dry yeast, such as SAF

1 cup warm low-fat or whole milk (110° to 115°F)

⅓ cup firmly packed light brown sugar

½ cup cold mashed sweet potatoes

2 large eggs, separated

3 tablespoons unsalted butter, softened

1½ teaspoons salt

3½ to 4 cups unbleached all-purpose flour

1 tablespoon cold water for brushing

1 tablespoon sesame seeds

1. In a large bowl, dissolve the yeast in the warm milk. Add a pinch of the sugar; let stand for 5 minutes. Add the remaining sugar, sweet potatoes, egg yolks, butter, salt, and 2 cups of the flour. Beat until smooth. Stir in enough of the remaining 1½ to 2 cups flour to form a soft dough.

2. Turn the dough out onto a floured surface, and knead until smooth and elastic, 6 to 8 minutes. Place in a bowl coated with nonstick cooking spray, turning once to coat the top. Cover and let rise in a warm place until doubled in size, about 1½ hours.

3. Turn the dough out onto a lightly floured surface and divide it into 28 balls of equal size. Roll each ball into a 10-inch-long rope; tie each rope with a loose knot. Place the rolls 2 inches apart on baking sheets coated with nonstick cooking spray. Cover and let rise again until double in size, about 30 minutes.

4. Preheat the oven to 375°F.

5. In a small bowl, beat the egg whites with the cold water, and brush the mixture over the rolls. Sprinkle the tops with sesame seeds. Bake until lightly browned, 15 to 18 minutes.

Rolled Turkey Breast with Prosciutto

B oneless turkey breast roasts are really easy to handle and come out of the cooker so very moist. You will need some kitchen twine to tie the roast. You can most certainly cook this roast with no filling; the simplified version will taste just as wonderful. If you make a half-breast roast, one that weighs 2 to 2½ pounds, cook it on LOW for half the amount of time, 4 to 5 hours, in a medium-size cooker, and cut the braising liquid measurements in half. ○ *Serves 8*

COOKER: Large round or oval
SETTING AND COOK TIME: HIGH for 4 to 5 hours, or LOW for 8 to 10 hours

2 large yellow onions, cut in half and sliced into half-moons
One 4- to 5-pound boneless turkey breast roast with skin, rinsed and patted dry
¼ cup (½ stick) unsalted butter, softened
4 to 6 fresh sage leaves
4 ounces paper-thin slices prosciutto
1 cup chicken broth or turkey stock
¼ cup dry white wine
Juice of 1 lemon
Salt and freshly ground black pepper to taste
1 recipe Sherry Cream Gravy (optional; recipe follows)

1. Coat the inside of the crock with olive oil– or butter-flavored nonstick cooking spray. Arrange the onion slices in the bottom of the slow cooker.

2. Cut the butcher netting off the turkey breast and, with your fingers, lift the skin to create a pocket between the skin and the meat. Rub inside the skin with the butter and position the sage leaves at even intervals across what will be the top of the roast. Turn the roast over and cover the meat with overlapping pieces of prosciutto. Starting at the short end, roll up the breast jellyroll fashion; tie it in 3 places with kitchen twine. Arrange the turkey breast, sage side up, on top of the onions; pour in the broth and wine. Pour the lemon juice over the top and sprinkle with salt and pepper.

3. Cover and cook on HIGH for 4 to 5 hours, or LOW for 8 to 10 hours. The turkey is done when an instant-read meat thermometer inserted into the thickest part registers 165° to 170°F.

4. When the turkey is cooked, transfer it to a platter, cover with aluminum foil, and let stand for 10 minutes before carving. (If you plan to serve the roast cold, let it cool in the braising liquid, then remove it. Discard the liquid or reserve it for use in soup. Wrap the breast in plastic wrap and store overnight in the refrigerator.)

5. Strain the cooking liquid through a cheesecloth-lined colander, pressing to squeeze the juice from the onions. Discard the onions. Place the broth in a small saucepan and prepare the gravy, if you like, or just serve the broth as is in a little pitcher alongside thick slices of the hot turkey.

Sherry Cream Gravy

We like this as a change of pace from regular turkey gravy. ◦ *Makes 2 to 2½ cups*

1 to 1½ cups turkey broth strained from the cooked turkey
⅓ cup dry sherry
¾ cup heavy cream
Salt and freshly ground black pepper to taste

Place the broth and sherry in a small saucepan, bring to a boil over high heat, and cook 1 minute. Add the cream and cook over medium-high heat until slightly thickened, 5 to 8 minutes. Season with salt and pepper and serve hot.

Turkey Legs with Mandarins

This is another creative Nancyjo Riekse recipe, which she calls Turkey Delight, reflecting her passion for fresh produce as director of the local farmers' market in Auburn, California. "Placer County in California, where I live," says Nancyjo, "is known for its seedless Satsuma mandarin oranges. With them available in every store and produce stand around in November, I thought the flavor combination of turkey and mandarins was one to explore." You can substitute regular tangerines or even navel oranges for the mandarins. The oval cooker fits the turkey legs better than a round shape. ○ *Serves 6*

COOKER: Large oval
SETTING AND COOK TIME: LOW for 5 to 6 hours, orange segments added during last hour

1 cup all-purpose flour seasoned with salt, pepper, and garlic powder
6 turkey legs (about 4½ pounds), skin removed
3 tablespoons unsalted butter
3 tablespoons olive oil
¾ cup freshly squeezed Meyer lemon juice
1½ cups freshly squeezed mandarin orange juice
⅓ cup honey
2 tablespoons soy sauce
1 tablespoon grated fresh ginger
6 to 8 Satsuma mandarins, peeled and segmented

1. Spray the inside of the crock with nonstick cooking spray. Put the seasoned flour into a brown paper bag, add the turkey legs, and shake to coat.

2. In a large, heavy skillet, heat 1 tablespoon of the butter and 1 tablespoon of the olive oil; brown 2 turkey legs until a deep golden brown, about 5 minutes. Remove to a plate. Repeat until all 6 turkey legs are browned, adding 1 tablespoon butter and 1 tablespoon oil for each batch. Transfer the turkey legs to the slow cooker. Turn the heat under the skillet to high, and add the lemon juice, orange juice, honey, soy sauce, and ginger, stirring and deglazing the pan as it comes to a boil. Pour the boiling liquid over the turkey legs in the cooker.

3. Cover and cook on LOW for 5 to 6 hours, until fork tender. During the last hour, add the mandarin segments. Serve hot.

Cold Poached Turkey Tenderloins with Chutney-Yogurt Sauce

For summer dining *al fresco* or for a buffet any time of year, here is a recipe concept originally created by the National Turkey Federation and adapted for the slow cooker. Boneless turkey tenderloins are as easy to poach as chicken breasts and every bit as good. The slow cooker is perfect for the job because it gently cooks the breast, giving you an extra-tender and -moist meat. Serve with a cold rice salad and sliced avocados and papayas. **○ *Serves 8***

COOKER: Large oval
SETTING AND COOK TIME: HIGH for 2½ to 3 hours

4 turkey tenderloins (about 3 pounds), left whole
Salt and freshly ground black pepper to taste
1 cup chopped celery with leaves
8 green onions (white and green parts), cut into sections
1 cup dry white wine

CHUTNEY-YOGURT SAUCE:
1 cup thick plain yogurt
1 cup mayonnaise
1 cup sour cream
1 tablespoon curry powder
1 tablespoon ground ginger
1½ teaspoons onion powder
½ cup mango chutney, chopped
Juice of ½ lemon
Salt to taste

1. Spray the inside of the crock with nonstick cooking spray. Arrange the tenderloins in a single layer in the bottom of the crock. Sprinkle with salt and pepper. Add the celery and onion, then the wine and enough hot water just to cover the turkey. Cover and cook on HIGH for 2½ to 3 hours, until the turkey is white throughout when cut with a knife. The internal temperature should read 170°F on an instant-read thermometer.

2. Remove the turkey from the broth and transfer to a rimmed platter. Discard the cooking liquid and vegetables. Cool the turkey slightly, cover with plastic wrap, and refrigerate for at least 4 hours or overnight. (If not using within 24 hours, cool completely in its liquid, then transfer to a covered container and refrigerate in the liquid for up to 2 days. If not using within 2 days, cool and portion the meat into small plastic freezer bags and freeze for up to 2 months.)

3. To make the sauce, in a small bowl, whisk together the yogurt, mayonnaise, sour cream, curry powder, ginger, onion powder, chutney, lemon juice, and salt. Alternatively, you can put all the ingredients into a food processor and pulse to combine. Spoon the sauce over the chilled tenderloins to cover completely. Reserve the extra sauce for serving. Chill for at least 1 hour.

4. When ready to serve, slice the tenderloins into thick medallions across the grain and arrange on a platter. Place the extra sauce in a small bowl and serve on the side.

White Meatloaf

E ver since eating at Max's Diner in San Francisco, Beth has been an advocate of white meatloaf. This is Max's original recipe, adapted for the slow cooker. The turkey is balanced with some ground veal, which keeps the loaf together nicely. A wonderful honey mustard glaze covers the whole thing, and it is served with a quick Madeira gravy. Make this tonight, and serve it with peas and mashed potatoes. Leftovers make great sandwiches the next day. ○ *Serves 8*

COOKER: Medium or large round or oval
SETTING AND COOK TIME: LOW for 7 to 9 hours; glaze added during last 30 minutes

MEATLOAF:
1 pound ground turkey meat
1 pound ground veal
2 large egg whites, beaten until foamy
½ pound French bread, cut into slices
⅓ cup skim milk

2 white boiling onions, minced

2 cloves garlic, minced

2 ribs celery, minced

1½ teaspoons salt

¼ teaspoon poultry seasoning

¼ teaspoon ground white pepper

¼ teaspoon ground nutmeg

HONEY-MUSTARD GLAZE:

3 tablespoons honey

2 tablespoons Dijon mustard

1 tablespoon sesame seeds

MADEIRA GRAVY:

One 1.8-ounce package turkey gravy mix

1 cup water

⅓ cup Madeira

1. To make the meatloaf, place the ground turkey and veal and the egg whites in a large bowl. Tear the bread slices into hunks, place in a food processor, and pulse until reduced to crumbs. Transfer the crumbs to the bowl. Add the milk, onions, garlic, celery, salt, poultry seasoning, white pepper, and nutmeg. Using your hands or a large fork, mix gently but thoroughly, being careful not to compact the meat.

2. Make an aluminum foil "cradle" to help you easily remove the meatloaf from the slow cooker when it is done. Place a sheet of heavy-duty aluminum foil that is about 24 inches long along the edge of the counter, and tear it in half the long way. Fold each piece in half lengthwise, then in half again lengthwise. Place the strips in the cooker in a cross shape, centering them. The edges of the strips will hang over the edge of the cooker. Place the meat mixture on top of the strips and shape it into an oval or round loaf, depending on the shape of your cooker, by pressing it gently, evening out the top, and shaping it to fit your cooker. Bend the foil strips in toward the meatloaf so they will not prevent the cover of the cooker from closing properly. Cover and cook on LOW for 6½ to 8½ hours.

3. About 30 minutes before the end of the cooking time, make the glaze. Combine the honey and mustard in a small bowl. Bend the foil strips out of the way and pour the glaze over the meatloaf. Sprinkle with the sesame seeds. Cover and continue to cook on LOW another 30 minutes, until an instant-read meat thermometer inserted into the center registers at least 180°F.

4. To make the gravy, combine the gravy mix, water, and Madeira in a small saucepan. Blend with a whisk and bring to a boil over high heat, stirring constantly. Reduce the heat to a simmer and cook until thickened, about 2 minutes.

5. To serve, lift the meatloaf onto a cutting board or serving platter, using the foil handles. Slide out and discard the strips. Slice the meatloaf and serve hot with the gravy.

Duck Breasts à l'Orange

When Batia Rabec and Julie went shopping for ingredients to prepare this recipe, they were delighted to find boneless, skin-on duck breasts sealed in a vacuum package in the freezer section at the market. The breasts defrost quickly if you place the unopened package in a bowl of cold water. You can certainly make this recipe with duck legs or with pieces of a duck that you have disjointed yourself, but the ready-to-go boneless breasts certainly make cooking (and eating) a breeze. Yes, duck is a high-fat meat, and most of the fat is right under the skin. But do cook the meat with the skin still on it. You will skim the fat from the sauce after the duck is cooked. If you are nervous about flaming the triple sec, you may skip it. Just add it to the duck in the skillet, bring it to a boil, and cook for a minute or two before removing the duck to the cooker. If you are going to flame the triple sec, be sure to use a skillet that does *not* have a nonstick coating; cast-iron or stainless steel works well. ◦ *Serves 8*

COOKER: Medium oval or large round or oval
SETTING AND COOK TIME: LOW for 6 to 7 hours

3 tablespoons unsalted butter
8 boneless duck breast halves, with skin on (about 3 pounds total)
2 teaspoons salt, or more to taste
¼ teaspoon freshly ground black pepper, or more to taste
⅔ cup triple sec or other orange-flavored liqueur
½ cup dry white wine
Juice and grated zest of 4 oranges

4 tablespoons cornstarch

½ cup whole or low-fat milk

6 tablespoons heavy cream

1. Melt the butter in a large skillet (not a nonstick one) over medium-high heat. When it foams, add as many pieces of the duck, skin side down, as will fit in a single layer without crowding, and cook until deep golden brown on both sides, 2 to 3 minutes per side. As the duck pieces are browned, use a slotted spoon to transfer them to the slow cooker, sprinkling with salt and pepper as you go. When the last pieces of duck have browned but are still in the skillet, add the triple sec and bring to a boil. Being careful of long sleeves and dangling hair, touch a long lit match to the liquid in the pan and turn off the stove. The liquid will catch fire and burn for about 30 seconds, then the flames will extinguish themselves. With a slotted spoon, transfer the duck to the slow cooker.

2. Add the wine to the skillet and bring to a boil again. Cook at a boil for a couple of minutes, scraping up any browned bits stuck to the pan. Pour the wine over the duck, as well as the orange juice, then sprinkle with the zest. Cover and cook on LOW for 6 to 7 hours.

3. Preheat the oven to 375°F. With a slotted spoon, transfer the duck to a shallow baking dish. Tent with aluminum foil and keep warm in the oven while you finish the sauce.

4. Skim and discard as much fat as possible from the liquid in the cooker, then transfer the liquid to a small saucepan. In a small bowl, stir the cornstarch into the milk to make a smooth slurry. Stir the cream into the sauce and bring to a boil. Add the slurry and cook, stirring, until it thickens, 3 to 4 minutes. Add salt and pepper, if desired. Serve the duck with the sauce on the side.

•• About Pheasant ••

Pheasant is a wonderful dish to prepare for guests, as these birds boast the largest and most succulent breast of all poultry. One pheasant typically weighs 2 to 3 pounds and serves 2 people. The meat is lean, delicate, and pale pink, and no growth hormones or steroids are used in the raising of pheasant. It is a wild bird that once flourished in the American northern woodlands in the millions. The brilliantly plumed bird was once more frequently served than chicken in the United States, until the chicken industry boom in the 1960s. The ring-necked pheasant, one of dozens of species of the bird, is the most available, and is farmed in California and Pennsylvania. The pheasant is also the historical food of the European nobleman, as you may have seen in so many beautiful paintings of that era featuring lavish feasts, with the bird shown intact on a platter.

Braised Pheasant with Mushrooms in Riesling

(P) heasant is a lean bird, with the domestic farm-raised strains being a bit meatier, especially around the breast, because they are not running around the woodlands. If you enjoy game birds, anything from chukar to squab, you will really like pheasant. This recipe will fit in a medium-size cooker; if you double it, be sure to use a large round or oval cooker. The timing for cooking will be determined by the age of your birds, so begin testing at 3½ hours. If you have any leftovers, you can pick the meat off the bones and toss it in a nice salad with a berry vinaigrette. This recipe is adapted from one of our favorite cookbooks, *The New England Cookbook*, by Brooke Dojny (The Harvard Common Press, 1999). Try serving it over egg noodles. ○ *Serves 6*

COOKER: Medium or large round or oval
SETTING AND COOK TIME: HIGH for 3½ to 5 hours

¼ pound salt pork, rind removed and finely diced

1 medium-size onion, cut in half and sliced into half-moons

2 large leeks (white parts and some of the green), thinly sliced

3 tablespoons unsalted butter

½ pound fresh shiitake or other meaty large mushrooms,
    stems removed and caps thickly sliced

⅓ cup all-purpose flour

½ teaspoon salt

⅛ teaspoon white pepper

2 pheasants (2 to 3 pounds each), each cut into 4 pieces, rinsed, and patted dry

2 cups slightly sweet white wine, such as a California Riesling

1 cup chicken broth

Pinch of dried or fresh thyme

1. Place the salt pork in a skillet and cook over medium-high heat until the fat is rendered and there are brown bits of meat, about 10 minutes. Remove the meat with a slotted spoon and drain on paper towels; set aside. Drain off and discard all but 2 tablespoons of the fat. Add the onion and leeks and cook, stirring, for about 5 minutes. Add the butter and mushrooms and cook, stirring, for 5 more minutes. Transfer the vegetables to the slow cooker.

2. Combine the flour, salt, and pepper on a plate, then roll the pheasant pieces in it. Add the pheasant to the hot skillet and lightly brown on both sides; transfer the pieces to the cooker on top of the vegetables. Add the wine, broth, and thyme. Cover and cook on HIGH until the meat is tender and an instant-read thermometer inserted into the thickest part registers 180°F, 3½ to 5 hours.

3. Transfer the vegetables and pheasant to warm plates or a platter and pull off the skin. Skim any fat off the top of the sauce in the cooker. Sprinkle in the reserved pork bits and stir. Serve the sauce in a bowl with a ladle alongside the pheasant.

Pheasant with Apple-Shallot Cream

When a dish is labeled "Val d'Auge," after a district in Normandy, France, it is describing a preparation with cream, apples, and apple cider or apple brandy. This dish is reminiscent of that. We'd like to be able to look down our noses at the use of condensed soup in this recipe, but, on the contrary, it makes this dish incredibly delicious and incredibly simple. This is a favorite way to cook pheasant, a tasty bird once only hunted in the wild that is now farm raised and easily bought at a butcher shop or specialty market. You can add a tablespoon or two of Calvados as part of the apple juice, if desired. ○ *Serves 6*

COOKER: Large round or oval (oval preferred)
SETTING AND COOK TIME: HIGH for 3½ to 5 hours

Two 10.75-ounce cans condensed cream of mushroom soup
Two 10.75-ounce cans condensed cream of chicken soup
⅓ cup all-purpose flour
3 large shallots, finely chopped
4 cloves garlic, crushed
¾ cup unfiltered apple juice or cider
¾ teaspoon sweet paprika
1½ tablespoons Worcestershire sauce
1 pound fresh mushrooms, quartered
Two 3- to 4-pound pheasants, cut into 4 pieces, rinsed, and patted dry

1. Coat the inside of the crock with nonstick cooking spray. In the slow cooker, combine the soups (do not add any water), flour, shallots, garlic, apple juice, paprika, and Worcestershire sauce with a whisk. Stir in the mushrooms. Push the pheasant down into the sauce and spoon some sauce over the top of the pheasant as well. Cover and cook on HIGH until the meat is tender and an instant-read thermometer inserted into the thigh registers 180°F, 3½ to 5 hours.

2. Transfer the pheasant to warm plates or a platter and pull off the skin. Skim off and discard any fat on the top of the sauce in the cooker. Serve the sauce in a bowl with a ladle alongside the pheasant.

•• About Rabbit ••

Rabbit is far more popular and available in Europe than it is here in the United States. Rabbits have lean meat and are raised with no steroids or hormones, making rabbit a healthful alternative to chicken. Rabbit does beautifully in a slow cooker environment, with mild white meat that in all respects can be handled like chicken. Older rabbits must be braised or stewed; they are just too tough otherwise. Small fryers are about 3 pounds, and roasters are 4 pounds and up. We usually have the butcher cut the rabbit into 8 pieces—the loin, four legs, two ribs, and the back (or saddle)—for easy handling in the crock. Please note that cooking with wild rabbit is a bit different than cooking with the farm-raised variety; wear rubber gloves when handling wild rabbit because of potentially harmful bacteria, which will die when cooked. But the domestic rabbits are so tasty and convenient that, unless you have a tradition of hunting in your family, there is no need to fuss with the wild kind. Most rabbit recipes are traditionally served with flat egg noodles, spaetzle (page 197), or potatoes.

Braised Rabbit with Prunes and Green Olives

Old-fashioned braised rabbit is a sophisticated, popular dish at many restaurants. There is a lot of resistance to eating rabbit in the United States because it is also an animal that is a favorite pet; professionals call it the "bunny rabbit syndrome." Little do people know that rabbit is very heart healthy and low in calories, and the entire animal is white meat. Plus, it's delicious! If you ask, your butcher will cut it into pieces for you. Here is a wonderful recipe that we adapted from Beth's friend, food writer and restaurant reviewer Janet Hazan. Janet had a French boyfriend named Gil in the late 1980s. Every time Beth would call her, she would be making this rabbit stew for Gil. You want those nice big green olives for this dish. Serve this over extra-wide egg noodles. ○ *Serves 4 to 6*

COOKER: Medium or large round or oval
SETTING AND COOK TIME: HIGH for 3 1/2 to 5 hours

2 tablespoons olive oil

¼ pound pancetta, cubed

One 3- to 3½-pound rabbit, cut into 8 pieces, rinsed, and patted dry

2 tablespoons all-purpose flour

1 large onion, cut in half and sliced into half-moons

2 to 4 cloves garlic (Janet uses 6), to your taste, minced

½ cup dry white wine

1 cup chicken broth

1 bouquet garni made of 2 sprigs fresh Italian parsley, 1 bay leaf, 1 sprig fresh thyme, and 8
    black peppercorns tied together in cheesecloth

1 heaping cup (about ½ pound) pitted prunes

1 heaping cup (one 9-ounce jar) unpitted green olives, drained

Salt and freshly ground black pepper to taste

1. In a large skillet over medium-high heat, heat the olive oil, then cook the pancetta, stirring, until golden, about 5 minutes. Set aside on paper towels to drain.

2. Dust the rabbit with the flour, add to the hot pan, and brown on all sides. Transfer to the slow cooker. Add the onion and garlic to the pan and cook, stirring, for 8 minutes, adding back the pancetta cubes at the end. Transfer the mixture to the cooker. Add the wine to the pan and cook, scraping up any browned bits stuck to the pan. Add the broth to the pan and bring to a boil. Pour over the rabbit in the cooker. Add the bouquet garni, prunes, and olives to the cooker. Cover and cook on HIGH until the rabbit is very tender and falling off the bone, 3½ to 5 hours.

3. Discard the bouquet garni. Season with salt and pepper and serve hot.

Stewed Rabbit with Red Wine and Wild Mushrooms

T his is a rich, wonderful, peasant-style dish generously shared with us by food writer and restaurateur-chef John Ash of Santa Rosa, California. We have adapted it for the slow cooker. If you like, you may prepare the rabbit, mushrooms, and sauce a day or two ahead and reheat them at serving time to top the polenta. There is quite a bit of braising liquid, which will be reduced before serving. It is a traditional touch to braise rabbit in red wine. ○ *Serves 8*

COOKER: Large round or oval
SETTING AND COOK TIME: HIGH for 3 1/2 to 5 hours,
    plus 30 minutes to reduce the sauce

Two 2 1/2- to 3-pound rabbits, each cut into 6 pieces, rinsed, and patted dry
1/4 cup all-purpose flour
Salt and freshly ground black pepper to taste
2 tablespoons olive oil
2 medium-size yellow onions, chopped
1 cup chopped carrots
1/2 cup chopped celery
2 cloves garlic, minced
One 15-ounce can diced tomatoes, undrained
2 teaspoons chopped fresh rosemary
2 teaspoons chopped fresh thyme
1 teaspoon fennel seeds
1 cup hearty red wine
3 cups chicken broth

MUSHROOMS:
2 tablespoons olive oil
1/2 ounce dried porcini mushrooms, soaked in boiling water to cover for
    1 hour, drained, and coarsely chopped
2 tablespoons minced shallots
4 cups (about 12 ounces) thickly sliced wild mushrooms, such as chanterelle,
    oyster, and/or shiitake

2 tablespoons slivered oil-packed sun-dried tomatoes

½ cup sliced drained olives

Zest of 1 lemon

Salt and pepper to taste

1 recipe Gorgonzola Polenta (page 194)

1. Dust the rabbit pieces with the flour and season liberally with salt and pepper. Heat the olive oil in a large skillet over medium-high heat and brown the rabbit on all sides. Transfer to the slow cooker. Add the onions, carrots, celery, and garlic to the pan and cook, stirring, until softened, about 5 minutes. Add the tomatoes with their juice, rosemary, thyme, fennel seeds, wine, and broth and bring to a boil. Pour the mixture over the rabbit. Cover and cook on HIGH until the rabbit is very tender and falling off the bone, 3½ to 5 hours.

2. Remove the rabbit from the cooker. Strain the sauce, returning all of the braising juices to the cooker. Cook, uncovered, on HIGH until slightly reduced, about 30 minutes.

3. Meanwhile, remove the meat from the rabbit bones and discard the bones and braising vegetables. Season the meat with salt and pepper and set aside, keeping warm.

4. While the braising liquid is reducing, prepare the mushrooms. Heat the olive oil in a large skillet over high heat. Add the porcini mushrooms and shallots and cook, stirring, until just beginning to color. Add the wild mushrooms and cook, stirring occasionally, until browned, about 5 minutes. Stir in the sun-dried tomatoes, olives, and lemon zest; season with salt and pepper. Set aside, keeping warm.

5. To serve, spoon the gorgonzola polenta into a large shallow bowl and make a well in the center. Place a portion of gorgonzola in the center and top with the rabbit meat and the mushroom mixture. Ladle the reduced sauce over all. Serve immediately.

Beef, Veal, and Venison

New-Fashioned Pot Roast with
Fresh Rosemary o 299

Sweet-and-Sour Cranberry
Pot Roast o 300

Barbacoa o 301

Pot-au-Feu o 303

Cholent o 304

Braised Oxtails (Rabo) o 306

Corned Beef with Cabbage and
Radicchio o 307

Beef Burgundy o 308

Paniolo Beef Stew o 310

Beef Stifado o 311

Beef Stew with Chestnuts o 313

Sauerbraten o 314

Beef Stroganoff with Porcini
Mushrooms o 316

Stuffed Sweet-and-Sour
Cabbage o 317

Frito Pie o 319

Jan's Tuscan Meatloaf with Roasted
Red Potatoes o 320

Barbecued Beef on Buns o 322

Devilishly Good Beef
Short Ribs o 323

Short Ribs of Beef with Sherry-Mustard
Sauce and Fennel Seed o 324

Korean Short Ribs of Beef
with Ginger o 325

Beer-Soaked Brats o 326

Italian Meatballs o 327

Veal Ragoût with Artichokes,
Brandied Raisins, and
Crème Fraîche o 328

Veal Stew with Champagne o 330

Ragoût of Veal for 20 ○ 331

Osso Buco ○ 332

Puchero ○ 334

Venison, Fruit, and Greens ○ 336

Venison Stew with
Dried Cherries ○ 337

There are legions of meat lovers, and for them, no other food satisfies quite like it. Despite the mood created by any current trendy diet, meat is the most dependable and popular source of protein available. While the main course need not be elaborate, a beef or veal stew, bread, wine, and salad are greatly appreciated foods to be shared with friends, especially during the colder months. Add a delectable rice or potato dish, and you have perfect fare for a formal party. They never fail to please.

Once you become familiar with the slow cooker and what it is capable of doing, there is an entire world of tougher-but-flavorful cuts of beef and veal that make a multitude of delicious dishes. If you are primarily a sautéer or griller, you may not be familiar with them, but these reasonably priced cuts of meats are perfect for the slow cooker, and lend themselves to succulent ragoûts, stews, roasts, tagines, curries, fricassees, and braises. Take a walk down the meat aisle at your local supermarket. You will notice that you look first at certain familiar areas for the types of beef you eat most and are most used to preparing for guests, such as the prime cuts of steak, which are great for the broiler or grill, but would toughen mercilessly if slow-cooked. Take the time to look at the cuts of beef you have never chosen before or have passed over because you don't know how to cook them. For many

people, these will include shank, brisket, chuck roasts, and short ribs, and they are the best choices at the meat market for slow cooker dishes. Also notice that these are the less expensive, more muscley, and fattier cuts. Despite all the bad press on excess fat in one's diet, remember that some fat is necessary for proper tenderness, juiciness, and flavor.

Many cooks prefer to cut their own stew meat from a large roast; we wish to encourage that practice. It is economical, and packaged stew meat is often cut from a section like the top round, which looks nice but cooks up dry and tough. Stew cuts have long been in the realm of French bistro cooking and are now showing up in more restaurants with the resurgence of the desire for slow-cooked food.

Although these cuts start out tough, the long, moist cooking time produces tender, luscious, deeply flavored dishes. As the stew sits undisturbed in the slow cooker environment, the disparate flavors meld together and create a kind of magic. Remember that it is important to have a flavor balance in a stew—the combination of meat, fresh vegetables, herbs, and seasonings is what will make your stew memorable and satisfying. Stews take less time to cook than braises do, because the meat is fully submerged in liquid.

Chuck roasts, often sold as a flat hunk rather than a tied round, should cook up moist and tender, never tough and stringy. Pot roast is a braise made with a 3- to 5-pound piece of meat that is slow-cooked in a small amount of liquid. We love both of these for informal entertaining. Small steaks can be cooked in this braising manner as well, just with proportionately less liquid. Pick out the meat by its shape and size for your size and shape of slow cooker. Chuck is the cut to use for portioning your own stew meat; you can also use beef cheeks or shin meat. Rolled and tied into a pot roast, flank steak is also excellent for crowds. Braciole, small pieces cut from the top or bottom round, are also used for braising as a roulade or as beef rolls.

Oxtail, a cut that traditionally demands special treatment, ended up being one of our favorite meats in the slow cooker. That special treatment is the slow, slow cooking process. Oxtail is the tail portion of cattle, cut into hunks. It is a humble meat not often cooked today, but once you try it, you will agree with us. Oxtail contains lots of collagen, giving it loads of flavor and a lush, silky texture. Buy ½ to 1 pound per person. Your guests will swoon.

Veal is well suited to the slow cooker environment, and we heartily recommend it for serving to company. It has lots of collagen, which melts enticingly into natural gelatin and makes superior, tender braises. Veal shoulder roasts, chuck, neck, cheeks, and blade roasts are really good for cutting up into stew meat, and they are the most economical. For roasts, use the breast, which is rolled and tied like flank steak and is ideal for stuffing for a special occasion. Veal shanks are a premium meat and a high-on-our-list meal for special guests. A popular restaurant cut of veal, shanks cook up almost silky. Please make our Osso Buco (page 332), and buy the hind shanks, if you can find them; they are meatier than the foreshanks.

Although veal remains a controversial meat in the United States, Europeans embrace it and have a multitude of recipes using it. You can choose formula-fed veal, which is pale pink, or grass-fed veal. Grass is what the animal eats when it is allowed to roam and graze, making for a ruddier and stronger-tasting meat.

As always, be aware of keeping all food preparation surfaces clean and free from bacterial contamination by washing your hands, counters, cutting boards, and knives with warm soapy water. *E. coli* is the pathogen most commonly associated with beef, but proper preparation will ensure no cross-contamination, and the cooking process will kill any existing bacteria. Never eat raw meat, and freeze any meat that you don't plan to use within 3 days of purchase. Thaw meat in the refrigerator or microwave, not at room temperature.

•• Important Tips for Braises and Stews ••

Braising, or slow-cooking in liquid, is the easiest way to tenderize meat and bring out its luscious flavors. A braise is not the same as a stew. A braise refers to a large cut of meat cooked in a small amount of liquid, while a stew is meat that is cut up into small pieces and cooked in plenty of savory liquid. Here's what we've learned about braises and stews made in the slow cooker:

- If you are making a stew, first place hard veggies such as potatoes and carrots into the cooker. Then brown the uniform-size pieces of meat in a heavy Dutch oven or skillet in uncrowded batches, adding the pieces to the crock as you finish browning them. Then brown onions and any other vegetables called for in the recipe, add the liquid to the skillet, and deglaze the pan.

- Deglazing gives the juices a deep color and a rich taste. Bring the liquid to a boil in the skillet before pouring it over the meat, then cover and start the slow cooker process. Because the crock is stoneware, there are no concerns about any of the ingredients reacting with the pan.

- In general, if you want the flavor of the meat to go into the liquid and don't care so much about texture, start with cold water and cook on LOW. If you want to keep more flavor in the meat, start with cold water but cook on HIGH for 1 hour before switching to LOW; this speeds up the cooking process. If you want the optimum texture and the most flavor to stay in the meat, pat the meat dry with paper towels and brown the meat in a separate skillet over high heat, then load it into the slow cooker with hot liquid. The searing process, important in traditional braises, caramelizes the surface of the meat, adding considerable flavor.

- Meat stews should always be cooked at a low simmer, never boiling, to fully develop their character and flavor, a process that is perfectly performed in the slow cooker. The collagen, a tough stringy substance found in all meat to some degree, converts to gelatin and thickens the sauce. That is why your sauce shimmers and your meat becomes tender. If you want to thicken your sauce further, see our tips on thickeners on pages 17–18.

- By all means, serve your stew or braise right from the stoneware crock, as its rusticity adds to the pleasure of the meal. For tips on degreasing, see pages 16–17.

- Beef stews and braises keep for up to 3 days in the refrigerator. They taste great when made a day or two in advance and then reheated, and they can be frozen for up to 3 months.

New-Fashioned Pot Roast with Fresh Rosemary

Here is a totally different pot roast, with a mild tomato base and the flavor of fresh rosemary. This is an all-day recipe from the Desperation Dinners gals, who write a syndicated newspaper column. This is great to serve a group. Use a nice wine vinegar here; we like a Zinfandel vinegar. Browning the meat is an optional step; here it is not necessary to make a luscious roast. Serve this with crusty ciabatta rolls and a green salad. ○ *Serves 8 to 10*

COOKER: Medium oval or large round or oval
SETTING AND COOK TIME: LOW for 8 to 10 hours

One 4- to 5-pound boneless chuck roast, trimmed of as much fat
    as possible and patted dry
3 medium-size yellow onions, thinly sliced
2 cups baby carrots (about 24)
8 to 12 medium-size red or white new potatoes, peeled or not and quartered
½ cup ketchup
¼ cup red wine vinegar
2 tablespoons Worcestershire sauce
1 teaspoon salt
¼ teaspoon freshly ground black pepper
2 tablespoons minced fresh rosemary
½ cup boiling water

1. Put the roast into the slow cooker. Add the onions, carrots, and potatoes.

2. In a small bowl, combine the ketchup, vinegar, Worcestershire, salt, pepper, rosemary, and boiling water; pour over the meat and vegetables. Cover and cook on LOW for 8 to 10 hours.

3. To serve, transfer the meat to a cutting board to carve. Serve slices of meat and vegetables with some of the fragrant juices poured over them.

Sweet-and-Sour Cranberry Pot Roast

huck roast makes a great pot roast, producing a silky, fork-tender meat. Cooking the beef in cranberry sauce sounds like an unlikely combination, but it is a favorite preparation, especially during the winter months and during the holidays. ○ *Serves 6 to 8*

COOKER: Medium oval or large round or oval

SETTINGS AND COOK TIMES: HIGH for 30 minutes, then LOW for 8 to 10 hours

One 16-ounce can tomato sauce

One 16-ounce can whole cranberry sauce

¼ cup dry red wine or water

3 shallots, chopped

2 ribs celery, chopped

3 tablespoons cider vinegar

1 tablespoon olive oil

1 tablespoon prepared horseradish

1 teaspoon dry mustard

One 3- to 4-pound boneless chuck roast, trimmed of as much fat
   as possible and patted dry

1. In the crock, stir together the tomato sauce, cranberry sauce, wine, shallots, celery, vinegar, oil, horseradish, and mustard. Cover and turn to HIGH; cook for 30 minutes.

2. Place the roast in the slow cooker and spoon some of the sauce over the top. Cover and cook on LOW for 8 to 10 hours.

3. To serve, transfer the meat to a cutting board. If the sauce is too thin, turn to HIGH and cook for a few minutes, uncovered, to thicken the sauce. Serve slices of meat and vegetables with some of the fragrant sauce on the side.

Barbacoa

Beth's friend Laura Quemada sent this recipe from her mother. "Here's a recipe for barbacoa my mom gave me. It translates into 'BBQ' in Spanish, but the meat really isn't barbecued, and not really stewed, so I'm not sure how to describe it. It uses a flavorful dry spice rub, then a nice spicy sauce. Mom uses salt, pepper, coriander, and rosemary in quantities to suit her taste. My dad would probably add New Mexican red chile powder and sage, but he's a little more adventurous (he watches the cooking channels). Now, if you ask my dad, he says you should add beer to the cooking process, about one-half can or bottle, but mom uses water. I've had it both ways, and they are both great. It is one of my favorites. I remember being served it at Mexican weddings and special birthday parties. It's great with sopa (Mexican rice), frijoles (beans), tortillas, and a green salad. I'm getting hungry just thinking about it." ○ *Serves 6 to 8*

COOKER: Medium or large, oval preferred

SETTING AND COOK TIME: HIGH for 6 to 6½ hours; need to turn meat at 2½ to 3 hours, barbecue sauce added at 5 hours

1 tablespoon salt

1 tablespoon chopped fresh rosemary or 1 teaspoon crumbled dried rosemary

1 teaspoon freshly ground black pepper

1 teaspoon ground coriander

1 tablespoon New Mexican red chile powder or chili powder, such as Gebhardt (optional)

1 teaspoon ground or crumbled dried sage (optional)

One 3- to 4-pound 7-bone roast or boneless chuck rump roast, patted dry

2 tablespoons olive oil

¾ cup water or beer

1 to 2 bay leaves, to your taste

1 to 2 tablespoons chopped garlic, to your taste

2 cups barbecue sauce of your choice, store-bought or homemade (page 110)

1. Combine the salt, rosemary, pepper, coriander, chile powder, and sage in a small bowl. Sprinkle the rub on both sides of the meat. In a heavy Dutch oven or a heavy, deep skillet, heat the oil over high heat. When hot, add the meat and brown well on both sides, 4 to 5 minutes per side.

2. Place the meat in the slow cooker. (If you are using a round slow cooker, you may have to cut the meat in half and stack the pieces.) Add the water, then the bay leaf and garlic. Cover and cook on HIGH for about 5 hours, turning the meat once about halfway through cooking, if desired or possible, to coat both sides evenly with the cooking liquid.

3. Add the barbecue sauce, cover, and cook on HIGH until the meat is fork tender, another 1 to 1½ hours. Slice and serve with the extra sauce on the side.

·· About Pot-au-Feu ··

Pot-au-feu, or the "pot in the fire," the French version of a boiled dinner, is an efficient, one-step approach to making a flavorful soup, a tender roast of beef, and some savory vegetables. It is a meal that takes to almost endless variations in both composition and presentation. You can start with different cuts of meat, add some smoked sausage or not, cook the vegetables separately or not. When all is cooked, you can treat the pot-au-feu as two courses—serving the broth as a separate first-course soup—or more casually, as one hearty, knife-and-fork supper-in-a-soup-plate. We confess that the latter is the way we prefer it. We like to offer some plain cooked white rice alongside for each diner to add to his or her soup plate.

We find our large, oval-shaped cookers ideal for pot-au-feu, because the oval roast and long carrots and leeks fit so nicely. A large round cooker will work as well, though you may have to stand your roast on its end to make it fit. If you find you don't have room for the carrots, turnips, and leeks, just refrigerate them until half an hour before serving time. Then cook them on the stovetop, using some of the broth from the cooker, if you like. If you have a gravy de-greaser, one of those oddly shaped measuring cups with a long spout coming up from the bottom, you will be able to skim the stock easily and quickly. If you don't, use a turkey baster or a large spoon to remove the fat.

As you look at the list of ingredients, you can see that space is an issue for this dish. Pack the crockery insert with care, tucking the ingredients in as efficiently as possible. If your roast is large, you may not have room for soup bones. One ingredient that takes up almost no space at all but adds flavor is dried porcini mushrooms, an addition we tried after reading the essay on boiled beef in Laurie Colwin's *More Home Cooking* (Harper Perennial, 2000).

In addition to eye of round, brisket and rump roast are other common cuts of meat for pot-au-feu. We like the leanness of the eye of round and find that its compact shape works well in the slow cooker. It also yields nicely shaped slices.

Pot-au-Feu

Here is a pot-au-feu formula we like. The one point that we always waver on is the chicken. If you accept the point of view that the chicken's purpose is to enhance the broth, then you'll want to line the bottom of your cooker with parts you're not going to eat: flattened wings or a bony chicken back. If you figure that, as long as you're cooking, you may as well have chicken to eat, too, then use thighs. As with any chicken cooked in water for a long time, the meat will be fairly bland. Serve the pot-au-feu as two courses—broth first, then meat and vegetables—or as one. We like to serve a grainy mustard alongside the meat. This recipe is best made in an oval cooker. ○ *Serves 8*

COOKER: Large oval or round
SETTING AND COOK TIME: LOW for 8 to 10 hours

About ¾ pound veal or beef soup bones (optional)
1 medium-size yellow onion
2 whole cloves
¼ cup coarsely chopped celery tops and leaves
4 sprigs fresh Italian parsley
½ bay leaf
2 cloves garlic
3 or 4 whole black peppercorns, to your taste
4 to 6 dried porcini mushrooms, or more, to your taste (optional)
4 chicken wings or 6 small chicken thighs
One 2- to 2½-pound eye of round roast beef
2 or 3 medium-size carrots, to your taste
2 or 3 medium-size turnips, to your taste
2 leeks
Salt and freshly ground black pepper to taste

1. Place the soup bones, if using, in the slow cooker. Peel the onion, quarter it, push the cloves into one of the onion quarters, and place in the cooker. Add the celery, parsley, bay leaf, garlic, peppercorns, and porcini mushrooms, if using.

2. If you are using chicken wings, flatten them and remove any loose pieces of fat. If using thighs, remove the skin and trim away the fat. Add to the crock. Place the roast in the crock, rearranging the chicken and vegetables as needed for the most efficient fit. Peel the carrots and cut in half lengthwise. Cut each long piece in half crosswise. Peel the turnips and cut into 6 or 8 wedges each. Trim the roots from the leeks and cut away most of the tough green leaves, leaving the white and a couple of inches of green. Split in half lengthwise and wash thoroughly, checking for sand between each layer. Add the carrots, turnips, and leeks to the crock. Add water to cover.

3. Cover and cook on LOW for 8 to 10 hours. (If you are going to be home at the beginning of cooking, you can ensure a clearer broth if you take the time to skim the broth. To do this, turn the cooker to HIGH to start. When the water comes to a boil, skim off any scum that has risen to the surface. Turn the cooker to LOW, cover, and cook for 6 to 8 hours more.)

4. To serve, transfer the carrots, turnips, and leeks to a large, warm, heatproof platter, and the beef to a carving board. If you have used chicken thighs, add them to the platter, too. Strain the broth very thoroughly, pouring it through a colander lined with a double layer of cheesecloth set over a bowl. Pour a few spoonfuls of the strained broth over the meat and the vegetables to keep them moist. Allow the broth to stand so that the fat rises to the surface and you can skim it. Meanwhile, slice the roast and arrange the slices on the platter. If desired, sprinkle the meat and vegetables with salt and pepper.

5. If you are going to serve the broth as a separate first course, cover the platter with aluminum foil and keep warm in a preheated 200°F oven. Skim the fat from the broth, season it with salt and pepper, and serve immediately. To serve together, place some meat, some chicken, if using, and some vegetables in each soup plate. Add some of the broth. You can pass the extra broth at the table, if you like.

Cholent

C holent is the hearty Sabbath stew of European Jews. Pronounced either CHO-lent or CHU-lent, the dish exists in an infinite number of variations that can be simple or lavish, but all versions have one thing in common: They are designed to cook ever so slowly during the hours of the Sabbath, when the work of cooking is forbidden. A slow cooker is easier to manage than the traditional cholent appliances—a wood-burning oven, or even a hearth—and provides the ideal environment for the necessary long, slow cooking. This cholent recipe comes from Julie's friend Batia Rabec, who is from Argentina. Batia loves the combination of black beans and barley, and we agree that the flavors and colors complement each other perfectly. And the amount of garlic is no misprint; the 15 cloves cook into creamy sweetness, imbuing the humble beans and barley with a deeply satisfying flavor. For the best taste and texture, we prefer to cook this on HIGH for a much shorter period of time than is traditional; of course, you can cook it on LOW for longer, if you wish. **○** *Serves 6 to 8*

COOKER: Medium or large round or oval
SETTING AND COOK TIME: HIGH for 5 to 6 hours

2 pounds cross-cut beef shank
1 cup dried black beans, rinsed and picked over
¾ cup pearl barley
15 cloves garlic
1 teaspoon salt
¼ teaspoon sweet paprika
⅛ teaspoon freshly ground black pepper
1 beef bouillon cube, crushed
4 cups water, or to cover

1. Place the ingredients in the slow cooker in the order in which they are listed. Cover and cook on HIGH until the beans are tender, 5 to 6 hours. The meat will probably have fallen away from the bones by this time.

2. Remove and discard the bones and any large pieces of marrow or fat. If any pieces of meat are larger than bite-size, transfer them to a cutting board, chop, and return them to the stew. Stir before serving hot.

Braised Oxtails (Rabo)

Oxtails are often ignored, and what a pity. When treated right—that is, when lightly browned, then braised for a long time with a few flavorful ingredients—they are a rich and silky treat. This spectacular recipe for rabo comes from Julie's friend Karin Schlanger, who grew up eating it in Buenos Aires, Argentina. Rabo means "tail" in Spanish, and this dish is indeed Spanish in origin. When you are shopping for oxtail, try to get as many of the larger, meatier pieces as possible. Yes, saffron is a luxury item, but its fragrant richness elevates this humble cut of meat to superstar status. Penzeys Spices, one of our favorite purveyors (800-741-7787 or www.penzeys.com), sells saffron by mail-order at very attractive prices. Serve this with rice or mashed potatoes. ❍ *Serves 8 to 10*

COOKER: Large round or oval
SETTING AND COOK TIME: LOW for 8 to 9 hours

¼ cup olive oil
5 pounds oxtails
6 large carrots, thinly sliced
4 medium-size onions, chopped
4 teaspoons sweet paprika
1½ teaspoons salt
1 teaspoon saffron threads
¼ teaspoon freshly ground black pepper
¼ cup water

1. In a large skillet, heat the oil over medium-high heat. When hot, add as many pieces of oxtail as will fit in a single layer, without crowding. Cook until lightly browned on all sides, turning as necessary and transferring to a plate as they are browned. When all the meat is browned, add the carrots and onions and cook, stirring occasionally, until softened but not browned, about 10 minutes. Add the paprika, salt, saffron threads, crumbling them between your fingers, and pepper. Stir to combine well.

2. Place about one-quarter of the vegetables in the slow cooker. Add as many of the oxtail pieces as will fit in a single layer, laying them flat. Spoon in some more of the vegetables, then arrange another layer of oxtail pieces. Continue in the same manner, layering vegetables in between the oxtail pieces. When you have added all of the oxtail pieces, pour the rest of the vegetables and any liquid remaining in the skillet into the crock. Add any juices from the plate that held the browned oxtails, and add the water. Cover and cook on LOW for 8 to 9 hours. Serve hot.

Corned Beef with Cabbage and Radicchio

Corned beef is a cut of meat prepared in a manner that recalls early American meat preservation, which involved salting in place of refrigeration. The name "corned beef" comes from the corn-size crystals of salt used to make the briny preservative. This twist on the more traditional corned beef and cabbage uses radicchio, a bitter red-leaf variety of chicory that braises beautifully.

Serves 8

COOKER: Medium oval or large round or oval
SETTINGS AND COOK TIMES: LOW for 9 to 11 hours, then HIGH for about 30 minutes; cabbage and radicchio added during last 30 minutes

One 3- to 4-pound corned beef brisket with seasoning packet, rinsed
1 medium-size yellow onion, coarsely chopped
2 bay leaves
2 cloves garlic, minced
1 medium-size head white cabbage, cut into 8 wedges, each tied with kitchen twine to keep
    from falling apart in the cooker
1 medium-size to large head radicchio, cut into 8 wedges, each tied with kitchen twine
½ cup Dijon mustard, for serving
½ cup prepared horseradish, for serving

1. Lay the corned beef in the slow cooker. If the meat is too big to lay flat in your cooker, cut it in half and stack the pieces one atop the other. Add water just to cover the brisket. Add the seasoning packet, onion, bay leaves, and garlic. Cover and cook on LOW for 9 to 11 hours.

2. Remove the corned beef and place in a serving casserole; cover with aluminum foil to keep warm.

3. Place the cabbage and radicchio in the slow cooker with the cooking liquid and turn the heat to HIGH. Cover and cook until crisp-tender, 20 to 30 minutes.

4. Slice the beef across the grain, and remove the twine from the wedges of cabbage and radicchio. Serve the beef, cabbage, and radicchio with the mustard and horseradish on the side.

Beef Burgundy

A well-made beef burgundy, the venerable braised *sauté de boeuf à la bourguignonne*, is a treasure; the meat melts in your mouth and the wonderful wine does its magic both as a flavor agent and as a tenderizer. It is a bistro standard and one of the most famous slow-cooked beef stews in the culinary world. We love the stew meat cut from the bottom round or even oxtails, as you wish. Please, no generic "burgundy" wines here; choose something nice (the wine makes a big difference) and let the flavor of this wonderful dish entertain your senses. In this version, the beef is not browned first, but if you'd prefer it that way, please go ahead; just pat the meat dry with paper towels before browning it. This requires marinating overnight, so plan accordingly. Serve this straight out of the crock with steamed potatoes and baby carrots. ○ *Serves 8 to 10*

COOKER: Large round or oval
SETTING AND COOK TIME: LOW for 8 to 9 hours

4 pounds stewing beef, trimmed of any excess fat and cut into 2-inch chunks
1¼ cups red Burgundy
¼ cup olive oil
1 teaspoon freshly ground black pepper
8 strips bacon, diced
1 large onion, diced
2 shallots, minced
1 pound white mushrooms, cut in half or quartered

2 cloves garlic, crushed (+)
¼ cup all-purpose flour
1 tablespoon tomato paste
1 teaspoon crushed dried thyme
½ cup beef broth
¼ cup Cognac (optional)
Bouquet of 4 sprigs fresh parsley, stems tied with kitchen twine
Salt to taste

1. Marinate the beef in the wine, oil, and pepper overnight in refrigerator (this can be done in the crockery insert, if you like).

2. In a large skillet over medium-high heat, cook the bacon until soft, but not browned. Add the onion and shallots to the bacon and cook, stirring, until softened; transfer to the slow cooker. You can dab up the bacon fat with a piece of paper towel if there is too much, but leave some in the pan. Add the mushrooms and cook until they give off some of their liquid and begin to brown. Add the garlic and cook less than a minute, just to take off the raw edge. Transfer the contents of the skillet to the crock. Drain the beef, reserving the marinade, and add the beef to the crock; sprinkle with the flour, turning to coat the meat.

3. Add the marinade, tomato paste, thyme, broth, and Cognac, if using, to the skillet. Bring to a boil, then pour into the crock. Nestle the parsley bouquet in the stew. Cover and cook on LOW for 8 to 9 hours.

4. Skim the fat from the surface, if desired, and discard the parsley. Season with salt and serve immediately.

26 JAN 2020 - for Cathy's birthday. Meat might have broken down too much. Still a couple of pieces were too large (after cooking) and needed to be cut in ½. Need full nine hours. Taste was excellent.

Paniolo Beef Stew

T his is a unique recipe adapted from The Orchid restaurant at Mauna Lani resort on the Big Island of Hawaii. *Paniolo* is the word for the Hawaiian cowboys who rode the old ranches that dot the islands. The ingredients reflect the Pacific Rim influence. Shop at an Asian grocery for the taro root and daikon. Serve this with good bread and a green salad. ◦ *Serves 8*

COOKER: Large round or oval
SETTING AND COOK TIME: LOW for 8 to 9 hours;
vegetables added at 6 hours

One 4-pound chuck roast, trimmed of excess fat and cut into 1- to 1½-inch chunks
3 tablespoons all-purpose or whole wheat pastry flour
Salt and freshly ground black pepper to taste
¼ cup olive oil
2 large or 3 medium-size yellow onions, finely chopped
1 cup drained canned diced tomatoes
⅓ cup tomato paste
3 cloves garlic (optional), crushed
4 coin-size ¼-inch-thick rounds fresh ginger
1 bay leaf
3 tablespoons chopped fresh Italian parsley
1 tablespoon chopped fresh thyme or rosemary
1 cup dry red wine
3 tablespoons unsalted butter
¾ cup cubed (1-inch) carrots
¾ cup cubed (1-inch) waxy white potatoes
¾ cup cubed (1-inch) celery
¾ cup peeled and cubed (1-inch) taro root
¾ cup peeled and cubed (1-inch) daikon radish
8 fresh shiitake mushrooms, stems removed and caps sliced
1 tablespoon all-purpose flour mashed together with
    1 tablespoon softened unsalted butter

1. In a large bowl, toss the beef with the flour, salt, and pepper until evenly coated.

2. In a large skillet over medium-high heat, warm 2 tablespoons of the oil until very hot. Add half of the chopped onion and cook, stirring, until limp, then place in the slow cooker. Add half the beef to the skillet and brown on all sides, about 5 minutes. Transfer to the crock. Repeat the browning with the remaining 2 tablespoons oil and beef. Add the tomatoes, tomato paste, garlic, if using, ginger, bay leaf, parsley, and thyme to the crock and stir to distribute evenly.

3. Lower the heat to medium and pour the wine into the skillet. Stir constantly, scraping up any browned bits stuck to the pan; it will reduce a bit. Pour into the crock and stir. Cover and cook on LOW for 6 hours.

4. In the same large skillet over medium-high heat, melt 2 tablespoons of the butter. Add the remaining chopped onion, the carrots, potatoes, and celery and cook 5 to 8 minutes (let the potatoes brown a dash). Transfer to the crock. Add the remaining 1 tablespoon butter to the skillet and cook the taro root, daikon, and mushrooms, stirring, about 5 minutes. Transfer to the crock, cover, and cook another 2 to 3 hours.

5. Season with salt and pepper, whisk in the flour-butter paste (the *beurre manié*), cover, and cook 10 minutes longer. Serve immediately.

Beef Stifado

A stifado is a Greek stew, and this one is a traditional favorite braised winter dish. It is customarily made with beef, venison, or rabbit and studded with plenty of tiny white boiling onions. The recipe varies from village to village and person to person, but the characteristic hint of whole mixed spices flavors all versions. Food writer Lynn Alley, who has a special love for Greek-style cooking and is the author of *The Gourmet Slow Cooker* (Ten Speed Press, 2003), contributed this recipe. Serve this with steamed rice. ○ *Serves 6*

COOKER: Medium or large round or oval
SETTING AND COOK TIME: LOW for 6 to 7 hours; onions added at 3 to 3½ hours

3 tablespoons olive oil

2 tablespoons all-purpose flour

Pinch of salt and freshly ground black pepper, plus more to taste

2 pounds boneless beef stew meat or top round steak, trimmed of fat
    and cut into 1½-inch chunks across the grain

24 white pearl onions, trimmed

One 28-ounce can crushed tomatoes, undrained

½ cup hearty red wine

3 bay leaves

Two 4-inch cinnamon sticks

2 cloves garlic, smashed flat

8 whole cloves

4 allspice berries

¼ pound feta cheese, crumbled, for serving

¾ cup coarsely broken walnut pieces, for serving

½ cup finely chopped fresh Italian parsley, for serving

1. In a large skillet over medium-high heat, warm 1½ tablespoons of the oil until very hot. While it is heating, combine the flour, salt, and pepper in a large zipper-top plastic bag. Add the beef chunks to the bag and shake until well coated. Add half the beef to the hot oil and brown on all sides, 3 to 4 minutes. Transfer to the slow cooker. Repeat the browning with the remaining 1½ tablespoons oil and remaining beef. (If you don't have the time, you can skip this step and step 2 and put the floured meat directly into the cooker, as well as the uncooked onions, tomatoes, and wine.)

2. Add the onions to the skillet and brown slightly, stirring, over medium-high heat; transfer to a bowl and set aside. Add the tomatoes and their juice and the wine to the pan and bring to a boil, scraping up the browned bits stuck to the pan; pour into the cooker.

3. Make a bouquet garni of the bay leaves, cinnamon sticks, garlic, cloves, and allspice berries by wrapping them in cheesecloth and tying the bundle with kitchen twine; submerge into the stew. Cover and cook on LOW for 3 to 3½ hours.

4. Add the sautéed onions, cover, and continue to cook on LOW until the meat is tender, another 3 to 3½ hours.

5. Remove the bouquet garni and season with salt and pepper. Stir gently so as not to break up the onions. Serve topped with the crumbled feta cheese, walnuts, and chopped parsley.

Beef Stew with Chestnuts

T his is adapted from a recipe from the Williams-Sonoma mail-order catalog some years back, developed by their wonderful test kitchen, which is overseen by founder Chuck Williams, for use with their brand of vacuum-packed steamed chestnuts. If you get their catalog, don't skip the recipes dotted throughout it; there are some gems! Serve this with broad egg noodles, steamed rice, or spaetzle dumplings (page 197). ○ *Serves 6*

COOKER: Medium or large round or oval
SETTING AND COOK TIME: LOW for 6 to 8 hours; mushrooms added at 3 to 4 hours

⅓ cup all-purpose or whole wheat pastry flour
Salt and freshly ground black pepper to taste
3 pounds stewing beef, trimmed of excess fat and cut into 1½-inch chunks
¼ cup olive oil
1 large yellow onion, finely chopped
2 cloves garlic, crushed
One 12-ounce bag baby carrots
3 stalks celery with leaves, chopped
½ pound new potatoes (cubed if large, halved or quartered if
    small, or left whole if baby creamers)
One 16-ounce can vacuum-packed steamed chestnuts, drained if necessary
2 tablespoons tomato paste
1½ cups beef broth
½ cup water
Pinch of dried thyme
1 cup dry red wine
2 tablespoons unsalted butter
3 fresh shiitake mushrooms, stems removed and caps sliced

1. Combine the flour, salt, and pepper in a large zipper-top plastic bag. Add the beef chunks to the bag and shake until well coated.

2. In a large skillet over medium-high heat, warm 2 tablespoons of the oil until very hot. Add half the beef and brown on all sides, 3 to 4 minutes. Transfer to the slow cooker. Repeat with the remaining 2 tablespoons oil and remaining beef.

3. Add the onion, garlic, carrots, celery, potatoes, chestnuts, tomato paste, broth, water, and thyme to the crock and stir to distribute evenly.

4. Lower the heat to medium and pour the wine into the skillet. Stir constantly, scraping up any browned bits stuck to the pan; pour into the cooker. Cover and cook on LOW for 3 to 4 hours.

5. In a small skillet over medium-high heat, melt the butter, then cook the mushrooms, stirring, until limp. Add to the stew, stir, cover, and continue to cook on LOW for another 3 to 4 hours. Season with more salt and pepper. Serve immediately.

Sauerbraten

(I) f you've never tried the tangy sweet-and-sour beef pot roast called sauerbraten, a German specialty, you are in for a treat. Serve it over egg noodles or mashed potatoes and you will be very lucky to have any leftovers at all. This recipe came from Gen Cantor of Albuquerque, New Mexico, a dear friend of Julie's mother. She started with a recipe from *Woman's World* magazine, then began adapting. We adapted further. If you are short on time, marinate the beef overnight, but for a tangier flavor, marinate for 2 days. If you won't be using your slow cooker for anything else, you can marinate the beef right in the crock—a nice little time- and mess-saver. Some people like raisins in their sauerbraten gravy; add them in the last step, if you like. Also, you don't need fancy gingersnaps here— the little hard ones sold in boxes in the supermarket cookie aisle are fine.

⊙ Serves 6 to 8

COOKER: Medium or large, oval preferred
SETTINGS AND COOK TIMES: HIGH while browning meat, then LOW for 6 to 8 hours

2 medium-size onions, thinly sliced into half-moons
2 bay leaves
1 teaspoon whole black peppercorns
¼ teaspoon whole cloves
½ cup firmly packed light brown sugar, or more to taste
1 cup cider vinegar

½ cup dry red wine

1 cup water

One 3- to 4-pound bottom round beef roast or rump roast

2 tablespoons vegetable, canola, or olive oil

Ten 2-inch gingersnaps

1 teaspoon salt

2 tablespoons dark raisins (optional)

1. In a large zipper-top plastic bag or in the crock, combine the onions, bay leaves, peppercorns, cloves, brown sugar, vinegar, wine, and water. Add the roast, turning to coat it with the marinade. Seal the bag or cover the crock. Refrigerate overnight or for up to 2 days, turning the roast every 6 to 12 hours or so, if possible.

2. Remove the roast from the marinade and pat dry with paper towels. If you have marinated the meat in a plastic bag, pour the marinade into the crock. Place the crock into the slow cooker base, cover, and turn the heat setting to HIGH.

3. Heat the oil in a large, heavy skillet (cast iron is perfect) over high heat. Brown the roast well on all sides, about 3 minutes per side. Place the roast in the crock; turn to coat it with marinade. Use a spoon to place some of the onions on top of the roast. Place the gingersnaps around the roast in the liquid, breaking them up, if necessary, so they don't stick out of the liquid. Cover, turn the cooker to LOW, and cook until the roast is tender but not falling apart, 6 to 8 hours.

4. Transfer the roast to a cutting board. Strain the liquid in the crock into a saucepan, discarding the onions and spices. To the liquid add the salt and the raisins, if using. Bring to a boil and let it continue to boil until thickened somewhat, about 5 minutes. Taste and add more brown sugar, if desired.

5. While the sauce is boiling, slice the beef across the grain. Arrange it in a shallow serving dish and cover it with some of the sauce. Serve hot and pass the remaining sauce on the side.

Beef Stroganoff with Porcini Mushrooms

Yes, we know that true beef stroganoff is a quick sauté and has absolutely no place in a slow cooker cookbook! But stroganoff has taken many paths, from stew to soup, and this version goes no further afield than many of the others. If you can't bear to call this delicious meal "stroganoff," just rename it "beef and mushrooms in a creamy sauce." This recipe is based on one from Julie's friend Batia Rabec, a slow cooker expert. Serve it with rice or rice pilaf. ● *Serves 6 to 8*

COOKER: Medium or large round
SETTING AND COOK TIME: HIGH for 4 hours; heavy cream added during last hour

About 1 ounce dried porcini mushrooms
2 tablespoons light olive oil or unsalted butter, plus more if needed
½ cup minced shallots
2 pounds lean stewing beef, trimmed of fat, cut into ½ × 2-inch strips, and patted dry
½ cup dry white wine
2 teaspoons salt
¼ teaspoon freshly ground black pepper
1 teaspoon Dijon mustard
⅔ cup heavy cream or crème fraîche, store-bought or homemade (page 90)

1. Place the mushrooms in a cup or small bowl. Add the hottest possible tap water just to cover them. Allow them to soak for at least 1 hour.

2. Meanwhile, heat the oil in a large skillet over medium-high heat. Add the shallots and cook, stirring, until softened, 2 to 4 minutes. Add the beef and cook, stirring, until lightly browned, 3 to 5 minutes. If the beef sticks, you may need to add additional oil. Transfer with a slotted spoon to the slow cooker.

3. To the skillet, add the wine, salt, pepper, and mustard and cook, scraping up any browned bits stuck to the pan. Pour the liquid over the beef. Remove the mushrooms from their soaking liquid and distribute them over the beef. Pour the soaking liquid through a fine-mesh strainer or coffee filter to remove the grit, then add to the crock and stir to combine. Cover and cook on HIGH for 3 hours.

4. Stir in the heavy cream. Cover and continue to cook on HIGH for another hour. Serve hot.

Stuffed Sweet-and-Sour Cabbage

T his recipe is modeled after one used by Julie's aunt, Rose Newman, a creative and discerning home cook. Many of the tips and techniques are hers—including the ingenious colander method for removing cabbage leaves from the head. Softening and separating the leaves is the most time-consuming part of making stuffed cabbage. Although it requires patience, it is not hard. You can do it a day ahead and refrigerate the leaves in a tightly closed plastic bag. Some people trim or shave away the thick stem ends of the cabbage; we find this isn't necessary, especially in the slow cooker, which will thoroughly cook and tenderize the entire leaf. This is a hearty dish with an abundance of thick sauce, which makes it just right for serving over a plate of buttered egg noodles or fluffy rice.

○ Makes 8 to 10 cabbage rolls; serves 4 to 5

COOKER: Medium or large round or oval
SETTING AND COOK TIME: LOW for 10 to 12 hours

1 medium-size head green cabbage

½ cup dark raisins

1 large egg

½ medium-size carrot, cut into chunks

½ medium-size onion, cut into chunks

1 pound lean ground beef

⅓ cup cooked long-grain white rice

¾ teaspoon salt

¼ teaspoon freshly ground black pepper, plus more for the sauce

¼ teaspoon ground ginger, plus more for the sauce

One 28-ounce can crushed tomatoes

2 tablespoons tomato paste

2 tablespoons cider vinegar, or to taste

3 tablespoons light or dark brown sugar, or to taste

1. Prepare the cabbage: Bring a large kettle or saucepan of water to a boil. You will need at least 2 quarts of boiling water. Meanwhile, wash the cabbage and use a sharp knife to cut out as much of the core as possible. You will be removing a cone-shaped piece from the bottom center of the cabbage. Set the cabbage, bottom up, in a colander in the sink. When the water boils, slowly and steadily pour about three-quarters of it over the cabbage, directing it into the hole where the cabbage core was and down the sides. Reserve the remaining hot water in case you need it to soften a particularly difficult leaf.

Alternatively, you can prepare the cabbage using a microwave oven. Wash and core the cabbage as directed above. Wrap the wet cabbage tightly in plastic wrap, being sure to cover it completely. Place in the microwave, core end down, and cook on HIGH until the outside leaves seem pliable, 7 to 10 minutes.

2. In either case, allow the cabbage to cool for a few minutes. Starting at the stem end, begin peeling away the leaves, one by one, using your fingers with care and a paring knife to detach any leaves that are still attached at the core. Do your best to remove the leaves without tearing them. If you are having difficulty, return the cabbage to the colander and re-douse it with boiling water, or re-wrap it and return it to the microwave. You will need about 8 to 10 large leaves. They should be as intact as possible, but it is okay if there are small tears. Set aside the intact leaves. Quarter the remaining cabbage and slice it crossways into ¼-inch-thick ribbons. You will need 3 to 4 cups of shredded cabbage. Arrange the shredded cabbage evenly in the crock. Sprinkle about half of the raisins on top.

3. Make the meat filling: In a blender or a food processor, combine the egg, carrot, and onion. Process until the vegetables are finely chopped. (Alternatively, you can grate the carrot and grate or mince the onion.) Place the meat in a medium-size bowl and pour the egg mixture over it. Add the rice, salt, pepper, and ¼ teaspoon ginger. Using your hands or a large fork, gently combine the beef with the other ingredients, being careful not to compact the meat.

4. Stuff the leaves: Place a cabbage leaf on a work surface, so that it curves upward like a bowl, stem end toward you. Place about ¼ cup of the meat mixture on the leaf, about 1 inch in from the bottom edge. Gently shape it into a thick log that runs sideways across the leaf. Fold the sides of the leaf in toward the filling, then bring up the stem end toward the filling. Roll up into a neat packet, keeping the sides tucked in and the whole thing as compact as possible. Place the completed roll on top of the shredded cabbage, seam side down. Continue stuffing and rolling leaves until you have used up all the meat filling. As you finish arranging each layer of rolls in the crock, sprinkle on some of the remaining raisins until they are used up.

5. Make the sauce: Place the tomatoes in a medium-size bowl. Stir in the tomato paste, vinegar, brown sugar, ⅛ teaspoon ginger, and a few grinds of pepper. Taste the sauce. It should be pleasantly sweet and tangy; adjust as desired with additional vinegar, brown sugar, ginger, and/or pepper. Unless you have used unsalted tomatoes, you will probably not need additional salt. Pour over the cabbage rolls. Cover and cook on LOW for 10 to 12 hours.

6. To serve, transfer the cabbage rolls to a platter. Serve them with a generous helping of the sauce, shredded cabbage, and raisins from the bottom of the crock.

Frito Pie

rito pie consists of chili con carne ladled over Fritos corn chips, and topped with shredded cheddar cheese and, if desired, raw onions. If you buy it at a carnival or street fair, the chili will probably be ladled right into a single-serving bag of Fritos. Ideally, the bag will have been placed flat on a plate and torn open on the side (not from the top, which would not provide enough surface area for the chili). If you make Frito pie at home, you'll place a handful of Fritos on the plate and put the chili on top.

The most famous version of Frito pie was the one served at the lunch counter at the Woolworth's on the Plaza in Santa Fe, New Mexico. (Woolworth's is gone, but its successor still sells the same Frito pie.) For Julie, though, the definitive Frito pie was the one dished up in the school cafeteria 60 miles away, in her hometown of Albuquerque. Our Frito pie is light on the meat and heavy on the low-fat, fiber-rich pinto beans and the lycopene-containing canned tomatoes.

When shopping, be sure to buy regular Fritos. The larger ones are too big to eat easily when laden with chili and soften too slowly. The flavored ones compete with the flavors of this warmly spiced chili. And don't even think of substituting tortilla chips! They will quickly go soggy under the weight of the chili. This is delightful for a casual gathering that includes kids—but the adults will get a kick out of it as well. ○ *Serves 12*

COOKER: Large round or oval
SETTING AND COOK TIME: LOW for 4 to 5 hours

2 pounds lean ground beef

8 to 10 cloves garlic, to your taste, chopped

2 to 4 tablespoons or more New Mexican red chile powder

4 teaspoons ground cumin

Two 28-ounce cans chopped tomatoes, undrained

Two 16-ounce cans pinto beans, rinsed and drained, or

   3½ to 4 cups homemade pinto beans (page 214)

Salt and freshly ground black pepper to taste

Two 12-ounce bags regular Fritos

1 pound mild or sharp cheddar cheese, shredded (4 cups)

1 large white onion (optional), chopped

1. Heat a medium-size nonstick skillet over medium heat. Add the ground beef and garlic and cook until there is no pink, using a wooden spoon or spatula to break up the meat. Drain the meat and place in the slow cooker. Add the ground chile, cumin, tomatoes with their juice, and pinto beans; stir well to combine. Cover and cook on LOW for 4 to 5 hours.

2. Season with salt and pepper. To serve, place a handful of Fritos on a dinner plate. Top with a ladleful of chili and some shredded cheese. Garnish with chopped onion, if desired.

Jan's Tuscan Meatloaf with Roasted Red Potatoes

We love meatloaf in all of its infinite varieties. Here it is studded with flavorful fennel seeds and topped with butter-tossed potatoes. All cook together and make a fine meal served hot from the crock, but we like to make this the day before and eat it cold just as much. ○ *Serves 6*

COOKER: Medium oval or round

SETTING AND COOK TIME: LOW for 6 hours; ketchup added during last 30 minutes

1½ pounds ground sirloin

3 regular-size or 2 large slices whole wheat or white bread

¾ cup finely chopped onion

1 clove garlic, minced

⅓ cup minced fresh Italian parsley

1½ teaspoons salt

¾ teaspoon freshly ground black pepper

1 teaspoon sweet paprika

¾ teaspoon crumbled dried oregano or marjoram

¾ teaspoon crumbled dried basil

½ teaspoon fennel seeds

6 to 8 medium-size red potatoes, quartered

2 tablespoons unsalted butter, melted

½ cup ketchup

1. Place the ground sirloin in a large mixing bowl. Tear the bread slices into quarters or eighths, place in a food processor, and pulse until reduced to crumbs. Transfer to the bowl. Add the onion, garlic, parsley, salt, pepper, ¾ teaspoon of the paprika, the oregano, basil, and fennel. Using your hands or a large fork, mix gently but thoroughly, being careful not to compact the meat.

2. Make an aluminum-foil "cradle" that will help you easily remove the meatloaf from the slow cooker when it is done. Tear a sheet of foil that is about 20 inches long. Place the foil along the edge of the counter and tear in half the long way. Fold each piece in half lengthwise, then again in half lengthwise. Place the foil strips in the crock in a cross shape, centering them. The edges of the strips will hang over the edge of the crock. Place the meat mixture in the crock, on top of the strips. Shape the meat into an oval or round loaf, depending on the shape of your cooker, by pressing it gently, evening out the top and shaping it to fit your crock. Bend the foil strips in toward the meatloaf so they will not prevent the cover from closing properly.

3. In a small bowl, toss the potatoes with the melted butter and the remaining ¼ teaspoon paprika; arrange on top of the meatloaf. Cover and cook on LOW until an instant-read thermometer inserted into the center of the meatloaf reads 160° to 165°F, about 6 hours.

4. About 30 minutes before the end of cooking time, remove the cover, transfer the potatoes to a dish, and keep warm. Pour the ketchup over the meatloaf. Cover and cook another 30 minutes on LOW.

5. To serve, lift the meatloaf onto a serving platter, using the foil handles. Slide out and discard the foil strips, and arrange the potatoes around the meatloaf. Slice the meatloaf and serve hot.

Barbecued Beef on Buns

T his is the real thing—moist, shredded meat simmered in a spicy tomato barbecue sauce and served on soft rolls. The surprise ingredient in the sauce is ginger ale. Don't skip it; it adds a lot of flavor. You might want to use a knife and fork to eat these sandwiches, because they will get messy.

○ Serves 10 to 12

COOKER: Medium or large round or oval
SETTING AND COOK TIME: LOW for 8 to 10 hours, or HIGH for 4 to 5 hours

One 3- to 3½-pound boneless beef chuck roast
2 cups ketchup
¼ cup cider vinegar
¼ cup ginger ale
¼ cup firmly packed light or dark brown sugar
3 tablespoons Worcestershire sauce
1 tablespoon Dijon mustard
2 cloves garlic, crushed
½ teaspoon salt
½ teaspoon freshly ground black pepper
¼ teaspoon red chile powder
1 dozen white, light wheat, or whole-grain soft hamburger buns, for serving

1. Place the chuck roast in the crock. Combine all of the remaining ingredients, except the buns, in a medium-size bowl and whisk until smooth. Pour over the roast. Cover and cook on LOW for 8 to 10 hours, or on HIGH for 4 to 5 hours.

2. Transfer the roast from the crock to a serving platter, cover with aluminum foil, and let stand for 10 minutes before shredding the meat with two forks. Place the shredded meat back in the cooker, and stir to coat evenly with the sauce. With tongs and an oversized serving spoon, pile the meat onto the bottom half of the sandwich buns, add a bit more sauce, if needed, and replace the top of the bun. Serve immediately.

Devilishly Good Beef Short Ribs

H ere's a rib-sticking classic from the BBQ Queens, Karen Adler and Judith Fertig, just for our entertaining book. When paired with garlic mashed potatoes and braised greens, this is home cooking at its finest, and a fabulously easy recipe that takes minutes to load into the slow cooker. ○ *Serves 6 to 10*

COOKER: Large round or oval
SETTING AND COOK TIME: LOW for 6 to 8 hours

6 pounds beef short ribs
1 cup beer of your choice, at room temperature
1 cup tomato-based barbecue sauce of your choice, store-bought or homemade (page 110)
2 teaspoons dry mustard
2 teaspoons light or dark brown sugar
2 teaspoons bottled liquid smoke flavoring

1. Place the short ribs in the slow cooker. In a medium-size bowl, whisk together all of the remaining ingredients until well blended. Pour over the ribs. Cook on LOW for 6 to 8 hours, until the ribs are fork tender and falling off the bone, and the cooking liquid has thickened to a sauce-like consistency.

2. During the last hour of cooking, leave the lid slightly askew so that more liquid will evaporate to thicken the sauce. Serve the ribs hot on a platter with the sauce.

Short Ribs of Beef with Sherry-Mustard Sauce and Fennel Seed

his sauce and short rib combo is really nice. We love lots of Worcestershire sauce and the touch of fennel seed. It is an adaptation of a dish by meat experts Bruce Aidells and Denis Kelly that they cook on the outdoor grill. You don't have to cook the sauce first; just place everything in the slow cooker at once. Serve this with a green salad, corn on the cob, and rice pilaf. ⚬ *Serves 6 to 10*

COOKER: Large round or oval
SETTING AND COOK TIME: LOW for 7 to 8 hours

½ cup Dijon mustard
¼ cup dry sherry
¼ cup Worcestershire sauce
¼ cup soy sauce
2 tablespoons olive oil
2 tablespoons cider vinegar
2 cloves garlic, crushed
3 tablespoons firmly packed light or dark brown sugar
1 tablespoon crushed fennel seeds
1½ teaspoons dried thyme
¾ teaspoon freshly ground black pepper
Pinch of cayenne pepper
6 pounds beef short ribs
2 medium-size yellow onions, chopped

1. Combine the mustard, sherry, Worcestershire sauce, soy sauce, olive oil, vinegar, garlic, brown sugar, fennel, thyme, black pepper, and cayenne pepper in the slow cooker and mix until smooth. Add the ribs to the cooker, submerging them in the sauce. Sprinkle the onions over the ribs. If you have a round cooker, stack the ribs and layer with the onions. Cover and cook on LOW until the meat is tender and starts to separate from the bone, 7 to 8 hours.

2. Let the sauce cool a bit, then spoon the liquid fat off the surface and discard. Serve immediately.

Beef ribs, called beef short ribs or beef chuck short ribs depending on what section they are cut from, come from the 12 ribs that transverse the lower belly area behind the brisket and just below the prime rib. Look for meaty, lean ribs. Often you can find ribs that are cut from the end of the standing rib roast, and these are outrageously good. Short ribs are also referred to as flanken (especially in German cookbooks), and they are a style cut across the rib bones. English-style ribs are cut into individual rectangles with a bit of bone left in; they are usually found in butcher shops. Korean-style short ribs are a thinner cut of flanken ribs and should be quickly grilled or broiled. They are not ideal for the slow cooker. Beef short ribs are often submerged in long-simmered Italian-style tomato sauces to give body to the sauce, which will be served over pasta. When purchasing beef ribs, figure ½ to 1 pound per person, more if you want leftovers.

Korean Short Ribs of Beef with Ginger

One of the most famous ways to cook short ribs of beef is in this Korean dish called *kalbi*. The marinade is scrumptious, with lots of ginger and Asian sesame oil. Serve with kimchee (hot pickled cabbage) and steamed jasmine rice. Do not use the thinly sliced Korean-style short ribs for this dish. ○ *Serves 6 to 10*

COOKER: Large round or oval
SETTING AND COOK TIME: LOW for 7 to 8 hours

½ cup Japanese or Korean soy sauce
2 cloves garlic, crushed
¼ cup firmly packed light brown sugar
2 tablespoons rice vinegar or cider vinegar
2 tablespoons Asian sesame oil
1 tablespoon ketchup
1 tablespoon minced fresh ginger
½ teaspoon red pepper flakes
6 pounds beef short ribs
Chopped green onions for garnish

1. Combine the soy sauce, garlic, brown sugar, vinegar, oil, ketchup, ginger, and red pepper flakes in a small bowl and mix well.

2. Arrange the ribs in the slow cooker and pour the sauce over them. If you have a round cooker, stack them. Cover and cook on LOW until the meat is tender and starts to separate from the bone, 7 to 8 hours.

3. Transfer the ribs to a platter and garnish with the chopped green onions. Serve immediately.

Beer-Soaked Brats

Beer-soaked bratwursts go with football season—they're perfect fare for watching the Big Game with friends. This recipe employs an outdoor grill to brown the outside of the sausages; you can use an indoor broiler or sauté pan, if you like. We like lots of fixings, such as sauerkraut, a variety of mustards, chopped onions, and chopped tomatoes. If you make a favorite potato salad, you'll have a feast. ○ *Serves 6 to 8*

COOKER: Medium or large round or oval
SETTINGS AND COOK TIMES: HIGH for 15 minutes, then LOW for 2 to 3 hours

6 to 8 precooked bratwurst sausages
½ cup beer of your choice
¾ cup water
½ medium-size white onion, sliced

1. Prepare a hot fire in your charcoal grill, or preheat a gas grill or an oven broiler. Grill or broil the brats until brown all over. With a knife, split each brat down one side.

2. Place the beer, water, and onion slices in the slow cooker. Turn to HIGH for 15 minutes to heat through.

3. Add the brats, cover the cooker, and simmer on LOW for 2 to 3 hours.

4. Just before serving, remove the brats from their hot bath and place back onto the grill or under the broiler for 1 minute.

Italian Meatballs

Here is our most delicious meatball recipe, loosely adapted from *Italian Country Cooking* (Villard Books, 1984), a fabulous Italian cookbook that is sadly out of print, by Spago associate Judy Gethers. No herbs in the sauce! No eggs in the meatballs! You can serve them over spaghetti (with Parmesan all over the top), over rice, or piled into a fresh sweet French roll for a hearty sandwich. Note the easy technique for patting the meat into a rectangle and cutting it into squares to form equally portioned meatballs. ○ *Serves 8*

COOKER: Large round or oval
SETTINGS AND COOK TIMES: HIGH to start, then LOW for 6 to 7 hours

SAUCE:
4 tablespoons olive oil
1 large yellow onion, finely chopped
Two 28-ounce cans plum tomatoes, drained and crushed with your hands
One 6-ounce can tomato paste
1 cup chicken broth
½ teaspoon salt
Freshly ground black pepper to taste

MEATBALLS:
1 pound lean ground beef
½ pound ground veal
½ pound ground pork
½ cup fresh bread crumbs
4 tablespoons grated Parmesan or Romano cheese
6 tablespoons minced fresh Italian parsley
2 cloves garlic, pressed
½ teaspoon salt
Freshly ground black pepper to taste

1. To make the sauce, heat the olive oil in a small skillet over medium-high heat. Add the onion and cook until soft, but not browned, about 3 minutes. Scrape with a spatula into the cooker. Add the tomatoes, tomato paste, broth, salt, and pepper to the crock. Stir to blend, cover, and cook on HIGH while you prepare the meatballs.

2. To make the meatballs, place the ground beef, veal, and pork in a medium-size mixing bowl, breaking it up a bit with your fingers or a large fork. Add the bread crumbs, Parmesan, parsley, garlic, salt, and pepper. Mix well using your hands or a large fork. Be careful not to compact the meat, which will make your meatballs tough. Divide the meat mixture in half. On a cutting board, lightly pat the meat mixture into 2 thick rectangles, about 8 × 6 inches. With a knife, cut a cross into the meat, dividing each rectangle into 4 equal portions; further divide the 4 portions in half, to make 8 equal portions. Gently shape each portion into a meatball, each a bit bigger than a golf ball. You will have a total of 16 meatballs.

3. Gently add the meatballs to the crock and spoon some sauce over them. Cover, turn the heat to LOW, and cook for 6 to 7 hours, until the meatballs are firm and register an internal temperature of 160°F on an instant-read thermometer. Serve immediately, or cool and refrigerate for up to 3 days or freeze for up to 2 months.

Veal Ragoût with Artichokes, Brandied Raisins, and Crème Fraîche

his recipe is from food writer Louise Fiszer, coauthor and recipe developer of *The California-American Cookbook* (Simon and Schuster, 1985), a book now out of print but one of our favorites. In the 1980s, Beth began teaching baking classes at Louise's Pantry. She often sat in on Louise's classes, and it was there that she learned this veal stew. It is simply one of the best, and she still makes it often for parties and catering. ○ *Serves 6 to 8*

COOKER: Medium or large round or oval
SETTINGS AND COOK TIMES: LOW for 7 to 8 hours (artichoke hearts, mushrooms, and raisins added at 3 1/2 to 4 hours), then HIGH for 10 minutes

1 cup golden raisins
1/3 cup brandy
3 pounds veal stew meat, trimmed of fat and cut into 1 1/2-inch chunks
1/2 cup (1 stick) unsalted butter
2 tablespoons all-purpose flour

1 cup chicken broth

¾ cup dry white wine

1 bouquet garni of 3 sprigs fresh Italian parsley, some celery leaves, 1 sprig fresh thyme, and 1 bay leaf tied together with kitchen twine

One 12-ounce package frozen artichoke heart halves, thawed

12 ounces white mushrooms, sliced

Salt and freshly ground black pepper to taste

1 cup crème fraîche, store-bought or homemade (page 90)

1. In a small bowl, cover the raisins with the brandy and let macerate for 1 hour.

2. Pat the veal dry with paper towels. In a large skillet over medium-high heat, melt ¼ cup (½ stick) of the butter until very hot. Add half the veal and cook until browned on all sides, 4 to 5 minutes. Transfer to the slow cooker. Repeat with 2 tablespoons of the remaining butter and the remaining veal. Add the remaining 2 tablespoons butter to the skillet and sprinkle with the flour. Cook for 2 minutes, stirring, to make a roux. Add the broth and wine, bring to a boil, and cook, scraping up any browned bits stuck to the pan, until the wine has thickened slightly, 1 to 2 minutes. Pour into the cooker and tuck in the bouquet garni. Cover and cook on LOW for 3½ to 4 hours.

3. Add the artichoke hearts, mushrooms, and plumped raisins, cover, and continue to cook on LOW until the veal is tender enough to cut with a fork, another 3½ to 4 hours.

4. When done, remove and discard the bouquet garni. Add salt and pepper and stir in the crème fraîche. Switch the setting to HIGH, cover, and cook for 10 minutes to heat through. Serve immediately.

Veal Stew with Champagne

C hampagne is a wonderful complement to veal and makes a flavorful stew. Be sure to cook the carrots separately before adding them to the slow cooker, so as not to end up with an overall too-sweet flavor. Serve this with steamed rice or boiled new potatoes in their jackets. ❍ *Serves 12 to 16*

COOKER: Medium or large round or oval

SETTING AND COOK TIME: LOW for 7 to 8 hours; carrots cooked separately and added at the end of cooking

2 tablespoons unsalted butter

4 tablespoons olive oil

6 pounds veal stew meat or boneless veal shoulder, trimmed of fat and cut into 2-inch cubes

4 medium-size yellow onions, chopped

6 tablespoons all-purpose flour

2½ cups chicken broth

2½ cups brut Champagne

1 teaspoon chopped fresh thyme

1 bay leaf

10 large carrots, cut into ¾-inch-thick rounds

½ cup heavy cream or crème fraîche, store-bought or homemade (optional; page 90)

Salt and freshly ground black pepper to taste

1. In a very large skillet over medium-high heat, warm 1 tablespoon of the butter and 2 tablespoons of the oil together until very hot. Add half the veal and cook until browned on all sides, 4 to 5 minutes. Transfer to the slow cooker. Repeat with the remaining 1 tablespoon butter and 2 tablespoons oil and the rest of the veal. Add the onions to the skillet and cook, stirring, until softened, about 5 minutes. Sprinkle with the flour and cook for 2 minutes, stirring, to make a roux. Add the broth and Champagne, bring to a boil, and cook, scraping up any browned bits stuck to the pan, until the wine has thickened slightly, 1 to 2 minutes. Add the thyme and bay leaf. Pour into the cooker and stir to combine with the veal. Cover and cook on LOW until the veal is tender enough to cut with a fork, 7 to 8 hours.

2. At the end of cooking, cook the carrots in boiling water until tender, about 8 minutes; drain and add the warm carrots to the stew. Stir in the heavy cream and season with salt and pepper. Serve hot.

Ragoût of Veal for 20

Every so often you need a good dinner party dish or family-style stew. Here is a luscious braised veal stew for those occasions. You must have a very large slow cooker for this recipe—6 or 7 quarts is best. Because of the large amount of pearl onions needed, we suggest you use frozen for convenience, but you may peel fresh baby pearl onions, if you prefer. Serve with a combination of white and wild rice, French bread with sweet butter, and a green salad.

○ *Serves 20*

COOKER: Large round or oval

SETTINGS AND COOK TIMES: HIGH for 1 hour, then LOW for 7 to 9 hours, then HIGH for 15 minutes; stew thickened and mushrooms added during last 30 minutes

9 pounds veal stew meat or boneless veal shoulder, trimmed of fat
    and cut into 1½-inch chunks

¾ cup all-purpose flour

2 teaspoons salt

2 teaspoons freshly ground black pepper

½ cup olive oil

2 cups dry white wine

5 cups chicken broth

¼ cup tomato paste

8 cloves garlic, skewered onto toothpicks or a bamboo skewer

1 tablespoon chopped fresh oregano

2 bouquet garni, each containing 3 sprigs fresh parsley, some celery leaves,
    and 1 bay leaf tied together with kitchen twine

Four 10-ounce packages frozen pearl onions, thawed

3 tablespoons unsalted butter, softened and mashed together with
    3 tablespoons all-purpose flour

¼ cup (½ stick) unsalted butter

2 pounds white or cremini mushrooms, stems removed and sliced

¼ cup chopped fresh dill

1. Pat the veal dry with paper towels. In a very large mixing bowl, combine the flour, salt, and pepper, then add the veal chunks and toss to coat evenly. In a large skillet over medium-high heat, heat the oil until very hot. Add the veal and cook until browned on all sides, 4 to 5 minutes. You will have to do this in batches. Transfer to the slow cooker. Add the wine to the skillet and bring to a boil, scraping up any browned bits stuck to the pan; add to the cooker. Add the broth, tomato paste, garlic, oregano, and bouquet garni to the cooker. Cover and cook on HIGH for 1 hour.

2. Add the onions, then turn the heat to LOW and cook until the veal is tender enough to cut with a fork, 7 to 9 hours.

3. Remove the garlic and discard, then taste for seasoning. Transfer the meat and onions to a large bowl with a slotted spoon, then add the butter-flour paste in pieces to the cooker. Cover and cook on LOW until thickened, about 15 minutes.

4. Meanwhile, melt the butter in a large skillet over medium-high heat. Add the mushrooms and cook until slightly browned; let any juice evaporate a bit.

5. Return the meat and onions to the thickened sauce and stir in the dill and cooked mushrooms. Cover and let heat for 15 minutes on HIGH. Serve hot.

Osso Buco

O sso buco is the classic Italian veal braise made with veal shanks. It is traditionally served with saffron risotto or Saffron Rice (page 190). In Italy, it is not unusual to see a diner digging out the marrow from the insides of the bones and spreading it on crusty bread. The parsley-lemon-garlic garnish called gremolata is a wonderful touch, so don't skip it. The shanks are sold in thick slices, so you can see the marrow inside the bone. ○ *Serves 8 to 12*

COOKER: Large round or oval
SETTINGS AND COOK TIMES: LOW for 7 to 8 hours, then HIGH for 10 minutes

8 pounds veal shanks
½ cup all-purpose flour
⅓ cup olive oil, plus more if needed
Salt and freshly ground black pepper to taste
2 large yellow onions, finely chopped

2 large carrots, finely chopped

4 ribs celery, finely chopped

1½ cups dry white wine

1½ cups chicken broth

Two 15-ounce cans diced stewed tomatoes, drained

GREMOLATA:

Peel of 2 lemons, cut off in strips

4 cloves garlic

½ cup chopped fresh Italian parsley

1. Pat the veal dry with paper towels and, in a large bowl, toss with the flour to coat. In a large skillet over medium-high heat, warm half the oil until very hot. Add half the veal and brown on all sides, about 5 minutes. Transfer to the slow cooker. Repeat with the remaining oil and veal. Season with salt and pepper.

2. Discard the grease in the skillet. Add the onions, carrots, and celery to the skillet; add another tablespoon of oil if it is too dry. Cook, stirring, until the onion is softened, about 5 minutes. Add the wine and chicken broth and bring to a boil. Add the tomatoes, stir, and pour everything into the crock, surrounding the shanks. Cover and cook on HIGH until the veal is tender enough to cut with a fork, 7 to 8 hours.

3. Transfer the shanks to a platter and cover with aluminum foil. Skim any fat off the cooking liquid, then turn the cooker to HIGH and let the liquid reduce, uncovered, until it reaches the desired thickened consistency, about 10 minutes. Some cooks use an immersion blender to puree the vegetable sauce; you can do this, coarsely mash it through a food mill, or leave it chunky.

4. To make the gremolata, in a small food processor or using a mortar and pestle, combine the lemon peel, garlic, and parsley. Pulse or grind until finely chopped or mashed. Pour the sauce from the cooker over the shanks and sprinkle with the gremolata. Serve immediately.

Puchero

Puchero is a mixed pot of meats, vegetables, and sometimes fruit that is made in Spain and throughout Latin America. The ingredients vary widely from place to place, based on what is locally available, but there is usually a combination of meats. Many versions include starchy plantain as well as delicate fruits such as peaches or pears. After cooking, the meat and other items are removed from the broth and divided among the diners. The broth, which acquires a complex and delicious flavor, is usually served as a separate course, but we confess, we like it all together, served in shallow soup plates. Today, the word *puchero* has acquired a modern meaning in addition to the traditional one: It is now the name of a Spanish-language computer program for organizing recipes. This recipe comes from Julie's friend Karin Schlanger, who is from Argentina. You will need your largest slow cooker (6 or 7 quarts), or you can divide the ingredients between two medium-size ones. The cooking time will remain the same if you use two smaller slow cookers. ◦ *Serves 6 to 8*

COOKER: Large round or oval, or 2 medium
SETTINGS AND COOK TIMES: HIGH for 1 hour, then LOW for 6 to 7 hours

2 large onions, quartered

3 large carrots, cut in half crosswise

4 medium-size boiling potatoes

2 chicken thighs, skin removed

3 pounds veal shanks

1 spicy smoked sausage (about 4 ounces), such as Polish or spicy turkey, cut in half crosswise

¼ head cabbage (about ½ pound), left in one piece

2 to 3 large ribs celery, cut into large chunks

1 leek, cut in half lengthwise

1 ear corn, shucked and cut in half crosswise

½ red bell pepper, seeded and cut in half

2 cloves garlic

1½ teaspoons salt

½ teaspoon dried thyme or 2 to 3 sprigs fresh thyme

1. Place all the ingredients in the slow cooker, beginning with the onions, carrots, and potatoes, then tucking in the pieces of meat and the other vegetables. Sprinkle with the salt and thyme and add water just to cover the ingredients. Cover and cook on HIGH for 1 hour.

2. Turn the cooker to LOW and cook until the meat and vegetables are tender, 6 to 7 hours longer.

3. Serve the broth as the first course and the vegetables and meat as the second course, or serve everything together in shallow bowls as a one-dish meal.

·· About Venison ··

Bright red venison, the king of game meats and the food of kings, has been a culinary staple in European and American diets for centuries, though now it is much less common in the United States. If you have not been blessed with a hunter in your family, don't worry: Farm-raised and flash-frozen venison is now available, and it is a superior lean meat. Species of deer have been brought to Texas and Wisconsin from exotic locations such as India and Manchuria to complement the United States' native wild breeds of white-tailed deer, mule deer, and black-tailed deer. Venison is being raised in New Zealand as well.

Surprisingly, venison is a low-fat alternative to beef, pork, chicken, and some fish. It is also a natural meat, with no added hormones or antibiotics, which is important to some cooks. Venison will vary in texture and flavor based on breed, age, the geographic area where it was raised, and muscle tone. Farm-raised venison is less gamey tasting and more tender than the wild varieties, and it will appeal to the most delicate palates. Because it is so lean, all venison must be cooked slowly to achieve the best texture.

The tougher cuts, which are excellent for stew meat—the shoulder, hind leg, and round steak—are throwbacks to campfire cooking, and in older cookbooks you may find recipes using coffee, chili, hot sauce, Worcestershire sauce, currant jelly, fruit, and lots of herbs and bacon. Marinades are essential for the meat of hunted game, especially the toughest shoulder and leg sections, but they are not necessary with the farm-raised variety. The more tender areas of the ribs, loin, and rump don't need marinating, but they will benefit from that extra boost in flavor. If you want to experiment, try marinades made with fruit juices, beer, or wine, and marinate no longer than 4 to 6 hours. You could also add some ground venison in combination with your ground beef in chili, or cut up chunks of chuck or round venison steak for stews or pot pies.

Venison, Fruit, and Greens

This is a wonderful way to serve venison and enjoy its remarkable flavor; the recipe is the handiwork of food entrepreneur and farmers' market co-ordinator Nancyjo Rieske. If you don't have access to venison, you can substitute dark chicken meat. Serve this stew over wild rice. ○ *Serves 10*

COOKER: Large round or oval
SETTING AND COOK TIME: LOW for 7 to 8 hours

3 to 4 pounds venison stew meat, trimmed of fat, tenderized by
    pounding, and cut into 1½-inch pieces
1 cup pitted dates
2 cups vegetable broth
2 cups Madeira or dry red wine
½ cup red wine vinegar
½ cup olive oil
6 cloves garlic, chopped
2 teaspoons crumbled dried thyme
8 juniper berries, crushed
4 black peppercorns, crushed
1 bay leaf
Pinch of ground cloves
¼ cup firmly packed light brown sugar or honey

GARNISHES:
4 strips thick-sliced bacon
1 bunch Swiss chard, spinach, or mustard greens, trimmed of
    heavy stems and cut into 1-inch-wide ribbons
2 cups coarsely chopped dried assorted fruits (apples, apricots,
    figs, peaches, and/or pears), steeped in boiling water for at least
    1 hour and drained

1. Place all the ingredients into the slow cooker except for the garnishes. Cover and cook on LOW for 7 to 8 hours, stirring occasionally.

2. Right before serving, chop the bacon into small pieces and brown in a large skillet over medium heat. Remove the bacon with a slotted spoon when crisp but still tender, and drain on paper towels. Add the Swiss chard to the bacon drippings and cook, stirring, until just wilted. Remove from the heat, add the bacon back to the skillet, and stir to mix.

3. Serve the stew hot, topped with the assorted chopped fruits and sautéed greens.

Venison Stew with Dried Cherries

T his is a very different stew from the previous one. It has the complementary addition of dried cherries, root vegetables such as parsnips, a hit of brandy, and some orange. You will find the venison and cherry pairing a delicious combination, and one that is perfect for guests. ○ *Serves 12*

COOKER: Large round or oval
SETTING AND COOK TIME: LOW for 8 to 9 hours

5 pounds venison stew meat, trimmed of fat, tenderized by pounding,
    and cut into 1-inch chunks
⅓ to ½ cup all-purpose or whole wheat pastry flour
Salt and freshly ground black pepper to taste
½ cup olive oil
4 medium-size yellow onions, diced
4 cups dry red wine, such as Cabernet Sauvignon
16 medium-size red potatoes, left whole or quartered
6 large carrots, diced
2 large parsnips, peeled and diced
6 ribs celery, diced
1 orange, peeled, seeded if necessary, and chopped
16 juniper berries, cracked
10 cloves garlic, or to your taste, minced
2 cups dried tart cherries, or a combination of dried cherries and golden raisins
Two 10.5-ounce cans low-sodium beef broth
½ cup brandy
2 tablespoons balsamic vinegar

1. Pat the venison dry with paper towels. Combine the flour, salt, and pepper in a large zipper-top plastic bag with the flour, add the venison chunks, and shake to coat the meat evenly. In a large skillet over medium-high heat, heat the oil, then brown the meat in batches; transfer to the slow cooker. Add the onions to the skillet and cook, stirring, just to brown slightly on the edges, about 3 minutes; transfer to the cooker. Add the wine to the skillet, bring to a boil, and cook, scraping up any browned bits stuck to the pan, until the wine has thickened slightly, 1 to 2 minutes. Pour into the cooker. Add the potatoes, carrots, parsnips, celery, orange, juniper berries, garlic, cherries, broth, and brandy to the cooker; stir to distribute evenly.

2. Cover and cook on LOW until the venison is tender enough to cut with a fork, 8 to 9 hours. Stir in the vinegar, season with salt and pepper, and serve hot.

Pork and Lamb

Cherry-Glazed Pork Pot Roast
with Herbs ○ 342

Pork Roast with Tomatoes and
Mushrooms ○ 343

Pernil ○ 344

Mexican Pork Roast with Tomatillo
Sauce ○ 346

Glazed Ham ○ 348

Asian Pork Tenderloins ○ 349

Ragoût of Pork and Mushrooms with
White Wine ○ 350

Chile Verde ○ 351

Oscar's Chile Colorado Mole ○ 352

Choucroute Garnie ○ 354

Chipotle and Orange Pork Ribs ○ 357

Honey Barbecue Pork Ribs ○ 358

Pork Ribs with No-Cook
Barbecue Sauce ○ 359

Braised Pork Ribs with Chiles and
Shallots ○ 360

Hawaiian Laulau ○ 361

French Country Terrine ○ 362

Potée Boulangère ○ 364

Lamb Roast with Lotsa Garlic and
Rosemary ○ 365

Lamb Navarin ○ 366

Lamb and Fruit Tagine ○ 368

Julie's Lamb and Quince Ragoût ○ 369

Moroccan-Style Lamb with
Preserved Lemons ○ 371

Lamb Shanks with White Wine and Wild
Mushroom Sauce ○ 373

Spiced Lamb Dolmas ○ 374

Pork has a rich character and plenty of flavor, and it is very lean. No longer fatty and indigestible, pork contains less cholesterol than beef, veal, lamb, and even dark-meat turkey and chicken. It is known as the world's most popular meat, and if you are looking for lean, pork is the meat you want to eat.

Because pork is so lean and contains much less collagen tissue than beef does, but instead has a unique type of connective tissue called elastin, it is important to buy those cuts that will cook best in the moist heat of the slow cooker. Overcook pork and it tends to shrink up rather than soften. Pork is never served rare; it is always cooked completely through to the bone and should register about 160°F on an instant-read thermometer. Testing with a thermometer is recommended for all cooking done with whole pork roasts.

The fresh shoulder and the upper part of the shoulder, called the Boston butt, ham hocks, blade roast, spareribs, and the picnic are the very best cuts for the slow cooker. The shoulder is what you want for the best pork stews. Spareribs take the spotlight in summer entertaining outdoors or at parties for kids. Pork is quite delicately flavored, so it will take on the essence of whatever your sauce is. It likes the sweet, including barbecue sauce and dried fruit, and the strong, such as peanut sauce, soy sauce and ginger, Hungarian paprika, and Southwestern chiles. The elegant pork tenderloin can be cooked in the slow cooker, too; if done carefully, it turns out flawless.

Hams are another cut of meat associated with celebratory dining. If you choose to prepare a ready-to-eat, fully cooked ham in your cooker, be sure to coordinate the meat with the size of your cooker. Half hams fit best. When buying a ham, calculate 6 to 8 ounces per person with a boneless ham; a tad more for bone-in ham. If you choose to cook one of the artisan country hams that are dry cured, such as Virginia Smithfield hams, be sure to soak it for at least 48 hours, because they are heavily salted; follow the instructions that come with the ham. Ham hocks are like miniature hams; cook them with greens, beans, and split peas, or in a soup or stock. After cooking, remove the skin and bones, then chop the meat.

If you use any type of pork sausages, unless you buy them fully cooked, you must brown and cook them before adding them to the slow cooker. Parcook or fully cook bacon or pancetta, as directed in specific recipe instructions for the slow cooker. Never add raw sausage or bacon to the slow cooker. The exceptions are Canadian bacon and prosciutto, which are precooked and cured, respectively; they can be chopped and added without pre-cooking.

Once only a springtime treat, today's lamb is fresh and of high quality year-round. Lamb is still a meat of celebration and traditional at many Easter dinners. For Beth as a child, many a happy Sunday dinner featured lamb as the main dish. Most lamb is between 6 and 12 months in age at slaughter. It has a sweet taste that goes well with vegetables of all kinds, fresh and dried fruits, mustard, wine, garlic, tomatoes, and nuts. Look for a dark reddish meat with a fine grain and a fresh smell.

Lamb shanks are one of the most succulent and exciting meats to prepare in the slow cooker; they end up melting off the bone, rather than getting a bit tough and dry as they often do with regular roasting methods. The shoulder is coveted for cutting into delicious stew meat. It takes lovingly to long braises, and you can flavor it in myriad ways, from Moroccan to French to Indian styles. Lamb is as tasty with the classic accompaniments of onion, carrot, celery, and mint jelly or pungent curries as it is in more unusual combinations, such as with eggplant, morels, and artichokes.

·· What Exactly Is Lard? ··

Lard is rendered clarified pork fat, a traditional and flavorful ingredient in many ethnic cuisines from Europe to South America and Mexico. The fat can come from many parts of the animal, but the most flavorful lard comes from the fat around the kidneys. We are talking about leaf lard, not the block of bleached, hydrogenated, and emulsified *manteca* in the red and white box on market shelves, which we equate with candle wax and is designed for a long shelf life. After processing, when it cools or is chilled, lard becomes a creamy white semi-solid, with a consistency similar to that of butter.

The surprising news is that after decades of bad press, it turns out lard is lower in fat and cholesterol than butter. It can be used as an ingredient, in the manner of butter or shortening, in making rich, flaky biscuits and other baked goods and pastries. It makes delicious flour tortillas, is used for sautéing and frying, and can be melted in a deep pot for deep-frying. Lard may be substituted in an exact measurement for butter, margarine, chicken fat, bacon fat, or solid vegetable shortening in recipes.

Although we do not call for lard in any of these recipes, you should certainly try some if you have the opportunity, especially in our Mexican recipes or for browning chicken. The best leaf lard is available from butcher shops and kept under refrigeration.

Cherry-Glazed Pork Pot Roast
with Herbs

This is one you have to try just to see how good it is. Pork is a natural complement to fruit, from applesauce and rhubarb to mango and pineapple. Here, we use cherry preserves made tart with vinegar as the glaze and braising liquid. And it uses fresh rosemary, whole sage leaves, and plenty of chopped parsley and thyme to make it even better. The slow cooker takes care of the basting.

◦ Serves 10

COOKER: Large round or oval
SETTINGS AND COOK TIMES: HIGH for 2 hours, then LOW for 6 hours

One 3½- to 4-pound rolled boneless pork loin roast
3 tablespoons chopped fresh Italian parsley
1 tablespoon chopped fresh rosemary
1 tablespoon chopped fresh thyme leaves
4 fresh sage leaves
3 cloves garlic, quartered
2 medium-size yellow onions, sliced
One 12-ounce jar tart cherry preserves
2 tablespoons honey
¼ cup red wine vinegar
¼ teaspoon ground cloves
¼ teaspoon ground cinnamon
¼ teaspoon salt
¼ cup slivered almonds

1. Remove the string from the pork roast and trim any visible fat. Sprinkle evenly with the chopped parsley, rosemary, and thyme; lay the sage leaves on top. Roll up and tie at 2-inch intervals with heavy string. Pierce the roast all over with the tip of a paring knife and insert the slivers of garlic. Spray the inside of the crock with nonstick cooking spray and place the onions on the bottom. Place the roast on top of the onions. Coat with a few blasts of the cooking spray. Cover and cook on HIGH for 2 hours.

2. Combine the preserves, honey, vinegar, cloves, cinnamon, and salt in a small saucepan. Bring to a boil over medium heat, then reduce the heat and simmer for 2 to 3 minutes, stirring frequently. Add the almonds. Pour the glaze over the pork roast, reduce the heat setting to LOW, cover, and cook for another 6 hours, until the meat is tender when pierced with the tip of a knife and an instant-read thermometer registers about 160°F.

3. Transfer to a platter, cover with aluminum foil, and let stand for 10 minutes before removing the string and carving into thick slices. Serve with the crock juices spooned over the top.

Pork Roast with Tomatoes and Mushrooms

T his is an excellent recipe adapted from one that ran in one of our favorite magazines, *Cooking Light*. It screams Italian home cooking, from the tomatoes to the mushrooms and on to the pasta. If you can find the canned golden tomatoes, definitely buy them and use them in this recipe. The pork loin roast is often sold already tied in meat departments; you just have to cut off the twine before serving. ○ *Serves 6*

COOKER: Medium or large round or oval
SETTINGS AND COOK TIMES: HIGH for 1 hour, then LOW for 7 hours

1 cup canned crushed red or golden tomatoes
3 tablespoons all-purpose flour
1½ tablespoons chopped fresh thyme or 2 teaspoons crumbled dried thyme
1 pound white mushrooms, cut in half
½ pound cremini mushrooms, cut in half
6 ounces fresh shiitake mushrooms, stems discarded and caps thickly sliced
1 large yellow onion, cut into 8 wedges
½ ounce sun-dried tomatoes (6 to 8 pieces), not oil packed, quartered
2 pounds boned and tied pork loin roast, trimmed of visible fat
Salt and freshly ground black pepper to taste
1 pound fresh egg noodles, cooked according to package directions, for serving

1. Combine ½ cup of the crushed tomatoes, the flour, and the thyme in the slow cooker; stir well with a whisk. Add all the mushrooms, the onion, and the sun-dried tomatoes. Sprinkle the pork with salt and pepper and arrange on top of the mushroom mixture. Pour the remaining ½ cup crushed tomatoes over the pork. Cover and cook on HIGH for 1 hour.

2. Reduce the heat setting to LOW and cook for another 7 hours.

3. Transfer the pork to a serving platter, cut away the twine, and cut the pork into thick slices. Serve with the hot noodles and ladle plenty of the mushroom sauce over everything.

Pernil

Pernil is a pork roast with a spicy rub and is normally slow-cooked in the oven for up to 6 hours. The dish is popular in somewhat different forms in Puerto Rico, Colombia, and several other Caribbean and South American cuisines. The original version of this recipe came via our former editor, Pam Hoenig, whose neighbor, Peggy Young, learned it from the mother of a Puerto Rican friend. This is the first time it has been written down and adapted for the slow cooker at the same time. We placed it on a bed of sliced onions so as to properly dry-cook the meat in the slow cooker, and it ended up adding to the deliciousness of the pork. During the testing we had trouble finding some of the ethnic ingredients, such as the adobo paste and Sazón Goya (look for them with the imported products or in a Latin American grocery), so you have a choice of Rub #1, the authentic mixture, or Rub #2, the easy, off-the-spice-rack mixture, just in case. For an even more intense flavor, you can season the roast, cover it with plastic wrap, and refrigerate it for up to 2 days before cooking. Serve piled on a platter with steamed white rice and black beans on either side. ○ *Serves 6 to 8*

COOKER: Large round or oval
SETTING AND COOK TIME: LOW for 10 to 12 hours

Olive oil for rubbing

1 to 2 large yellow onions, to your taste, thickly sliced

One 3-pound Boston pork butt with rind intact

RUB #1:

1 head garlic, cloves separated and peeled

1½ teaspoons dried oregano

1½ teaspoons adobo paste

One 2-ounce package Sazón seasoning with achiote and cilantro,
   such as Goya brand

1 tablespoon olive oil

RUB #2:

3 large cloves garlic, chopped

3 tablespoons chili powder

1 tablespoon salt

1 to 1½ tablespoons olive oil

1. Rub the inside of the crock with oil and place the onions in the slow cooker, covering the entire bottom. Pierce the roast all over the top with the tip of a paring knife to make small slits about ½ inch deep. In a small bowl, mortar with pestle, or small food processor, combine the rub ingredients of choice; beat, crush, or pulse until smooth. Pull open the little slits in the roast and fill with the rub mixture. Place the roast on the bed of onions in the cooker. Cover and cook on LOW until the pork is fork tender, 10 to 12 hours.

2. Remove the roast from the cooker and shred the meat with a fork. Serve hot.

Mexican Pork Roast with Tomatillo Sauce

Pork and green tomatillos make a wonderful taste combination in this authentic Southwestern recipe. The tomatillo sauce is known as *salsa verde*, or green sauce. You can make your own, if you like, instead of using bottled or canned. Serve this with corn tortillas. This is a fabulous recipe for entertaining and an excellent way to cook a pork roast; don't miss it. ● *Serves 6*

COOKER: Medium or large oval
SETTING AND COOK TIME: LOW for 6 to 7 hours

One 2½- to 3-pound bone-in pork loin roast, trimmed of fat and tied
    with kitchen twine at 1-inch intervals
3 tablespoons olive oil
¼ teaspoon salt
¼ teaspoon freshly ground black pepper
1 medium-size white onion, chopped
1 medium-size Anaheim green chile, seeded and chopped
1 jalapeño chile, seeded and minced
2 cloves garlic, minced
1 cup jarred or canned green tomatillo salsa or fresh *salsa verde* (recipe follows)
½ cup chicken broth
¼ cup minced fresh cilantro

1. Pat the meat dry with paper towels. In a large skillet over medium-high heat, heat 2 tablespoons of the oil until very hot. Add the meat and cook until browned on all sides, about 10 minutes. Transfer to a plate and season with the salt and pepper. Add the onion, Anaheim and jalapeño chiles, and garlic to the skillet along with the remaining 1 tablespoon oil. Cook, stirring, until the onion is softened, about 5 minutes; transfer to the slow cooker. Add the salsa and chicken broth to the cooker; arrange the roast and any accumulated juices on top. Cover and cook on LOW for 6 to 7 hours, until an instant-read thermometer inserted into the center registers at least 165°F.

2. Remove the pork to a serving platter and tent with aluminum foil. Using an immersion blender or removing the vegetables and juices to a blender, add the cilantro and puree. If necessary to reheat, return the pureed sauce to the cooker, cover, turn to HIGH, and bring to a boil. Slice the roast and serve with the sauce on the side.

Salsa Verde

○ *Makes about 1 cup*

¾ **pound fresh tomatillos**
¾ **cup chopped fresh cilantro**
1 tablespoon rice vinegar
1 small white boiling onion, quartered
Pinch of sugar
Pinch of salt

1. Bring a large saucepan filled with water to a boil over high heat. Place the whole tomatillos into the saucepan and let boil for 10 minutes. Remove with a slotted spoon to drain. When cool enough to handle, remove the husks with your fingers.

2. Place the whole tomatillos in a food processor or blender. Add the cilantro, vinegar, onion, sugar, and salt. Process until you have a smooth salsa consistency.

3. Transfer the mixture to a medium-size saucepan and simmer over medium-low heat for 10 minutes. Use immediately, or store in an airtight container in the refrigerator for up to 1 week.

Glazed Ham

Y ou can choose a precooked ham of any type and prepare it beautifully in your slow cooker. The trick is to obtain the right size ham for your cooker. A 5-pound smoked or cured ham will fit in a large, 6-quart cooker; choose a 2½- to 3½-pound ham for a medium-size, 4- to 5-quart cooker. If you have a ham that is already glazed and you wish to heat it, just add the liquid to the cooker and skip the glazing. When choosing your glaze from the options below, pick a complementary liquid; the hot pepper jelly or maple glazes are good with apple juice, the mustard-fruit glaze is good with Madeira or port, and the orange-bourbon glaze is good with orange or cranberry juice. The following glazes are proportioned for a large ham, so if you have a small one, cut the recipe in half.

o *Serves 6 to 10, depending on size of ham*

COOKER: Medium or large round or oval
SETTING AND COOK TIME: LOW for 5 to 8 hours

One 3- to 5-pound boneless cooked ham, depending on the size of your slow cooker
⅓ cup water, apple juice, pear juice, orange juice, cranberry juice cocktail,
    sparkling apple cider, hard cider, Madeira, or port

HOT PEPPER JELLY GLAZE:
⅔ cup hot pepper jelly, heated in the microwave or a small saucepan until liquid
2 tablespoons orange juice or tequila

MUSTARD-FRUIT GLAZE:
⅔ cup jam or fruit preserves, such as apricot or cherry
2 tablespoons corn syrup
¼ cup Dijon mustard

MAPLE GLAZE:
⅓ cup firmly packed light brown sugar
3 tablespoons pure maple syrup (Grade B, if possible)
1 tablespoon whiskey (optional)
1 tablespoon Dijon or other mustard

ORANGE-BOURBON GLAZE:
⅔ cup orange marmalade
2 tablespoons bourbon or orange liqueur

1. Coat the inside of the crock with nonstick cooking spray. Place the ham in the slow cooker and add the liquid of your choice.

2. If glazing, in a small bowl, combine the glaze ingredients of your choice and spoon or spread the glaze over the ham. Cover and cook on LOW for 5 to 6 hours for a small ham, or 6 to 8 hours for a large ham, until an instant-read thermometer inserted into the center registers at least 165°F. Some cooks like to baste the ham a few times during cooking.

3. Transfer the ham to a platter. Slice and serve hot or at room temperature.

Asian Pork Tenderloins

We just adore tenderloins cooked ι sauce and served over jasmine ric minutes using standard pantry items. Th company dinner. ◦ *Serves 12 to 16*

COOKER: Large oval
SETTING AND COOK TIME: HIGH for 3 1/2 t

4 whole pork tenderloins (about 4 pounds), tι
½ cup low-sodium soy sauce
⅓ cup rice vinegar
2 tablespoons hoisin sauce
2 tablespoons ketchup
2 tablespoons dark brown sugar
3 cloves garlic, crushed
2 tablespoons minced fresh ginger
1½ tablespoons cornstarch

GARNISHES (CHOOSE WHAT YOU LIKE):
⅔ cup diagonally sliced green onions (white and green parts)
⅔ cup chopped dry-roasted peanuts
⅔ cup chopped fresh cilantro

1. Spray the inside of the crock with nonstick cooking spray and arrange the tenderloins inside. In a small bowl, combine the soy sauce, rice vinegar, hoisin sauce, ketchup, brown sugar, garlic, and ginger; whisk in the cornstarch. Pour over the tenderloins.

2. Cover and cook on HIGH for 3½ to 4½ hours. Transfer the pork to a heatproof platter or cutting board and cover with aluminum foil; let stand for 10 minutes. Pour the cooking liquid into a heatproof bowl; let stand for 10 minutes, then skim any fat from the surface. Cut each tenderloin into 8 slices, arrange on a platter, and sprinkle with the green onions, peanuts, and cilantro. Serve the cooking liquid on the side, gravy style.

Ragoût of Pork and Mushrooms with White Wine

This delightful stew is an adaptation from a favorite book called *Private Collection* (Wimmer Cookbooks, 1984), put together by the Junior League of Palo Alto, California. The two volumes are slim but packed with some of the best recipes in print, especially for entertaining. Use a really good Sauvignon Blanc in this dish, then serve the same wine as an accompaniment if you are drinking wine with dinner. Serve this with egg noodles and hot biscuits. ○ *Serves 6*

COOKER: Large round or oval
SETTING AND COOK TIME: LOW for 7½ to 9½ hours;
  mushrooms added during last 20 to 30 minutes

1 large yellow onion, chopped
2 large carrots, sliced
2 cloves garlic, minced
2 pounds boneless pork shoulder, cut into 1-inch cubes
3 tablespoons olive oil
3 tablespoons all-purpose flour
1½ cups chicken broth
1¼ cups dry white wine
½ teaspoon crumbled dried rosemary
¼ teaspoon crumbled dried thyme

½ teaspoon salt

⅛ teaspoon freshly ground black pepper

2 tablespoons unsalted butter

1 pound fresh white or brown mushrooms, sliced

¼ cup chopped fresh Italian parsley

2 tablespoons freshly squeezed lemon juice

1. Coat the inside of the crock with nonstick cooking spray. Layer the onion, carrots, and garlic in the slow cooker.

2. Pat the meat dry with paper towels. In a large skillet over medium-high heat, warm half the oil until very hot. Add half the meat and cook until browned on all sides, 4 to 5 minutes. Transfer to the cooker. Repeat with the remaining oil and meat. Sprinkle the pan with the flour and stir for 1 minute. Add the broth and 1 cup of the wine, scraping up any browned bits from the bottom of the pan; add the rosemary, thyme, salt, and pepper; cook and stir with a whisk until thickened. Pour over the meat and vegetables in the cooker. Cover and cook on LOW until the pork is fork tender, 7 to 9 hours.

3. In a large skillet over medium heat, melt the butter and gently cook the mushrooms, stirring, until soft. Add to the slow cooker along with the remaining ¼ cup wine, the parsley, and the lemon juice; cover and cook for 20 to 30 minutes. Serve hot.

Chile Verde

Carne de puerco en chile verde is a popular home-cooked dish in Latin communities from Los Angeles to New Mexico. It is simply a pork stew with mild green chiles added. The fresh chiles are roasted to give them a smoky flavor; they can be done over an open flame, under the broiler, or on an outdoor grill, but canned chiles work fine as well. There is not much water added here; you want this to be nice and thick. Serve with corn or flour tortillas.

○ *Serves 8 to 10*

COOKER: Medium or large round or oval
SETTING AND COOK TIME: LOW for 6 to 8 hours

3 pounds boneless pork shoulder or Boston butt, trimmed of visible fat
   and cut into ½-inch cubes

2 tablespoons olive or peanut oil

1 large yellow onion, diced

3 cloves garlic, crushed

2 large ripe or 5 to 6 canned tomatoes, chopped

12 to 15 Anaheim chiles, roasted (page 134), seeded, peeled, and cut into
   ½- to 1-inch-wide strips, or four 4-ounce cans roasted whole green chiles,
   drained and cut into ½- to 1-inch-wide strips

Pinch of ground cumin

½ teaspoon salt, or to taste

Freshly ground black pepper to taste

1. Pat the meat dry with paper towels. In a large skillet over medium-high heat, warm 1 tablespoon of the oil until very hot. Add the meat in batches and cook until browned on all sides, 4 to 5 minutes, adding the remaining oil as necessary. Transfer to the slow cooker along with all but 1 tablespoon of the pan juices.

2. Add the onion and garlic to the skillet and cook, stirring, until limp; add to the slow cooker along with the tomatoes, chiles, and cumin. Add water just to cover. Cover and cook on LOW until the pork shreds easily when pressed with a spoon, 6 to 8 hours. Season with the salt and pepper and serve hot.

Oscar's Chile Colorado Mole

Τhe spicy Mexican stews called moles are a delightful collection of regional dishes ranging in color from green to deep brown. The best-known versions in the United States contain a dash of chocolate in the sauce, which adds depth of flavor. Beth's friend and chef Oscar Mariscal likes to make this with a slab of bone-in pork shoulder for extra flavor and shreds the pork after cooking. The unusual addition of the potato is for its thickening quality. Serve with pinto beans cooked up with a dash of cumin, oregano, and garlic. Tuck the meat and beans into a large flour tortilla, roll up, and enjoy a fabulous homemade burrito accompanied by romantic mariachi music on the stereo. ∘ *Serves 6 to 8*

One 2- to 2½-pound bone-in pork shoulder, loin roast, or Boston butt

2 tablespoons olive or peanut oil

1 medium-size yellow onion, diced

3 cloves garlic, crushed

1 medium-size russet potato, peeled and cubed

One 8-ounce can tomato sauce

¼ cup New Mexican red chile powder

1 teaspoon dried oregano

½ teaspoon ground cumin

1 jalapeño chile, seeded and minced

½ of a 4-ounce Hershey milk chocolate bar

1 heaping tablespoon creamy peanut butter

½ teaspoon salt, or to taste

Freshly ground black pepper to taste

1. Pat the meat dry with paper towels. In a large skillet over medium-high heat, heat the oil until very hot. Add the meat and cook until browned on all sides, 4 to 5 minutes. Transfer to the slow cooker. Drain off all but 1 tablespoon of the fat from the skillet. Add the onion and garlic to the skillet and cook, stirring, until softened, about 5 minutes. Add to the cooker along with the potato, tomato sauce, chile powder, oregano, cumin, and jalapeño. Add water just to cover. Cover and cook on LOW until the pork shreds easily when pressed with a spoon, 8 to 10 hours.

2. Transfer the meat to a platter and shred with a fork or cut into cubes; discard the bones. Add the chocolate and peanut butter to the slow cooker; stir to combine and melt the chocolate. Season with the salt and pepper, return the meat to the cooker, and stir to blend. Serve hot.

Choucroute Garnie

We know. It is hard to pronounce but, once you get the hang of it, fun to say (say shoo-CREWT gar-NEE). And, by gosh, what is it? Well, it's a French family meal of sausage, smoked pork chops, and sauerkraut. Choucroute is an Alsatian classic and, since Beth is part Alsatian from her maternal grandfather, it has become one of her signature dishes. It is tart, smoky, salty, spicy, sour, and meaty all in one. Beth first cooked it out of the Madeleine Kamman classic *The Making of a Cook* (Atheneum, 1978), with leftover Champagne and a mélange of wonderful homemade sausages after a trip to the Coralitos meat market near Watsonville, California. We have omitted the goose fat from this version, because olive oil works just fine. Traditionally, this dish contains a small hunk of blanched slab bacon or a smoked pork hock as well; please do add it if you like. Served with light rye bread, whipped unsalted butter, a variety of mustards, and boiled new potatoes, it will be a feast to be remembered. Since it is a bit of a to-do, it's perfect for a group. The leftovers are great—if you are lucky enough to have any. Juniper berries are easily available on a supermarket spice rack; if you can't find them, add a splash of gin to the mix. ○ *Serves 8*

COOKER: Large round or oval
SETTING AND COOK TIME: LOW for 9 to 10 hours

½ cup olive oil or unsalted butter
2 medium-size yellow onions, chopped
2¼ cups dry white wine or dry Champagne
2¼ cups chicken broth
8 juniper berries
8 whole black peppercorns
1 bay leaf
½ teaspoon caraway seeds
8 assorted precooked sausages, such as bockwurst, bratwurst, turkey or
   duck sausages, or Polish kielbasa
Four 1-pound bags fresh sauerkraut, rinsed, then spread on a thick towel and squeezed dry
8 smoked pork chops (get these at a deli or butcher shop)

1. In a large skillet over medium-high heat, heat the oil and cook the onions, stirring, until softened, about 5 minutes. Add the wine, broth, juniper berries, peppercorns, bay leaf, and caraway seeds; bring to a boil. Add the sausages and cook until just browned on all sides, 4 to 5 minutes.

2. Arrange one-third of the sauerkraut in the slow cooker, then add some of the onion-wine mixture. Arrange the sausages over that, then cover with more sauerkraut and the rest of the onion-wine mixture. Set the pork chops on top and cover the entire mixture with the rest of the sauerkraut. Cover and cook on LOW for 9 to 10 hours.

3. Discard the bay leaf. To serve, mound the sauerkraut on a large, deep platter, surround it with the meats, and pour the cooking juices over everything.

•• About Pork Ribs ••

The slow cooker excels at cooking ribs, a favorite party food that is easy to prepare in large amounts with a large slow cooker. Slow-cooking, plus a good marinade/sauce, adds up to some tasty, succulent meat. Although ribs cooked on a grill or roasted in an oven can be chewy, slow-cooked ribs are fall-apart tender. And, while cooking ribs on the grill or in the oven can make a big mess, using the slow cooker is mess free, except, of course, for the fingers and face during eating. Ribs can be made with so little fuss that you might buy a slow cooker for that alone.

When eating ribs, there is lots of bone and a little meat, and you never use a fork. You eat with your fingers, just like our primal ancestors, tearing the ribs apart to get at the meat that holds them together and sucking the delicious glaze off the bones. Ribs are a food that combines heritage, style, atmosphere, and theater all in one.

Ribs are also a food that cannot be cooked dry; they need a sauce and/or marinade to be properly cooked and tenderized. Ribs are naturally a bit fatty, so they stay nice and moist during long, slow cooking, and they soak up whatever sauce you braise them in. Although you won't get the smoky flavor that you would get from outdoor cooking with soaked wood chips, we guarantee you won't miss it with these recipes. One advantage with the slow cooker is that you can use sauces with all sorts of proportions of sugar, because there is no chance of the glaze burning on the meat, as so often happens when cooking over an open fire.

Ribs come in a slab of 2 to 3 pounds, with varying amounts of meat and fat attached, feeding 2 to 3 eaters. Carefully inspect your slab before purchase so that you can be sure to get one with plenty of meat and the least amount of fat. You can cook your slab whole, divide it into sections to stack in your round slow cooker, or divide it into serving-size portions. You need not precook the ribs in boiling water; the slow cooker does the job perfectly with no fussy preparation. Just load up the cooker and go.

When cooking pork ribs, you have three choices. The family includes spareribs, baby back ribs, and country-style ribs. With all three cuts, buy only USDA 1 graded pork, and buy fresh for the best flavor. Spareribs are the most popular pork ribs to cook due to their meatiness and wonderful flavor; they are cut from the lower rib cage of the animal, down by the belly, after the bacon is removed. Usually if you conjure a mental picture of a plate of ribs, they will be spareribs with a coating of tomato-based barbecue sauce. There is as much bone as meat, but the meat is good eating. They come in slabs of about 3 pounds each, containing 13 ribs.

Baby back ribs are a familiar part of upscale American restaurant rib culture, but they are by far not the meatiest ribs. Baby backs are smaller and more delicate than a regular sparerib, often with the boneless meat separated off, leaving only a small amount of meat. They often show up as appetizers, as they are very tender and small. A slab feeds only 1 to 2 people, so you will need to fill the slow cooker to the top to feed a group with these ribs.

Country-style ribs are different from regular ribs. They have a high meat-to-bone ratio and are more like little loin pork chops, because they are from the part of the upper rib that modulates into the loin. Often they have been butterflied or split. They are very popular in the southern United States, and to most people they are the tastiest choice, because they are so meaty. They are inexpensive for the amount of meat they contain and are a favorite for braising in the slow cooker.

Chipotle and Orange Pork Ribs

T here is something elusive and downright deliciously satisfying about the combination of chiles and pork; they are a natural flavor match. This is a recipe from prolific food writer Leslie Mansfield of the Napa Valley in California, adapted for the slow cooker. She serves these earthy ribs with cold brut Champagne. We add fresh corn tortillas and a black bean chili. ○ *Serves 6 to 8*

COOKER: Large round or oval
SETTING AND COOK TIME: LOW for 8 to 10 hours

2 medium-size onions, chopped
¼ cup minced canned chipotle chiles in adobo sauce
½ cup orange marmalade
½ cup firmly packed light brown sugar
½ cup cider vinegar
2 tablespoons soy sauce
2 tablespoons olive oil
1 teaspoon ground cumin
4 pounds pork spareribs or baby back ribs, cut into serving pieces of 3 to 4 ribs,
    or country-style ribs

1. Combine the onions, chipotles, marmalade, brown sugar, vinegar, soy sauce, olive oil, and cumin in a medium-size bowl and mix until smooth; brush over both sides of the ribs.

2. Arrange the ribs in the slow cooker, pouring over any extra sauce. If you have a round cooker, stack the ribs with sauce in between the layers. Cover and cook on LOW until tender and the meat starts to separate from the bone, 8 to 10 hours. Serve immediately.

Honey Barbecue Pork Ribs

This glaze is ridiculously simple and splendidly delicious. When a friend of Beth's had to make a slow cooker pot of ribs for a local wine bar's appetizer hour, this is what she made. Do provide lots of napkins along with the drinks.

○ *Serves 8 to 10*

COOKER: Large round or oval
SETTING AND COOK TIME: LOW for 8 to 9 hours

8 pounds pork spareribs or baby back ribs, cut into serving pieces of 3 to 4 ribs,
    or country-style ribs
2 yellow onions, sliced
1 quart barbecue sauce of your choice, store-bought or homemade (page 110)
1 cup mild-flavored honey

1. Arrange the rib portions in the slow cooker, layering them with the onion slices. Combine the barbecue sauce and honey in a large bowl and mix until smooth; spoon over the ribs. If you have a round cooker, stack the ribs with sauce in between the layers. Cover and cook on LOW for 8 to 9 hours, until the meat is tender and starts to separate from the bone.

2. Transfer the ribs to a platter and serve immediately. If there is extra sauce on the bottom of the cooker, pour it into a bowl and serve on the side.

Pork Ribs with No-Cook Barbecue Sauce

Company coming and no time to do anything but pop some ribs in the cooker? Here is a no-cook tomato barbecue sauce that beats all. Turn to this, which you mix in minutes in the food processor, instead of a bottled sauce. If you have any sun-dried tomatoes packed in oil, toss them in, too. This recipe is a favorite. ○ *Serves 8 to 10*

COOKER: Large round or oval
SETTING AND COOK TIME: LOW for 8 to 9 hours

3 cloves garlic or 3 shallots
2 cups ketchup
1 cup dry red wine
⅓ cup olive oil
⅓ cup soy sauce (we use reduced sodium)
⅓ cup white wine vinegar or white balsamic vinegar
2 tablespoons dry mustard
2 tablespoons chili powder
1 tablespoon crumbled dried marjoram or oregano
8 pounds pork spareribs or baby back ribs, cut into serving pieces of 3 to 4 ribs,
     or country-style ribs

1. Place the garlic in a food processor and process to chop. Add the ketchup, wine, oil, soy sauce, vinegar, dry mustard, chili powder, and marjoram and process until smooth.

2. Arrange the rib portions in the slow cooker. Pour the sauce over the ribs. If you have a round cooker, stack the ribs with sauce in between the layers.

3. Cover and cook on LOW for 8 to 9 hours, until the meat is tender and starts to separate from the bone. Serve immediately. If there is extra sauce on the bottom of the cooker, pour it into a bowl and serve on the side.

Braised Pork Ribs with Chiles and Shallots

T his recipe, from the Singapore Symphony Orchestra Ladies League, is for true Asian-flavored ribs. It is easy to distinguish between light and dark soy sauces, as the light is thinner. The dark is a bit sweet. Look for *pak si yau* (light) and *hak si yau* (dark). The little fresh red chiles are known as *chilli padi* or bird's eye chile (*mirchi* in Indian markets). Left longer on the plant to ripen and turn from green to red, they are an important flavor in this dish, so don't skip them. Be sure to wear thin, disposable rubber gloves when handling the chiles.

○ *Serves 8*

COOKER: Large round or oval
SETTINGS AND COOK TIMES: HIGH for 30 to 45 minutes, then LOW for 8 to 10 hours; optional final step to brown ribs in the oven for 1 hour

4 pounds pork spareribs or baby back ribs, cut into serving pieces of 3 to 4 ribs,
   or country-style ribs
¼ cup oyster sauce
¼ cup dark soy sauce
¼ cup light soy sauce
2 tablespoons sugar
10 small shallots
10 cloves garlic
5 small fresh red bird's eye chiles, seeded
1 to 2 tablespoons sesame oil, to your taste
1 cinnamon stick
8 whole cloves
1 cup dry white wine, ⅓ cup rice wine, or ¼ cup dry sherry

1. Arrange the ribs in the slow cooker. If you have a round cooker, stack them. Combine the oyster sauce, dark and light soy sauces, and sugar in a small bowl. Pour over the ribs and let marinate for 30 minutes.

2. Combine the shallots, garlic, and chiles in a small food processor or with a mortar and pestle and work until a mash is formed. Heat the oil in a small sauté pan over medium heat, add the shallot mixture, and fry until fragrant, 3 to 4 minutes. Add to the cooker along with the cinnamon stick and cloves. Add the wine and enough cold water just to cover the ribs. Cover and cook on HIGH to bring to a simmer, 30 to 45 minutes.

3. Turn the cooker to LOW and cook until the meat is tender and starts to separate from the bone, 8 to 10 hours.

4. If you wish to brown the ribs in the oven (this is optional), preheat the oven to 350°F. Remove the ribs from the cooker and place on an aluminum foil–lined baking sheet. Bake for up to 1 hour to brown them before serving. Serve immediately.

Hawaiian Laulau

Hawaiian (Polynesian) home cooking is a realm unto itself and not often experienced off the popular vacation islands. Most visitors to Hawaii never see an authentic luau, or outdoor feast, which includes a *kalua*—a wild pig—steam-roasted in an *imu,* or underground oven, with bananas, breadfruit, and sweet potatoes. This authentic recipe is from Marilyn Ige, a former copyeditor at the *Honolulu Star-Bulletin*. You can serve mai tais or mango daiquiris while you let the slow cooker do all the work! Look for luau leaves in specialty ethnic markets; you can substitute spinach or chard leaves, if desired. Luau leaf needs preliminary parboiling to collapse the leaves slightly, then a full 9 hours in the crock, stewing away, to break down the calcium oxalate crystals that will otherwise cause an itch in the mouth; you absolutely do not want them undercooked. This recipe has pork only, but you could experiment by substituting beef, chicken thighs, or even taro chunks for part of the pork. Hawaiian salt is a locally harvested coarse white sea salt (there is also a red variety colored by algae); substitute coarse sea salt or kosher salt. Serve this dish with French bread, Twice-Crocked Stuffed Potatoes with Macadamia Nuts (page 150), Carrots Glazed with Marmalade, Brown Sugar, and Butter (page 132), and steamed asparagus with sesame seeds. ○ *Serves 8*

3 pounds luau leaves, large spinach leaves, or green Swiss chard leaves
One 3-pound boneless pork loin roast, cut into 2-inch chunks
2½ tablespoons Hawaiian white or red salt
¾ cup water

1. Wash the luau leaves and remove the stems and fibrous parts of the veins. Fill a large stockpot with water and bring to a full boil. Add the leaves and boil until wilted, about 3 minutes. Drain well.

2. Rub the pork with the salt, kneading it in thoroughly. Layer the wilted luau leaves with the pork chunks in the slow cooker; add the water. Cover and cook on LOW until the luau leaves are totally soft, 9 to 10 hours.

French Country Terrine

T his is a classic homemade *pâté de campagne*. In France, many meals begin with a crock or terrine of refrigerator-cold, homemade pâté that is more like a fine meatloaf, coarse-grained Pommery or Dijon mustard, and fresh country bread sitting in the center of the table. At her very first wedding catering job, Beth offered three different homemade French terrines, with sides of chutney, special mustards, and sour gherkin cornichons, with great success. Be sure to keep all the ingredients as cold as possible while you are working, as they are highly perishable, and don't be tempted to use meats with no fat; it is that fat that will keep the terrine moist. This recipe is still made in a terrine container and bain-marie water bath, but the slow-cooking assures a beautiful, moist loaf. Leftovers will keep for up to 1 week in the refrigerator. ● *Serves 10*

COOKER: Large oval
SETTING AND COOK TIME: LOW for 8 to 9 hours

2 tablespoons unsalted butter
3 cloves garlic, chopped

1 medium-size yellow onion, finely chopped

1 shallot, chopped

Salt to taste

2 teaspoons dried thyme

Leaves from ½ bunch fresh Italian parsley

1 pound pork liver, rinsed, trimmed, cubed, and chilled, or ground chicken

1 pound ground round beef

1 pound ground pork

2½ teaspoons salt

1 teaspoon freshly ground black pepper

½ teaspoon ground white pepper

¼ teaspoon ground allspice

¼ teaspoon ground ginger

Pinch of ground cloves

Pinch of ground cinnamon

¼ cup Cognac or brandy

2 tablespoons port wine

3 large eggs, beaten

3 tablespoons all-purpose flour

5 strips thick-sliced bacon

6 bay leaves

1 tablespoon whole black peppercorns

1. In a medium-size skillet, melt the butter over medium heat and cook the garlic, onion, and shallot, stirring, until soft; add a pinch of salt and ½ teaspoon of the thyme. Set aside and let cool to room temperature.

2. Place a trivet in the slow cooker and fill the cooker with 2 inches of water. Cover and turn to HIGH to heat the water.

3. Chop the parsley in a food processor to make ½ cup; transfer to a large bowl. When the onion mixture is cooled, place in the food processor along with the pork liver; process until coarsely ground. Transfer to the bowl and add the ground beef, pork, and the salt. Add the black and white peppers, allspice, ginger, cloves, cinnamon, Cognac, port, eggs, and flour, and mix thoroughly. Pack the mixture into a heavy 6-cup terrine (don't use a metal pan; ceramic or the enameled ones made by Le Creuset are perfect). Smooth the top with the back of a large spoon and whack the terrine firmly several times on the counter to help settle the contents and make the texture even. Cover the top completely with the strips of bacon. Gently press the bay leaves, black peppercorns, and the remaining 1½ teaspoons thyme on top of the bacon. Cover the terrine tightly with aluminum foil and cut 3 slits in it to allow steam to escape.

4. Carefully place the terrine on the trivet in the slow cooker. Carefully pour in very hot tap water to reach about halfway up the sides of the terrine. Cover, turn the heat setting to LOW, and cook for 8 to 9 hours, checking to make sure the water doesn't boil or evaporate lower than the halfway mark and adding more hot water if necessary. Check for doneness by inserting an instant-read thermometer through the foil. When done, the center of the terrine will register 160° to 165°F. When it does, turn the slow cooker off and let the terrine stand in the cooker until slightly cooled, up to 1 hour.

5. With oven mitts, remove the terrine from the water bath and place a weight, such as a tin of canned tomatoes or an iron, on the top while it cools to room temperature (no longer). Wipe off the sides and bottom of the terrine with a wet towel and cover with clean foil and the terrine lid; refrigerate for 2 to 4 days before serving.

6. To serve, remove the spices on top. Unmold the terrine by running a knife around the sides and turning it out onto a serving platter. Serve in thin slices.

Potée Boulangère

This is a slow cooker version of *baeckeoffe*, or "baker's stew," a traditional Alsatian casserole that can contain anything from mutton to a pig's tail. In days gone by, European housewives would take a layered stew like this to the bakery and let it cook in the big oven after the bread baking was done. It would simmer all day in a casserole sealed shut with a paste of flour and water around the lid so that not a bit of steam could escape. The wine is important; the recipe traditionally calls for Sylvaner or Riesling. Since Sylvaner is difficult to find outside Alsace, Sauvignon Blanc is a good substitute. The meat needs to marinate overnight before cooking, so plan accordingly. ○ *Serves 6 to 8*

COOKER: Medium or large oval
SETTING AND COOK TIME: LOW for 8 to 9 hours

1 pound boneless beef chuck, cut into 2-inch pieces
½ pound boneless pork shoulder, cut into 2-inch pieces

½ pound boneless lamb shoulder, cut into 2-inch pieces

1 cup dry white wine, such as Sauvignon Blanc

2 tablespoons chopped fresh Italian parsley

¼ teaspoon dried thyme

½ of a bay leaf

Pinch of ground cloves

¼ teaspoon salt

¼ teaspoon freshly ground black pepper

1 tablespoon unsalted butter, softened

4 large yellow onions, cut in half and sliced into half-moons

4 large russet potatoes, peeled and sliced

1. Combine the meats, wine, parsley, thyme, bay leaf, cloves, salt, and pepper in a large bowl, plastic container, or zipper-top plastic bag. Cover or seal and let marinate overnight in the refrigerator.

2. Rub the inside of the crock with the butter. Cover the bottom with a layer of one-quarter of the onions and then one-quarter of the potatoes. Top with one-third of the meat mixture, removing it from the marinade with a slotted spoon. Continue to layer, ending with potatoes. Pour the marinade from the meat over the top. Cover and cook on LOW until the meat is fork tender, 8 to 9 hours. Serve hot.

Lamb Roast with Lotsa Garlic and Rosemary

T his recipe comes from Jesse Cool, executive chef and proprietor of Flea Street Café and jZcool Eatery & Catering, both in Menlo Park, California, and the Cool Café, which is adjacent to the art museum at Stanford University. All of Jesse's restaurants take full advantage of seasonal, organic ingredients. In her spare time, Jesse is a cookbook writer and a cooking teacher who has taught and written about slow cooker cuisine. Use a lamb shoulder or butt for this recipe; a cut that is well marbled with fat is a necessity. For Jesse, the potatoes, slow-cooked in the juices of the lamb along with the garlic and rosemary, are just as delicious as the lamb. Serve this with steamed artichokes and green beans, jellied cranberry sauce, a fruit chutney or mint jelly, and crusty bread. ○ *Serves 6*

COOKER: Large round or oval
SETTING AND COOK TIME: LOW for 8 to 9 hours

One 3-pound lamb roast
4 to 5 large new potatoes, cut into large pieces
Cloves from 1 head garlic, sliced
1 tablespoon chopped fresh rosemary
4 whole cloves
1 tablespoon salt
½ teaspoon freshly ground black pepper

1. Place the roast in the slow cooker and arrange the potatoes around it. Sprinkle with all of the remaining ingredients.

2. Cover and cook on LOW until the lamb is fork tender, 8 to 9 hours. Slice the lamb and serve hot with the potatoes.

Lamb Navarin

B raised young lamb is the basis for this classic French ragoût with spring vegetables, known as *à la printanière*. Julia Child, in *The French Chef Cookbook* (Knopf, 1968), devoted her sixty-fourth TV show to navarin. For stew meat, she recommended a combination of the breast, for fat and texture; shoulder, for lean, solid pieces; ribs, for texture and flavor; and neck, for texture and sauce consistency. She also called for sprinkling the stew meat with sugar as it cooks; you may do so, if you like. The baby vegetables are worth searching out, and do shell your own peas if you can, as fresh peas are a treat; try a farmers' market or specialty produce stand. You can also add whole baby new potatoes and white boiling onions, if you like, to make it the traditional way. You could also certainly make this with just onions and turnips for vegetables and still be totally French in spirit. Serve with hot French bread and butter, or with a side of mashed potatoes. Julia said not to forget to enjoy it with a glass of Bordeaux or Beaujolais.

○ *Serves 6*

COOKER: Large round or oval
SETTINGS AND COOK TIMES: HIGH for 1 hour, then LOW for 6 to 7 hours; vegetables are parcooked and added during last 30 to 60 minutes

1 to 2 tablespoons olive oil, as needed
3 pounds lamb shoulder, trimmed of fat and cut into 3-inch chunks
1 large white or yellow onion, chopped
3 tablespoons chopped fresh tarragon
2 cups chicken, lamb, or beef broth
¾ cup dry white wine
2 tablespoons all-purpose flour kneaded into 2 tablespoons unsalted butter, for thickening
14 to 16 baby carrots (about 10 ounces)
10 to 12 baby turnips (about ½ pound), peeled and left whole or halved
1 pound asparagus, ends trimmed and cut diagonally into 2-inch lengths
1 cup fresh (about ¾ pound unshelled) peas or thawed frozen petite peas
Salt and freshly ground black pepper to taste

1. In a large nonstick skillet over medium-high heat, heat the oil and brown the lamb on all sides. Transfer to the slow cooker. Add the onion to the skillet and cook for about 5 minutes, stirring, to soften; add to the crock. Add 1½ teaspoons of the tarragon, the broth, and wine. Cover and cook on HIGH for 1 hour.

2. Reduce the heat to LOW and cook until the lamb is very tender, 5½ to 6 hours.

3. Add the kneaded butter (*beurre manié*) in pieces to the cooker and stir until thickened.

4. Bring a small pot of water to a boil and parcook the carrots and turnips separately for 5 minutes each. Drain and add to the crock with the remaining 1½ teaspoons tarragon, the asparagus, and peas. Cover and cook on LOW until the vegetables are cooked, 30 minutes to 1 hour longer. Season with salt and pepper and serve hot.

Lamb and Fruit Tagine

Tagines are the stews of Morocco, and many of them combine fruit and meat for a sweetish and substantial main dish. This one is really something special. If you can find them, please do choose California dried apricot halves instead of the less expensive Turkish ones. We find the domestic product to be moister and much more flavorful, adding a great deal of depth to the stew. Also, choose the leanest lamb you can find; well-trimmed leg meat is perfect. Shoulder is flavorful but often is not lean enough. If you bone the meat yourself and your slow cooker is large enough, brown the bones, too, and put them in with the other ingredients; they will add flavor and body to the stew. (Count the bones so you can be sure to remove all of them before serving.) We like to serve this tagine with fragrant basmati rice cooked with a cinnamon stick, a couple of whole green cardamom pods, and a pinch of saffron threads. ○ *Serves 6 to 8*

COOKER: Large round or oval
SETTING AND COOK TIME: LOW for 6 to 8 hours

3 pounds lean boneless lamb, preferably from the leg or shoulder,
    trimmed of some fat and cut into 1- to 1½-inch cubes
Salt and freshly ground black pepper to taste
2 tablespoons olive oil
2 large yellow onions, chopped
4 to 5 cloves garlic, to your taste, cut in half
One 3-inch cinnamon stick
6 green cardamom pods
2 medium-size turnips, peeled and cut into 1- to 1½-inch pieces
½ cup dried California apricot halves
½ cup pitted prunes, cut in half
1 cup water
One 28-ounce can chopped tomatoes, undrained
1 tablespoon brown mustard seeds
Small pinch of saffron threads (optional)

1. Pat the lamb dry with a paper towel and season with salt and pepper. In a large skillet, heat the oil over medium-high heat. Brown the lamb on all sides, working in batches. As it browns, remove to a plate. Add the onions and garlic to the skillet and cook, stirring, until the onions have softened, about 5 minutes. Transfer to the slow cooker, spreading them evenly over the bottom. Place the cinnamon stick and cardamom pods on top. If you are worried about your guests eating them by accident, tie them into a small square of cheesecloth so you can remove them easily when serving. Next, add the turnips to the crock, spreading them out evenly. Place the apricots and prunes on top, then cover them with the browned meat, spreading it evenly.

2. Pour the water into the skillet and bring it to a boil, scraping up any browned bits from the bottom of the pan; pour into the slow cooker. Open the can of tomatoes and stir in the mustard seeds. Crumble the saffron, if using, into the tomatoes. Pour the tomatoes and their juices evenly over the meat. Cover and cook on LOW until the meat, fruit, and vegetables are tender, 6 to 8 hours.

3. Season with salt and pepper, and remove the cinnamon stick and, if desired, the cardamom pods. Serve hot.

Julie's Lamb and Quince Ragoût

T he quince is not the friendliest of fruits—despite their lovely, fuzzy, yellow-green outer appearance, they are as hard as rocks. Also, their season (fall) is short, and even when they are in season, they are difficult to find in all but specialty grocery stores. Astringent when fresh, they must be peeled, cored, and cooked to transform them. Once conquered, their distinctive, perfumey taste makes them well worth all of the trouble. Another thing quinces have going for them is that, unlike apples or pears, they retain some texture after cooking. That's what makes them so delightful when paired with lamb and mild spices in this recipe. Serve this over mounds of fluffy white rice or couscous. ○ *Serves 6 to 8*

COOKER: Medium or large, oval preferred
SETTING AND COOK TIME: HIGH for 2½ to 3 hours, or LOW for 4 to 5 hours

2 large or 3 small quinces (about 1½ pounds)

2 tablespoons olive oil

2 large yellow onions, cut in half and sliced into half-moons

2 tablespoons all-purpose flour

2 pounds boneless lamb or 3 pounds lamb stew meat with bones, cut into 1½-inch cubes

One 14.5-ounce can diced tomatoes, undrained

½ cup water

1 teaspoon salt

½ teaspoon freshly ground black pepper

½ teaspoon sweet paprika

½ teaspoon ground cinnamon

½ teaspoon ground turmeric

¼ teaspoon sugar

1. Peel the quinces, cut them into wedges, and cut out the cores. If the wedges are very large, cut each in half. Place them in the slow cooker.

2. In a large skillet, heat 1 tablespoon of the oil over medium-high heat. Add the onions and cook, stirring a few times, until softened, 3 to 5 minutes. Place the onions on top of the quinces in the crock.

3. Place the flour in a large zipper-top plastic bag. Pat the lamb pieces dry with a paper towel, then place a handful of them into the bag. Holding the bag closed, gently shake until the pieces of meat are coated with flour. Remove the meat, shaking off any excess flour, and place on a plate. Repeat with the remaining meat.

4. In the skillet, heat the remaining 1 tablespoon oil over medium-high heat. Add the meat, allowing it to brown lightly on the first side before turning to brown on the other sides. This process will take 5 to 7 minutes total. When the lamb is lightly browned on all sides, add the tomatoes with their juice, the water, and the salt, pepper, paprika, cinnamon, turmeric, and sugar. Bring the mixture to a boil, stirring to distribute the seasonings evenly. Let it boil for 2 to 3 minutes, until the liquid has reduced slightly. Pour the contents of the skillet into the crock, distributing the meat evenly over the onions and quinces.

5. Cover and cook on HIGH for 2½ to 3 hours, or cook on LOW for 4 to 5 hours. Serve hot.

Moroccan-Style Lamb with Preserved Lemons

This is a simple lamb stew that cooks the couscous right in the slow cooker after the stew is completed. You will need to prepare the preserved lemons about 2 weeks ahead to make this dish with authentic flavor. You can omit them, but that changes the dish quite a bit. Serve with a chopped fresh spinach salad with canned chickpeas and a dash of saffron in your vinaigrette, mashed roasted eggplant with pita, and fruit. ○ *Serves 6*

COOKER: Medium or large round or oval
SETTINGS AND COOK TIMES: LOW for 7 to 9 hours,
   then HIGH for about 10 minutes

2 pounds lamb shoulder, trimmed of fat and cut into 1½-inch cubes
2 large onions, cut into wedges
2 cups chopped canned or fresh tomatoes
1 cup carrots, cut into 1-inch-thick rounds
2 cups chicken broth
¼ cup chopped preserved lemons (recipe follows)
1½ teaspoons ground cumin
½ teaspoon ground turmeric
¼ teaspoon red pepper flakes
One 10-ounce box quick-cooking couscous
¼ cup dried currants or raisins

1. Combine the meat, onions, tomatoes, and carrots in the slow cooker. Add the broth, preserved lemons, cumin, turmeric, and red pepper flakes. Cover and cook on LOW until the lamb is fork tender, 7 to 9 hours.

2. Just before serving, turn the cooker to HIGH. Using a slotted spoon, transfer the meat to a serving bowl and cover with aluminum foil to keep warm. Skim the fat from the cooking juices. Stir the couscous and currants into the cooking juices in the cooker. Cover and cook until the couscous is tender, 5 to 7 minutes. Serve the meat over the couscous.

Preserved Lemons

Preserved lemons result from soaking lemons in a brine solution made of the juice from the lemons and salt until the lemons turn pulpy and soft. They are used as a distinctive condiment or flavor accent in Moroccan cuisine, adding a salty element as well as a deeply lemony flavor to foods. To use, finely chop the lemons and add to a dish during cooking, or at the end. ○ *Makes 1 quart*

6 to 8 fresh, juicy lemons (thin-skinned Meyers, if possible)
About ⅔ cup fine kosher salt
Clean 1-quart glass jar with a tight-fitting lid

1. Wash and dry the lemons thoroughly. Using a clean, dry knife, quarter the lemons, remove any seeds, and trim and discard the ends. Sprinkle about 1 tablespoon salt into the bottom of the jar. Layer the lemons in the jar, alternating each layer with salt and adding 1 tablespoon salt for each whole lemon. As you reach the top of the jar, press down on the lemons to cram in as many pieces as possible. (As you do this, the lemons will exude their juice.) When the jar is tightly packed, the level of juice will have risen to or near the top of the jar. Seal the jar with a tight-fitting lid and gently shake to mix the salt and juice. If you are having trouble submerging the lemons, fill the space at the top of the jar with a piece of crumpled plastic wrap.

2. Place the jar on a countertop out of direct sunlight and shake gently every day. In the first few days, as the lemons begin to soften, they may pack down enough to allow you to add another lemon or two. Do so if you can to keep the jar full. The lemons are ready to use when they are mushy and the juice is syrupy. This will take a few weeks. Once you begin to use the lemons, store the jar in the refrigerator, where they will keep for several months.

Lamb Shanks with White Wine and Wild Mushroom Sauce

L amb shanks are succulent, moist, rich tasting, and oh so fragrant as they cook. They are also a real bargain, allowing you to put a beautiful meal on the table for very little money or, as in this recipe, leaving room in the budget for a small indulgence: dried wild mushrooms. These flavorful little beauties add so much depth to the sauce. Look for them in cellophane packets in the produce section. We recommend porcini, morels, or a dried mushroom blend for this recipe; shiitakes alone are too strongly flavored. ○ *Serves 8 to 12*

COOKER: Large round or oval
SETTING AND COOK TIME: LOW for 7 to 8 hours

1 ounce dried porcini or morel mushrooms or a dried wild mushroom blend
6 tablespoons olive oil
8 lamb shanks (8 to 10 pounds), trimmed of fat
2 large onions, cut in half and sliced into half-moons
1 cup dry white wine
1 teaspoon Dijon mustard or ½ teaspoon dry mustard
Three to four 2-inch sprigs fresh oregano or 2 teaspoons dried oregano
Three to four 2-inch sprigs fresh mint or 2 teaspoons dried mint
One to two 2-inch sprigs fresh rosemary or ¾ teaspoon dried rosemary
2 teaspoons salt, or more to your taste
¼ teaspoon freshly ground black pepper, or more to your taste
2 tablespoons cornstarch
¼ cup water

1. Place the dried mushrooms in a small cup. Barely cover them with the hottest possible tap water and allow to soak while you proceed with the recipe.

2. In a large skillet, heat the oil over medium-high heat and cook the shanks until golden brown on all sides, 5 to 7 minutes in all. You may have to do this in batches. As they brown, transfer to a plate. Pour off all but about 1 tablespoon of oil. Add the onion to the skillet and cook, stirring a few times, until softened, about 5 minutes. Make a bed of the onions in the bottom of the slow cooker. Remove the mushrooms from their soaking liquid, reserving the liquid, and distribute the mushrooms over the onions. Pour the soaking liquid through a fine-mesh strainer or a coffee filter to remove any grit, and add the liquid to the cooker. Arrange the shanks on top of the onions.

3. Add the wine to the skillet and bring to a boil over high heat, scraping up any browned bits stuck to the bottom. Stir in the mustard, then pour the mixture over the lamb. If you are using fresh herbs, tie the sprigs together with string and tuck in between two of the shanks. If using dried herbs, sprinkle over the lamb. Sprinkle with the salt and pepper. Cover and cook on LOW until the lamb is fork tender, 7 to 8 hours.

4. Preheat the oven to 400°F. With a slotted spoon or tongs, transfer the shanks to a shallow baking dish and put in the oven to keep warm while you finish the sauce. If you have used a fresh herb bundle, remove and discard it.

5. Remove and discard as much fat as possible from the sauce. Strain the sauce, reserving the onions and mushrooms, and pour it into a small saucepan. In a small cup, stir the cornstarch into the water to form a smooth paste. Add this slurry to the sauce and cook, stirring, over medium-high heat until it comes to a boil and thickens, about 3 minutes. Stir in the onions and mushrooms and cook, stirring, to heat through. Season with salt and pepper as needed.

6. Serve the lamb shanks whole, or remove the meat from the bones in large chunks. Spoon some of the mushroom sauce over each portion.

Spiced Lamb Dolmas

S tuffed grape leaves, called dolmas, are one of our favorite appetizers, and we love them cold, packed for lunch boxes or picnics. We often see them featured on cold assorted salad plates in Middle Eastern and Mediterranean restaurants, and they are also sold in many delicatessens, as well as being available canned. But once you have made your own, you will not want to go back to ready-made! If you are lucky enough to have your own grapevine, just blanch the leaves for a minute or two in salted water before using them. Most of us, though, have to buy our grape leaves for stuffing—they are sold in jars, packed in brine. This recipe makes enough filling for about half a jar of grape leaves; if you have a large slow cooker and want to make more, just double the filling recipe. (You can put the unused leaves back into the jar and fill it with salt water. They will keep for several weeks.) The slow cooker makes dolmas perfectly. We find the cleanup is easier than on the stove, and it is easy to monitor them while they are cooking because of the slow cooker's glass lid. ○ *Serves 6 to 8 as an appetizer, 4 as a main dish*

COOKER: Medium or large round or oval
SETTING AND COOK TIME: HIGH for 2 to 3 hours

One 1-pound jar grape leaves, or about 30 fresh grape leaves
    blanched in salt water and drained
¼ cup extra-virgin olive oil
1 cup finely chopped onion (1 medium-large onion)
3 tablespoons slivered almonds
½ pound lean ground lamb
¾ cup grated carrot (1 large carrot)
¾ cup converted rice
3 tablespoons dried currants
1 tablespoon chopped fresh mint
1 tablespoon chopped fresh Italian parsley
1 teaspoon salt
½ teaspoon ground allspice
½ teaspoon ground cinnamon
½ teaspoon freshly ground black pepper
3 to 4 cups water
1 cup plain yogurt, for serving (optional)

1. Drain the jarred grape leaves, carefully remove them from the jar, and rinse under cold running water. Set aside in a colander to drain.

2. In a large skillet, heat 2 tablespoons of the olive oil over medium-high heat. Add the onion and cook, stirring a few times, until softened, about 5 minutes. Add the almonds and continue to cook, stirring, until they begin to brown, about 2 minutes more. Transfer the onion mixture to a large bowl. Add the lamb, carrot, rice, currants, mint, parsley, salt, allspice, cinnamon, and pepper to the bowl and mix gently with a fork to combine without mashing the meat.

3. Before you begin stuffing the grape leaves, line the bottom of the slow cooker with a few of the torn leaves.

4. To stuff the leaves, place a perfect leaf, shiny side down, rib side up, on your work surface. Trim off the stem, if there is one. Depending on the size of the leaf, place 1 teaspoon to 1 tablespoon of the filling in the center of the leaf. Shape it into a little log, running side to side across the leaf. Fold the sides of the leaf in, as you would to make an envelope, and roll up the leaf jellyroll fashion to make a small, plump cylinder. Don't roll it too tightly; the rice will expand as it cooks. If you have any tears, snip off a lobe and patch it from the inside. Place the stuffed leaf in the slow cooker, making sure the loose end is tucked firmly underneath the roll. Continue to stuff leaves until you run out of filling, stacking them in the crock as you go. Stack them close, side by side, but don't jam them in. Make as many layers as necessary.

5. Gently pour the water over the dolmas. When you press gently on the top layer, the water should almost cover the top layer of dolmas. If it doesn't, add more water. Drizzle the remaining 2 tablespoons olive oil over the dolmas. Place a small, heatproof plate over them to keep them in place and put the lid on the cooker. Cook on HIGH until the rice is cooked through but not mushy, 2 to 3 hours. You will have to cut into a dolma in the center of the cooker to check.

6. Let the dolmas cool, uncovered, in their liquid. Remove them from the liquid and serve just slightly warm or at room temperature. If not serving right away, refrigerate them. Serve with yogurt for dipping, if desired. They will keep, tightly covered, for up to 1 week in the refrigerator.

Slow Cooker Puddings, Cakes, and Breads

Tapioca Pudding ● 379

Steamed Chocolate Pudding ● 380

New Orleans–Style Vanilla Bread
Pudding with Whiskey Sauce ● 382

Sticky Steamed Pumpkin
Pudding ● 384

Gingerbread with Blackberry
Sauce ● 386

Blueberry Cake ● 388

Lemon Cornmeal Cake in Fragrant Fig
Leaves ● 389

Vanilla Pan de Maiz ● 391

Crock-Baked Salsa Cornbread ● 392

Steamed Maple-Raisin Brown
Bread ● 393

Steamed Brown Bread with
Rum Fruits ● 394

There are some desserts that work very nicely in the slow cooker, without fuss or special equipment. The slow cooker makes beautiful, creamy puddings like tapioca and chocolate pudding, which are delightful old-fashioned desserts. You can use either whole pearl tapioca or quick-cooking tapioca (whole tapioca run through a machine like a coffee grinder) in slow cooker recipes. The key to perfect silky puddings is not to overcook them, and the slow cooker is perfect for assuring that.

Bread puddings, containing milk and eggs, are usually cooked on the HIGH setting. Because of the eggs, you don't want the mixture to sit at too low a temperature for a long period. And they must be watched carefully at the end to prevent burning or overcooking. Bread puddings, while a hearty, home-style dessert, are still a very attractive and appreciated dessert for company.

We especially like the slow cooker for steaming dessert puddings as an alternative to the stovetop. Depending on the mold you use for the pudding, you can use a trivet or not; the heating element is around the sides in the cooker, so there is no bottom contact with direct heat like there would be on a stovetop.

Our quick breads and cakes are cooked directly on the crock floor. These desserts are especially convenient if you are in a kitchen with no oven, or in a facility with limited appliances, like on a sailboat or in a studio room without any kitchen. Don't pass up our dried and fresh fruit and spice steamed puddings and cakes. They are not overly sweet and hark back to our baking ancestors, who cooked them in kettles over an open fire.

You can serve the cakes with one of our sauces, whipped cream, ice cream, a favorite frosting, powdered sugar sprinkled on top, or just plain.

Please note that most of the baking recipes are cooked on the HIGH heat setting; the LOW setting does not set the texture of breads and cakes properly.

Tapioca Pudding

T his is lovely served with sliced or chopped fruit (try peaches, blueberries, or pineapple) and whipped cream, but it's also comfortingly delicious served on its own. ○ *Serves 8*

COOKER: Medium or large round
SETTING AND COOK TIME: LOW for 3 to 3½ hours; eggs added in last 30 minutes

4 cups whole or low-fat milk
1 cup sugar
½ cup small pearl tapioca
1½ teaspoons pure vanilla extract
2 large eggs

1. Place the milk, sugar, tapioca, and vanilla extract in the crock. Stir well to combine thoroughly. Cover and cook on LOW for 2½ to 3 hours, until most of the tapioca balls are completely transparent. Some of them will still have a white dot at their centers; that is okay.

2. Break the eggs into a small bowl and whisk or beat well with a fork. Lift the cover and stir the pudding thoroughly to break up any tapioca clumps. Spoon a few tablespoons of the hot tapioca into the bowl with the egg and beat well. Pour the egg mixture back into the cooker and stir well to combine. Replace the cover and cook on LOW for an additional 30 minutes. Serve warm, or pour into a bowl, let cool, cover, and chill.

Steamed Chocolate Pudding

A dapted from our book *The Ultimate Rice Cooker Cookbook* (The Harvard Common Press, 2003), this is one of our favorite chocolate puddings. Enticingly called *Mohr im hemd*, or the Moor in a shirt, it is a Viennese steamed chocolate-almond pudding served warm with cool vanilla whipped cream to make a stunning black-and-white dessert for special occasions. It has a delicate spongy texture with an almost oozy center, which is exactly the way it should be. ○ *Serves 8*

COOKER: Large round or oval
SETTING AND COOK TIME: HIGH for 2½ to 3 hours

4 ounces semisweet chocolate, chopped
1 ounce unsweetened chocolate
½ cup (1 stick) unsalted butter
1 teaspoon all-purpose flour
1 cup blanched whole almonds
1½ cups coarsely ground fresh bread crumbs made from 3 slices white bread
    with the crusts removed (leave the crumbs in the food processor)
⅔ cup warm heavy cream
¼ teaspoon pure almond extract
4 large eggs
⅔ cup granulated sugar
Pinch of salt
2 cups cold heavy cream
3 tablespoons sifted confectioners' sugar
1 teaspoon pure vanilla extract or ½ teaspoon orange oil

1. Place the semisweet and unsweetened chocolates and the butter in a small, heavy saucepan over low heat and melt together, stirring constantly. Remove from the heat as soon as the mixture is melted and smooth; set aside. Butter a 1½-quart pudding mold and lid, ceramic soufflé dish, heatproof bowl, slow cooker crock, or other ceramic baking dish that fits comfortably inside your crock with at least 1 inch of clearance all around to allow steam to circulate freely. Sprinkle the inside with the flour and set aside.

2. Add the almonds to the bread crumbs in the food processor and process until finely ground. Transfer to a large bowl and add the warm heavy cream and almond extract. Stir and let stand for 5 minutes.

3. With an electric mixer in a medium-size bowl, beat the eggs, granulated sugar, and salt together on high speed until thick and lightly colored, about 3 minutes. Meanwhile, with a large rubber spatula, add the melted chocolate to the soaked crumbs. Fold the egg mixture into the chocolate-crumb mixture. Scrape the batter into the prepared mold, smoothing the top with a rubber spatula. If using a baking dish without a cover, cover tightly with a double layer of aluminum foil; tie a string around the rim of the bowl to hold the foil in place. Gently lower the dish into the crock.

4. Carefully add hot water until it comes up about 2 inches high on the side of the mold. Place the lid on the slow cooker and cook on HIGH for 2½ to 3 hours, taking care not to let the water boil off; add a bit more hot water, if needed. Check the pudding; it should feel set to the touch, yet slightly moist. It will be puffed, rising to fill the mold, and a cake tester inserted into the center should come out clean. If not cooked, cover and continue to cook, checking again in increments of 15 to 20 minutes.

5. Meanwhile, in a medium-size bowl with an electric mixer, whip the cold heavy cream until just thickened; add the confectioners' sugar and vanilla extract and beat until soft peaks form. Cover with plastic wrap and refrigerate until ready to serve.

6. Carefully remove the pudding from the slow cooker to a rack. Remove the lid or foil. Allow the pudding to cool for 10 minutes, then turn the mold upside down onto a serving plate and remove the mold. Serve slices warm or at room temperature with spoonfuls of the whipped cream.

New Orleans–Style Vanilla Bread Pudding with Whiskey Sauce

T his is a wonderful recipe adapted from Elaine Corn's book *Gooey Desserts: The Joy of Decadence* (Crown Publishing, 1995). Elaine's mother visited New Orleans while accompanying her husband to a convention. To keep busy, she took a cooking class at the New Orleans School of Cooking. This is the recipe made in class that day, except with a bit less sugar, raisins, coconut, and pecans to accommodate the slow cooker method. If you use fresh bread, place it on a baking sheet and toast for 10 to 15 minutes at 350°F. This bread pudding is so addictive that you might find yourself eating it right out of the crock, and the heck with the sauce. This is a grand dessert for company after a light meal. ○ *Serves 8*

COOKER: Medium round
SETTING AND COOK TIME: HIGH for 2½ hours, plus 15 minutes uncovered

6 to 7 cups crumbled stale French bread
¾ cup dark raisins
¾ cup sweetened shredded dried coconut
¾ cup chopped pecans
4 cups whole milk
1¾ cups sugar
3 large eggs
½ cup (1 stick) unsalted butter, melted and cooled
1 teaspoon ground cinnamon
1 teaspoon ground nutmeg
2 tablespoons pure vanilla extract
1 recipe Whiskey Sauce (recipe follows), for serving

1. Coat the inside of the crock with butter-flavored nonstick cooking spray.

2. Place the bread, raisins, coconut, and pecans in the slow cooker. In a large bowl, whisk together the milk, sugar, eggs, melted butter, cinnamon, nutmeg, and vanilla extract until smooth. Pour into the cooker over the bread cubes and push the bread down to moisten it evenly. Cover and cook on HIGH until puffed and a knife inserted into the center comes out clean, about 2½ hours. An instant-read thermometer inserted into the center should register 190°F.

3. Remove the lid and cook on HIGH for another 15 minutes.

4. Turn off the cooker, cover, and let the pudding cool before serving warm or at room temperature with the warm whiskey sauce. Store both the pudding and the sauce, covered, in the refrigerator for up to 3 days.

Whiskey Sauce

○ *Makes about 1½ cups*

½ cup (1 stick) unsalted butter
1½ cups confectioners' sugar
2 large egg yolks
¼ to ⅓ cup bourbon or Scotch, to your taste

Place the butter and confectioners' sugar in a medium-size saucepan over medium heat. Let the butter melt, then beat with a handheld immersion blender or whisk until smooth. Beat in the egg yolks. Remove from the heat and slowly beat in the bourbon. The sauce will thicken as it cools. You may keep it warm in a small slow cooker, covered, set on LOW until ready to serve.

Sticky Steamed Pumpkin Pudding

D ates make this moist, cake-like steamed pudding "sticky," and a final drizzle of silken butterscotch sauce makes it utterly irresistible. When our ovens are filled to capacity for holiday entertaining, we turn to this comforting slow cooker dessert for its luscious flavor as much as for its convenience. This is from cookbook writer and dear friend Peggy Fallon. ● *Serves 8 to 10*

COOKER: Large round or oval
SETTING AND COOK TIME: HIGH for 3 to 3 1/2 hours

½ pound pitted dates

1 tablespoon unsalted butter, softened

1½ cups all-purpose flour

1½ teaspoons baking soda

1 teaspoon ground cinnamon

1 teaspoon ground ginger

½ teaspoon salt

¼ teaspoon ground nutmeg

2 large eggs

One 15-ounce can pumpkin puree

1½ cups firmly packed dark brown sugar

½ cup vegetable or canola oil

1½ teaspoons grated orange zest

1½ teaspoons pure vanilla extract

1 recipe Spirited Butterscotch Sauce (recipe follows) and/or
   sweetened whipped cream, for serving

1. Using lightly oiled kitchen scissors, cut each date into 3 or 4 pieces; set aside. Select a 2½-quart pudding mold with a lid, ceramic soufflé dish, heatproof bowl, small slow cooker crock, or other ceramic baking dish that fits comfortably inside your crock with at least 1 inch of clearance all around to allow steam to circulate freely. Generously coat the inside of the mold and lid or baking dish with the softened butter.

2. In a medium-size bowl, whisk together the flour, baking soda, cinnamon, ginger, salt, and nutmeg. In a large bowl, whisk the eggs until lightly beaten. Whisk in the pumpkin puree, brown sugar, oil, orange zest, and vanilla extract. Stir in the dates. Gradually stir in the flour mixture just until blended. Scrape the batter into the prepared mold, smoothing the top with a rubber spatula. If using a dish without a cover, cover the dish tightly with a double layer of aluminum foil; tie a string around the rim of the bowl to hold the foil in place. Gently lower the mold into the crock.

3. Carefully add hot water until it comes up about 2 inches high on the side of the mold. Place the lid on the slow cooker and cook on HIGH for 3 to 3½ hours, taking care not to let the water boil off; add a bit more hot water if needed. Check the pudding; it should feel set to the touch, yet slightly moist. A cake tester inserted into the center should come out clean.

4. Leave the mold in the cooker, uncovered, for 10 minutes to cool slightly, then carefully remove the mold to a rack. Remove the cover or foil from the mold. Allow the pudding to cool for 10 minutes, then turn it upside down onto the rack to let the pudding slide out. Serve slightly warm or at room temperature, cut into wedges and topped with the butterscotch sauce and/or whipped cream. Store leftovers, wrapped in plastic, in the refrigerator for up to 3 days.

Spirited Butterscotch Sauce

While designed to be served with Sticky Steamed Pumpkin Pudding, we also like this butterscotch sauce on ice cream or gingerbread, or even with a slice of Steamed Chocolate Pudding (page 380). ● *Makes about 1½ cups*

COOKER: Small round
SETTING AND COOK TIME: LOW for 1 hour

½ cup (1 stick) unsalted butter, cut into pieces
1 cup firmly packed light brown sugar
½ cup heavy cream or heavy whipping cream
Pinch of salt
1 tablespoon Scotch, brandy, or dark rum or 1 teaspoon pure vanilla extract

1. Combine the butter, brown sugar, cream, and salt in the slow cooker. Cover and cook on LOW for 1 hour.

2. Add the Scotch, whisking until well blended and heated through. Serve warm. You may keep the sauce warm on LOW for up to 1 hour before serving. If made in advance, store in the refrigerator in an airtight container for up to 1 week.

Gingerbread with Blackberry Sauce

One of the oldest cakes in the civilized world, gingerbread is reinvented with every baking, its warm, intoxicating fragrance filling the kitchen with the promise of good eating. English cookbooks still call for dark or light treacle in gingerbread recipes, but we use molasses. Use the unsulfured Barbados variety of molasses rather than blackstrap, which is bitter. You may also substitute pure cane syrup or Lyle's Golden Syrup for a mellower flavor. Use plenty of fresh ground ginger (buy a new bottle every six to nine months) to get the most concentrated hot and fiery flavor. To make a white gingerbread, substitute cane syrup, maple syrup, or honey for the molasses. If you don't have time to make the fruit sauce, you can serve this with whipped cream. o *Serves 6*

COOKER: Medium or large round
SETTING AND COOK TIME: HIGH for 2¼ to 2½ hours

1 cup all-purpose flour
¼ cup sugar
2 teaspoons instant espresso powder
1½ teaspoons ground ginger
1 teaspoon ground cinnamon
½ teaspoon ground cloves
¼ teaspoon ground nutmeg
Pinch of ground allspice
½ teaspoon baking soda
¼ teaspoon salt
⅔ cup full-fat sour cream
3 tablespoons unsalted butter, melted
⅓ cup light or dark molasses
1 large egg
1 recipe Blackberry Sauce (recipe follows), for serving
1 cup crème fraîche, store-bought or homemade (page 90), or heavy cream whipped
   to stiff peaks, for serving

1. Line the bottom of the crock with a round of parchment paper. Coat the paper and one-third of the way up the side of the crock with butter-flavored nonstick cooking spray.

2. In a medium-size bowl, combine the flour, sugar, espresso powder, ginger, cinnamon, cloves, nutmeg, allspice, baking soda, and salt. In a small bowl, combine the sour cream, melted butter, molasses, and egg; beat until smooth. Add to the dry ingredients and beat until smooth and fluffy. Spread the batter evenly in the crock.

3. Cover and cook on HIGH until puffed and a cake tester inserted into the center comes out clean, 2¼ to 2½ hours.

4. Uncover and let stand for 30 minutes to cool before cutting small wedges to serve warm or at room temperature straight out of the crock. To remove, run a knife around the edge inside the crock and lift out the cake in one piece with a large rubber spatula. To serve, place a spoonful of the sauce on each dessert plate. Place a wedge of gingerbread on top of the sauce and top with cold crème fraîche.

Blackberry Sauce

○ *Makes about 2 cups*

2 cups fresh blackberries or one 16-ounce package individually frozen blackberries (not packed in syrup), thawed
2 tablespoons Cognac, apple juice, or water
¼ cup superfine sugar, or to taste

1. In a small bowl, sprinkle the berries with the Cognac and sugar. Let stand for 1 hour at room temperature.

2. Pass through a sieve to remove the seeds. Store in the refrigerator in an airtight container for up to 4 days.

Blueberry Cake

I n the past 25 years, large, firm, deep-blue blueberries have transformed from a local specialty to a mass-cultivated fruit that has captured the hearts and palates of food lovers all over America. They are excellent cooked in cakes and pies, as well as stewed. Blueberries are fresh in summer, but also available frozen all winter, and these retain the delicious qualities of the fresh variety. For oven-baked recipes you can toss still-frozen berries into the batter, but in crock-baked cakes, the berries must be thawed first. ○ *Serves 6*

COOKER: Medium or large round
SETTING AND COOK TIME: HIGH for 2¼ to 2½ hours

3 tablespoons unsalted butter, softened
½ cup sugar
2 large eggs
½ teaspoon pure vanilla extract
½ cup full-fat sour cream
1 cup plus 2 tablespoons all-purpose flour
½ teaspoon baking soda
¼ teaspoon salt
1½ cups fresh or frozen blueberries, picked over for stems if fresh,
    thawed and drained on paper towels if frozen

1. Line the bottom of the crock with a round of parchment paper. Coat the paper and one-third of the way up the side of the crock with butter-flavored nonstick cooking spray.

2. With an electric mixer, cream the butter and sugar together in a medium-size bowl until fluffy. Add the eggs, one at a time, the vanilla extract, and the sour cream; beat well on medium-low speed for 30 seconds. Add 1 cup of the flour, the baking soda, and the salt and beat on medium-high speed until thick and fluffy, about 30 seconds. Do not overbeat. Sprinkle the blueberries with the remaining 2 tablespoons flour and gently fold them into the mix. Spread the batter evenly in the crock.

3. Cover and cook on HIGH until puffed and a cake tester inserted into the center comes out clean, 2¼ to 2½ hours.

4. Uncover and let stand for 30 minutes before cutting small wedges to serve warm or at room temperature straight out of the crock. To remove, run a knife around the edge inside the crock and lift out the cake in one piece with a large rubber spatula.

Lemon Cornmeal Cake in Fragrant Fig Leaves

Since we love cornmeal so much, here is a simple little single-layer cake to serve with berries and whipped cream. This is a lot more delicate than regular cornbread. Based on ancient cooking techniques that called for lining earthenware dishes with leaves before baking cakes, we line the crock with fresh fig leaves, then pour in the batter. When serving, you just peel back the leaves from the side of the cake and leave the cake on its natural platter. If you don't have access to fig leaves, just bake this directly in the crock as with our other cakes. ○ *Serves 8*

COOKER: Medium or large round
SETTING AND COOK TIME: HIGH for 2½ to 2¾ hours

2 large fresh fig leaves, washed and patted dry
¾ cup yellow cornmeal, sifted
¾ cup all-purpose flour
Pinch of salt
1 teaspoon baking powder
¾ cup (1½ sticks) unsalted butter, softened
1 cup sugar
3 large eggs
¼ cup full-fat sour cream
Grated zest of 1 lemon
Squeeze of fresh lemon juice
¼ teaspoon pure lemon extract or lemon oil

1. Line the bottom of the crock with a round of parchment paper. Coat the paper and one-third of the way up the side of the crock with butter-flavored nonstick cooking spray. Spread the fig leaves flat and cut out the thick stem and lower part of the vein. Arrange the two leaves in the bottom of the cooker, stem side ends overlapping, so that the entire bottom of the crock is covered and the lobed leaves are pressed up against the sides of the crock. Sprinkle with 1 tablespoon of the cornmeal.

2. In a medium-size bowl, combine the remaining cornmeal with the flour, salt, and baking powder. In another medium-size bowl, beat the butter with an electric mixer until fluffy. Add the sugar, beat until light, and then beat in the eggs until just smooth. Beat in the sour cream, lemon zest, lemon juice, and lemon extract until smooth. Add the dry mixture to the wet mixture and stir until well combined. Spread the batter evenly in the crock and smooth the top.

3. Cover and cook on HIGH until a cake tester inserted into the center comes out clean, 2½ to 2¾ hours.

4. Uncover and let stand for 30 minutes to cool before cutting small wedges to serve warm or at room temperature straight out of the crock. To remove, run a knife around the edge inside the crock and lift out in one piece with a large rubber spatula.

Vanilla Pan de Maiz

T his sweet, moist cornbread has the delicate aroma of vanilla paired with the grainy texture of cornmeal. It is utterly divine served with sliced fresh papaya and sweet butter as an unusual breakfast bread, as a base for Jacquie's Southwest-Style Poached Eggs with Chipotle Gravy (page 270), or plain and warm from the crock with a home-cooked bowl of beans. ○ *Serves 8*

COOKER: Medium round
SETTING AND COOK TIME: HIGH for 2¼ to 2½ hours

1 cup yellow cornmeal, preferably stone-ground
1 cup all-purpose flour
¾ cup confectioners' sugar
½ teaspoon salt
½ teaspoon baking powder
½ teaspoon baking soda
2 large eggs
1 cup buttermilk
1 tablespoon pure vanilla extract
6 tablespoons (¾ stick) unsalted butter, melted

1. Line the bottom of the crock with a round of parchment paper. Coat the paper and one-third of the way up the side of the crock with butter-flavored nonstick cooking spray.

2. In a medium-size bowl, combine the cornmeal, flour, confectioners' sugar, salt, baking powder, and baking soda. In another medium-size bowl, mix the eggs, buttermilk, vanilla extract, and melted butter together with a whisk. Add to the dry mixture and, with a few vigorous strokes, stir until just blended. Spread the batter evenly in the crock.

3. Cover and cook on HIGH until a cake tester inserted into the center comes out clean, 2¼ to 2½ hours.

4. Uncover and let stand for 30 minutes to cool before cutting small wedges to serve warm or at room temperature straight out of the crock. To remove, run a knife around the edge inside the crock and lift out in one piece with a large rubber spatula.

Crock-Baked Salsa Cornbread

O kay, here's one for those days when you want to mix something up quickly. It makes a great savory side dish for a chili party! You can top it with a bit of sour cream and chopped green onion, if you wish. ● *Serves 10 to 12*

COOKER: Medium round
SETTING AND COOK TIME: HIGH for 2¼ to 2½ hours

One 15-ounce can creamed corn
2 large eggs
½ cup full-fat sour cream
One 4-ounce can diced roasted green chiles, undrained
2 tablespoons unsalted butter, softened
Two 8-ounce boxes corn muffin mix
3 to 4 tablespoons chunky salsa of your choice

1. Line the bottom of the crock with a round of parchment paper. Coat the paper and one-third of the way up the side of the crock with butter-flavored nonstick cooking spray.

2. In a medium-size bowl, combine the creamed corn, eggs, sour cream, chiles, and butter. Whisk together until well combined. Add the corn muffin mix, stirring well to combine. Pour the batter into the crock, then spoon the salsa over the top and cut into the batter with a butter knife or rubber spatula, using a swirling motion to marble the batter.

3. Cover and cook on HIGH until a cake tester inserted into the center comes out clean, 2¼ to 2½ hours.

4. Uncover and let stand for about 15 minutes. Loosen the sides with a knife and invert onto a large plate. If a little of the top sticks to the bottom of the crock or the parchment paper, place a dollop of salsa over it.

Steamed Maple-Raisin Brown Bread

We love maple syrup in brown bread, a pure New England touch. You can substitute plain whole wheat flour for the graham flour, but the graham flour has a lovely sweet flavor all its own. Graham flour is available in most supermarkets in the flour section, or check your local natural foods store. ○ *Serves 8*

COOKER: Medium or large round
SETTING AND COOK TIME: HIGH for 2 to 2½ hours

1 large egg
⅓ cup pure maple syrup
¾ cup buttermilk
¾ cup graham flour
½ cup all-purpose flour
½ cup yellow cornmeal
1½ teaspoons baking soda
½ teaspoon salt
½ cup dark or golden raisins

1. Grease and flour a 1½-quart (6-cup) pudding mold, heatproof bowl, or small slow cooker crock that will fit inside your slow cooker with an inch or so of clearance all around.

2. In a medium-size bowl, beat together the egg, maple syrup, and buttermilk. In another medium-size bowl, whisk together the graham flour, all-purpose flour, cornmeal, baking soda, and salt. Add to the buttermilk mixture and stir until thoroughly combined. Stir in the raisins. Pour the batter into the prepared mold. Place the cover on the mold or, if you are using a bowl, cover it tightly with a double layer of aluminum foil; tie a string around the rim of the bowl to hold the foil in place.

3. Lower the mold inside the crock and carefully add hot water until it comes up about 2 inches high on the sides of the mold. Place the lid on the slow cooker and cook on HIGH for 2 hours. To determine if the bread is done, carefully remove the cover or foil and gently touch the center of the bread. It should spring back into place. If your finger leaves an impression, re-cover the bread and continue to steam it, checking at 30-minute intervals.

4. When the bread is done, carefully remove the mold to a rack. Let the bread cool, uncovered, for 10 minutes. Run a table knife around the inside of the mold to loosen the bread. Invert onto a rack and remove the mold to cool the bread. Cut into wedges or slices to serve.

Steamed Brown Bread with Rum Fruits

 ere is another variation of Boston brown bread with a distinctly special touch. If you don't want to use the rum, substitute your favorite fruit juice.

○ *Serves 8*

COOKER: Medium or large round
SETTING AND COOK TIME: HIGH for 2 to 2½ hours

¼ **cup chopped pitted dates**
¼ **cup chopped dried apricots**
3 tablespoons dark rum
1 large egg
1 tablespoon unsalted butter, melted
1 cup buttermilk
½ **cup whole wheat flour**
½ **cup all-purpose flour**
½ **cup rye flour**
⅓ **cup yellow cornmeal**
2 tablespoons light or dark brown sugar
1¼ **teaspoons baking soda**
½ **teaspoon salt**

1. Grease and flour a 1½-quart (6-cup) pudding mold, heatproof bowl, or small slow cooker crock that will fit inside your slow cooker with an inch or so of clearance all around.

2. Combine the dates, apricots, and rum in a small bowl; let stand for 30 minutes at room temperature to macerate.

3. In a medium-size bowl, beat together the egg, melted butter, and buttermilk. In another medium-size bowl, whisk together the whole wheat flour, all-purpose flour, rye flour, cornmeal, brown sugar, baking soda, and salt, then add to the buttermilk mixture and stir just until thoroughly combined. Stir in the dried fruits and rum. Pour the batter into the prepared mold. Place the cover on the mold or, if you are using a bowl, cover it tightly with a double layer of aluminum foil; tie a string around the rim of the bowl to hold the foil in place.

3. Lower the mold inside the crock and carefully add hot water until it comes up about 2 inches high on the sides of the mold. Cover and cook on HIGH for 2 hours. To determine if the bread is done, carefully remove the lid or foil and gently touch the center of the bread. It should spring back into place. If your finger leaves an impression, re-cover the bread and continue to steam it, checking at 30-minute intervals.

4. When the bread is done, carefully remove the mold to a rack. Let the bread cool, uncovered, for 10 minutes. Run a table knife around the inside of the mold to loosen the bread. Invert onto a rack and remove the mold to cool the bread. Cut into wedges or slices to serve.

Fruit Desserts and Compotes

Crock-Baked Apples with Honey, Orange, and Dates o 399

Lady Marmalade Bananas o 400

Cherries Jubilee o 401

Caramel Peaches o 402

Poached Peaches with Brandied Custard Sauce o 403

Slow-Poached Pears with Marsala and Fruit Sauce o 405

Slow-Poached Pears with Port, Ice Cream, and Raspberry Drizzle o 406

Slow-Poached Pears with Warm Chocolate Sauce o 408

Slow-Poached Pears in Raspberries and Red Wine o 409

Stewed Quinces in Late-Harvest Wine Syrup o 410

Rhubarb-Strawberry Crumble o 411

Apple Crumble with Maple Crème Fraîche o 412

Fruit Buckle o 413

Stewed Dried Fruit o 415

Apricot, Peach, and Cherry Compote o 416

Winter Fruit Compote o 417

Spiced Orange Plums o 418

Vanilla Figs and Dried Cherries o 418

Seasonal fruit can be the star of any party menu. The slow cooker, with its gentle, even heat, makes lovely fruit desserts, such as gently spiced compotes and poached fresh whole fruit, desserts that somehow often get ignored as too old-fashioned or simple for today's diners. We disagree! This is pure comfort food, softly cooked, warm, and sweet. These are not elaborate desserts to prepare, but they will dazzle when served to guests. We especially favor poached pears, in a variety

of poaching liquids and served with a special finishing sauce. For the most elegant presentation, we plate them individually. We also included an old favorite, Cherries Jubilee (page 401), the hallmark of another era in dessert making, for a return to the gracious dining room.

Poached fresh and dried fruit have a charm all their own. They are still special and dependable desserts on European tables, and most bistros and trattorias offer some type of poached fruit with a bit of their syrup. We want them on our tables as well. Depending on the type of fruit, they can be poached whole, halved, or in pieces, and in a thick or thin sugar syrup. You can make a compote out of a single fruit or a combination of two or more fruits, called a *compote composée*. They are just plain gorgeous in a serving bowl surrounded by their syrup. Fruits can be poached in water, wine, or fruit juice, or a combination thereof. The slow cooker poaches gently, even though we poach most fruits on the HIGH setting. Although poached prunes are the most familiar

cooked dried fruit, relegated sadly to only the breakfast table, all sorts of other dried fruits lend themselves well to the gentle cooking and sweet aromatic bath required for a nice compote. For your next holiday dinner or brunch, prepare one of our compotes a day ahead.

Some of the same rules of savory slow cooker cooking apply as well to fruit desserts. Some liquid is required: anywhere from a dash to full submersion. None of these is left to cook all day because they are too delicate, so you must be around to supervise the timing. You want whole fruit to retain its shape, not end up like apple or pear sauce.

Cooked fruits are traditionally served still gently warm or at room temperature, but they are also good served cold as a garnish to vanilla cheesecake and a battery of plain old-fashioned cakes, including angel food cake, sponge cake, golden cake, and pound cake. We think you will be delightfully surprised.

We also offer recipes for a number of fresh fruit crumbles, the British version of our crisp with a slightly heartier topping, usually with rolled oats added. Remember that baking in the slow cooker crock does not encourage browning, so the crumbly top will be pale, but it will be cooked through. We offer seasonal versions, and with these recipes as a template, you can substitute your own fruit combinations.

Crock-Baked Apples with Honey, Orange, and Dates

 ere is a tasty variation on plain old baked apples. ○ *Serves 6*

COOKER: Medium or large round or oval

SETTING AND COOK TIME: HIGH for $2^{1}/_{2}$ to $3^{1}/_{2}$ hours
(the time will vary somewhat based on the size of the apple)

6 large firm baking apples (about ½ pound each), such as Golden Delicious,
    Granny Smith, Rome Beauty, or Fuji
⅓ cup chopped pitted dates
⅓ cup dark or golden raisins or dried tart or sweet cherries
¼ cup honey
⅓ cup water
⅓ cup orange juice
¼ cup sweet white wine, such as a Gewürztraminer,
    late-harvest Riesling, or ice wine

1. Grease the crock with some butter or coat with butter-flavored nonstick cooking spray.

2. Using a paring knife, vegetable peeler, or corer, remove the cores of the apples without going all the way through to the bottom (leave ½ inch at the bottom). Peel off a strip of skin around the top of each apple. Stuff each apple with a heaping tablespoon each of the dates and raisins, then drizzle evenly with the honey. Stand each apple in the cooker, right side up, fitting 2 or 3 on the bottom and stacking the rest on top, offset, not squarely on top of the others. Add the water, orange juice, and wine to the cooker. Cover and cook on HIGH until the apples are soft when pierced with the tip of a small knife, 2½ to 3½ hours. You want them firm enough to hold their shape, but soft enough to cut with a spoon or fork. They will soften a bit more as they cool.

3. Turn off the cooker, remove the lid, and let the apples cool a bit. Serve warm or at room temperature. To serve cold, refrigerate the apples in their liquid, covered, for at least 4 hours. They will keep for several days in the refrigerator.

Lady Marmalade Bananas

Baked bananas with orange marmalade is an unusual and surprisingly delicious combination. Essencia is an orange-flavored dessert wine that, if you can find it, will add nicely to the finished flavor. ○ *Serves 6*

COOKER: Medium round or oval
SETTING AND COOK TIME: LOW for 1 to 2 hours

3 tablespoons unsalted butter, softened
6 large, firm, slightly under-ripe bananas
2 tablespoons freshly squeezed lemon juice
3 to 4 tablespoons orange marmalade
3 tablespoons fruity dessert wine, such as cream sherry or Essencia
Vanilla or chocolate ice cream for serving

1. Spread the bottom of the crock with half the butter. Peel the bananas, cut them in half lengthwise, and then cut each piece in half crosswise to make 4 pieces per banana. Place in the slow cooker and sprinkle with the lemon juice. Spoon over the marmalade and dot with the remaining butter. Add the wine. Cover and cook on LOW for 1 to 2 hours.

2. Serve immediately, spooned over the ice cream.

Cherries Jubilee

C herries jubilee is strictly adult fare. Beth has fond memories of going to her first elegant restaurant as a child and watching her little sister dip each cherry into her water glass to wash off the brandy taste before eating it. Serve this over the best-quality vanilla ice cream or gelato you can find, and ladle the sauce over the ice cream at the table. This is a simple, elegant dessert that will please the fussiest dessert eaters. ○ *Serves 12*

COOKER: Medium round

SETTINGS AND COOK TIMES: LOW for 2 to 3 hours, then HIGH for 15 minutes

Four 16-ounce cans pitted Bing cherries in juice
1½ cups sugar
3 tablespoons freshly squeezed lemon juice
Grated zest of 2 small lemons
6 tablespoons cornstarch
1 cup brandy
Vanilla ice cream for serving

1. Set aside ¾ cup of the cherry juice in a small cup. Combine the cherries, the remaining cherry juice, the sugar, lemon juice, and lemon zest in the slow cooker. Cover and cook on LOW for 2 to 3 hours.

2. About 15 minutes before serving time, stir the cornstarch into the reserved cherry juice until it makes a smooth slurry with no lumps. Slowly stir the slurry into the cherry sauce in the slow cooker. Cover, turn the cooker to HIGH, and cook until the liquid is glossy and thick, about 15 minutes.

3. Stir in the brandy, reserving an oversized spoonful. Turn off the cooker. Holding the spoonful of brandy over the hot mixture, carefully ignite the brandy in the spoon with a long-handled match, being careful of long sleeves and dangling hair. When the flame subsides, stir the brandy into the mixture. Serve immediately over vanilla ice cream.

Caramel Peaches

ooking fresh peach halves in a cream-and-sugar mixture makes a luscious caramel sauce almost by magic. You must use fresh rather than canned or frozen fruit for this to turn out properly. ○ *Serves 6*

COOKER: Medium round or oval
SETTING AND COOK TIME: LOW for 4 to 5 hours

6 large ripe peaches, peeled, pitted, and cut in half
1 tablespoon freshly squeezed lemon juice
1¼ cups firmly packed light brown sugar
¼ cup (½ stick) unsalted butter, melted
⅓ cup heavy cream
½ teaspoon ground cinnamon

1. In a large bowl, toss together the peaches and lemon juice.

2. In the slow cooker, combine the brown sugar, melted butter, heavy cream, and cinnamon; the mixture will be thick. Add the peaches and toss gently with a wooden spoon to coat with the brown sugar mixture. Make sure the peaches end up cut side down in the mixture. Cover and cook on LOW for 4 to 5 hours.

3. Place 2 peach halves on each dessert plate and drizzle with the caramel sauce from the crock. Serve hot or warm.

Poached Peaches with Brandied Custard Sauce

P oaching peaches on the stovetop is sometimes a hit-or-miss procedure—too high a heat and you end up with mashed peaches floating in liquid when you want perfect whole ones for serving. But the low simmer in the slow cooker provides just the gentle cooking the peach needs to stay whole. ○ *Serves 6*

COOKER: Medium round or oval
SETTING AND COOK TIME: HIGH for about 2 hours

3 cups water
1 cup sugar
Juice of 1 lemon
3 lemon slices
6 firm but ripe peaches, dipped into boiling water for 5 seconds,
    and skins slipped off
1 recipe Brandied Custard Sauce (recipe follows)

1. Combine the water, sugar, lemon juice, and lemon slices in the slow cooker. Add the whole peaches; they will float in the liquid. Cover and cook on HIGH for about 2 hours. Do not stir at any time during the cooking or you might bruise the fruit. Check the consistency of the peaches by piercing their flesh with the tip of a small knife; you want them firm, but slightly soft. They will soften a bit more as they cool.

2. Remove the peaches from the liquid with a slotted spoon to a serving bowl. Let cool to room temperature.

3. When cooled, pour the poaching liquid from the cooker over the peaches. Cover, and refrigerate for at least 4 hours or up to overnight.

4. To serve, remove the peaches from their liquid with a slotted spoon, cut each in half, and remove the pit. Pour some of the custard sauce onto each plate and place 2 halves on top. Serve chilled.

Brandied Custard Sauce

Custard sauce is good on just about any type of poached fruit or any kind of cake, as well as on gingerbread. It is so delicious that it would be a shame to skip making it.

○ *Makes 2 cups*

1 cup heavy cream
1 cup half-and-half
⅓ cup sugar
3 large eggs
2 tablespoons cream sherry
2 tablespoons Calvados or brandy
1 teaspoon pure vanilla extract
1 teaspoon rum

1. In a medium-size heavy saucepan over medium heat, heat the heavy cream and half-and-half together until bubbles form around the edges of the pan.

2. In a medium-size bowl or food processor, combine the sugar and eggs. Beat hard with a whisk or process briefly until light colored and foamy. Whisking constantly, or with the machine running, gradually add the hot cream to the egg mixture. Pour back into the saucepan and place over medium heat. Cook the sauce gently, stirring constantly with a whisk, until it is just slightly thickened and will coat the back of a spoon; do not boil.

3. Stir in the sherry, Calvados, vanilla extract, and rum, and cook for 30 seconds longer. Let cool for 15 minutes, pour into an airtight container, cover, and refrigerate until serving time or up to 2 days.

Slow-Poached Pears with Marsala and Fruit Sauce

This is a showstopper dessert, beautiful and so refreshing. Because you make it entirely ahead, it's perfect for a party. (And you can serve it, sans the whipped cream, to anyone on a low-fat diet.) Spend a bit of time choosing the pears. They must be firm and slightly under-ripe or else they will fall apart during cooking. Nice large Comice pears would be a top choice. Marsala is a fortified Italian wine that is made domestically as well. Look for it near the port and sherry. If you choose a sweet Marsala, you will want to use less white sugar when you are finishing the sauce. Also spend a bit of time selecting the right serving dishes. You want something that is about the size of the pear and deep enough to cradle it in the sauce. The idea is to make it easy for the diners to enjoy some sauce with each bite of fruit.

This recipe comes from Julie's friend Batia Rabec, and it was the grand finale at a tasting party of 10 slow cooker dishes. The guests thought they were full, but one bite of the sweet and tender fruit convinced them otherwise. It was an unqualified hit! o *Serves 6*

COOKER: Medium or large round or oval
SETTING AND COOK TIME: HIGH for 3 to 4 hours

6 large, firm Comice or other pears, such as Bosc or D'Anjou
¼ cup apricot jam
¼ cup seedless raspberry jam
½ cup firmly packed light brown sugar
2 cups Marsala, or more depending on your slow cooker
⅓ to ½ cup granulated sugar, or more as needed
Lightly sweetened whipped cream for serving
Chopped toasted pecans for serving

1. Leaving the stems intact, peel the pears. As you peel them, place them in the slow cooker. If you must stack them, do so carefully, arranging them large end down, so that the slender tops are protected from being squashed by another pear.

Use a spoon to dollop the apricot and raspberry jams on top of the pears. Sprinkle the brown sugar over the top. Pour in enough Marsala to cover the pears. (If you do not have enough Marsala to cover, you will need to open the cooker halfway through and rearrange the fruit, so every part gets cooked in the Marsala.) Cover and cook on HIGH for 3 to 4 hours.

2. Turn the cooker off, remove the lid, and let the pears cool until you can handle them. Carefully place them in a container large enough to hold them in a single layer. Cover and refrigerate until serving time.

3. Pour the liquid remaining in the crock through a fine-mesh strainer into a small saucepan. Add ½ cup granulated sugar (⅓ cup if you used sweet Marsala). Bring the liquid to a boil over medium-high heat and let boil until it has reduced to a syrupy consistency, about 15 minutes. Taste the syrup (careful: it's hot!), adding more sugar if desired. Let the syrup cool, then cover and refrigerate until serving time.

4. To serve, place each pear in a serving dish or small bowl, discarding any liquid that has escaped from the pears while chilling in the refrigerator. Pour the cold syrup over the pears and top each with whipped cream and chopped pecans.

Slow-Poached Pears with Port, Ice Cream, and Raspberry Drizzle

Here is another fabulous do-ahead entertaining dessert from Batia Rabec. Serve each guest an ice cream–topped pear half in a shallow bowl. In high season, make the drizzle with fresh raspberries. If you find frozen raspberries packed in syrup, you may not need to sweeten the sauce. If you don't have superfine sugar, just whirl some regular granulated sugar in a dry blender or food processor to grind it. The perfect time to do this is right before you puree the raspberries. For a dessert that looks like it came from a restaurant kitchen, transfer the raspberry drizzle to a clean plastic squeeze bottle. Then you can use it to "paint" an artistic squiggle or zigzag pattern on the pear. ◦ *Serves 6*

COOKER: Small or medium round or oval
SETTING AND COOK TIME: HIGH for 3 to 4 hours

3 large, firm Comice or other pears, such as Bosc or D'Anjou
½ cup firmly packed light brown sugar
1 to 2 cups port, or more depending on your slow cooker
½ cup granulated sugar, or more as needed

RASPBERRY DRIZZLE:
½ pint fresh raspberries or one 10-ounce package frozen raspberries, thawed and drained
2 tablespoons superfine sugar, or more as needed

Vanilla ice cream for serving
Chopped toasted almonds for serving (optional)

1. Peel the pears, placing each in the slow cooker as you finish with it. If you must stack them, do so carefully, arranging them large end down so that the slender tops are protected from being squashed by another pear. Sprinkle the brown sugar over the pears. Pour in enough port to cover the pears. (If you do not have enough port, you will need to open the cooker halfway through and rearrange the fruit so that every part gets cooked in the port.) Cover and cook on HIGH for 3 to 4 hours.

2. Turn the cooker off, remove the lid, and let the pears cool until you can handle them. Carefully place them in a container large enough to hold them in a single layer. Cover and refrigerate until cold.

3. Meanwhile, pour the liquid remaining in the cooker through a fine-mesh strainer into a small saucepan. Add the granulated sugar, bring to a boil over medium-high heat, and let boil until reduced to a syrupy consistency, about 15 minutes. Taste the syrup (careful: it's hot!), adding more sugar if desired. Let the syrup cool, then refrigerate it, covered, until serving time.

4. After the pears are cold, cut each in half lengthwise. Use an apple corer (or a small teaspoon) to neatly scoop out the core. If not serving right away, return the pears to the refrigerator.

5. To make the raspberry drizzle, puree the raspberries in a blender. Press the puree through a fine-mesh strainer to remove the seeds. Stir in superfine sugar to taste, starting with 2 tablespoons.

6. To serve, place each pear half in a serving dish or small bowl, flat side up, discarding any liquid that has escaped from the pears in the refrigerator. Pour the cold syrup over the pears and top each one with a small scoop of vanilla ice cream. Top the ice cream with raspberry drizzle. Sprinkle on some chopped almonds, if using, and serve.

Slow-Poached Pears with Warm Chocolate Sauce

A nice Italian twist on poached pears is to serve them with a bittersweet chocolate sauce. Called *pere con cioccolato*, it is a surprise pairing and a really great summer dessert that is light and decadent at the same time.

o Serves 6

COOKER: Medium round
SETTING AND COOK TIME: HIGH for 3 to 4 hours

1 cup dry white wine
1 cup water
1½ cups sugar
2 teaspoons whole cloves
6 slightly under-ripe D'Anjou pears, peeled, cut in half, and cored
2 tablespoons freshly squeezed lemon juice
1 recipe Bittersweet Chocolate Sauce (page 435) or
    warmed chocolate sauce of your choice

1. Combine the wine, water, sugar, cloves, pears, and lemon juice in the slow cooker. Cover and cook on HIGH for 3 to 4 hours. Do not stir at any time during the cooking to avoid bruising the fruit. Check the consistency of the pears by piercing their flesh with the tip of a small knife; you want them firm, but slightly soft. They will soften a bit more as they cool.

2. Turn the cooker off, remove the lid, and let cool to room temperature before serving. To serve cold, refrigerate the pears in their liquid, covered, for at least 4 hours or up to overnight.

3. To serve, remove the poached pears from their liquid with a slotted spoon to a dessert bowl. Serve 2 pear halves for each person with warm chocolate sauce poured on the side or over the top.

Slow-Poached Pears in Raspberries and Red Wine

When buying pears for slow cooker recipes like this one, choose ones that are hard and under-ripe, not close to the consistency you would want if you were to eat them out of hand. The long, gentle cooking will transform them.

o Serves 6 to 8

COOKER: Medium round
SETTING AND COOK TIME: HIGH for 3 to 4 hours

3 cups dry red wine, such as Merlot or Pinot Noir
Two 10-ounce packages frozen raspberries in syrup, thawed and drained, reserving the syrup
1⅓ cups sugar
One ½-inch-long piece vanilla bean or 2 teaspoons pure vanilla extract
One 3-inch cinnamon stick
1 long strip orange peel, 1 teaspoon orange oil, or ½ teaspoon pure orange extract
6 to 8 slightly under-ripe Bartlett, Comice, D'Anjou, or Bosc pears, with a circular strip of peel removed from around the middle and stem left intact
6 to 8 whole cloves
Whipped cream for serving (optional)

1. Combine the wine, reserved raspberry syrup, sugar, vanilla bean, cinnamon stick, and orange peel in the slow cooker. Press a clove into the blossom end of each pear. Place the pears in the cooker on their sides or standing on end. Cover and cook on HIGH for 3 to 4 hours. Do not stir at any time during the cooking to avoid bruising the fruit. Check the consistency of the pears by piercing their flesh with the tip of a small knife; you want them firm, but slightly soft. They will soften a bit more as they cool.

2. Turn off the cooker, remove the lid, and let cool to warm or room temperature. If you desire a thicker sauce, remove the whole spices and transfer the liquid to a saucepan. Over high heat, reduce until you achieve the desired consistency. To serve cold, refrigerate the pears in their sauce, covered, for at least 4 hours or up to overnight.

3. To serve, remove the pears from the sauce with a slotted spoon to a dessert plate. Serve warm or chilled in a pool of the raspberry-wine sauce and some whipped cream, if desired.

Stewed Quinces in Late-Harvest Wine Syrup

Quinces have a short season in the autumn, and Beth has been blessed with her own tree. For years she struggled to find ways to prepare and cook the wildly old-fashioned and out-of-vogue fruit, sort of a relic of a bygone era of home cooking. Here, it is lovingly and simply poached. The cooking time is not too long because you are cooking slices. Serve warm or chilled from the fridge topped with some chopped candied ginger. ○ *Serves 6*

COOKER: Medium round or oval
SETTINGS AND COOK TIMES: HIGH for 30 to 45 minutes, then LOW for 1½ to 2 hours

4 large or 8 small quinces (about 3 pounds)
½ cup (1 stick) unsalted butter
½ cup sugar
½ cup mild honey
1½ cups late-harvest white wine, such as a Riesling, ice wine, Sauternes, Muscat, or Gewürztraminer (you can also use half water, half wine)
Juice of ½ lemon

1. Cut the quince in half, remove the seeds, and core with a melon baller or sharp paring knife. Peel the quinces, then cut the halves into ¼- to ½-inch-thick slices, or use the ¼-inch slicer disc on a food processor (a great way to cut all the hard fruit evenly and quickly).

2. Place the quince slices and butter in the slow cooker. Cover and cook on HIGH for 30 to 45 minutes to sweat the fruit and coat with the butter; stir occasionally.

3. Reduce the heat to LOW and stir in the sugar, honey, wine, and lemon juice. Cover and cook until the fruit is tender when pierced with the tip of a knife, 1½ to 2 hours. Transfer the quince slices, along with their cooking liquid, to an airtight container and refrigerate for at least 5 hours. Serve chilled.

Rhubarb-Strawberry Crumble

T here are never enough recipes for rhubarb, in our opinion. Combined with strawberries, a fruit not often served cooked, you have one of the most famous pairings in the culinary world. ◦ *Serves 8*

COOKER: Medium round or oval or large round
SETTINGS AND COOK TIMES: HIGH for 30 minutes, then LOW for 2½ to 3 hours

FRUIT MIXTURE:
1 pound fresh rhubarb, leaves removed and stalks cut into 1-inch pieces to equal about 4 cups
2 pints fresh strawberries, hulled and cut in half
1 cup granulated sugar
¼ cup all-purpose flour
2 tablespoons cornstarch
Pinch of salt

TOPPING:
1¾ cups quick-cooking rolled oats
1 cup firmly packed light brown sugar
½ cup all-purpose flour
1 teaspoon baking powder
¾ teaspoon ground cinnamon or apple pie spice
¼ teaspoon salt
½ cup (1 stick) cold unsalted butter, cut into pieces

Vanilla ice cream or whipped cream for serving (optional)

1. Coat the crock with nonstick cooking spray or grease with butter. To prepare the fruit mixture, place the rhubarb and strawberries in the crock; sprinkle with the granulated sugar, flour, cornstarch, and salt, and toss to coat the fruit. Cover and cook on HIGH for 30 minutes.

2. Meanwhile, to make the topping, place half the rolled oats in a food processor; pulse to make a flour. Add the remaining rolled oats, the brown sugar, flour, baking powder, cinnamon, and salt. Cut in the butter by pulsing to make coarse crumbs. After cooking the fruit for 30 minutes, spread the topping evenly over the fruit, leaving a ½-inch border all the way around the edge to prevent burning.

Cover, set the heat to LOW, and cook until the fruit is tender, 2½ to 3 hours. Test by sticking a knife into the center of the crumble; when it passes through the fruit with little resistance, the crumble is done.

3. Uncover and let cool for 10 minutes in the crock before serving. If desired, top each serving with ice cream or whipped cream.

Apple Crumble with Maple Crème Fraîche

A good cooking apple needs to keep its shape during baking. Its flavor, sour-sweet when raw, mellows delightfully when cooked. We like baking with medium-size to large Pippin, Granny Smith, and Fuji apples; Golden Delicious and McIntosh are wonderful if very firm, and Rome Beauties and Gravensteins are delightful early-season apples. For a sophisticated taste, toss the apples with 2 tablespoons Grand Marnier or Calvados. ○ *Serves 8*

COOKER: Medium round or oval or large round
SETTINGS AND COOK TIMES: HIGH for 30 minutes, then LOW for 2½ to 3 hours

½ cup whole unsalted nuts, such as walnuts, hazelnuts, macadamia nuts, or pecans
2 pounds (5 to 6 large) cooking apples, peeled, cored, and sliced ¾ inch thick
2 tablespoons granulated sugar
½ teaspoon ground cinnamon
2 tablespoons cornstarch

TOPPING:
1 cup all-purpose flour
¼ cup quick-cooking rolled oats
⅓ cup firmly packed light brown sugar
¼ cup granulated sugar
½ teaspoon ground cinnamon
½ cup (1 stick) cold unsalted butter, cut into pieces

MAPLE CRÈME FRAÎCHE:
1½ cups crème fraîche, store-bought or homemade (page 90)
5 tablespoons pure maple syrup

1. Preheat the oven to 350°F. Toast the nuts in the oven until lightly toasted, about 5 minutes. Let cool, then chop.

2. Coat the crock with nonstick cooking spray or grease with butter. Place the apples in the slow cooker; sprinkle with the granulated sugar, cinnamon, and cornstarch and toss to coat the fruit. Cover and cook on HIGH for 30 minutes.

3. Meanwhile, to make the topping, place the flour, oats, brown sugar, granulated sugar, and cinnamon in a small bowl or food processor. Cut in the butter with two knives or your fingertips or pulse to make coarse crumbs. Add the nuts and toss to coat. After cooking the apples for 30 minutes, spread the topping evenly over the fruit, leaving a ½-inch border all the way around the edge to prevent burning. Cover, set the heat to LOW, and cook until the fruit is tender, 2½ to 3 hours. Test by sticking a knife into the center of the crumble. When it passes through the apples with little resistance, the crumble is done.

4. Uncover and let cool for 10 minutes in the crock before serving. Meanwhile, to make the maple crème fraîche, place the crème fraîche in a small bowl. Whisk in the maple syrup until smooth. Dollop on top of each portion of crumble before serving.

Fruit Buckle

This is certainly one of the simplest desserts to make, as well as one of the most delicious. Fresh fruit is scattered over a plain yellow cake batter and then bakes up into an appealing fruit-topped cake that is as flavorful as it is tender. Favorite fruits for this recipe include pitted sweet cherries from the local farmers' market; peeled and pitted ripe summer peaches in combination with Santa Rosa plums, apricots, or nectarines; field-grown red rhubarb; delicate winter pears; or big raspberries, blueberries, or blackberries. We always make it with plums, a favorite summer fruit. You can use frozen, canned, or fresh fruit, because the fruit is cooked a bit before placing it over the cake batter. The buckle is best served the day it is made, either warm or at room temperature, accompanied by a pitcher of cold heavy cream. ○ *Serves 6*

COOKER: Medium or large round

SETTING AND COOK TIME: HIGH for 2 to 2½ hours

CAKE BATTER:

1 cup all-purpose flour

½ cup sugar

1 teaspoon baking powder

¼ teaspoon salt

⅓ cup whole milk or evaporated milk

1 large egg

2 tablespoons unsalted butter, melted

1½ teaspoons pure vanilla extract

FRUIT TOPPING:

3½ to 4 cups pitted and halved or sliced fresh fruit or berries (see above)

½ cup sugar (more or less, depending on sweetness of the fruit)

⅔ cup water

2 tablespoons complementary fruit brandy, such as Poire William, Calvados, framboise, or Grand Marnier, or freshly squeezed juice of
½ lemon or orange

Grated zest of 1 lemon or orange

1. Coat the crock with butter-flavored nonstick cooking spray.

2. To make the cake batter, in a medium-size bowl, combine the flour, sugar, baking powder, and salt. In a measuring cup, combine the milk, egg, melted butter, and vanilla, then add to the dry ingredients and beat until smooth and fluffy. Spread evenly in the crock.

3. To make the topping, in a medium-size saucepan, combine the fruit and sugar. Add the water, brandy, and zest, bring to a boil, and boil for 15 to 30 seconds. Gently spoon the hot fruit over the batter; do not stir.

4. Cover and cook on HIGH until puffed and a cake tester inserted into the center comes out clean, 2 to 2½ hours.

5. Let stand for 30 minutes in the covered crock before using an oversized spoon to serve warm. Or let cool with the lid off to serve at room temperature straight out of the crock.

Stewed Dried Fruit

Dried fruit is great when cooked until nice and plump to serve with baked ham or turkey on the buffet table. You can also use it as a topping for cottage cheese at breakfast, or dollop it with whipped cream and serve it for dessert. It is also one of our favorite ways to dress up a slice of pound cake or chiffon cake for dessert. Any combination of dried fruit or just one fruit will do. Consider prunes, apricots, apples, pears, or peaches (we especially like dried apples). You can leave out the honey or sugar, if you wish, and the compote will still be excellent. ○ *Makes about 3 cups to serve 6*

COOKER: Medium round
SETTING AND COOK TIME: LOW for 3 to 4 hours

2½ cups water
⅓ cup honey or sugar (optional)
12 ounces mixed dried fruit or all of one type
½ cup dried cranberries, cherries, or raisins

1. Combine the water, honey, if using, and all the dried fruit in the slow cooker. Cover and cook on LOW for 3 to 4 hours.

2. Turn off the cooker, remove the lid, and let cool a bit before serving warm or at room temperature. Or pour into an airtight container, cover, and refrigerate overnight. You may store in the refrigerator for up to 1 week.

Apricot, Peach, and Cherry Compote

This is a simple compote, combining just three canned and dried fruits, but we think it is one of the best. You use the juice in the canned fruit for part of the poaching liquid. We like this around the holidays with roasted meats or for brunch with quiche. Serve in a pretty cut-glass bowl with a sliver-plated serving spoon and enjoy the colors. ◦ *Serves 6*

COOKER: Medium round
SETTING AND COOK TIME: LOW for 2½ to 3 hours

½ cup firmly packed light brown sugar
½ cup orange juice
¼ cup freshly squeezed lemon juice
Grated zest of 1 orange
Grated zest of 1 lemon
12 ounces dried apricots
One 16-ounce can sliced peaches in light or heavy syrup, undrained
One 16-ounce can Bing cherries in juice, undrained

1. Combine the brown sugar, orange and lemon juices, orange and lemon zests, and dried and canned fruits with their liquids in the slow cooker. Cover and cook on LOW for 2½ to 3 hours.

2. Turn off the cooker, remove the lid, and let cool a bit before serving warm or at room temperature. Or transfer to an airtight container, refrigerate, and serve cold. You may store in the refrigerator for up to 1 week.

Winter Fruit Compote

T his is a pantry compote, one you can whip up in minutes. It is wonderful to serve to a group during the holidays. While the canned mandarins work well in this recipe, the flavor component goes up a notch if you substitute sectioned fresh tangerines. ❍ *Serves 10 to 12*

COOKER: Medium round
SETTING AND COOK TIME: HIGH for 1½ to 2 hours;
  prunes added during last 30 minutes

½ **pound dried apricots**
1 cup unsweetened apple or pear juice
¼ **cup sugar**
Juice and grated zest of 1 lemon
1 cup pitted whole dried prunes
One 8-ounce can pineapple chunks in unsweetened juice, undrained
One 16-ounce can sliced peaches in unsweetened juice, undrained
One 11-ounce can mandarin oranges in unsweetened juice or syrup, undrained,
  or 2 tangerines, peeled, sectioned, and seeded
2 cups seedless green or red grapes
1½ cups fresh or thawed individually frozen raspberries
⅓ **cup slivered blanched almonds**
2 tablespoons chopped candied ginger or candied orange peel

1. Place the apricots, apple juice, sugar, and lemon juice and zest in the slow cooker. Cover and cook on HIGH until the apricots are soft, 1 to 1½ hours.

2. Add the prunes, cover, and cook on HIGH for another 30 minutes.

3. Turn off the cooker and stir in the pineapples, peaches, and oranges and their juices. Let cool until warm, covered, then stir in the grapes, raspberries, almonds, and candied ginger. Serve slightly warm or chilled. The compote will keep for up to 2 days refrigerated in an airtight container.

Spiced Orange Plums

J ust in case you hadn't heard the news, prunes are now being called dried plums. When you make this rich brew of stewed prunes in orange juice and wine, you'll never think of prunes (excuse us, dried plums) in the same way again. This is wonderful served on its own or with vanilla ice cream.

○ Serves 6 to 8

COOKER: Medium round
SETTING AND COOK TIME: LOW for 3 to 4 hours

2 cups orange juice
¼ cup red wine or sparkling white wine, such as Asti Spumante
2 tablespoons light or dark brown sugar
1 pound dried prunes
1 strip lemon peel
½ teaspoon ground cinnamon
½ teaspoon ground cloves
½ teaspoon ground nutmeg

1. Combine all of the ingredients in the slow cooker. Cover and cook on LOW for 3 to 4 hours.

2. Turn off the cooker, remove the lid, and let cool a bit before serving warm or at room temperature. Or transfer to an airtight container, refrigerate, and serve cold. You may store in the refrigerator for up to 1 week.

Vanilla Figs and Dried Cherries

O ur collection would not be complete without a poached fig recipe. We like all manner of dried figs, whether they are black or green, moist or dehydrated. The tart dried cherries are a must; they balance the sweet nature of the figs. ○ *Serves 6*

COOKER: Medium round

SETTING AND COOK TIME: LOW for 3 to 4 hours

2 cups water
½ to ¾ of a whole vanilla bean, split in half but halves left attached at the end
½ cup mild honey
¼ cup sugar
½ pound whole dried figs
⅓ cup dried tart cherries
1 recipe Rum Whipped Cream (recipe follows)

1. Combine the water, vanilla bean, honey, sugar, figs, and cherries in the slow cooker. Cover and cook on LOW until the figs are soft, 3 to 4 hours.

2. Turn off the cooker, remove the lid, and let cool a bit before serving warm or at room temperature with the whipped cream. Or transfer to an airtight container, refrigerate, and serve cold. You may store in the refrigerator for up to 1 week.

Rum Whipped Cream

○ *Makes 2¼ cups*

1 cup cold heavy cream
2 tablespoons confectioners' or superfine sugar
2 tablespoons golden rum
½ cup full-fat sour cream

1. Place a medium-size bowl and the beaters of an electric mixer in the freezer for at least 1 hour to chill thoroughly.

2. Combine the heavy cream, sugar, and rum in the chilled bowl. Whip on high speed with an electric mixer until soft peaks form, about 3 minutes. Fold in the sour cream. Serve immediately, or cover and refrigerate for up to 6 hours before serving.

Dessert Fondues, Sweet Sauces, and Chocolate Truffles

Toblerone Fondue ● 423

Perfumed Chocolate Fondue ● 424

Chocolate Chip Fondue ● 424

White Chocolate Piña Colada
Fondue ● 425

Bittersweet Chocolate–Coconut
Fondue ● 426

Spur-of-the-Moment Chocolate-
Marshmallow Fondue ● 427

Hot Honey Cherry Sauce ● 428

Brandied Prune Sauce ● 429

Warm Berry Sauce ● 430

Ice Cream Parlor Butterscotch
Sauce ● 431

Maple-Caramel Sauce ● 432

Peggy's Killer Hot Fudge Sauce ● 432

Low-Fat Mocha Fudge Sauce with
Kahlúa ● 434

Warm Chocolate Honey ● 434

Bittersweet Chocolate Sauce ● 435

Chocolate-Cognac Sauce ● 437

Narsai's Chocolate Sauce ● 438

Creamiest Fudge ● 438

Black-on-Black Truffles ● 440

Raspberry Truffles ● 441

Low-Fat Chocolate-Nut
Truffles ● 442

The slow cooker was made for fondue. Prepare it in the slow cooker, serve it in the slow cooker—no need to run out and get a special fondue pot. Fondues fell out of fashion for a time, but they've come back with a vengeance over the past several years, and dessert fondues are showing up regularly on dessert menus. We love them for impromptu gatherings at home.

In 1966, a group of American journalists were served a Swiss fondue meal, from beginning to end, during a press conference in New York City. Dessert was melted Toblerone chocolate in a ceramic fondue pot served with bread cubes, broken shortbread cookies, and fruit chunks for dipping. It was a smash success, and the recipe was published in many newspapers. It proved so popular that it became a signature dish at the Plaza Hotel in New York City. We include that recipe here.

There is not a slice of pound cake, sponge cake, gold cake, even banana bread, nor bowl of ice cream, frozen yogurt, Tofutti nondairy ice cream, or ice cream pie that will not benefit from our wonderful selection of dessert sauces. We have climbed the heights beyond hot fudge and butterscotch to reach the peaks of hot cherry sauce, maple caramel sauce, and warm chocolate honey sauce. These are an absolute snap to put together, sometimes literally involving merely pulling jars or boxes off the pantry shelf and emptying them directly into the slow cooker. The small slow cooker is also great for keeping a sauce warm and waiting, just like in the ice cream parlor, so that it will pour nicely over that favorite bowl of ice cream.

Why bother making truffles in a slow cooker? Because the heat is so low and so even, the slow cooker works even better than a double boiler for melting chocolate. Chocolate truffles are rolled into rough balls that look like their namesakes, the earthy subterranean fungi that are a culinary delicacy. That is where the resemblance ends, though; real truffles are an acquired taste, whereas chocolate truffles are an instant epiphany. To be devoured in a single bite, they are intensely sweet, a satisfying treat for the most discerning chocolate addict. Is the homemade version just as good as what you can get in the upscale shops? "The results are amazing," says our colleague Aleta Watson, a food writer at the *San Jose Mercury News*. "Smooth, creamy, and decadently rich. The better the ingredients, the more impressive the results. I made very nice truffles with bars of Ghirardelli dark chocolate from the grocery store, but the truffles made with Valrhona Le Noir Gastronomie or Scharffen Berger's bittersweet home chef's bar were competitive with all but the top chocolatiers." So go ahead and dazzle your guests.

Toblerone Fondue

H ere is that famous classic recipe that started the dessert fondue craze. The honey and nuts in the Toblerone chocolate bars make for a very special flavor that you won't get with plain chocolate. Serve this with sweet white bread or pound cake cubes, rolled fresh crêpes or blini, slices of pear and apple, fresh mandarin orange sections, cherries, banana chunks, and/or grapes. People have even been known to dip large marshmallows.

○ *Makes about 4 cups to serve 12 to 16*

COOKER: Small round
SETTING AND COOK TIME: LOW for 1 to 2 hours; will keep on LOW for another hour

1½ cups heavy cream
Twelve 3.52-ounce bars Toblerone chocolate, broken into pieces
4 tablespoons Cognac, rum, or whole or low-fat milk

1. Combine the cream and chocolate pieces in the slow cooker. Cover and cook on LOW for 1 to 2 hours.

2. Add the Cognac and stir until the fondue is smooth. You can serve the fondue immediately, keep it warm on LOW for an hour or so, or let it cool, uncovered, and store at room temperature in an airtight container for up to 4 hours. Reheat it before you are ready serve, letting it warm on LOW for 30 minutes to 1 hour.

Perfumed Chocolate Fondue

This is a subtly flavored fondue. Beth adores the quince jelly, added to give a haunting, perfumey quality to the fondue. Serve this with pound cake cubes, ladyfingers, or slices of apples and/or pears.

○ *Makes about 4 cups to serve 12 to 16*

COOKER: Small round
SETTING AND COOK TIME: LOW for 1 to 2 hours; will keep on LOW for another hour

2 cups heavy cream
16 ounces bittersweet chocolate, broken into small chunks
5 to 6 tablespoons quince jelly, bittersweet orange marmalade, or mixed berry jam

1. Combine the cream and chocolate chunks in the slow cooker. Cover and cook on LOW for 1 to 2 hours.

2. Add the jelly and stir until the fondue is smooth. You can serve the fondue immediately, keep it warm on LOW for an hour or so, or let it cool, uncovered, and store at room temperature in an airtight container for up to 4 hours. Reheat it before you are ready to serve, letting it warm on LOW for 30 minutes to 1 hour.

Chocolate Chip Fondue

Here's a quick, super-simple fondue that won't break the bank. Kids love it. Serve it with bananas, pears, dried apricots, strawberries, angel food cake cubes, and/or graham crackers. ○ *Makes about 2 cups to serve 6 to 8*

COOKER: Small round
SETTING AND COOK TIME: LOW for 1 to 2 hours; will keep on LOW for another hour

One 12-ounce bag semisweet chocolate chips
⅔ cup half-and-half
2 teaspoons pure vanilla extract

1. Combine the chocolate chips, half-and-half, and vanilla extract in the slow cooker. Cover and cook on LOW for 1 to 2 hours.

2. Stir until the fondue is smooth. You can serve the fondue immediately, keep it warm on LOW for an hour or so, or let it cool, uncovered, and store at room temperature in an airtight container for up to 4 hours. Reheat it before you are ready to serve, letting it warm on LOW for 30 minutes to 1 hour.

White Chocolate Piña Colada Fondue

T his white fondue has all the flavors of the fun tropical drink it is named after. Be sure to get high-quality white chocolate; the less expensive brands do not produce a good result. If you're a fan, go ahead and add the sweetened flaked coconut, but some people don't like anything chunky to disturb the smoothness of a fondue. And be sure to use cream of coconut, not coconut milk. Complete the piña colada theme by dunking chunks of dried or fresh pineapple. This is also great with fresh strawberries, dried apricots, ladyfingers, and/or cubes of chocolate or vanilla pound cake. ○ *Makes about 3 cups to serve 8 to 12*

COOKER: Small round
SETTING AND COOK TIME: LOW for 1 to 2 hours; will keep on LOW for another hour

⅔ cup canned cream of coconut (such as Coco López)
¼ cup dark rum
1 pound best-quality white chocolate, chopped into ½- to 1-inch pieces
1 cup sweetened flaked coconut (optional)

1. Combine the cream of coconut, rum, and chopped white chocolate in the slow cooker. Cover and cook on LOW for 1 to 2 hours.

2. Stir until the fondue is smooth, then stir in the coconut, if using. You can serve the fondue immediately, keep it warm on LOW for an hour or so, or let it cool, uncovered, and store at room temperature in an airtight container for up to 4 hours. Reheat it before you are ready to serve, letting it warm on LOW for 30 minutes to 1 hour.

Bittersweet Chocolate–Coconut Fondue

This has an entirely different flavor than the fondue of coconut and white chocolate on page 425. Both recipes, though, use cream of coconut, not coconut milk. Dunk cubes of pound cake, biscotti, ladyfingers, or fresh strawberries.

○ *Makes about 3 cups to serve 8 to 12*

COOKER: Small round
SETTING AND COOK TIME: LOW for 1 to 2 hours; will keep on LOW for another hour

Two 15-ounce cans cream of coconut (such as Coco López)
1½ pounds bittersweet chocolate, chopped into ½- to 1-inch pieces
1 cup heavy cream or evaporated milk
1 teaspoon pure coconut extract

1. Combine the cream of coconut, chopped chocolate, heavy cream, and coconut extract in the slow cooker. Cover and cook on LOW for 1 to 2 hours.

2. Stir until the fondue is smooth. You can serve the fondue immediately, keep it warm on LOW for an hour or so, or let it cool, uncovered, and store at room temperature in an airtight container for up to 4 hours. Reheat it before you are ready to serve, letting it warm on LOW for 30 minutes to 1 hour.

Spur-of-the-Moment Chocolate-Marshmallow Fondue

I f you keep marshmallows around for microwave s'mores, as Julie's family does, and chocolate chips in case the urge to bake suddenly strikes, then you can make this fondue anytime. This simple fondue rises above its humble ingredients to become a thick and even elegant dessert that has just the right texture to cling without clumping to whatever is being dipped into it. It's sweet as chocolate fondues go, so our favorite dippers are not overwhelmingly sweet, to balance out the flavors. We like to serve this with firm banana slices, sweet-tart strawberries, ladyfingers, and a rich, but not overly sweet, pound cake. This is Julie's daughter's favorite birthday dessert. ○ *Makes about 2 cups to serve 6 to 8*

COOKER: Small round
SETTING AND COOK TIME: LOW for 1 to 2 hours; will keep on LOW for another hour

3 tablespoons unsalted butter
¼ cup whole milk
1 cup semisweet chocolate chips
16 large marshmallows

1. Combine the butter, milk, chocolate chips, and marshmallows in the slow cooker. Cover and cook on LOW for 1 to 2 hours.

2. Cover and stir until the fondue is smooth. You can serve the fondue immediately, keep it warm on LOW for an hour or so, or let it cool, uncovered, and store at room temperature in an airtight container for up to 4 hours. Reheat it before you are ready to serve, letting it warm on LOW for 30 minutes to 1 hour.

Hot Honey Cherry Sauce

W hen Julie offered a bowl of vanilla ice cream with this sauce to her cousin Jim, a real cherry lover, he handed it back, saying, "I can still see the ice cream." This luscious, versatile sauce is good on more than vanilla and chocolate ice cream, though. Try it spooned over cold cheesecake or pound cake, or on its own in a bowl topped with sour cream. Once you have thickened the sauce, do not let it boil on the HIGH setting; reheat it gently in the slow cooker (or in a microwave). This sauce is not overly sweet, which is how we prefer it. If you like a sweeter sauce, add an extra tablespoon or two of honey. Julie uses Montmorency red tart pitted cherries packed in cherry juice that she gets from Trader Joe's market, but you can use regular canned pie cherries as well. ○ *Makes about 4 cups*

COOKER: Medium round

SETTINGS AND COOK TIMES: LOW for 3 to 4 hours, then HIGH for 15 minutes

One 24-ounce jar or two 12-ounce cans pitted tart cherries in juice
½ cup red currant jelly
2 tablespoons crème de cassis, kirsch, or Cherry Marnier
2 tablespoons freshly squeezed lemon juice
1 tablespoon mild honey
One 3-inch cinnamon stick
2 tablespoons cornstarch

1. Set aside ¼ cup of the cherry juice in a small cup.

2. Combine the cherries and the remaining juice, the jelly, crème de cassis, lemon juice, honey, and cinnamon stick in the slow cooker. Cover and cook on LOW for 3 to 4 hours.

3. About 15 minutes before serving time, stir the cornstarch into the reserved cherry juice until it makes a smooth slurry with no lumps. Slowly stir the slurry into the cherry sauce. Cover, turn the cooker to HIGH, and cook until the liquid is glossy and thick, about 15 minutes. Serve hot, warm, or cold. You may refrigerate in an airtight container for up to 1 week.

Brandied Prune Sauce

A dapted from an elegant restaurant dessert menu, this is an entirely different interpretation of prunes from the ones poached in orange juice and wine on page 418. It is heady, luscious, unctuous, and decadent. For your fancy dinner party, serve it over vanilla, toasted almond, or chocolate ice cream with some butter cookies on the side. ○ *Make about 2½ cups*

COOKER: Medium round
SETTING AND COOK TIME: LOW for 3 to 4 hours

1½ cups water
1½ cups sugar
⅓ cup Calvados or Cognac
1 whole star anise
1 vanilla bean, split
One 4-inch cinnamon stick
One 1-inch piece fresh ginger or 2 pieces candied ginger
1 pound dried pitted jumbo prunes

1. Combine the water, sugar, Calvados, star anise, vanilla bean, cinnamon stick, ginger, and prunes in the slow cooker. Cover and cook on LOW for 3 to 4 hours. Carefully remove the lid twice during cooking to allow for a burst of steam to be released from the wine reducing.

2. At the end of the cooking time, carefully remove the lid, allowing the steam to escape. The fruit will be plump and tender. With a wooden spoon, stir a few times. Turn off the cooker and let cool. Remove and discard the whole spices. Puree with a handheld immersion blender, or leave the prunes whole in the thickened sauce, as desired. Serve warm or at room temperature, or pour into an airtight container, cover, and refrigerate overnight to serve cold. You may store in the refrigerator for up to 2 weeks.

Warm Berry Sauce

T his is a lovely embellishment for pound cake, whether it be homemade or frozen store-bought, plain or toasted gently. Also, we love this warm over cold vanilla custard or sliced fresh peaches or pears. Don't cook the berries so long that they break down totally; but even if they do, the sauce will still be a winner. Originally the sauce had sugar, but we use jam instead; it sweetens and flavors at the same time. If you don't have marmalade on hand, use sugar to taste.

○ *Makes 4 cups*

COOKER: Small or medium round
SETTING AND COOK TIME: LOW for 2 to 3 hours

1 pint fresh strawberries, hulled and cut in half
1 pint fresh blueberries, picked over for stems
1½ pints fresh blackberries
Juice of 1 orange
½ cup orange marmalade
2 tablespoons Grand Marnier or other orange liqueur (optional)

1. Combine the strawberries, blueberries, blackberries, orange juice, and marmalade in the slow cooker. Cover and cook on LOW until warm, but not super hot, 2 to 3 hours.

2. Stir in the liqueur, if desired. If you can, bring the crock to the table with a nice ladle and serve warm. Refrigerate any leftover sauce and use cold. You may store the sauce in an airtight container in the refrigerator for up to 1 week.

Ice Cream Parlor Butterscotch Sauce

Golden, thick, and unctuous homemade butterscotch simply dwarfs the store-bought stuff in a jar. Serve with steamed puddings, over ice cream, or in a pool under a slice of apple pie or strudel. ○ *Makes about 1 ¾ cups*

COOKER: Small or medium round
SETTINGS AND COOK TIMES: HIGH for 30 minutes, then LOW for 1 hour

1 cup firmly packed light brown sugar
1½ cups heavy cream
¼ cup (½ stick) unsalted butter, cut into pieces
3 tablespoons light corn syrup
Dash of salt
1½ teaspoons pure vanilla extract
¼ teaspoon cider vinegar or freshly squeezed lemon juice

1. Combine the brown sugar, heavy cream, butter, corn syrup, and salt in the slow cooker. Cover and cook on HIGH until thick and bubbly, about 30 minutes.

2. Stir with a whisk until smooth. Turn the cooker to LOW and cook for 1 hour.

3. Stir in the vanilla extract and vinegar. Serve hot. You may refrigerate in an airtight container for up to 1 week.

Butter Pecan Sundae Sauce: Omit the salt and add ½ cup toasted salted pecan halves or pieces at the end along with the vanilla extract.

Maple-Caramel Sauce

everyone loves creamy caramel sauce, a favorite with non-chocoholics. This one is an easy alternative to boiling the sugars before making the sauce and is every bit as good. The combination of liquid and solid sugars, each with different molecular structures, makes for a silky-smooth sauce.

Makes about 2 cups

COOKER: Medium round
SETTING AND COOK TIME: HIGH for 1 to 1½ hours

1 cup firmly packed light brown sugar
¼ cup granulated sugar
¼ cup pure maple syrup
¼ cup light corn syrup
1¼ cups heavy cream

1. Combine all the ingredients in the slow cooker. Cover and cook on HIGH until thick, 1 to 1½ hours. Insert a candy thermometer; the mixture should register 220°F.

2. Stir with a whisk until smooth. Let cool for 30 minutes and serve warm. You may refrigerate in an airtight container for up to 5 days.

Peggy's Killer Hot Fudge Sauce

there are many variations on hot fudge sauce, a favorite in ice cream shops and a simple sauce not made often enough at home. Just scoop some ice cream into a bowl or footed dessert dish and drizzle with warm hot fudge sauce. Garnish with whipped cream out of the can, chocolate or multicolored sprinkles, toasted nuts, and/or a maraschino cherry, and you've got a party in a bowl. Or try it simply drizzled over pound cake or ice cream pie. *Makes about 2 cups*

COOKER: Small or medium round
SETTING AND COOK TIME: LOW for 2 to 2½ hours; chocolate and vanilla
   extract added during last 30 minutes

¾ cup sugar
½ cup (1 stick) unsalted butter
½ cup heavy cream
¼ cup light corn syrup
Dash of salt
4 ounces semisweet or bittersweet chocolate, chopped
4 ounces unsweetened chocolate, chopped
2 teaspoons pure vanilla extract

1. Combine the sugar, butter, cream, corn syrup, and salt in the slow cooker. Cover and cook on LOW for 1½ hours.

2. Stir with a whisk until smooth to make sure the sugar is dissolved. Stir in the chopped semisweet and unsweetened chocolates and vanilla extract. Cover and continue to cook on LOW for another 30 minutes to 1 hour.

3. Stir until smooth. Serve warm. You may refrigerate the sauce in an airtight container for up to 3 weeks.

Peppermint Hot Fudge Sauce: Omit the vanilla extract and add ¼ teaspoon peppermint extract.

Orange Hot Fudge Sauce: Add 2 tablespoons Grand Marnier or other orange liqueur, 1½ teaspoons orange oil, or ¾ teaspoon orange extract along with the vanilla extract.

Brandied Hot Fudge Sauce: Add 2 tablespoons Cognac or brandy along with the vanilla extract.

Low-Fat Mocha Fudge Sauce with Kahlúa

We love this hot chocolate sauce, adapted from pastry baker Nancy Silverton, because it has a strong chocolate flavor and is made without any butter or cream. ○ *Makes about 1½ cups*

COOKER: Small round
SETTINGS AND COOK TIMES: HIGH for 20 minutes, then LOW for 30 minutes

⅔ cup strong brewed coffee *or* ⅔ cup boiling water mixed with
  1 tablespoon instant espresso powder
½ cup light corn syrup
¾ cup Dutch-processed unsweetened cocoa powder
¼ cup sugar
½ pound bittersweet chocolate, chopped
3 tablespoons Kahlúa or Frangelico

1. Combine the coffee, corn syrup, cocoa powder, and sugar in the slow cooker; whisk to combine. Cover and cook on HIGH for 20 minutes.

2. Add the chopped chocolate. Cover, turn the cooker to LOW, and cook until melted and smooth, about another 30 minutes.

3. Stir in the liqueur and serve hot. You may refrigerate the sauce in an airtight container indefinitely.

Warm Chocolate Honey

This is a totally different chocolate topping for ice cream. The honey melts into a smooth pool. Use a really good-quality unsweetened chocolate, such as Scharffen Berger or Peter's from Nestlé; it will make all the difference. Serve over vanilla or coffee ice cream, top with whipped cream and toasted almonds or macadamia nuts, and you've got yourself one dandy dessert.

○ *Makes about 1½ cups*

COOKER: Small round

SETTING AND COOK TIME: LOW for 1 to 1½ hours

1 cup mild honey
½ pound unsweetened chocolate, chopped

Combine the honey and chopped chocolate in the slow cooker. Cover and cook on LOW for 1 to 1½ hours to melt the chocolate and liquefy the honey; stir with a whisk to combine. Serve warm. You may refrigerate the sauce in an airtight container indefinitely.

Bittersweet Chocolate Sauce

Y ou want hot chocolate sauce, but you have only cocoa powder. This recipe makes a sauce every bit as good as those with solid chocolate; some say the best. The type of cocoa you use will dictate the final flavor. We use anything from Scharffen Berger and Poulain to Droste. If you can get organic heavy cream and flowery Tahitian vanilla, this sauce will be all the better. ○ *Makes 2½ cups*

COOKER: Small round

SETTING AND COOK TIME: LOW for 1½ to 2 hours

1 cup heavy cream
¾ cup sugar
2 tablespoons light corn syrup
½ cup (1 stick) unsalted butter, cut into pieces
1 cup Dutch-processed unsweetened cocoa powder
½ teaspoon pure vanilla extract

1. Combine the heavy cream, sugar, corn syrup, butter, and cocoa powder in the slow cooker. Stir with a whisk until smooth. Cover and cook on LOW for 1½ to 2 hours.

2. Stir in the vanilla extract and serve hot or warm. You may refrigerate the sauce in an airtight container for up to 1 week.

•• Adobe Ice Cream Pie ••

A classic and festive dessert, adobe ice cream pie is a perfect use for one of our hot fudge sauces. ○ Serves 8

One 8.5-ounce package Nabisco Famous Chocolate Wafer cookies

6 tablespoons (¾ stick) unsalted butter, melted

1 tablespoon Kahlúa

1 recipe Peggy's Killer Hot Fudge Sauce (page 432) or Low-Fat Mocha Fudge Sauce
    with Kahlúa (page 434), at room temperature

1½ pints vanilla ice cream

1½ pints coffee ice cream

2 ounces bittersweet chocolate, coarsely grated

1. Preheat the oven to 350°F. Butter the bottom of an extra-deep 9-inch pie plate.

2. Place the cookies in the food processor and finely grind. Add the melted butter and Kahlúa; process until the mixture just clumps. Remove from the bowl and press evenly into the bottom and sides of the pie plate until firmly packed (pressing down with another pie plate of the same size works well). Bake for 8 to 10 minutes. Let cool to room temperature, then place in the freezer for 15 minutes. Pour a thin layer of the fudge sauce into the pie shell; freeze until firm, at least 1 hour.

3. Meanwhile, place the vanilla ice cream in the refrigerator until softened but not melted, 15 to 30 minutes.

4. Using a plastic spatula, quickly spread the softened vanilla ice cream in an even layer over the fudge in the pie shell, mounding it slightly in the center. Cover with plastic wrap and freeze until firm, about 30 minutes. Meanwhile, place the coffee ice cream in the refrigerator to soften, 15 to 30 minutes.

5. Spread the softened coffee ice cream in an even layer over the vanilla ice cream, mounding it slightly in the center. Sprinkle with the grated chocolate. Cover and freeze for at least 4 hours.

6. When ready to serve, reheat the remaining fudge sauce and serve it alongside, not over, each slice of pie.

Chocolate-Cognac Sauce

 This one is for adults only. Garnish whatever you're drizzling it over with sliced fresh strawberries and toasted almonds. ○ *Makes about 3 cups*

COOKER: Medium round
SETTING AND COOK TIME: LOW for 1½ to 2 hours; chocolate and
Cognac added during last 30 to 60 minutes

¾ **cup water**
¾ **cup heavy cream**
⅓ **cup light corn syrup**
9 tablespoons unsalted butter, cut into pieces
1½ pounds semisweet chocolate, chopped
⅓ **cup Cognac**

1. Combine the water, heavy cream, corn syrup, and butter in the slow cooker. Cover and cook on LOW for 1 hour.

2. Stir with a whisk until smooth. Add the chopped chocolate and Cognac. Cover and continue to cook on LOW until melted, 30 minutes to 1 hour. Stir with a whisk to combine and smooth out the sauce. Serve hot. You may refrigerate the sauce in an airtight container for up to 3 weeks.

Narsai's Chocolate Sauce

his is a pretty infamous recipe, because at the time of its creation in the 1980s it was a quite revolutionary pairing of chocolate with red wine. It comes from the food environs of the San Francisco Bay Area and was created by Narsai David, one of the local restaurateurs and TV and radio food personalities. It still works for us—over ice cream, pound cake, angel food cake, or poached pears. ○ *Makes about 1¾ cups*

COOKER: Small round
SETTING AND COOK TIME: LOW for 1½ to 2 hours

1 cup Cabernet Sauvignon
8 ounces semisweet chocolate, chopped

1. Combine the wine and chocolate in the slow cooker. Cover and cook on LOW for 1½ to 2 hours.

2. Stir with a whisk until smooth. Serve hot or warm. You may refrigerate the sauce in an airtight container for up to 1 week.

Creamiest Fudge

his is a real treat and one that absolutely couldn't be easier when made in the slow cooker. The cooker keeps the heat very low and even, so it is even more effective than a double boiler when making fudge. If you start with chocolate chips, you don't even have to chop any chocolate! This fudge is great for host and hostess or teacher gifts, a perfect addition to a tray of holiday sweets, or a little luxury to keep in the fridge for yourself. For a gourmet version, use a high-quality chocolate and take the time to chop it into small pieces for even melting. If you want to cut the finished fudge into bars for gift giving, you can sprinkle the top with extra chocolate chips before refrigerating it; it looks really nice that way.

○ *Makes about 1½ pounds (sixty-four 1-inch pieces if made in an 8 × 8-inch pan)*

COOKER: Small round

SETTING AND COOK TIME: LOW for about 1 hour

1 pound semisweet or bittersweet chocolate, finely chopped

3 tablespoons unsalted butter, cut into pieces

One 14-ounce can sweetened condensed milk

½ cup finely chopped walnuts, pecans, or pine nuts (optional)

Paper or foil candy cups (optional)

1. Line an 8-inch square or 11 × 7-inch rectangular metal baking pan with parchment paper so that it hangs over two of the edges by at least 2 inches (to aid in removing the fudge from the pan). Butter the pan well or coat with butter-flavored nonstick cooking spray, especially on the sides of the pan not covered with parchment; set aside.

2. Place the chopped chocolate and butter pieces in the slow cooker. Cover and cook on LOW until melted, about 1 hour.

3. Stir with a wooden spoon, then stir in the condensed milk until smooth. Stir in the nuts, if using. Pour the mixture into the prepared pan and smooth the top to make an even layer. Refrigerate, uncovered, until set and firm, about 4 hours.

4. When the fudge is firm, dip a knife into hot water and use it to loosen the edges of the fudge that directly touch the pan. Pull on the 2 edges of the parchment paper to lift out the fudge in one piece. With the hot knife, cut the fudge into 1-inch squares. Place in paper or foil candy cups, if desired, or store in an airtight container with the layers of fudge separated by parchment or waxed paper. The fudge will keep for about 2 weeks in the refrigerator. Let rest for 30 minutes at room temperature before serving.

Black-on-Black Truffles

T his very basic recipe is adapted from *Chocolate Desserts by Pierre Hermé* (Little, Brown, 2001) by Dorie Greenspan. Make the truffles ahead and serve at your next party in small cut-crystal bowls after dinner.

○ *Makes about 40 truffles*

COOKER: Small round
SETTING AND COOK TIME: LOW for 45 minutes to 1 hour

9 ounces bittersweet chocolate, preferably Valrhona, chopped
1 cup heavy cream
3½ tablespoons unsalted butter, cut into 6 pieces, softened
About ½ cup Dutch-processed unsweetened cocoa powder
Paper or foil candy cups (optional)

1. Combine the chopped chocolate and heavy cream in the slow cooker. Cover and heat on LOW until melted, 45 minutes to 1 hour.

2. Stir gently with a whisk until smooth to complete the melting. Turn the cooker off. Add the pieces of butter one at a time, and stir after each addition until melted and smooth. If you can, remove the crock from the machine and let cool; otherwise, transfer the ganache to a bowl. Cover with plastic wrap pressed directly onto the surface of the chocolate to prevent a skin from forming and chill for about 4 hours or overnight to firm up.

3. Line a baking sheet with parchment paper. Place the cocoa powder in a shallow bowl. If the ganache is very hard, let stand at room temperature for 30 minutes until slightly malleable. When you are ready to shape the truffles, scoop up a scant tablespoonful for each truffle. A melon baller or #100 scoop works well. Dust the palms of your hands with more cocoa powder and, one by one, roll mounds of ganache between your palms to form balls. Don't worry about making them even—they're supposed to be gnarled and misshapen. As you shape each truffle, drop it into the bowl of cocoa, turning it over until well coated, then gently toss between your palms to shake off excess cocoa. Place finished truffles on the baking sheet. When done, cover with plastic wrap and chill, at least 4 hours and up to overnight.

4. When hardened, place the truffles in candy cups, if desired, transfer to an airtight plastic container, and refrigerate for up to 2 weeks, or freeze indefinitely. Let come to room temperature for 1 hour before serving.

Raspberry Truffles

A very easy method of shaping truffles calls for slicing the chilled ganache into little squares with a knife dipped into hot water. This square truffle is subtly flavored with raspberry jam. We make this recipe with a 9.7-ounce bar of Scharffen Berger bittersweet chocolate, a truly gourmet artisan chocolate made in our own San Francisco Bay Area. Any way you shape them, though, homemade truffles are an especially thoughtful gift. ○ *Makes about 40 truffles*

COOKER: Small round
SETTING AND COOK TIME: LOW for 45 minutes to 1 hour

10 ounces bittersweet chocolate, chopped
¼ cup seedless raspberry jam
⅔ cup heavy cream
1 tablespoon framboise or Chambord
About ½ cup Dutch-processed unsweetened cocoa powder
Paper or foil candy cups (optional)

1. Combine the chopped chocolate, jam, and heavy cream in the slow cooker. Cover and heat on LOW until melted, 45 minutes to 1 hour.

2. Stir gently with a whisk until smooth to complete the melting. Turn the cooker off. Add the framboise and stir in one direction until smooth.

3. Line a 9 × 5-inch loaf pan with plastic wrap, letting the ends hang over the edges of the pan, and pour the ganache in, carefully leveling the top with a rubber spatula. Place the pan in the refrigerator until cooled, then cover with plastic wrap and chill for about 4 hours or overnight to firm up.

4. Remove the pan from the refrigerator. Grasp the edges of the plastic wrap, lift the ganache out of the pan, and set on a cutting board. If it is very hard, let stand at room temperature for 30 minutes, until slightly malleable and soft enough to slice easily. Dip a sharp knife into hot water and slice the ganache in half lengthwise. Clean the knife in hot water and slice both pieces lengthwise again (you will have 4 long bars), cleaning the knife after each cut. Now slice crosswise at 1-inch intervals, dipping the knife into hot water as needed, until you have about 40 small squares.

5. Place the cocoa powder in a shallow bowl. One or two at a time, carefully place the squares into the cocoa and gently roll about until all sides are dusted. Shake off any excess. Place in candy cups, if desired. Serve immediately, or store in an airtight container in the refrigerator for up to 1 week or in the freezer indefinitely. Let come to room temperature for 1 hour before serving.

Low-Fat Chocolate-Nut Truffles

L ow-fat truffles? You bet, and they are delicious. In place of the cream, we use prune butter. The result is a smashing, low-fat truffle with a pure balance of flavor. Sweetened prune filling (available in the baking section), prune lekvar (available in the kosher section), or prune baby food can be substituted, but homemade puree is best, as well as easy. The inspiration for this unlikely combination of chocolate and a fruit puree comes from Stephen Durfee, former pastry chef of The French Laundry restaurant in Yountville, California, and recipient of the 1999 James Beard Pastry Chef of the Year Award. ○ *Makes 24 truffles*

COOKER: Small round
SETTING AND COOK TIME: LOW for 45 minutes to 1 hour

8 ounces bittersweet chocolate, such as Lindt, Callebaut, or Guittard, chopped
½ cup Prune Butter (recipe follows)
1½ tablespoons unsalted butter
1 tablespoon liqueur of your choice (see variations below)
¾ cup nuts of your choice
Paper or foil candy cups (optional)

1. Combine the chopped chocolate, prune butter, butter, and liqueur in the slow cooker. Cover and heat on LOW until melted, 45 minutes to 1 hour.

2. Stir gently with a whisk until smooth to complete the melting. Turn the cooker off. If you can, remove the crock from the cooker and let cool; otherwise, transfer the mixture to a bowl. Cover with plastic wrap pressed directly onto the surface of the chocolate to prevent a skin from forming and chill for about 4 hours or overnight to firm up.

3. To toast the nuts, preheat the oven to 350°F. Chop the nuts fine and place on a baking sheet. Toast the nuts in the oven until fragrant, about 5 minutes. Allow to cool, then place the nuts in a shallow plate or cake tin.

4. Line a baking sheet with parchment paper. If the truffle mixture is very hard, let stand at room temperature for 30 minutes until slightly malleable. Using a teaspoon, scoop out a small round the size of a big cherry and roll it between your palms to form a rough ball. Roll each ball in the chopped nuts and place on the baking sheet. Cover with plastic wrap and chill for about 4 hours or overnight.

5. When hardened, place the truffles in candy cups, if desired, transfer to an airtight plastic container, and refrigerate for up to 2 weeks, or freeze indefinitely. Let come to room temperature for 1 hour before serving.

Amaretto Truffles: Add amaretto to the melted chocolate mixture and roll the balls in chopped almonds.

Orange-Pistachio Truffles: Add Grand Marnier to the melted chocolate mixture and roll the balls in chopped pistachios.

Rum-Pecan Truffles: Add dark rum to the melted chocolate mixture and roll the balls in chopped pecans.

Raspberry-Almond Truffles: Add framboise or Chambord to the melted chocolate mixture. Tuck a frozen whole raspberry into the center when forming the ball, and roll the balls in Dutch-processed unsweetened cocoa powder. Stud each truffle with 4 almond slivers.

Brandied Chestnut Truffles: Add Cognac or brandy to the melted chocolate mixture. Tuck a piece of chestnut packed in vanilla-flavored syrup (available in cans in the jam section of upscale supermarkets) into the center when forming the ball, and roll the balls in Dutch-processed unsweetened cocoa powder.

Cherry-Walnut Truffles: Add Cherry Marnier to the melted chocolate mixture and roll the balls in chopped walnuts.

Hazelnut Truffles: Add Frangelico to the melted chocolate mixture and roll the balls in chopped hazelnuts.

Prune Butter

Dried fruit butters are indispensable for low-fat baking and make an excellent complement to chocolate. Since this puree keeps for up to 3 weeks in the refrigerator, make a big batch to have on hand for spur-of-the-moment baking, or even just for spreading on toast. ❍ *Makes 1¹/₂ cups*

One 12-ounce bag dried pitted prunes
¾ cup boiling water

Place the prunes and ¼ cup of the boiling water in a food processor (it will be too thick for a blender) and process, adding the remaining boiling water in a thin stream through the feed tube while the machine is running, until a thick, smooth paste forms. It will look a bit chunky from the skins; that's okay, but if it bothers you, press the mixture through a sieve. Use immediately, or refrigerate, tightly covered, for up to 3 weeks.

Measurement Equivalents

Please note that all conversions are approximate.

Liquid Conversions

U.S.	Metric	U.S.	Metric
1 tsp	5 ml	1 cup	240 ml
1 tbs	15 ml	1 cup + 2 tbs	275 ml
2 tbs	30 ml	1¼ cups	300 ml
3 tbs	45 ml	1⅓ cups	325 ml
¼ cup	60 ml	1½ cups	350 ml
⅓ cup	75 ml	1⅔ cups	375 ml
⅓ cup + 1 tbs	90 ml	1¾ cups	400 ml
⅓ cup + 2 tbs	100 ml	1¾ cups + 2 tbs	450 ml
½ cup	120 ml	2 cups (1 pint)	475 ml
⅔ cup	150 ml	2½ cups	600 ml
¾ cup	180 ml	3 cups	720 ml
¾ cup + 2 tbs	200 ml	4 cups (1 quart)	945 ml
			(1,000 ml is 1 liter)

Weight Conversions

U.S. / U.K.	Metric		U.S. / U.K.	Metric
½ oz	14 g		7 oz	200 g
1 oz	28 g		8 oz	227 g
1½ oz	43 g		9 oz	255 g
2 oz	57 g		10 oz	284 g
2½ oz	71 g		11 oz	312 g
3 oz	85 g		12 oz	340 g
3½ oz	100 g		13 oz	368 g
4 oz	113 g		14 oz	400 g
5 oz	142 g		15 oz	425 g
6 oz	170 g		1 lb	454 g

Oven Temperature Conversions

°F	Gas Mark	°C
250	½	120
275	1	140
300	2	150
325	3	165
350	4	180
375	5	190
400	6	200
425	7	220
450	8	230
475	9	240
500	10	260
550	Broil	290

Index

Adobe Ice Cream Pie, 436
Almond(s)
    Amaretto Truffles, 443
    Country Captain, 261–62
    Malabar, 47–48
    -Raspberry Truffles, 443
    Steamed Chocolate Pudding,
        380–81
    Tamari, 46–47
Amaretto Truffles, 443
Ancho Chile Sauce, 108–9
Anchovies
    Bagna Cauda, 37–38
    Caesar Dressing, 201
Appetizers, 27–53
    Always Smooth Chile con
        Queso, 31–32
    Bagna Cauda, 37–38
    Barbecued Chicken Wings for a
        Crowd, 271
    Blue Cheese Dip, 274–75
    Buttermilk Fondue, 44–45
    Buttery Rosemary Pecan
        Halves, 48
    Caramel Brie, 39
    Champagne Fondue, 43–44
    Chili Olive Dip, 34–35
    Chipotle Hummus from the
        Prado in Balboa Park, 219

Creamy Refried Bean Dip,
    35–36
Crocked Buffalo Chicken
    Wings, 274–75
Curry Mixed Nuts, 52
Eggplant Caponata, 139–40
Fondue Neuchâtel, 42–43
Fondue with Sparkling Apple
    Cider, 45–46
Garlic and Lime Chicken
    Wings with Chipotle Mayon-
    naise, 275–76
Glazed Walnuts, 265
Herb Fondue, 43
Hot Artichoke Dip with Pita
    Crisps, 29
Hot Crab Supreme, 36
Hot Sausage Dip, 38
Hot Spinach Dip, 31
Hummus with Tofu and
    Roasted Vegetables, 218–19
Jacquie's Black Bean–Jalapeño
    Dip, 33–34
Julie's Hummus, 217–18
Layered Artichokes and Green
    Chiles, 30
Malabar Almonds, 47–48
Maple-Glazed Pecans, 49
New Year's Black-Eyed Peas,
    220–21
Plum Sauce Chicken Wings,
    277

Potato Fondue, 46
Retro Party Mix, 52–53
Shrimp Fondue, 43
Smoky Black Bean and Ched-
    dar Dip, 33
Spiced Lamb Dolmas, 374–75
Spicy Walnuts, 50
Sugared Walnuts, 51
Sujata's Curried Chicken
    Wings, 273–74
Tamari Almonds, 46–47
Tomato Fondue, 41
Walnuts and Ginger, 50–51
Welsh Rabbit, 40
Apple Cider
    Cider-Braised Turnips, 156
    Mulled Cider with Cardamom
        and Saffron, 58
    Potato Fondue, 46
    Sparkling, Fondue with,
        45–46
    Spiked Wassail, 80
Apple Juice
    Hot Mulled, The Best, 57
    Jamaica, 63–64
    "Rum" and Cherry Cider, 59
    Spiced Apple and Chamomile
        Tea, 66–67
    Spiked Wassail, 80
Apple(s)
    and Chamomile Tea, Spiced,
        66–67

Apple(s) *(continued)*
  and Cranberries, Candied
    Yams with, 156–57
  Crock-Baked, with Honey,
    Orange, and Dates, 399–400
  Crumble with Maple Crème
    Fraîche, 412–13
  Ponche, 64–65
  Spiked Wassail, 80
Apricot Nectar, Hot, 62
Apricot(s)
  Dried, Pecans, and Cherries,
    Wild Rice with, 173–74
  Honey Cornbread with, 240–41
  Lamb and Fruit Tagine,
    368–69
  Peach, and Cherry Compote,
    416
  Red Wine, and Honey, Red
    Cabbage with, 132
  Steamed Brown Bread with
    Rum Fruits, 394–95
  Winter Fruit Compote, 417
Arizona Vegetable and Herb
  Bread Stuffing, 179
Armenian Rice and Vermicelli
  Pilaf, Victoria's, 191–92
Artichoke(s)
  Brandied Raisins, and Crème
    Fraîche, Veal Ragoût with,
    328–29
  Dip, Hot, with Pita Crisps, 29
  and Green Chiles, Layered, 30
  and Peas, Ragoût of, with Tar-
    ragon, 146
  preparing for slow cooker, 127
  Slow-Steamed, 129–30
Arugula
  and Asparagus, Risotto with,
    171
  Christmas Limas with Greens,
    225
Asian Chicken Broth, 92
Asian Cucumber Bisque, 91
Asian Pork Tenderloins, 349–50
Asparagus
  and Arugula, Risotto with, 171
  Braised Spring Vegetables, 161
  Lamb Navarin, 366–67
  preparing for slow cooker, 128
  Ragoût of Baby Vegetables, 162
Athole Brose, 81

B

Bacon
  adding to slow cooker, 340
  Chestnuts, and Dried Cherries,
    Cornbread Stuffing with,
    184–85
  Eggs Benedict, 269
  Slow Cooker Cassoulet,
    226–27
Bagna Cauda, 37–38
Baja Tomato Juice, 66
Balsamic Syrup, 172–73
Bananas, Lady Marmalade, 400
Barbacoa, 301–2
Barbecued Beef on Buns, 322
Barbecued Chicken Wings for a
  Crowd, 271
Barbecued Pinto Beans, Hickory,
  228
Barbecue Honey Pork Ribs, 358
Barbecue Sauces
  Chinese-Style, 111
  KC, Our Basic, 110
  Red Wine, 109–10
  in slow cooker recipes, 113
  Tequila and Pineapple, 112
Barbecue Spice, BBQ Queens',
  271
Barley
  Cholent, 304–5
Basil
  Paste, Pistou, 88–89
  Risotto Verde, 166–67
  Vinaigrette, 207
Basmati Rice, 188
BBQ Queens' Barbecue Spice,
  271
Bean(s)
  Bake, Calico, 230
  Baked, Indian, 229
  Bean, Roasted Vegetable Chili,
    237–38
  Black, and Cheddar Dip,
    Smoky, 33
  Black, and Pumpkin Soup,
    99–100
  Black, Cuban, 215–16
  Black, –Jalapeño Dip,
    Jacquie's, 33–34

Braised Flageolets with Herbs,
  223
for chili, traditional types, 211
Chili Olive Dip, 34–35
Chipotle Hummus from the
  Prado in Balboa Park, 219
Cholent, 304–5
Christmas Limas with Greens,
  225
cooked, freezing, 211
cooked, storing, 211
cooking liquid for, 211
cornbread accompaniments for,
  239–42
dried, yield from, 220
Elizabeth Taylor's Chili,
  234–35
Fava, Fresh, with Tomatoes
  and Saffron, 221–22
French Vegetable Soup with
  Pesto, 88–89
Fresh Shell, Braised, 130
Frito Pie, 319–20
Gringo Chili for a Crowd,
  231–32
Hielem, 100–101
Hummus with Tofu and
  Roasted Vegetables, 218–19
Julie's Hummus, 217–18
New Year's Black-Eyed Peas,
  220–21
Pinto, Chili with Mexican
  Sausage, 232–33
Pinto, Hickory Barbecued, 228
preparing for slow cooker, 129
pre-soaking, 213, 216
Red, Stew and Rice, 224
Refried, Dip, Creamy, 35–36
salting, after cooking, 211
Slow Cooker Cassoulet,
  226–27
slow cooker cooking time chart,
  212–13
Slow Cooker Pot of, 214–15
slow cooking, tips for, 216
Spicy Lentil Soup with Saffron
  and Cilantro, 98–99
stocking, for slow cooker
  recipes, 21
Vegetable Curry, 158–59
White, Turkey Chili with,
  235–36

Beef. *See also* Veal
  Barbacoa, 301–2
  Barbecued, on Buns, 322
  Beefy Tomato Sauce with
    Sausage and Fennel, 121–22
  Beer-Soaked Brats, 326
  Borscht, Hearty, with Cabbage,
    97–98
  Braised Oxtails (Rabo), 306–7
  Burgundy, 308–9
  Chili Colorado, 242–43
  Chili con Carne, 244–45
  Cholent, 304–5
  chuck roasts, about, 297
  Corned, with Cabbage and
    Radicchio, 307–8
  Elizabeth Taylor's Chili,
    234–35
  French Country Terrine,
    362–64
  Frito Pie, 319–20
  Gringo Chili for a Crowd,
    231–32
  internal temperatures, 16
  Italian Meatballs, 327–28
  Jan's Tuscan Meatloaf with
    Roasted Red Potatoes,
    320–21
  New-Fashioned Pot Roast with
    Fresh Rosemary, 299
  oxtails, about, 297
  Pot-au-Feu, 303–4
  pot-au-feu, about, 302
  Potée Boulangère, 364–65
  pot roast, about, 297
  Prune Chili, 245–46
  safe handling of, 297
  Sauerbraten, 314–15
  short ribs, about, 325
  Short Ribs, Devilishly Good,
    323
  Short Ribs of, Korean, with
    Ginger, 325–26
  Short Ribs of, with Sherry-
    Mustard Sauce and Fennel
    Seed, 324
  Stew, Red Chile, 243
  stews, best cuts for, 297
  Stew with Chestnuts, 313–14
  Stifado, 311–12
  stocking, for slow cooker
    recipes, 22

Stroganoff with Porcini Mush-
    rooms, 316
  Stuffed Sweet-and-Sour Cab-
    bage, 317–18
  Sweet-and-Sour Cranberry Pot
    Roast, 300
Beer-Soaked Brats, 326
Beets
  Crock-Baked, 131
  Hearty Beef Borscht with Cab-
    bage, 97–98
  preparing for slow cooker, 127
Belgian Endive, Braised, 140–41
Berry(ies)
  Blackberry Sauce, 387
  Blueberry Cake, 388–89
  Blueberry Vinaigrette, 206
  Candied Yams with Apples and
    Cranberries, 156–57
  Cranberry "Nog," 59–60
  Raspberry-Almond Truffles,
    443
  Raspberry Drizzle, 407
  Raspberry Truffles, 441–42
  Rhubarb-Strawberry Crumble,
    411–12
  Sauce, Warm, 430
  Slow-Poached Pears in Rasp-
    berries and Red Wine, 409
  Strawberry–White Wine
    Punch, 77
  Sweet-and-Sour Cranberry Pot
    Roast, 300
  Winter Fruit Compote, 417
Beurre manié, thickening liquid
    with, 17–18
Beverages, 55–82
  Athole Brose, 81
  Baja Tomato Juice, 66
  The Best Hot Mulled Apple
    Juice, 57
  Chai, 68–69
  Champurrado, 71
  Cranberry "Nog," 59–60
  Ginger-Lemon Tea, 67–68
  Glögg, 78
  Hot Apricot Nectar, 62
  Hot Buttered Rum, 82
  Hot Cranberry-Orange Punch,
    60–61
  Hot Eggnog, 72
  Hot Peppermint Milk, 72–73

Hot Spiced Grape Juice, 61–62
  Hot Tomato Virgin Mary, 65
  Irish Coffee, 74
  Jamaica, 63–64
  Lemongrass Cordial, 62–63
  Mexican Coffee with Brandy
    and Kahlúa, 73–74
  Moroccan Mint Tea, 70
  Mulled Cider with Cardamom
    and Saffron, 58
  Mulled Wine, 75
  Ponche, 64–65
  Port Wine Negus, 79
  "Rum" and Cherry Cider, 59
  Spiced Apple and Chamomile
    Tea, 66–67
  Spiked Wassail, 80
  Strawberry–White Wine
    Punch, 77
  Warm Cranberry Zinfandel, 76
Black Bean(s)
  and Cheddar Dip, Smoky, 33
  Cholent, 304–5
  Cuban, 215–16
  –Jalapeño Dip, Jacquie's,
    33–34
  and Pumpkin Soup, 99–100
Blackberry Sauce, 387
Black-Eyed Peas, New Year's,
    220–21
Blueberry(ies)
  Cake, 388–89
  Vinaigrette, 206
  Warm Berry Sauce, 430
Blue Cheese
  Dip, 274–75
  Gorgonzola Polenta, 194–95
  Mushroom-Gorgonzola Risotto
    in Radicchio Wraps with Bal-
    samic Syrup, 172–73
  –Sour Cream Mashers, 154
Borscht, Hearty Beef, with Cab-
    bage, 97–98
Braises
  adding wine to, 25
  defined, 298
  preparing, tips for, 298
Brandy
  Brandied Chestnut Truffles,
    443
  Brandied Chicken with Hazel-
    nuts, 255–56

Brandy (continued)
Brandied Custard Sauce, 404
Brandied Hot Fudge Sauce,
433
Brandied Prune Sauce, 429
Brandied Raisins, Artichokes,
and Crème Fraîche, Veal
Ragoût with, 328–29
Brandied Red Onion Soup
Gratinée, 87
Cherries Jubilee, 401
and Kahlúa, Mexican Coffee
with, 73–74
Mulled Wine, 75
Brats, Beer-Soaked, 326
Bread Pudding
slow cooking, tips for, 378
Thanksgiving Sausage, 182–83
Vanilla, New Orleans–Style,
with Whiskey Sauce, 382–83
Breads
Chile Cornsticks, 240
Crock-Baked Salsa Cornbread,
392
Honey Cornbread with Apri-
cots, 240–41
Pita Crisps, 29
Pumpkin Cornmeal Muffins,
239
slow cooking, tips for, 378
Sour Cream Cornmeal Muffins,
241
Steamed Brown, Maple-Raisin,
393–94
Steamed Brown, with Rum
Fruits, 394–95
Sweet Potato Dinner Rolls, 279
Toast Soldiers, 238
Vanilla Pan de Maiz, 391
Bread Stuffing
Cornbread, with Bacon, Chest-
nuts, and Dried Cherries,
184–85
Prosciutto, Parmesan, and
Pine Nut Holiday, 185–86
Vegetable and Herb, Arizona,
179
Whole Wheat, Mushroom-
Chard, 181–82
Brie, Caramel, 39
Broccoli, preparing for slow
cooker, 128

Broth, Asian Chicken, 92
Broth, for slow cooker recipes, 21
Brown Rice, Short-Grain, 190
Brussels sprouts, preparing for
slow cooker, 128
Buffalo Chicken Wings, Crocked,
274–75
Bulgur, Basic, 194
Butter, Prune, 444
Butter, thickening soup or sauce
with, 18
Buttermilk Fondue, 44–45
Butter Pecan Sundae Sauce, 431
Butterscotch Sauce
Ice Cream Parlor, 431
Spirited, 385

Cabbage. See also Sauerkraut
Chinese Vegetable Hot Pot,
160–61
French Vegetable Soup with
Pesto, 88–89
Hearty Beef Borscht with,
97–98
preparing for slow cooker,
128
Puchero, 334–35
and Radicchio, Corned Beef
with, 307–8
Red, with Red Wine, Apricots,
and Honey, 132
Stuffed Sweet-and-Sour,
317–18
Caesar Dressing, 201
Caesar Salad, 201–2
Cakes
Blueberry, 388–89
Gingerbread with Blackberry
Sauce, 386–87
Lemon Cornmeal, in Fragrant
Fig Leaves, 389–90
slow cooking, tips for, 378
Calico Bean Bake, 230
Calrose Rice, 189
Camembert, Champagne, and
Port, Onion Soup with, 86
Candied Yams with Apples and
Cranberries, 156–57

Caponata, Eggplant, 139–40
Caramel
Brie, 39
-Maple Sauce, 432
Peaches, 402
Cardoons, preparing for slow
cooker, 127
Carrot(s)
Chinese Vegetable Hot Pot,
160–61
Cream of Root Vegetable Soup
Normandy, 89–90
French Vegetable Soup with
Pesto, 88–89
Glazed with Marmalade,
Brown Sugar, and Butter,
132–33
Lamb Navarin, 366–67
New-Fashioned Pot Roast with
Fresh Rosemary, 299
and Potatoes, Mashed, with
Crisp Bacon and Chives, 155
preparing for slow cooker, 127
Ragoût of Baby Vegetables, 162
-Sweet Potato Soup, Gingered,
93
Veal Stew with Champagne,
330
Vegetable Curry, 158–59
Venison Stew with Dried Cher-
ries, 337–38
Cassoulet, Slow Cooker, 226–27
Cauliflower
preparing for slow cooker, 128
Vegetable Curry, 158–59
Celeriac, preparing for slow
cooker, 127
Celery
preparing for slow cooker,
128
Victor, 133–34
Chai, 68–69
Chai, Sweetened Milk for, 69
Chamomile and Apple Tea,
Spiced, 66–67
Champagne
Chicken in, 252
Fondue, 43–44
Port, and Camembert, Onion
Soup with, 86
Veal Stew with, 330
Champurrado, 71

Chard
　Hawaiian Laulau, 361–62
　Hielem, 100–101
　-Mushroom Whole Wheat
　　Bread Stuffing, 181–82
　preparing for slow cooker, 128
Cheddar
　and Black Bean Dip, Smoky, 33
　Creamy Refried Bean Dip,
　　35–36
　Double Corn Spoonbread, 178
　Layered Artichokes and Green
　　Chiles, 30
　Raja Rellenos, 134–35
　Scalloped Potatoes, 151
　Tortino di Zucchini, 157–58
　Welsh Rabbit, 40
Cheese
　Always Smooth Chile con
　　Queso, 31–32
　Blue, Dip, 274–75
　Blue, –Sour Cream Mashers,
　　154
　Brandied Red Onion Soup
　　Gratinée, 87
　Buttermilk Fondue, 44–45
　Caesar Dressing, 201
　Caramel Brie, 39
　Champagne Fondue, 43–44
　Chicken Mole Enchilada
　　Casserole, 251–52
　Chili Olive Dip, 34–35
　Creamy Refried Bean Dip,
　　35–36
　Double Corn Spoonbread, 178
　Fondue Neuchâtel, 42–43
　Fondue with Sparkling Apple
　　Cider, 45–46
　Frito Pie, 319–20
　Gnocchi alla Romana, 196
　Goat, Salad of Greens with,
　　203–4
　Gorgonzola Polenta, 194–95
　Herbed Chèvre Sauce, 124
　Herb Fondue, 43
　Hot Artichoke Dip with Pita
　　Crisps, 29
　Hot Sausage Dip, 38
　Hot Spinach Dip, 31
　Layered Artichokes and Green
　　Chiles, 30
　Mashed Potato Casserole, 152

　Mushroom-Gorgonzola Risotto
　　in Radicchio Wraps with
　　Balsamic Syrup, 172–73
　Onion Soup with Champagne,
　　Port, and Camembert, 86
　Pistou Basil Paste, 88–89
　Potato Fondue, 46
　Prosciutto, Parmesan, and
　　Pine Nut Holiday Stuffing,
　　185–86
　Pumpkin-Sage Risotto, 168–69
　Raja Rellenos, 134–35
　Risotto Milanese, 165–66
　Risotto Verde, 166–67
　Risotto with Asparagus and
　　Arugula, 171
　Salsa Alfredo, 123
　Scalloped Potatoes, 151
　Shrimp Fondue, 43
　Shrimp Risotto with Parsley
　　and Basil, 170
　Smoky Black Bean and Ched-
　　dar Dip, 33
　stocking, for slow cooker
　　recipes, 22
　Tomato Fondue, 41
　Tortino di Zucchini, 157–58
　Twice-Crocked Stuffed Potatoes
　　with Macadamia Nuts, 150
　Welsh Rabbit, 40
Cherry Cider and "Rum," 59
Cherry(ies)
　Dried, and Vanilla Figs,
　　418–19
　Dried, Bacon, and Chestnuts,
　　Cornbread Stuffing with,
　　184–85
　Dried, Venison Stew with,
　　337–38
　Dried Apricots, and Pecans,
　　Wild Rice with, 173–74
　-Glazed Pork Pot Roast with
　　Herbs, 342–43
　Honey Sauce, Hot, 428
　Jubilee, 401
　Peach, and Apricot Compote,
　　416
　-Walnut Truffles, 443
Chestnut(s)
　Bacon, and Dried Cherries,
　　Cornbread Stuffing with,
　　184–85

　Beef Stew with, 313–14
　Truffles, Brandied, 443
Chèvre Sauce, Herbed, 124
Chicken
　Brandied, with Hazelnuts,
　　255–56
　Broth, Asian, 92
　in Champagne, 252
　Coq au Cabernet, 258–59
　Country Captain, 261–62
　Crème de Cassis, 262–63
　with Glazed Walnuts and
　　Grand Marnier, 264–65
　Homemade Pho with, 95–97
　Honey-Mustard, 253
　with Mango and Coconut, 257
　Marsala, 254–55
　Mole Enchilada Casserole,
　　251–52
　with Orange Sauce, 259–60
　Pot-au-Feu, 303–4
　Puchero, 334–35
　Spicy Turmeric, 266–67
　stocking, for slow cooker
　　recipes, 22
　Thighs with Garlic and
　　Sparkling Wine, 267–68
　Wings, Barbecued, for a Crowd,
　　271
　Wings, Buffalo, Crocked,
　　274–75
　wings, buying, 272
　Wings, Curried, Sujata's,
　　273–74
　wings, disjointing, 272
　Wings, Garlic and Lime, with
　　Chipotle Mayonnaise,
　　275–76
　Wings, Plum Sauce, 277
Chickpeas
　Calico Bean Bake, 230
　Chipotle Hummus from the
　　Prado in Balboa Park, 219
　Hummus with Tofu and
　　Roasted Vegetables, 218–19
　Julie's Hummus, 217–18
Chile(s)
　Ancho, Sauce, 108–9
　Chile Verde, 351–52
　Chili Olive Dip, 34–35
　Chipotle and Orange Pork
　　Ribs, 357

Chile(s) *(continued)*
  Chipotle Gravy, 270
  Chipotle Hummus from the
    Prado in Baboa Park, 219
  Chipotle Mayonnaise, 276
  Colorado, 242–43
  con Queso, Always Smooth,
    31–32
  Cornsticks, 240
  Crock-Baked Salsa Cornbread,
    392
  Green, and Artichokes, Lay-
    ered, 30
  Green, Grits, 177
  Jacquie's Black Bean–Jalapeño
    Dip, 33–34
  Mole Poblano Sauce, 107
  Nancyjo's Tofu and Corn
    Posole, 138–39
  Oscar's Chile Colorado Mole,
    352–53
  powders, for chili, 214
  preparing for slow cooker, 128
  Raja Rellenos, 134–35
  Red, Beef Stew, 243
  Red, Sauce, 243
  Roasted Vegetable White Bean
    Chili, 237–38
  and Shallots, Braised Pork
    Ribs with, 360–61
Chili
  Chile Verde, 351–52
  chili powders for, 213–14
  Colorado, 242–43
  con Carne, 244–45
  cornbread accompaniments for,
    239–42
  Elizabeth Taylor's, 234–35
  Gringo, for a Crowd, 231–32
  Olive Dip, 34–35
  Oscar's Chile Colorado Mole,
    352–53
  Pinto Bean, with Mexican
    Sausage, 232–33
  Prune, 245–46
  Roasted Vegetable White Bean,
    237–38
  Turkey, with White Beans,
    235–36
Chili powder, for chili, 213–14
Chinese-Style Barbecue Sauce,
  111

Chinese Vegetable Hot Pot,
  160–61
Chipotle and Orange Pork Ribs,
  357
Chipotle Gravy, 270
Chipotle Hummus from the
  Prado in Balboa Park, 219
Chipotle Mayonnaise, 276
Chocolate
  Adobe Ice Cream Pie, 436
  Amaretto Truffles, 443
  Bittersweet, –Coconut Fondue,
    426
  Bittersweet, Sauce, 435
  Black-on-Black Truffles,
    440–41
  Brandied Chestnut Truffles,
    443
  Brandied Hot Fudge Sauce,
    433
  Champurrado, 71
  Cherry-Walnut Truffles, 443
  Chip Fondue, 424–25
  -Cognac Sauce, 437
  Creamiest Fudge, 438–39
  Fondue, Perfumed, 424
  Hazelnut Truffles, 443
  Honey, Warm, 434–35
  Low-Fat Mocha Fudge Sauce
    with Kahlúa, 434
  -Marshmallow Fondue, Spur-
    of-the-Moment, 427
  Mexican Coffee with Brandy
    and Kahlúa, 73–74
  Mole Poblano Sauce, 107
  -Nut Truffles, Low-Fat,
    442–43
  Orange Hot Fudge Sauce, 433
  Orange-Pistachio Truffles, 443
  Peggy's Killer Hot Fudge
    Sauce, 432–33
  Peppermint Hot Fudge Sauce,
    433
  Pudding, Steamed, 380–81
  Raspberry-Almond Truffles,
    443
  Raspberry Truffles, 441–42
  Rum-Pecan Truffles, 443
  Sauce, Narsai's, 438
  stocking, for slow cooker
    recipes, 22
  Toblerone Fondue, 423

  White, Piña Colada Fondue,
    425
Cholent, 304–5
Choucroute Garnie, 354–55
Chowder, Monterey Clam, 94–95
Christmas Limas with Greens,
  225
Chutney-Yogurt Sauce, 283–84
Cilantro
  and Saffron, Spicy Lentil Soup
    with, 98–99
  Tomatillo Sauce, 347
Clam Chowder, Monterey, 94–95
Coconut
  –Bittersweet Chocolate Fon-
    due, 426
  and Mango, Chicken with,
    257
  New Orleans–Style Vanilla
    Bread Pudding with
    Whiskey Sauce, 382–83
  and Raisins, Wild Rice with,
    176
  White Chocolate Piña Colada
    Fondue, 425
Coconut milk
  Chicken with Mango and
    Coconut, 257
  Thai Peanut Sauce, 114
  Vegetable Curry, 158–59
Coffee
  Irish, 74
  Low-Fat Mocha Fudge Sauce
    with Kahlúa, 434
  Mexican, with Brandy and
    Kahlúa, 73–74
Cognac-Chocolate Sauce, 437
Condiments
  Balsamic Syrup, 172–73
  Harissa, 101–2
  Prune Butter, 444
  Red Chile Sauce, 243
  Roasted Garlic, 141–42
  stocking, for slow cooker
    recipes, 22
Coq au Cabernet, 258–59
Cordial, Lemongrass, 62–63
Corn
  Chile Cornsticks, 240
  on the Cob, Fresh, Crock-
    Roasted, 137
  in Cream, 136

Crock-Baked Salsa Cornbread, 392
Double, Spoonbread, 178
preparing for slow cooker, 129
and Tofu Posole, Nancyjo's, 138–39
Cornbread
Salsa, Crock-Baked, 392
Stuffing with Bacon, Chestnuts, and Dried Cherries, 184–85
Vanilla Pan de Maiz, 391
Cornmeal
Chile Cornsticks, 240
Crock-Baked Salsa Cornbread, 392
Double Corn Spoonbread, 178
Dumplings, Slow Cooker, 195
Gorgonzola Polenta, 194–95
Honey Cornbread with Apricots, 240–41
Lemon Cake in Fragrant Fig Leaves, 389–90
Muffins, Pumpkin, 239
Muffins, Sour Cream, 241
Vanilla Pan de Maiz, 391
Cornsticks, Chili, 240
Country Captain, 261–62
Couscous, 193
Moroccan-Style Lamb with Preserved Lemons, 371
Crab Supreme, Hot, 36
Cranberry(ies)
and Apples, Candied Yams with, 156–57
"Nog," 59–60
Pot Roast, Sweet-and-Sour, 300
Cranberry Juice
Cranberry "Nog," 59–60
Cranberry Vinaigrette, 206
Hot Cranberry-Orange Punch, 60–61
Spiked Wassail, 80
Warm Cranberry Zinfandel, 76
Cream
Athole Brose, 81
Corn in, 136
Crème Fraîche, 90
and Fresh Herb Sauce, 122
Herbed Chèvre Sauce, 124
Salsa Alfredo, 123

Cream cheese
Chili Olive Dip, 34–35
Hot Artichoke Dip with Pita Crisps, 29
Hot Sausage Dip, 38
Hot Spinach Dip, 31
Mashed Potato Casserole, 152
Crème de Cassis Chicken, 262–63
Crème Fraîche, 90
Crème Fraîche, Maple, 412–13
Creole Tomato Sauce with Shrimp, 118–19
Cuban Black Beans, 215–16
Cucumber Bisque, Asian, 91
Cumberland Sauce, Garnet, 115
Curry
Country Captain, 261–62
Dressing, Simple Creamy, 207
Malabar Almonds, 47–48
Mixed Nuts, 52
Paste, Sujata's, 273
Sujata's Curried Chicken Wings, 273–74
Thai Peanut Sauce, 114
Vegetable, 158–59
Custard Sauce, Brandied, 404

Daikon radish, preparing for slow cooker, 127
Dal, Yellow Split Pea, with Mango, 103–4
Dates
Honey, and Orange, Crock-Baked Apples with, 399–400
Steamed Brown Bread with Rum Fruits, 394–95
Sticky Steamed Pumpkin Pudding, 384–85
Desserts
Adobe Ice Cream Pie, 436
Amaretto Truffles, 443
Apple Crumble with Maple Crème Fraîche, 412–13
Apricot, Peach, and Cherry Compote, 416
Bittersweet Chocolate–Coconut Fondue, 426

Bittersweet Chocolate Sauce, 435
Black-on-Black Truffles, 440–41
Blueberry Cake, 388–89
Brandied Chestnut Truffles, 443
Brandied Hot Fudge Sauce, 433
Brandied Prune Sauce, 429
Butter Pecan Sundae Sauce, 431
Caramel Peaches, 402
Cherries Jubilee, 401
Cherry-Walnut Truffles, 443
Chocolate Chip Fondue, 424–25
Chocolate-Cognac Sauce, 437
Creamiest Fudge, 438–39
Crock-Baked Apples with Honey, Orange, and Dates, 399–400
Fruit Buckle, 413–14
Gingerbread with Blackberry Sauce, 386–87
Hazelnut Truffles, 443
Hot Honey Cherry Sauce, 428
Ice Cream Parlor Butterscotch Sauce, 431
Lady Marmalade Bananas, 400
Lemon Cornmeal Cake in Fragrant Fig Leaves, 389–90
Low-Fat Chocolate-Nut Truffles, 442–43
Low-Fat Mocha Fudge Sauce with Kahlúa, 434
Maple-Caramel Sauce, 432
Narsai's Chocolate Sauce, 438
New Orleans–Style Vanilla Bread Pudding with Whiskey Sauce, 382–83
Orange Hot Fudge Sauce, 433
Orange-Pistachio Truffles, 443
Peggy's Killer Hot Fudge Sauce, 432–33
Peppermint Hot Fudge Sauce, 433
Perfumed Chocolate Fondue, 424
Poached Peaches with Brandied Custard Sauce, 403

Desserts *(continued)*
    Raspberry-Almond Truffles, 443
    Raspberry Truffles, 441–42
    Rhubarb-Strawberry Crumble, 411–12
    Rum-Pecan Truffles, 443
    Slow-Poached Pears in Raspberries and Red Wine, 409
    Slow-Poached Pears with Marsala and Fruit Sauce, 405–6
    Slow-Poached Pears with Port, Ice Cream, and Raspberry Drizzle, 406–7
    Slow-Poached Pears with Warm Chocolate Sauce, 408
    Spiced Orange Plums, 418
    Spur-of-the-Moment Chocolate-Marshmallow Fondue, 427
    Steamed Chocolate Pudding, 380–81
    Stewed Dried Fruit, 415
    Stewed Quinces in Late-Harvest Wine Syrup, 410
    Sticky Steamed Pumpkin Pudding, 384–85
    Tapioca Pudding, 379
    Toblerone Fondue, 423
    Vanilla Figs and Dried Cherries, 418–19
    Warm Berry Sauce, 430
    Warm Chocolate Honey, 434–35
    White Chocolate Piña Colada Fondue, 425
    Winter Fruit Compote, 417
Dips. *See also* Fondue
    Always Smooth Chile con Queso, 31–32
    Bagna Cauda, 37–38
    Black Bean and Cheddar, Smoky, 33
    Black Bean–Jalapeño, Jacquie's, 33–34
    Blue Cheese Dip, 274–75
    Chili Olive, 34–35
    Chipotle Hummus from the Prado in Balboa Park, 219
    Chipotle Mayonnaise, 276
    Hot Artichoke, with Pita Crisps, 29
    Hot Crab Supreme, 36
    Hummus with Tofu and Roasted Vegetables, 218–19
    Julie's Hummus, 217–18
    Layered Artichokes and Green Chiles, 30
    Refried Bean, Creamy, 35–36
    Sausage, Hot, 38
    Spinach, Hot, 31
    Welsh Rabbit, 40
Dolmas, Spiced Lamb, 374–75
Duck
    Breasts à l'Orange, 286–87
    buying, 249
    Slow Cooker Cassoulet, 226–27
Dumplings
    about, 195
    Cornmeal, Slow Cooker, 195
    Gnocchi alla Romana, 196
    Matzo Balls, 199
    Potato, German, 198–99
    Spaetzle, 197

Edamame, preparing for slow cooker, 129
Eggnog, Hot, 72
Eggplant
    Caponata, 139–40
    preparing for slow cooker, 128
Eggs
    Benedict, 269
    Poached, Jacquie's Southwest-Style, with Chipotle Gravy, 270
    Poached, Slow Cooker, 268–69
Elizabeth Taylor's Chili, 234–35
Enchilada Casserole, Chicken Mole, 251–52
Endive, Belgian, Braised, 140–41
Entertaining, 1–3
    buffet parties, 2–3
    cocktail parties, 3
    sit-down meals, 3

Fat, removing from cooking liquids, 16–17
Fava Beans, Fresh, with Tomatoes and Saffron, 221–22
Fennel
    and Potatoes, 149
    preparing for slow cooker, 128
Fig Leaves, Fragrant, Lemon Cornmeal Cake in, 389–90
Figs, Vanilla, and Dried Cherries, 418–19
Fish. *See* Anchovies
Flageolets, Braised, with Herbs, 223
Flour, thickening liquids with, 17–18
Fondue
    Bittersweet Chocolate–Coconut, 426
    Buttermilk, 44–45
    Champagne, 43–44
    Chocolate, Perfumed, 424
    Chocolate Chip, 424–25
    Chocolate-Marshmallow, Spur-of-the-Moment, 427
    Herb, 43
    Neuchâtel, 42–43
    Potato, 46
    Shrimp, 43
    with Sparkling Apple Cider, 45–46
    Toblerone Fondue, 423
    Tomato Fondue, 41
    White Chocolate Piña Colada, 425
French Country Terrine, 362–64
French Vegetable Soup with Pesto, 88–89
Frito Pie, 319–20
Fruit(s). *See also specific fruits*
    Buckle, 413–14
    dried, for slow cooker recipes, 22
    Dried, Stewed, 415
    and Lamb Tagine, 368–69
    and Marsala Sauce, Slow-Poached Pears with, 405–6

-Mustard Glaze, 348
Rum, Steamed Brown Bread with, 394–95
slow cooking, tips for, 398
Venison, and Greens, 336–37
Fudge, Creamiest, 438–39

Game birds
Braised Pheasant with Mushrooms in Riesling, 288–89
buying, 249
Duck Breasts à l'Orange, 286–87
pheasant, about, 288
Pheasant with Apple-Shallot Cream, 290
Slow Cooker Cassoulet, 226–27
Garlic
Gremolata, 333
and Lime Chicken Wings with Chipotle Mayonnaise, 275–76
Lotsa, and Rosemary, Lamb Roast with, 365–66
Roasted, 141–42
Garnet Cumberland Sauce, 115
German Potato Dumplings, 198–99
Ginger
Gingerbread with Blackberry Sauce, 386–87
Gingered Carrot–Sweet Potato Soup, 93
Korean Short Ribs of Beef with, 325–26
-Lemon Tea, 67–68
Walnuts and, 50–51
Glazes
Hot Pepper Jelly, 348
Maple, 348
Mustard-Fruit, 348
Orange-Bourbon, 348
Glögg, 78
Gnocchi alla Romana, 196
Goat Cheese
Herbed Chèvre Sauce, 124
Salad of Greens with, 203–4

Grains. *See also* Cornmeal; Oats; Rice
Basic Bulgur, 194
Cholent, 304–5
Green Chile Grits, 177
Grand Marnier and Glazed Walnuts, Chicken with, 264–65
Grape Juice, Hot Spiced, 61–62
Grape leaves
Spiced Lamb Dolmas, 374–75
Gravy
Chipotle, 270
Sherry Cream, 281
Green Beans
Braised, Italian-Style, 142
French Vegetable Soup with Pesto, 88–89
preparing for slow cooker, 128–29
Vegetable Curry, 158–59
Greens. *See also* Cabbage; Spinach
Braised Peas with Lettuce, 147
Caesar Salad, 201–2
Christmas Limas with, 225
Hawaiian Laulau, 361–62
Hielem, 100–101
leafy, preparing for slow cooker, 128
Mushroom-Chard Whole Wheat Bread Stuffing, 181–82
Risotto with Asparagus and Arugula, 171
Salad of, with Goat Cheese, 203–4
Venison, Fruit, and, 336–37
Gremolata, 333
Gringo Chili for a Crowd, 231–32
Grits, Green Chile, 177

Ham
buying, 340
Glazed, 348–49
Prosciutto, Parmesan, and Pine Nut Holiday Stuffing, 185–86

Red Bean Stew and Rice, 224
Rolled Turkey Breast with Prosciutto, 280–81
slow cooking, 340
Split Pea Soup with, 102–3
Harissa, 101–2
Hawaiian Laulau, 361–62
Hazelnuts, Brandied Chicken with, 255–56
Hazelnut Truffles, 443
Herb(s). *See also specific herbs*
adding to slow cooker, 19, 23
Fondue, 43
Fresh, and Cream Sauce, 122
fresh, buying, 23
fresh, how to dry, 24
fresh, how to freeze, 26
fresh, most commonly used, 23–24
Herbed Chèvre Sauce, 124
and Vegetable Bread Stuffing, Arizona, 179
Hickory Barbecued Pinto Beans, 228
Hielem, 100–101
High altitude slow cooking, 20
Hollandaise Sauce, 269
Honey
Barbecue Pork Ribs, 358
Cherry Sauce, Hot, 428
Cornbread with Apricots, 240–41
-Mustard Chicken, 253
Warm Chocolate, 434–35
Hors d'oeuvres. *See* Appetizers
Hot Pot, Chinese Vegetable, 160–61
Hummus
Chipotle, from the Prado in Balboa Park, 219
Julie's, 217–18
with Tofu and Roasted Vegetables, 218–19

Ice Cream Pie, Adobe, 436
Indian Baked Beans, 229
Indian Spices, Pullao with, 191
Indian Tomato Sauce, 117

Irish Coffee, 74
Italian Meatballs, 327–28

Jalapeño–Black Bean Dip,
    Jacquie's, 33–34
Jamaica, 63–64
Jams and jellies, for slow cooker
    recipes, 22
Jasmine Rice, 189
Jerusalem artichokes, preparing
    for slow cooker, 127

Kahlúa and Brandy, Mexican
    Coffee with, 73–74
Korean Short Ribs of Beef with
    Ginger, 325–26

Lamb
    best cuts for slow cooking,
      341
    buying, 341
    Dolmas, Spiced, 374–75
    and Fruit Tagine, 368–69
    internal cooking temperatures,
      16
    Moroccan-Style, with Pre-
      served Lemons, 371
    Navarin, 366–67
    Potée Boulangère, 364–65
    and Quince Ragoût, Julie's,
      369–70
    Roast with Lotsa Garlic and
      Rosemary, 365–66
    Shanks with White Wine and
      Wild Mushroom Sauce,
      373–74
    stew, best cuts for, 341
    stocking, for slow cooker
      recipes, 22
Lard, about, 341

Leeks
    Braised, 143
    Braised Spring Vegetables,
      161
    preparing for slow cooker, 128
Lemongrass Cordial, 62–63
Lemon(s)
    -Chive Vinaigrette, 205
    Cornmeal Cake in Fragrant
      Fig Leaves, 389–90
    -Ginger Tea, 67–68
    Gremolata, 333
    Preserved, 372
Lentil Soup, Spicy, with Saffron
    and Cilantro, 98–99
Lettuce
    Braised Peas with, 147
    Caesar Salad, 201–2
Limas
    Calico Bean Bake, 230
    Christmas, with Greens, 225
Lime and Garlic Chicken Wings
    with Chipotle Mayonnaise,
    275–76
Liver
    French Country Terrine,
      362–64

Macadamia Nuts, Twice-Crocked
    Stuffed Potatoes with, 150
Main dishes (beans)
    Elizabeth Taylor's Chili,
      234–35
    Fresh Fava Beans with Toma-
      toes and Saffron, 221–22
    Gringo Chili for a Crowd,
      231–32
    New Year's Black-Eyed Peas,
      220–21
    Pinto Bean Chili with Mexican
      Sausage, 232–33
    Red Bean Stew and Rice, 224
    Roasted Vegetable White Bean
      Chili, 237–38
    Slow Cooker Cassoulet,
      226–27
    Turkey Chili with White
      Beans, 235–36

Main dishes (beef, veal and
    venison)
    Barbacoa, 301–2
    Barbecued Beef on Buns, 322
    Beef Burgundy, 308–9
    Beef Stew with Chestnuts,
      313–14
    Beef Stifado, 311–12
    Beef Stroganoff with Porcini
      Mushrooms, 316
    Beer-Soaked Brats, 326
    Braised Oxtails (Rabo), 306–7
    Chili Colorado, 242–43
    Chili con Carne, 244–45
    Cholent, 304–5
    Corned Beef with Cabbage and
      Radicchio, 307–8
    Devilishly Good Beef Short
      Ribs, 323
    Frito Pie, 319–20
    Italian Meatballs, 327–28
    Jan's Tuscan Meatloaf with
      Roasted Red Potatoes,
      320–21
    Korean Short Ribs of Beef with
      Ginger, 325–26
    New-Fashioned Pot Roast with
      Fresh Rosemary, 299
    Osso Buco, 332–33
    Paniolo Beef Stew, 310–11
    Pot-au-Feu, 303–4
    Prune Chili, 245–46
    Puchero, 334–35
    Ragoût of Veal for 20, 331–32
    Red Chile Beef Stew, 243
    Sauerbraten, 314–15
    Short Ribs of Beef with Sherry-
      Mustard Sauce and Fennel
      Seed, 324
    Stuffed Sweet-and-Sour Cab-
      bage, 317–18
    Sweet-and-Sour Cranberry Pot
      Roast, 300
    Veal Ragoût with Artichokes,
      Brandied Raisins, and
      Crème Fraîche, 328–29
    Veal Stew with Champagne,
      330
    Venison, Fruit, and Greens,
      336–37
    Venison Stew with Dried Cher-
      ries, 337–38

Main dishes (pork and lamb)
Asian Pork Tenderloins, 349–50
Braised Pork Ribs with Chiles and Shallots, 360–61
Cherry-Glazed Pork Pot Roast with Herbs, 342–43
Chile Verde, 351–52
Chipotle and Orange Pork Ribs, 357
Choucroute Garnie, 354–55
French Country Terrine, 362–64
Glazed Ham, 348–49
Hawaiian Laulau, 361–62
Honey Barbecue Pork Ribs, 358
Julie's Lamb and Quince Ragoût, 369–70
Lamb and Fruit Tagine, 368–69
Lamb Navarin, 366–67
Lamb Roast with Lotsa Garlic and Rosemary, 365–66
Lamb Shanks with White Wine and Wild Mushroom Sauce, 373–74
Mexican Pork Roast with Tomatillo Sauce, 346–47
Moroccan-Style Lamb with Preserved Lemons, 371
Oscar's Chile Colorado Mole, 352–53
Pernil, 344–45
Pork Ribs with No-Cook Barbecue Sauce, 359
Pork Roast with Tomatoes and Mushrooms, 343–44
Potée Boulangère, 364–65
Ragoût of Pork and Mushrooms with White Wine, 350–51
Spiced Lamb Dolmas, 374–75
Main dishes (poultry)
Barbecued Chicken Wings for a Crowd, 271
Braised Pheasant with Mushrooms in Riesling, 288–89
Braised Rabbit with Prunes and Green Olives, 291–92
Brandied Chicken with Hazelnuts, 255–56

Chicken in Champagne, 252
Chicken Marsala, 254–55
Chicken Mole Enchilada Casserole, 251–52
Chicken Thighs with Garlic and Sparkling Wine, 267–68
Chicken with Glazed Walnuts and Grand Marnier, 264–65
Chicken with Mango and Coconut, 257
Chicken with Orange Sauce, 259–60
Cold Poached Turkey Tenderloins with Chutney-Yogurt Sauce, 283–84
Coq au Cabernet, 258–59
Country Captain, 261–62
Crème de Cassis Chicken, 262–63
Crocked Buffalo Chicken Wings, 274–75
Duck Breasts à l'Orange, 286–87
Garlic and Lime Chicken Wings with Chipotle Mayonnaise, 275–76
Honey-Mustard Chicken, 253
Old-Fashioned Turkey Breast with Pan Gravy, 278–79
Pheasant with Apple-Shallot Cream, 290
Plum Sauce Chicken Wings, 277
Rolled Turkey Breast with Prosciutto, 280–81
Spicy Turmeric Chicken, 266–67
Stewed Rabbit with Red Wine and Wild Mushrooms, 293–94
Sujata's Curried Chicken Wings, 273–74
Turkey Legs with Mandarins, 282
White Meatloaf, 284–85
Main dishes (vegetables and seafood)
Chinese Vegetable Hot Pot, 160–61
Nancyjo's Tofu and Corn Posole, 138–39

Shrimp Risotto with Parsley and Basil, 170
Vegetable Curry, 158–59
Malabar Almonds, 47–48
Mandarins, Turkey Legs with, 282
Mango
and Coconut, Chicken with, 257
Country Captain, 261–62
Yellow Split Pea Dal with, 103–4
Maple (syrup)
-Caramel Sauce, 432
Crème Fraîche, 412–13
Glaze, 348
-Glazed Pecans, 49
-Raisin Brown Bread, Steamed, 393–94
Margarita Mayonnaise Dressing, 207
Marmalade, Brown Sugar, and Butter, Carrots Glazed with, 132–33
Marmalade Bananas, Lady, 400
Marshmallow-Chocolate Fondue, Spur-of-the-Moment, 427
Matzo Balls, 199
Mayonnaise, Chipotle, 276
Mayonnaise Dressing, Margarita, 207
Meatballs, Italian, 327–28
Meatloaf, Jan's Tuscan, with Roasted Red Potatoes, 320–21
Meatloaf, White, 284–85
Meats. See also Beef; Lamb; Pork; Rabbit; Veal; Venison
defrosting, before adding to slow cooker, 13
Mexican Coffee with Brandy and Kahlúa, 73–74
Mexican Pork Roast with Tomatillo Sauce, 346–47
Milk
Champurrado, 71
Hot Peppermint, 72–73
Sweetened, for Chai, 69
Mint
Harissa, 101–2
Hot Peppermint Milk, 72–73

Mint (continued)
Peppermint Hot Fudge Sauce, 433
Sauce, Old-Fashioned, 116
Tea, Moroccan, 70
Mocha Fudge Sauce, Low-Fat, Sauce with Kahlúa, 434
Mole Poblano Sauce, 107
Monterey Clam Chowder, 94–95
Monterey Jack cheese
Always Smooth Chile con Queso, 31–32
Creamy Refried Bean Dip, 35–36
Moroccan Mint Tea, 70
Moroccan-Style Lamb with Preserved Lemons, 371
Mozzarella
Brandied Red Onion Soup Gratinée, 87
Buttermilk Fondue, 44–45
Hot Spinach Dip, 31
Tomato Fondue, 41
Muffins
Pumpkin Cornmeal Muffins, 239
Sour Cream Cornmeal, 241
Mulled Apple Juice, Hot, The Best, 57
Mulled Cider with Cardamom and Saffron, 58
Mulled Wine, 75
Mung bean sprouts, preparing for slow cooker, 129
Mushroom(s)
Arizona Vegetable and Herb Bread Stuffing, 179
Beef Burgundy, 308–9
Braised Pheasant with, in Riesling, 288–89
-Chard Whole Wheat Bread Stuffing, 181–82
Chicken in Champagne, 252
Chicken Marsala, 254–55
Coq au Cabernet, 258–59
Forestière on Toast, 143–45
-Gorgonzola Risotto in Radicchio Wraps with Balsamic Syrup, 172–73
Pheasant with Apple-Shallot Cream, 290

Porcini, Beef Stroganoff with, 316
and Pork, Ragoût of, with White Wine, 350–51
Ragoût of Veal for 20, 331–32
stocking, for slow cooker recipes, 21
Thanksgiving Sausage Bread Pudding, 182–83
and Tomatoes, Pork Loin Roast with, 343–44
Wild, and Red Wine, Stewed Rabbit with, 293–94
Wild, and White Wine Sauce, Lamb Shanks with, 373–74
Mustard-Fruit Glaze, 348

New Orleans–Style Vanilla Bread Pudding with Whiskey Sauce, 382–83
Noodles
Homemade Pho with Chicken, 95–97
Victoria's Armenian Rice and Vermicelli Pilaf, 191–92
Nut(s). See also Almond(s); Pecan(s); Walnut(s)
Apple Crumble with Maple Crème Fraîche, 412–13
Beef Stew with Chestnuts, 313–14
Brandied Chestnut Truffles, 443
Brandied Chicken with Hazelnuts, 255–56
-Chocolate Truffles, Low-Fat, 442–43
Cornbread Stuffing with Bacon, Chestnuts, and Dried Cherries, 184–85
Curry Mixed, 52
Hazelnut Truffles, 443
Macadamia, Twice-Crocked Stuffed Potatoes with, 150
Orange-Pistachio Truffles, 443
Pine, Prosciutto, and Parmesan Holiday Stuffing, 185–86
Retro Party Mix, 52–53

stocking, for slow cooker recipes, 22

Oats
Apple Crumble with Maple Crème Fraîche, 412–13
Rhubarb-Strawberry Crumble, 411–12
Oils
Bagna Cauda, 37–38
types of, 21
Okra, preparing for slow cooker, 129
Olive(s)
Chili Dip, 34–35
Eggplant Caponata, 139–40
Green, and Prunes, Braised Rabbit with, 291–92
Onion(s)
Beef Stifado, 311–12
Brandied Chicken with Hazelnuts, 255–56
preparing for slow cooker, 128
Ragoût of Baby Vegetables, 162
Ragoût of Veal for 20, 331–32
Red, Soup Gratinée, Brandied, 87
Rosemary-Balsamic, 145
Soup with Champagne, Port, and Camembert, 86
spring, preparing for slow cooker, 128
Orange(s)
-Bourbon Glaze, 348
and Chipotle Pork Ribs, 357
-Cranberry Punch, Hot, 60–61
Duck Breasts à l'Orange, 286–87
Garnet Cumberland Sauce, 115
Honey, and Dates, Crock-Baked Apples with, 399–400
Hot Fudge Sauce, 433
-Pistachio Truffles, 443
Plums, Spiced, 418
Rice, 192
Sauce, Chicken with, 259–60
Turkey Legs with Mandarins, 282

-Walnut Wild Rice, 175
Winter Fruit Compote, 417
Osso Buco, 332–33
Oxtails, Braised (Rabo), 306–7

Paniolo Beef Stew, 310–11
Parmesan
    Caesar Dressing, 201
    Gnocchi alla Romana, 196
    Hot Artichoke Dip with Pita
        Crisps, 29
    Pistou Basil Paste, 88–89
    Prosciutto, and Pine Nut Holi-
        day Stuffing, 185–86
    Pumpkin-Sage Risotto, 168–69
    Risotto Milanese, 165–66
    Risotto Verde, 166–67
    Risotto with Asparagus and
        Arugula, 171
    Salsa Alfredo, 123
    Shrimp Risotto with Parsley
        and Basil, 170
Parsley
    Gremolata, 333
    Risotto Verde, 166–67
Parsnips
    preparing for slow cooker, 127
    Venison Stew with Dried Cher-
        ries, 337–38
Party Mix, Retro, 52–53
Pasta and noodles
    Couscous, 193
    Fresh Fava Beans with Toma-
        toes and Saffron, 221–22
    Hielem, 100–101
    Homemade Pho with Chicken,
        95–97
    stocking, for slow cooker
        recipes, 21
    Victoria's Armenian Rice and
        Vermicelli Pilaf, 191–92
Peach(es)
    Apricot, and Cherry Compote,
        416
    Caramel, 402
    Poached, with Brandied Cus-
        tard Sauce, 403
    Winter Fruit Compote, 417

Peanut Sauce, Thai, 114
Pears, Slow-Poached
    with Marsala and Fruit Sauce,
        405–6
    with Port, Ice Cream, and
        Raspberry Drizzle, 406–7
    in Raspberries and Red Wine,
        409
    with Warm Chocolate Sauce,
        408
Pea(s)
    and Artichokes, Ragoût of, with
        Tarragon, 146
    Black-Eyed, New Year's,
        220–21
    Braised, with Lettuce, 147
    Braised Spring Vegetables, 161
    Lamb Navarin, 366–67
    preparing for slow cooker, 129
    Ragoût of Baby Vegetables, 162
    Split, Soup with Ham, 102–3
    Yellow Split, Dal with Mango,
        103–4
Pecan(s)
    Butter, Sundae Sauce, 431
    Caramel Brie, 39
    Dried Apricots, and Cherries,
        Wild Rice with, 173–74
    Halves, Buttery Rosemary, 48
    Maple-Glazed, 49
    New Orleans–Style Vanilla
        Bread Pudding with
        Whiskey Sauce, 382–83
    -Rum Truffles, 443
Pepper Jelly, Hot, Glaze, 348
Peppermint Hot Fudge Sauce,
    433
Peppermint Milk, Hot, 72–73
Pepper(s). See also Chile(s)
    Braised Spring Vegetables, 161
    Chinese Vegetable Hot Pot,
        160–61
    Country Tomato Sauce with
        Roasted Vegetables, 119–20
    Harissa, 101–2
    Hummus with Tofu and
        Roasted Vegetables, 218–19
    preparing for slow cooker, 128
    Red Bell, Sauce with Saffron,
        113
    Roasted Vegetable White Bean
        Chili, 237–38

Yellow Bell, Sauce with Thyme,
    113
Pernil, 344–45
Pheasant
    about, 288
    with Apple-Shallot Cream, 290
    Braised, with Mushrooms in
        Riesling, 288–89
    buying, 249
Pho, Homemade, with Chicken,
    95–97
Pie, Adobe Ice Cream, 436
Pie, Frito, 319–20
Pilaf, Rice and Vermicelli, Victo-
    ria's Armenian, 191–92
Piña Colada White Chocolate
    Fondue, 425
Pineapple
    Ponche, 64–65
    and Tequila Barbecue Sauce,
        112
    Winter Fruit Compote, 417
Pine Nut(s)
    Prosciutto, and Parmesan Hol-
        iday Stuffing, 185–86
Pistachio-Orange Truffles, 443
Pistou Basil Paste, 88–89
Pita Crisps, 29
Plums, dried. See Prune(s)
Plum Sauce Chicken Wings, 277
Polenta, Gorgonzola, 194–95
Ponche, 64–65
Pork. See also Bacon; Ham; Pork
    sausages
    best cuts for slow cooking, 340
    Chile Verde, 351–52
    Choucroute Garnie, 354–55
    Country Tomato Sauce with
        Roasted Vegetables, 119–20
    Elizabeth Taylor's Chili,
        234–35
    French Country Terrine,
        362–64
    Hawaiian Laulau, 361–62
    internal cooking temperatures,
        16
    Italian Meatballs, 327–28
    lard, about, 341
    and Mushrooms, Ragoût of,
        with White Wine, 350–51
    Oscar's Chile Colorado Mole,
        352–53

Pork *(continued)*
  Potée Boulangère, 364–65
  Pot Roast, Cherry-Glazed, with
    Herbs, 342–43
  ribs, about, 355–56
  Ribs, Braised, with Chiles and
    Shallots, 360–61
  ribs, buying, 355–56
  Ribs, Chipotle and Orange, 357
  Ribs, Honey Barbecue, 358
  ribs, slow-cooking, 355–56
  Ribs with No-Cook Barbecue
    Sauce, 359
  Roast, Mexican, with Tomatillo
    Sauce, 346–47
  Roast with Tomatoes and
    Mushrooms, 343–44
  Slow Cooker Cassoulet, 226–27
  stew, best cuts for, 340
  stocking, for slow cooker
    recipes, 22
  Tenderloins, Asian, 349–50
Pork sausages
  adding to slow cooker, 340
  Beefy Tomato Sauce with
    Sausage and Fennel, 121–22
  Hot Sausage Dip, 38
  Pinto Bean Chili with Mexican
    Sausage, 232–33
  Prune Chili, 245–46
  Puchero, 334–35
  Red Bean Stew and Rice, 224
  Slow Cooker Cassoulet,
    226–27
  Thanksgiving Sausage Bread
    Pudding, 182–83
Posole, Nancyjo's Tofu and Corn,
  138–39
Potato(es). *See also* Sweet
    Potato(es)
  Blue Cheese–Sour Cream
    Mashers, 154
  Cream of Root Vegetable Soup
    Normandy, 89–90
  Dumplings, German, 198–99
  and Fennel, 149
  Fondue, 46
  Lamb Roast with Lotsa Garlic
    and Rosemary, 365–66
  Mashed, and Carrots with
    Crisp Bacon and Chives, 155
  Mashed, Casserole, 152

  Mashed, Good Old-Fashioned,
    152–53
  mashed, keeping warm in slow
    cooker, 153
  Monterey Clam Chowder,
    94–95
  New, with Fresh Lemon-Herb
    Butter, 148
  New-Fashioned Pot Roast with
    Fresh Rosemary, 299
  Oven-Roasted, 200
  Potée Boulangère, 364–65
  preparing for slow cooker, 127
  Ragoût of Baby Vegetables,
    162
  Red Chile Beef Stew, 243
  Roasted Red, Jan's Tuscan
    Meatloaf with, 320–21
  Scalloped, 151
  Twice-Crocked Stuffed, with
    Macadamia Nuts, 150
  Vegetable Curry, 158–59
  Venison Stew with Dried Cher-
    ries, 337–38
Poultry. *See also* Chicken; Game
    birds; Turkey
  buying, 249
  defrosting, before adding to
    slow cooker, 13
  internal cooking temperatures,
    16
  safe handling of, 250
  slow cooking, tips for, 248–50
Preserves, for slow cooker
    recipes, 22
Prosciutto
  adding to slow cooker,
    340–41
  Parmesan, and Pine Nut Holi-
    day Stuffing, 185–86
  Rolled Turkey Breast with,
    280–81
Prune(s)
  Butter, 444
  Chili, 245–46
  and Green Olives, Braised
    Rabbit with, 291–92
  Lamb and Fruit Tagine,
    368–69
  Sauce, Brandied, 429
  Spiced Orange Plums, 418
  Winter Fruit Compote, 417

Puchero, 334–35
Pudding
  slow cooking, tips for, 378
  Steamed Chocolate, 380–81
  Steamed Pumpkin, Sticky,
    384–85
  Tapioca, 379
  Vanilla Bread, New
    Orleans–Style, with
    Whiskey Sauce, 382–83
Pullao with Indian Spices, 191
Pumpkin
  and Black Bean Soup,
    99–100
  Cornmeal Muffins, 239
  Pudding, Sticky Steamed,
    384–85
  -Sage Risotto, 168–69

Quince(s)
  and Lamb Ragoût, Julie's,
    369–70
  Stewed, in Late-Harvest Wine
    Syrup, 410

Rabbit
  about, 291
  Braised, with Prunes and
    Green Olives, 291–92
  Stewed, with Red Wine and
    Wild Mushrooms, 293–94
Radicchio
  and Cabbage, Corned Beef
    with, 307–8
  Wraps, Mushroom-Gorgonzola
    Risotto in, with Balsamic
    Syrup, 172–73
Raisin(s)
  Brandied, Artichokes, and
    Crème Fraîche, Veal Ragoût
    with, 328–29
  and Coconut, Wild Rice with,
    176
  Country Captain, 261–62

Crock-Baked Apples with Honey, Orange, and Dates, 399–400
-Maple Brown Bread, Steamed, 393–94
New Orleans–Style Vanilla Bread Pudding with Whiskey Sauce, 382–83
Ponche, 64–65
Raja Rellenos, 134–35
Raspberry(ies)
  -Almond Truffles, 443
  Drizzle, 407
  and Red Wine, Slow-Poached Pears in, 409
  Truffles, 441–42
  Winter Fruit Compote, 417
Rhubarb-Strawberry Crumble, 411–12
Rice
  Basmati, 188
  best types, for risotto, 21, 169
  best types, for slow cookers, 21–22, 164
  Calrose, 189
  Jasmine, 189
  Mushroom-Gorgonzola Risotto in Radicchio Wraps with Balsamic Syrup, 172–73
  Orange, 192
  Pullao with Indian Spices, 191
  Pumpkin-Sage Risotto, 168–69
  Red Bean Stew and, 224
  Risotto Milanese, 165–66
  Risotto Verde, 166–67
  Risotto with Asparagus and Arugula, 171
  Saffron, 190
  Short-Grain Brown, 190
  Shrimp Risotto with Parsley and Basil, 170
  Spiced Lamb Dolmas, 374–75
  and Vermicelli Pilaf, Victoria's Armenian, 191–92
  Wild, Basic, 193
  Wild, Orange-Walnut, 175
  Wild, with Coconut and Raisins, 176
  Wild, with Dried Apricots, Cherries, and Pecans, 173–74

Yellow Split Pea Dal with Mango, 103–4
Risotto
  with Asparagus and Arugula, 171
  best rice for, 21, 169
  Milanese, 165–66
  Mushroom-Gorgonzola, in Radicchio Wraps with Balsamic Syrup, 172–73
  preparing, in slow cooker, 167
  Pumpkin-Sage, 168–69
  Shrimp, with Parsley and Basil, 170
  Verde, 166–67
Rolls, Sweet Potato Dinner, 279
Rosemary-Balsamic Onions, 145
Rosemary Pecan Halves, Buttery, 48
Roux, thickening liquids with, 17
Rum
  Fruits, Steamed Brown Bread with, 394–95
  Hot Buttered, 82
  -Pecan Truffles, 443
  Whipped Cream, 419
  White Chocolate Piña Colada Fondue, 425
"Rum" and Cherry Cider, 59
Rutabaga, preparing for slow cooker, 127

S

Saffron Rice, 190
Salad dressings
  Basil Vinaigrette, 207
  Blueberry Vinaigrette, 206
  Caesar, 201
  Cranberry Vinaigrette, 206
  Curry, Simple Creamy, 207
  Lemon-Chive Vinaigrette, 205
  Margarita Mayonnaise, 207
  Shallot Vinaigrette, 206
  Thousand Island, 208
  vinaigrettes, preparing, 205
  Walnut Vinaigrette, 205
Salads
  buffet, types of, 202
  Caesar, 201–2

of Greens with Goat Cheese, 203–4
plated, types of, 202
Salt, adding to recipes, 23
Sandwiches
  Barbecued Beef on Buns, 322
Sauces, 105–24
  Ancho Chile, 108–9
  Barbecue, Chinese-Style, 111
  barbecue, in slow cooker recipes, 113
  Barbecue, Our Basic KC, 110
  Barbecue, Red Wine, 109–10
  Barbecue, Tequila and Pineapple, 112
  Berry, Warm, 430
  Blackberry, 387
  Butter Pecan Sundae, 431
  Butterscotch, Ice Cream Parlor, 431
  Chipotle Gravy, 270
  Chocolate, Bittersweet, 435
  Chocolate, Narsai's, 438
  Chocolate-Cognac, 437
  Chutney-Yogurt, 283–84
  Custard, Brandied, 404
  Fresh Herb and Cream, 122
  Garnet Cumberland, 115
  Herbed Chèvre, 124
  Hollandaise, 269
  Honey Cherry, Hot, 428
  Hot Fudge, Brandied, 433
  Hot Fudge, Orange, 433
  Hot Fudge, Peggy's Killer, 432–33
  Hot Fudge, Peppermint, 433
  Maple-Caramel, 432
  Mint, Old-Fashioned, 116
  Mocha Fudge, Low-Fat, with Kahlúa, 434
  Mole Poblano, 107
  Peanut, Thai, 114
  Prune, Brandied, 429
  Raspberry Drizzle, 407
  Red Bell Pepper, with Saffron, 113
  Red Chile, 243
  Salsa Alfredo, 123
  Sherry Cream Gravy, 281
  Spirited Butterscotch, 385
  Tomatillo, 347

Sauces (continued)
  Tomato, Beefy, with Sausage and Fennel, 121–22
  Tomato, Country, with Roasted Vegetables, 119–20
  Tomato, Creole, with Shrimp, 118–19
  Tomato, Family-Style Winter, 120–21
  Tomato, Indian, 117
  Warm Chocolate Honey, 434–35
  Whiskey, 383
  Yellow Bell Pepper, with Thyme, 113
Sauerkraut
  Choucroute Garnie, 354–55
Sausage(s)
  adding to slow cooker, 340
  Bread Pudding, Thanksgiving, 182–83
  Choucroute Garnie, 354–55
  Dip, Hot, 38
  and Fennel, Beefy Tomato Sauce with, 121–22
  Mexican, Pinto Bean Chili with, 232–33
  Prune Chili, 245–46
  Puchero, 334–35
  Red Bean Stew and Rice, 224
  Slow Cooker Cassoulet, 226–27
  stocking, for slow cooker recipes, 22
Seafood. See Anchovies; Shellfish
Shallot Vinaigrette, 206
Shellfish
  Creole Tomato Sauce with Shrimp, 118–19
  Hot Crab Supreme, 36
  Monterey Clam Chowder, 94–95
  Shrimp Fondue, 43
  Shrimp Risotto with Parsley and Basil, 170
Sherry Cream Gravy, 281
Shrimp
  Creole Tomato Sauce with, 118–19
  Fondue, 43
  Risotto with Parsley and Basil, 170

Sides (beans)
  Braised Flageolets with Herbs, 223
  Calico Bean Bake, 230
  Chipotle Hummus from the Prado in Balboa Park, 219
  Christmas Limas with Greens, 225
  Cuban Black Beans, 215–16
  Hickory Barbecued Pinto Beans, 228
  Hummus with Tofu and Roasted Vegetables, 218–19
  Indian Baked Beans, 229
  Julie's Hummus, 217–18
  Slow Cooker Pot of Beans, 214–15
Sides (grains)
  Arizona Vegetable and Herb Bread Stuffing, 179
  Basic Bulgur, 194
  Basic Wild Rice, 193
  Basmati Rice, 188
  Calrose Rice, 189
  Cornbread Stuffing with Bacon, Chestnuts, and Dried Cherries, 184–85
  Double Corn Spoonbread, 178
  Gorgonzola Polenta, 194–95
  Green Chile Grits, 177
  Jasmine Rice, 189
  Mushroom-Chard Whole Wheat Bread Stuffing, 181–82
  Mushroom-Gorgonzola Risotto in Radicchio Wraps with Balsamic Syrup, 172–73
  Orange Rice, 192
  Orange-Walnut Wild Rice, 175
  Prosciutto, Parmesan, and Pine Nut Holiday Stuffing, 185–86
  Pullao with Indian Spices, 191
  Pumpkin-Sage Risotto, 168–69
  Risotto Milanese, 165–66
  Risotto Verde, 166–67
  Risotto with Asparagus and Arugula, 171
  Saffron Rice, 190
  Short-Grain Brown Rice, 190
  Thanksgiving Sausage Bread Pudding, 182–83

Victoria's Armenian Rice and Vermicelli Pilaf, 191–92
  Wild Rice with Coconut and Raisins, 176
  Wild Rice with Dried Apricots, Cherries, and Pecans, 173–74
Sides (pasta and dumplings)
  Couscous, 193
  German Potato Dumplings, 198–99
  Gnocchi alla Romana, 196
  Matzo Balls, 199
  Slow Cooker Cornmeal Dumplings, 195
  Spaetzle, 197
Sides (stovetop or oven)
  Basic Bulgur, 194
  Basic Wild Rice, 193
  Basmati Rice, 188
  Caesar Salad, 201–2
  Calrose Rice, 189
  cornbread accompaniments for chili, 239–42
  Couscous, 193
  German Potato Dumplings, 198–99
  Gnocchi alla Romana, 196
  Gorgonzola Polenta, 194–95
  Jasmine Rice, 189
  Matzo Balls, 199
  Orange Rice, 192
  Oven-Roasted Potatoes, 200
  Oven-Roasted Spaghetti Squash, 200–201
  Pullao with Indian Spices, 191
  Saffron Rice, 190
  Salad of Greens with Goat Cheese, 203–4
  Short-Grain Brown Rice, 190
  Spaetzle, 197
  Victoria's Armenian Rice and Vermicelli Pilaf, 191–92
Sides (vegetables)
  Blue Cheese–Sour Cream Mashers, 154
  Braised Belgian Endive, 140–41
  Braised Fresh Shell Beans, 130
  Braised Leeks, 143
  Braised Peas with Lettuce, 147
  Braised Spring Vegetables, 161

Caesar Salad, 201–2
Candied Yams with Apples and Cranberries, 156–57
Carrots Glazed with Marmalade, Brown Sugar, and Butter, 132–33
Celery Victor, 133–34
Cider-Braised Turnips, 156
Corn in Cream, 136
Crock-Baked Beets, 131
Crock-Roasted Fresh Corn on the Cob, 137
Eggplant Caponata, 139–40
Good Old-Fashioned Mashed Potatoes, 152–53
Italian-Style Braised Green Beans, 142
Mashed Potato Casserole, 152
Mashed Potatoes and Carrots with Crisp Bacon and Chives, 155
Mushrooms Forestière on Toast, 143–45
New Potatoes with Fresh Lemon-Herb Butter, 148
Oven-Roasted Potatoes, 200
Oven-Roasted Spaghetti Squash, 200–201
Potatoes and Fennel, 149
Ragoût of Baby Vegetables, 162
Ragoût of Peas and Artichokes with Tarragon, 146
Raja Rellenos, 134–35
Red Cabbage with Red Wine, Apricots, and Honey, 132
Rosemary-Balsamic Onions, 145
Salad of Greens with Goat Cheese, 203–4
Scalloped Potatoes, 151
Slow-Steamed Artichokes, 129–30
Tortino di Zucchini, 157–58
Twice-Crocked Stuffed Potatoes with Macadamia Nuts, 150
Silk squash
    Asian Cucumber Bisque, 91
Slow cookers
    adapting conventional recipes to, 18–20
    bean cooking time chart, 212–13
    cooking beans in, tips for, 216
    cooking method used by, 9
    cook times, 15
    first-time use, 4, 5
    guidelines for use, 10–13
    helpful equipment for, 9–10
    high altitude adjustments, 20
    internal temperature of food, 15
    keeping mashed potatoes warm in, 153
    leftovers from, handling, 12
    lifting lid, during cooking, 10
    liquids in, removing fat from, 16–17
    liquids in, thickening, 17–18
    newer features, 6
    panic-proof pantry ingredients for, 20–26
    placing ingredients in, 11–12, 14
    power outages and, 13
    preparing ingredients for, 13
    preparing vegetables for, 126–29
    programmable models, 8–9, 14
    recipe headnotes, about, 18
    safety guidelines, 10–13, 250
    shapes of, 5–6
    sizes of, 7–8
    specialty models, 8–9
    stoneware inserts, handling, 6, 12–13
    stoneware inserts, shapes of, 5–6
    temperature settings, 11, 14
    useful cooking techniques, 16–20
    wattage used by, 4, 10
Smart-Pot, 8, 14
Soups, 83–104
    Asian Cucumber Bisque, 91
    Black Bean and Pumpkin, 99–100
    Brandied Red Onion, Gratinée, 87
    French Vegetable, with Pesto, 88–89
    garnishes for, 85
    Gingered Carrot–Sweet Potato, 93
    Hearty Beef Borscht with Cabbage, 97–98
    Hielem, 100–101
    Homemade Pho with Chicken, 95–97
    Lentil, Spicy, with Saffron and Cilantro, 98–99
    Monterey Clam Chowder, 94–95
    Onion, with Champagne, Port, and Camembert, 86
    Root Vegetable, Cream of, Normandy, 89–90
    slow cooking, tips for, 84–85
    Split Pea, with Ham, 102–3
    Yellow Split Pea Dal with Mango, 103–4
Sour Cream Cornmeal Muffins, 241
Southwest-Style Poached Eggs, Jacquie's, with Chipotle Gravy, 270
Spaetzle, 197
Spaghetti Squash, Oven-Roasted, 200–201
Spice mixes
    BBQ Queens' Barbecue Spice, 271
    chili powders, types of, 213–14
    Sujata's Curry Paste, 273
Spinach
    Christmas Limas with Greens, 225
    Dip, Hot, 31
    Hawaiian Laulau, 361–62
    preparing for slow cooker, 128
    Risotto Verde, 166–67
Split Pea
    Soup with Ham, 102–3
    Yellow, Dal with Mango, 103–4
Spoonbread, Double Corn, 178
Squash
    Black Bean and Pumpkin Soup, 99–100
    French Vegetable Soup with Pesto, 88–89
    Pumpkin Cornmeal Muffins, 239
    Pumpkin-Sage Risotto, 168–69

Squash (continued)
  Spaghetti, Oven-Roasted, 200–201
  Sticky Steamed Pumpkin Pudding, 384–85
  summer, preparing for slow cooker, 129
  Tortino di Zucchini, 157–58
  Vegetable Curry, 158–59
  winter, preparing for slow cooker, 127
Squash, silk
  Asian Cucumber Bisque, 91
Stews. See also Chili
  adding wine to, 25
  beef, best cuts for, 297
  Beef, Paniolo, 310–11
  Beef, with Chestnuts, 313–14
  Beef Burgundy, 308–9
  Beef Stifado, 311–12
  Chili Colorado, 242–43
  cutting up meat for, 296
  Julie's Lamb and Quince Ragoût, 369–70
  lamb, best cuts for, 341
  Lamb and Fruit Tagine, 368–69
  Lamb Navarin, 366–67
  Moroccan-Style Lamb with Preserved Lemons, 371
  pork, best cuts for, 340
  Potée Boulangère, 364–65
  preparing, tips for, 298
  Ragoût of Pork and Mushrooms with White Wine, 350–51
  Ragoût of Veal for 20, 331–32
  Red Bean, and Rice, 224
  Red Chile Beef, 243
  Veal, with Champagne, 330
  Veal Ragoût with Artichokes, Brandied Raisins, and Crème Fraîche, 328–29
  Venison, Fruit, and Greens, 336–37
  Venison, with Dried Cherries, 337–38
Stock, for slow cooker recipes, 21
Strawberry(ies)
  -Rhubarb Crumble, 411–12
  Warm Berry Sauce, 430
  -White Wine Punch, 77

Stroganoff, Beef, with Porcini Mushrooms, 316
Stuffings
  Bread, Vegetable and Herb, Arizona, 179
  Cornbread, with Bacon, Chestnuts, and Dried Cherries, 184–85
  preparing in slow cooker, tips for, 180
  Prosciutto, Parmesan, and Pine Nut Holiday, 185–86
  Thanksgiving Sausage Bread Pudding, 182–83
  Whole Wheat Bread, Mushroom-Chard, 181–82
Sugared Walnuts, 51
Sweet Potato(es)
  -Carrot Soup, Gingered, 93
  Dinner Rolls, 279
  preparing for slow cooker, 127
Swiss chard. See Chard
Swiss cheese
  Buttermilk Fondue, 44–45
  Champagne Fondue, 43–44
  Fondue Neuchâtel, 42–43
  Fondue with Sparkling Apple Cider, 45–46
  Herb Fondue, 43
  Potato Fondue, 46
  Shrimp Fondue, 43
  Twice-Crocked Stuffed Potatoes with Macadamia Nuts, 150
Syrup, Balsamic, 172–73

Tagine, Lamb and Fruit, 368–69
Tahini
  Chipotle Hummus from the Prado in Balboa Park, 219
  Hummus with Tofu and Roasted Vegetables, 218–19
  Julie's Hummus, 217–18
Tamari Almonds, 46–47
Tapioca Pudding, 379
Tea
  Chai, 68–69
  Ginger-Lemon, 67–68

Moroccan Mint, 70
  Spiced Apple and Chamomile, 66–67
Tequila and Pineapple Barbecue Sauce, 112
Terrine, French Country, 362–64
Thai Peanut Sauce, 114
Thousand Island Dressing, 208
Toast Soldiers, 238
Toblerone Fondue, 423
Tofu
  Chinese Vegetable Hot Pot, 160–61
  and Corn Posole, Nancyjo's, 138–39
  and Roasted Vegetables, Hummus with, 218–19
Tomatillo(s)
  preparing for slow cooker, 128
  Roasted Vegetable White Bean Chili, 237–38
  Sauce, 347
Tomato(es). See also Tomato Sauces
  canned, for recipes, 21
  Country Captain, 261–62
  Eggplant Caponata, 139–40
  Fondue, 41
  French Vegetable Soup with Pesto, 88–89
  Frito Pie, 319–20
  Gringo Chili for a Crowd, 231–32
  Hot, Virgin Mary, 65
  Hot Sausage Dip, 38
  Italian Meatballs, 327–28
  Italian-Style Braised Green Beans, 142
  Juice, Baja, 66
  and Mushrooms, Pork Loin Roast with, 343–44
  New Year's Black-Eyed Peas, 220–21
  Pinto Bean Chili with Mexican Sausage, 232–33
  preparing for slow cooker, 128
  and Saffron, Fresh Fava Beans with, 221–22
  Stuffed Sweet-and-Sour Cabbage, 317–18

Turkey Chili with White Beans, 235–36
Vegetable Curry, 158–59
Tomato Sauces. *See also* Barbecue Sauces
Ancho Chile, 108–9
Beefy, with Sausage and Fennel, 121–22
canned, for recipes, 21
Country, with Roasted Vegetables, 119–20
Creole, with Shrimp, 118–19
Family-Style Winter, 120–21
Indian, 117
Mole Poblano Sauce, 107
Tortillas
Chicken Mole Enchilada Casserole, 251–52
Tortino di Zucchini, 157–58
Truffles
Amaretto, 443
Black-on-Black, 440–41
Brandied Chestnut, 443
Cherry-Walnut, 443
Chocolate-Nut, Low-Fat, 442–43
Hazelnut, 443
Orange-Pistachio, 443
Raspberry, 441–42
Raspberry-Almond, 443
Rum-Pecan, 443
Turkey
Breast, Old-Fashioned, with Pan Gravy, 278–79
Breast, Rolled, with Prosciutto, 280–81
buying, 249
Chili with White Beans, 235–36
Legs with Mandarins, 282
stocking, for slow cooker recipes, 22
Tenderloins, Cold Poached, with Chutney-Yogurt Sauce, 283–84
White Meatloaf, 284–85
Turmeric Chicken, Spicy, 266–67
Turnips
Cider-Braised, 156
Cream of Root Vegetable Soup Normandy, 89–90

Lamb and Fruit Tagine, 368–69
Lamb Navarin, 366–67
preparing for slow cooker, 127
Ragoût of Baby Vegetables, 162
Tuscan Meatloaf, Jan's, with Roasted Red Potatoes, 320–21

V

Vanilla Figs and Dried Cherries, 418–19
Vanilla Pan de Maiz, 391
Veal
best cuts for slow cooking, 297
buying, 297
internal cooking temperatures, 16
Italian Meatballs, 327–28
Osso Buco, 332–33
Puchero, 334–35
Ragoût of, for 20, 331–32
Ragoût with Artichokes, Brandied Raisins, and Crème Fraîche, 328–29
Stew with Champagne, 330
stocking, for slow cooker recipes, 22
White Meatloaf, 284–85
Vegetable(s). *See also specific vegetables*
Baby, Ragoût of, 162
Chinese, Hot Pot, 160–61
Curry, 158–59
and Herb Bread Stuffing, Arizona, 179
preparing, for slow cooker, 126–29
Roasted, and Tofu, Hummus with, 218–19
Roasted, Country Tomato Sauce with, 119–20
Roasted, White Bean Chili, 237–38
Root, Cream of, Soup Normandy, 89–90
slow-cooking, tips for, 126–27
Soup, French, with Pesto, 88–89

Spring, Braised, 161
stocking, for slow cooker recipes, 22
Venison
about, 335
Fruit, and Greens, 336–37
internal cooking temperatures, 16
Stew with Dried Cherries, 337–38
Vermicelli and Rice Pilaf, Victoria's Armenian, 191–92
Vinaigrettes
Basil, 207
Blueberry, 206
Cranberry, 206
Lemon-Chive, 205
preparing, 205
Shallot, 206
Walnut, 205
Vinegars, 21

W

Walnut(s)
-Cherry Truffles, 443
and Ginger, 50–51
Glazed, 265
Glazed, and Grand Marnier, Chicken with, 264–65
-Orange Wild Rice, 175
Spicy, 50
Sugared, 51
Walnut Vinaigrette, 205
Wassail, Spiked, 80
Water chestnuts
Chinese Vegetable Hot Pot, 160–61
preparing for slow cooker, 127
Welsh Rabbit, 40
Whipped Cream, Rum, 419
Whiskey
Athole Brose, 81
Irish Coffee, 74
Sauce, 383
Spirited Butterscotch Sauce, 385
White Bean(s)
Roasted Vegetable Chili, 237–38

White Bean(s) *(continued)*
  Turkey Chili with, 235–36
White Chocolate Piña Colada
    Fondue, 425
Wild Rice
  Basic, 193
  with Coconut and Raisins, 176
  with Dried Apricots, Cherries,
    and Pecans, 173–74
  Orange-Walnut, 175
Wine
  adding to stews and braises, 25
  Glögg, 78
  Mulled, 75
  Narsai's Chocolate Sauce, 438
  Onion Soup with Champagne,
    Port, and Camembert, 86
  Port, Negus, 79
  Red, Apricots, and Honey, Red
    Cabbage with, 132
  Red, Barbecue Sauce, 109–10

Sherry Cream Gravy, 281
Slow-Poached Pears with Port,
    Ice Cream, and Raspberry
    Drizzle, 406–7
Sparkling, and Garlic, Chicken
    Thighs with, 267–68
Warm Cranberry Zinfandel, 76
White, –Strawberry Punch, 77

Yams
  Candied, with Apples and
    Cranberries, 156–57
  preparing for slow cooker,
    127
Yellow Split Pea Dal with Mango,
    103–4
Yogurt-Chutney Sauce, 283–84

Zucchini
  French Vegetable Soup with
    Pesto, 88–89
  Tortino di, 157–58
  Vegetable Curry, 158–59